THE VAINGLORIOUS WAR
1854-56

ALSO BY A. J. BARKER

Principles of Small Arms
The March on Delhi
Suez: The Seven Day War
Eritrea 1941
The Neglected War: Mesopotamia 1914–1918
Townshend of Kut
The Civilised Mission
German Infantry Weapons of World War II
British and American Infantry Weapons of World War II
Pearl Harbour

THE VAINGLORIOUS WAR 1854-56

A. J. BARKER

WEIDENFELD AND NICOLSON
5 Winsley Street London W1

© A. J. Barker 1970

SBN 297 00215 5

Printed and Bound in Great Britain by
The Garden City Press Limited, Letchworth, Hertfordshire

'There is only one way of dealing with a power like Russia, and that is the way of courage.'

Karl Marx

New York Tribune, 30 December 1853

CONTENTS

ILLUSTRATIONS

The author and publishers are grateful to the following for permission to reproduce the pictures: 1, 2, 3, 5, 6, 8, 9, 11, 13, 15–24, The Radio Times Hulton Picture Library; 10 and 12, The Victoria and Albert Museum; 14, the Mansell Collection.

MAPS

CHRONOLOGY

1854
February | Advance contingents of the British and French armies sail for Turkey in anticipation of hostilities.

27 and 28 March | France and Britain declare war.

30 May | The British and French armies establish themselves at Varna in Bulgaria.

7 September | The allied armies sail for Russia, and on 14 September land unopposed at Eupatoria.

20 September | The Russians defeated in the Battle of the Alma.

26 September | The British encamp at Balaclava.

25 October | The Battle of Balaclava and Charge of the Light Brigade.

5 November | The Russians repulsed at the Battle of Inkerman.

1855
25 May | Allied troops destroy the Russian base on the peninsula in the Sea of Azov.

6 June | The Mamelon Vert captured by the French.

17 June | Attacks on the Redan and Malakoff beaten off with severe allied losses.

16 August | The Russians defeated in the Battle of the Tchernaya.

8 September | The British again defeated in an attack on the Redan.

The Malakoff captured by French troops.

9 September | Evacuation of Sebastopol by the Russians.

1856
28 February | An armistice is announced.

ACKNOWLEDGEMENTS

If I had not been able to borrow so generously from the library of the Royal United Service Institution and the Reading Public Library, or able to call upon the services of the British Museum, the National Army Museum and the Ministry of Defence Library, this book could not have been written. For the help of those who most kindly lent me manuscript material or books, who advised me and patiently answered my questions, I am also grateful. It is therefore with the greatest of pleasure that I thank the library staffs concerned; Miss Margaret Aldred for the diary of General Matthew Dixon, V.C.; Colonel J. M. Forbes of the Green Howards for his file 'Echoes of the Crimea'; Mr D. F. W. B. Williams for extracts from the diaries of his great-grandparents – Major and Mrs Arthur Wellesley Williams, 12th Lancers; Mr T. Ellis for his information on communicating and signalling in the Crimea; Aydin Kut Bey and Mr V. Mosey for their researches on my behalf, and the editor of *Soldier* for the co-operation which led to my uncovering some sources of information which would not otherwise have been available to me.

A large number of people sent me single letters, maps and books (some of them privately printed), or helped in some other way. These include Captain R. A. Bonner, Major A. C. E. Daniel, Mr J. H. W. Eyre, Major-General A. R. Fyler, O.B.E., M.C., Brigadier P. H. C. Hayward, C.B.E., Canon W. M. Lummis, M.C., and Mr W. A. Thorburn, Keeper of the Scottish United Services Museum.

Regimental archives yielded a rewarding harvest, and I must record the assistance of Major C. J. Airey, RHQ The Grenadier Guards; Colonel H. C. B. Cook, O.B.E., RHQ The Staffordshire Regiment; Colonel H. J. Darlington, O.B.E., D.L.; Major J. H. Davis, RHQ The Duke of Wellington's Regiment; Colonel D. A. D. Eykyn, D.S.O., D.L., RHQ The Royal Scots; Lieut.-Col. G. P. Gofton-Salmond, O.B.E., RHQ The Sherwood Foresters; Lieut.-Col. R. B. Humphreys, RHQ The Durham Light Infantry; Major T. Purdam, The King's Own Border Regimental Association;

Lieut.-Col. A. Rowland, O.B.E., M.C., 1st The Queen's Dragoon Guards; Lieut.-Col. P. Rogers, RHQ The Loyal Regiment; Colonel G. A. Rusk, D.S.O., M.C., and Major A. V. M. Chapman, M.B.E., T.D., RHQ The Black Watch; Major T. P. Shaw, M.B.E., RHQ The Lancashire Fusiliers; Major T. R. Stead, RHQ The Royal Anglian Regiment; Lieut.-Col. F. T. Stear, Secretary, Royal Engineers Historical Society; Major J. L. Sutro, M.C., Queen's Royal Irish Hussars; Lieut.-Col. J. Turnball, M.C., 11th Hussars (P.A.O.); Lieut.-Col. U. O. V. Verney, O.B.E., RHQ The Royal Green Jackets; Lieut.-Col. J. G. Vyvyan D.L., RHQ The Royal Welsh Fusiliers; Colonel F. Walden, D.L., RHQ The Queen's Regiment; and Captain A. J. Wilson, The Royal Highland Fusiliers.

PREFACE

Never had the prestige of a Tsar stood higher than that of Nicholas I in the summer of 1853. Five years earlier a revolutionary tide had rolled across Europe, sweeping Louis-Philippe off the throne of France, causing the Emperor of Austria to flee from his capital, King Frederick IV of Prussia to leave Berlin, Hungary to break away from Austria and provoking Italy's revolt against Habsburg rule. Nicholas had come to the rescue, effectively intervening on behalf of his neighbours and using his army to crush the Hungarian insurrectionists. Nicholas was taking no chances with liberal movements; he stood for stability and order.

Inflated by his success, encouraged by his courtiers, and corrupted by power, the 'Autocrat of all the Russias' decided that the time had come to bring new lustre to the Russian Crown. All the great Tsars had added territory to the Russian Empire and Nicholas certainly considered himself to be a great Tsar. His eyes focused on the crumbling Ottoman Empire and Constantinople, which the Russians had coveted for a thousand years. Russia had already fought seven wars against Turkey, and it was not difficult to pick a quarrel. A Russian envoy was sent to Constantinople demanding certain concessions for the Orthodox Church at shrines in Jerusalem and recognition of Russia as the protector of the Sultan's Christian Slavs. At the same time Nicholas summoned the British Minister in St Petersburg and blandly suggested partitioning Turkey's European possessions between England and Russia.

Britain, suspicious of Russia's motives, doubted the sincerity of Nicholas's sanctimonious arguments, and she entered into an alliance with Napoleon III – the nephew of the man against whom Britain had fought so long and desperately when France had threatened the liberties of Europe. The British Ambassador in Constantinople was told to advise the Sultan to concede the Tsar's demand for Orthodox rights in Jerusalem but flatly to reject that of a Russian protectorate over Turkey's Christian subjects.

But Nicholas had gone too far to draw back. It was clear that

Britain and France would side with Turkey, yet he found it difficult
to believe they would actually go to war in defence of a ramshackle
empire for which it was well known the Western Powers had little
sympathy. Come what may he was determined to resolve the
'Eastern Question', as it was called in diplomatic circles. To the
accompaniment of a good deal of talk about duty to God and
Christianity, a Russian 'liberation' army crossed the Prut on 2 July
1853 and marched into the Danubian provinces of Moldavia and
Wallachia which were then tributary to Turkey. The pretext was
that Russia was holding this territory as a pledge for her just
demands. The Turks demanded that the Russians retire and when
no notice was taken they mobilized. Three months later they
declared war on Russia.

When Nicholas rejected a joint ultimatum presented by Britain,
France and Austria urging an immediate withdrawal from the
Danubian principalities, war between the great powers was inevitable. Both sides had gone too far to give way without loss of
prestige; an alliance was made between the Western Powers and
Turkey and in March 1854 war was declared 'to protect Europe
from the dominance of a power which violates treaties and defies the
civilized world'.

Little of the background was clear to the majority of people in
Britain and France, and it is difficult to believe that people, in the
midst of an economic depression, shivering in an unusually cold
winter, and rioting because work on the land had stopped and with
it their miserable nine shillings a week, felt particularly enthusiastic
about the prospect of war. But highly coloured descriptions of the
destruction of a Turkish fleet at Sinope had roused intense feelings
and in both countries the Press had been building up to a crescendo
of abuse in its references to Nicholas and praise for the 'brave but
weak' Turks. Many of those whose dull little lives were constrained
by the field and factory, probably welcomed the excitement and
quickening of national life which the crisis aroused.

No real consideration had been given to the problem of where
Russia would be brought to heel. When war was declared it appeared certain the lower Danube would be the main theatre of
operations and the Caucasus the secondary theatre. In the event
the Black Sea was to become the seat of hostilities and the Crimean
Peninsula – which was to become the scene of the land fighting –
gave the war the name by which it is usually known. Except for the
naval base at Sebastopol, the Crimea had little strategic importance and if the Russians had abandoned it in 1854 the British and
French would have found it difficult to fight a land campaign. But

prestige demanded that the peninsula should be defended, and with the enormous numerical superiority which the Russians enjoyed the fighting was bound to be hard and bitter. (In those days soldiers fought standing shoulder to shoulder in ranks, exchanging fire with the enemy at point-blank range; fortunately weapons were inaccurate and casualties light by modern standards.) For the British army a long period of non-intervention in large-scale wars and the effects upon Parliament of strong pacifist propaganda had brought a decline in organization and administration. In consequence the British troops suffered extreme privations. The French, who did not do so much fighting, were better prepared and better organized for the campaign and they did not suffer to the same extent as the British. Wellington, it is said, once likened the organization of his army to a harness made of rope, and the French organization to one of leather. (The theory was that rope could be knotted and it would still function, whereas repairs to a leather harness were less simple.) In the Crimea what was left of Wellington's rope proved less durable than what the French had developed from Napoleon's leather.

In its effects the war against Russia was far from being the 'vain' campaign which some early twentieth-century historians dubbed it. In the field the British and French armies invariably defeated the Russians and inflicted on them such appalling casualties that they ceased to menace their neighbours for more than a generation. In Russia itself the internal economy suffered, and revolutionary propaganda which was finally to bring about the fall of the Tsarist Empire and the rise of the Soviet Union from its ruins was provided with fertile material. With the growth of the new Soviet Empire the advantages derived by Britain and France from their sacrifices in the Crimea may well seem nebulous. But it must be remembered that British soldiers were never called upon to fight in Europe between the fall of Sebastopol and the German invasion of Belgium in 1914, and in the same period Russia never attempted to interfere with French interests.

The Crimean War is remembered principally by a cavalry charge and the heroism of a woman. Two films have been made of the famous Charge of the Light Brigade; none, surprisingly, of the Battle of the Alma when Her Majesty's Guards, in full regalia, marched magnificently into battle – in step and in perfect lines. The name of Lord Cardigan – the 'Noble Yachtsman' who led the charge and refused to share with his troops the rigours of camp life – has passed into the English language as an article of clothing. Florence Nightingale, the 'Lady with the Lamp' who devoted herself to the care of the sick and wounded, is credited with establishing the first system of hygienic hospital care for the wounded. The campaign showed how sea power could maintain comparatively small armies in the territory of a gigantic continental enemy and defeat every force that land power could bring against them, so long as their sea communications remained secure. This fact was not forgotten for a long time, but nowadays few people appreciate that much of the fighting of the campaign set the pattern of the wars which followed up to 1918. Balaclava, with its cavalry charges and 'thin red line', was but an echo from the wars of the past and it was soon superseded by the trench warfare which siege operations and high-velocity rifles imposed. Explosive shells had been in limited use up to 1854, but in the Crimea shell-fire was used to a degree unequalled in earlier wars.

This was also the beginning of the rifle era. At the Alma, Inkerman and the Tchernaya the rifle and bayonet were the decisive weapons and they remained so until the coming of the machine-gun, the tank and the aeroplane. Rifles had been used in the eighteenth century but the rate of fire was slow and they were so clumsy that with all its faults the old smooth-bore musket was considered to be the best all-round weapon. Between the close of the Napoleonic wars and the outbreak of the war with Russia, however, the rifle was being developed and from the 1830s onwards most European armies were being rearmed with one form or another of it. When tests showed that the Minié rifle with which the French army was being re-equipped was superior to the British Baker rifles which had been used by the British army in the Peninsula war, the British Government decided to set up a factory at Enfield to manufacture an 'Enfield' rifle of a design which incorporated the best features of the Minié and several other types then being made in Europe and America. The Crimean War caught the British army in the process of rearming, so that some units found themselves with the new Enfield, others with the Minié and a few with the Baker.

Among other innovations were the light military railway which linked the base at Balaclava with the front towards the end of the siege; the first electric telegraph to be used in war – enabling politicians to exercise a closer control over the generals than had ever been possible hitherto; the first professional war correspondent, W. H. Russell of *The Times*; and the first war photographer, Roger Fenton. This was the last important campaign in which the British soldier fought in full dress uniform, the last in which regiments carried their colours, and the last in which the infantry marched into battle behind their regimental bands. The battles of the Crimea are more than a hundred years away; we have seen two world wars and several sizeable 'little' wars since then, and presumably we ought to know something more of what sets cannon roaring and bombs falling. In England there are still plenty of public houses, terraces and cottages named after Alma, Balaclava and Inkerman to remind people of a war that was primarily an infantry war.

According to Ecclesiastes, 'The thing that hath been, it is that which shall be; and that which is done is that which shall be done: and there is no new thing under the sun.' The story of *The Vainglorious War* is full of the old lessons we live to forget and the traditions we shall remember. More than a century has elapsed since the events recaptured in the following pages. During that time there have been many cultural, technical and scientific advances. But nations' characters remain basically the same, and on this we should reflect.

PROLOGUE

'Who is to have Constantinople? That is always the crux of the problem.' [1]

So wrote Napoleon to his ambassador in St Petersburg in May 1808. The French fleet had been destroyed at Trafalgar two and a half years earlier, and the Emperor was nervous of Russian activity in the Mediterranean. 'If Russia should hold the Dardanelles', he explained in the same letter, 'she would be at the gates of Toulon, of Naples, and Corfu'.

With the Turkish empire crumbling to decay this question of the future guardianship of the Dardanelles was destined to become one of the perpetual headaches of the statesmen of Europe.

The problem was of long standing. After Tuesday 29 May 1453, when Constantinople, the capital of the Byzantine Empire, fell to the conquering hordes of Sultan Mahmud II, the Turks remained in a chronic state of dissension with their Christian neighbours for more than four hundred years. But in 1683, when another Sultan was driven back from the walls of Vienna, the tide of Turkish conquest slowly began to recede. This was the end of an epoch, after which the Turks ceased to produce great leaders, and under a succession of weak sultans their empire – so grandly conquered – began to disintegrate. Pashas of distant provinces sought to make themselves independent of the central authority of Constantinople; bribery and corruption flourished throughout the administration, and unrest in the army paralysed the Sultan's authority at a time when he needed all the power he could muster to resist enemies from without.

Russia, in the early stages of her struggle for world power – the apogee of which she would reach four centuries later – had been casting predatory glances at the Ottoman Empire since the sixteenth century. Two hundred years later the expansion of her realms at Turkey's expense had become the object of Russian policy and the mainstay of every Tsar's ambition. At the conclusion of the Napoleonic wars, the Ottoman Sultan still controlled vast slices of territory stretching from the Polish border to the valley of the

Euphrates, but two wars with Russia in the first half of the nineteenth century saw a further decline in Turkish power in Eastern Europe. Russia's gains at Turkey's expense were now beginning to excite concern among other European nations however, and the conflict between the two countries was the principal element in what was popularly known in Western Europe as the 'Eastern Question'. 'The Franks,' Sultan Mahmud II observed perceptively, 'envy us our possession in Europe, and must sooner or later drive us into Asia. This would have been done twenty years before I mounted the throne had it been possible to divide Constantinople between them; but like a beautiful female captive, she has remained inviolate in the bosom of banditti. They cannot yet agree whose prize she is to be.'[2]

By the middle of the nineteenth century Britain was certainly not prepared to see Constantinople become Russia's prize. Whether or not the crescent flew over the dome of St Sophia had been a matter of indifference before the development of her commercial interests in the Far East and the conquest of India. To Britain the core of the Eastern Question was the control of the trade routes to the East. Neither the Suez Canal nor Middle Eastern oil supplies had yet arrived to complicate the issue, and the problem was confined to the overland route to the Indies. As this followed the old caravan route through the Middle East, across the mountains of Asia Minor or Syria and down the valley of the Euphrates, the Ottoman Empire was an essential link between Europe and the East. If Russia took over from Turkey, Europe could be cut off from the East altogether, and the growing realization that in fifty years Russia had nearly doubled her empire in Europe, advanced her frontiers 850 miles towards Vienna, Berlin, Dresden, Munich and Paris, 450 miles nearer Constantinople and to within a few miles of the capital of Sweden; that she was occupying the capital of Poland; and stretched forward about 1,000 miles towards India and the same distance towards the capital of Persia all stimulated British solicitude for peace in the Middle East. According to the map, a Russian regiment stationed on Muscovite territory on the western shores of the Caspian was farther from St Petersburg than from Lahore, and Russian battalions on the Persian border were nearer to Delhi than to their metropolitan base. A number of so-called buffer states still separated India from the dominions of the Tsar but those in Westminster now felt that any Russian advance in Central Asia occasioned grave suspicion.

In retrospect it is surprising how quickly the British attitude had changed. In 1854 British politicians frequently referred to the Turks as Britain's 'ancient allies' although it would have been more logical to have called them Europe's 'ancient enemies'. Not so very many years had passed since Turkish misgovernment and barbarities had been viewed with disgust by every country in Europe. In 1821 when the Greeks took up arms against their Turkish overlords, sentiment in Europe was overwhelmingly pro Greek, and a mixture of self-interest and sentiment led to European interference on the side of the Greeks. Russia, posing as the philanthropic and disinterested champion of an oppressed minority, saw the possibility of establishing in Greece a satellite state carved out of her rival in the Black Sea. Britain and France, yielding to the pull of the classical association of people called Greeks fighting for liberty, were both concerned with their maritime interests in the eastern Mediterranean and did not wish to see Constantinople become a Russian stronghold. By the efforts of a British Prime Minister, George Canning, however, the three nations were welded into an uneasy alliance. Without consulting the Turks, a conference was assembled in London at which the three countries concerned set about arranging the affairs of the Ottoman Empire to their own satisfaction. In the event the Turks showed complete indifference to the suggestions, remonstrances, menaces and armed demonstrations which stemmed from this conference. But three admirals, British, French and Russian struck the ultimate blow for Greek freedom when their combined fleets annihilated the Turkish navy at Navarino.

A peace treaty was signed in 1829, but with the loss of Greece, combined with the loss of prestige occasioned by Russian victories in Asia Minor, the Ottoman Empire had suffered further demoralization. And it had scarcely had time to recover before a new menace appeared to threaten its existence. Mohammed Ali, the Sultan's Viceroy in Egypt, was a man of considerable ability and insatiable ambition, whose aim was to sever Egypt's 300-year connection with the Porte* and to set himself up as an independent monarch. The time appeared to be opportune; his army was small but efficient, and his fleet of seven sail of the line and twelve frigates was superior to what remained of the Turkish fleet after Navarino. Above all he had a son, Ibrahim, who had studied the art of war and who had fought with distinction against the Greeks. A pretext for going to war was soon found. In the autumn of 1831 some thousands of fellaheen – Egyptian peasants – who had fled from Egypt to dodge

---

* An abbreviation for the 'Sublime Porte'. Originally the gateway to the palace where the Sultan or his Grand Vizier conducted official business, 'the Porte' came to mean either the Ottoman Government itself, or the empire.

Mohammed Ali's tax collectors were sheltering in Syria. Mohammed Ali asked the Pasha of Syria to send them back, and when his neighbours refused to co-operate an army of 30,000 infantry and 8,000 cavalry, under the command of Ibrahim, was sent to enforce the demand. Syria was invaded and every Turkish army sent against him – including one of 18,000 men – was defeated. When the last remaining Turkish army was crushed at Konya the road to Constantinople lay open. Fortunately for the Sultan, Ibrahim – like Hannibal before him – sat back, inactive, for a month and when he resumed his advance it was too late to achieve the ultimate success that his earlier successes might have won for him.

Seen from Europe, Mohammed Ali's revolt and his son's victories threatened the entire disruption of Turkish power. News of Ibrahim's achievements had spread like wildfire from the Euphrates to the Danube, from the Caspian to the Mediterranean, and there was every possibility either that the Ottoman Empire would fragment into chaos as many of its subject peoples overthrew their Turkish masters, or that it would be replaced by a more vigorous regime. Both alternatives were unacceptable – a fact which the Sultan had quickly appreciated. But Britain could not help; since Waterloo her army and navy had been drastically reduced and she was hardly in a condition to defend her own interests let alone help Turkey. France, to whom the Sultan appealed next, was equally disinclined to send any troops to the Middle East. Only Russia remained and she answered the Sultan's *cri du coeur*, with what afterwards seemed to be almost indecent haste. Hoping to establish the right to intervene in any future crisis affecting the Ottoman Empire, a Russian fleet and a Russian army were sent to Constantinople and the Egyptian advance was halted.

If Britain and France were undecided as to whether Mohammed Ali should take over the leadership of the Faithful, they were both agreed that Constantinople was no place for the Russians. A three-cornered diplomatic battle resulted in a convention by which the Sultan, pressed by Britain and France, made Mohammed Ali Pasha of Syria to keep him quiet and by which the Russian troops and fleet had to leave the Bosphorus when the Egyptian army had withdrawn to Syria. At the time it seemed that Tsar Nicholas had derived no advantage from the philanthropic rescue of his neighbour – except a treaty of alliance, which was a mutual compliment rather than a mutual advantage. Three months later Britain and France had a rude shock when they learned that this treaty contained a secret clause by which Russian warships were given the sole right to enter the Dardanelles. Mohammed, indignant at the supposed humiliation to which he had been subjected, had decided that his best ally was Turkey's old enemy. Russia's influence in the Black Sea was now predominant, and there was little that Britain and France could do about it except to protest.

For six years the Eastern Question remained dormant, until in 1839 there was a complication which brought Britain and France to the verge of war with each other. Encouraged by promises of French support Mohammed Ali was again the cause, but this time it was the Sultan who was the aggressor. Burning for revenge on his former viceroy and believing that Britain would support him, the sultan precipitated a new crisis when his troops invaded Syria. As in 1833 his army suffered a disastrous series of defeats, and after an equally disastrous naval battle, Achmed Fauzi Pasha, the admiral commanding the Sultan's fleet, was compelled to surrender his ships at Alexandria. In such circumstances it was to be expected that the Sultan would invoke the six-year-old treaty with Russia and ask the Tsar to stage another rescue operation. But Russian policy had taken a sudden turn and the Tsar – who had been trying to reach an understanding with Britain in order to reconcile British and Russian interests in Europe and Asia – saw a golden opportunity to widen the existing breach between Britain and France. The treaty with Turkey, he declared, would be allowed to lapse, and he was prepared to negotiate a settlement of the Turkish-Egyptian question with others who were interested.

Under the direction of Lord Palmerston, the British Foreign Secretary, a conference attended by Russia, France, Austria, Britain, Prussia and Turkey was called to discuss Mohammed Ali's future. What everybody except France had in mind appears to have been a solution which supported Turkey. But public opinion in France saw in Mohammed Ali a man who could be useful if there was a clash of French and British maritime interests in the Mediterranean, and the government of Louis-Philippe* could not afford to ignore popular sentiment. When it became plain to Palmerston that the French were intriguing outside the conference with both Mohammed Ali and the Porte, he decided to seek a solution which excluded France. Sultan Mohammed died in June 1839. A year later – without telling France – Palmerston persuaded Russia, Austria and Prussia to agree to coerce Mohammed Ali into a settlement with Sultan Mohammed's successor, Abdul Medjid. Provided

* The liberal regime of Louis-Philippe – who became king of France in 1830 – shrivelled up so decidedly that he lost his throne, and in 1848 the monarchy gave place to a republic. Under the presidency of Louis Napoleon – the great Bonaparte's nephew – this republic, in turn, was replaced by the Second Empire in 1852.

Mohammed Ali accepted within ten days of the offer being made, the recalcitrant pasha could have the hereditary pashalic of Egypt and be Pasha of southern Syria for life; after this he was to be excluded from Syria, and if he should hold out for another ten days Sultan Abdul Medjid was to be pledged to nothing.

Believing that France would support him, Mohammed Ali rejected this ultimatum. But French help never came and his downfall quickly followed. A combined British, Austrian and Turkish fleet appeared off the coast of Syria and there was a mutiny in Egypt. Beirut and Acre were taken by the allied fleet and Sir Charles Napier, its British commander-in-chief, threatened to bombard the Pasha's palace in Alexandria. When Ibrahim was compelled to evacuate Syria, Mohammed Ali agreed to abandon his claim to Syria in return for the promise of Egypt for himself and his heirs. The Turkish-Egyptian dispute was settled, and Europe had shown that it was willing to prop up the 'Sick Man'* of Europe. But the underlying motive had been fear of Russia, and the jealousies of the European states were more responsible for Mohammed Ali's downfall than any real objection to him wresting power from the Porte or any real love of the Turks. When the furore over Mohammed Ali subsided, the main question – the fate of Turkey – was no nearer solution. But the problem had been recognized, and in an attempt to prevent friction in the future a treaty, closing the Dardanelles to all non-Turkish warships, was signed in 1841 by all the great powers.†

For the next ten years the Middle East enjoyed a period of comparative peace and tranquillity. But throughout this decade Nicholas kept his eyes firmly fixed on Constantinople, and made several ineffectual attempts to arrange a contingent treaty with Britain which would operate in the event of the death of the 'Sick Man'. Successive British governments rejected the Tsar's overtures. Palmerston, who, with brief intervals, controlled British foreign policy for thirty years, had no love for Russia and was determined to maintain the integrity of the Ottoman Empire at all costs.

The trouble to which the outbreak of the Crimean war may be directly attributed erupted in 1850. Among the heterogeneous population of the Ottoman Empire were at least 15 million Orthodox

---

* It was Tsar Nicholas who first referred to Turkey as a 'Sick Man' who might suddenly die 'and be on our hands'. With Sir Hamilton Seymour, British Ambassador at St Petersburg, he discussed the disposal of the 'Sick Man's' property.

† As this treaty remained in force until the Crimean war and has considerable bearing on what might be considered NATO's Eastern Question, its provisions are quoted in Appendix 1.

Christians – adherents of the Greek Church – to whom the Tsar of Russia was the acknowledged champion of their religion. At the same time the role of France as the 'Protector of Latin Christians in the East' had been established by treaties with the Ottoman Empire – the most recent being in 1740. Living in the Holy Land were the representatives of several Roman Catholic orders who were supposed to carry out certain stipulated duties of upkeep and repair of the shrines which, in the Sultan's view, entitled the Catholics of Western Europe to the privilege of worshipping there. Since 1758, however, these orders had neglected their responsibilities and many of their functions had been taken over by Greek Orthodox Christians, who, in turn, were given firmans or grants of authority by the Sultan in compensation for their efforts. In the early nineteenth century a series of disputes had developed as a result of the Catholic orders and the Greek Orthodox Church possessing duplicate firmans which in many cases gave them the same rights and privileges as each other. These disputes revolved round such points as worship at particular shrines, and the holding of keys to them.* As the differences were local, chiefly ecclesiastical and could hardly be considered to be of world-shattering importance, it is hardly to be wondered that the tendency of the Sultan was to remain profoundly indifferent to the rivalries of those whom his religion taught to regard as infidel dogs. In 1819 the differences led to diplomatic negotiations which were provoked, suspended and temporarily lost in the upheaval caused by the Greek struggle for independence during the 1820s. But the issues involved were not forgotten in France where the clerical party never ceased to press for the support of Catholic interests in Palestine.

In 1850, the monks in Bethlehem quarrelled over possession of the keys to the Church of the Holy Sepulchre, and Louis Napoleon – the self-created Emperor of France – reasserted France's interest in the dispute. In the dispute the new Napoleon saw an opportunity to appease the clerics in his own country and to impress himself on Tsar Nicholas as an imperial figure of some consequence. Accordingly, the French ambassador in Constantinople was instructed to remind the Sultan of the 'unalterable rights' of the Catholics in Jerusalem and to demand the restitution to the Catholics of the seventeen sanctuaries 'usurped' by the Greeks. With customary Oriental procrastination, the Turks decided to appoint a commission

---

* The main questions were whether the Catholics had the right to keys of the main door of the Church of Bethlehem and to each of the two doors of the Manger, and whether they were entitled to place a silver star in the Sanctuary of the Nativity. They also wanted to have a cupboard and a lamp in the Tomb of the Virgin at Gethsemane.

to investigate the state of affairs at the Holy Places. Greek annoyance, converging rapidly along the usual diplomatic channels, produced a corresponding vibration in St Petersburg where the Tsar saw French demands as a prospective change in the *status quo* which violated the principles of 1815. Tsar Nicholas did not believe in revolutions and the fact that Louis Napoleon was, in effect, a child of revolution did not help matters. Nicholas was a man of firm convictions and when, in December 1852, the Sultan decided in favour of the Catholic Christians he sent a special envoy to Constantinople. The Turks needed to be reminded of Russian strength, Nicholas felt, and force seemed to be the only language they understood. For this mission of intimidation Prince Menschikoff – an imperious bully whose attitude to the Turks had been hardened by bitterness over his emasculation by a shot from a Turkish gun – was selected.

Menschikoff arrived in Constantinople breathing arrogance and insult in a Russian warship and was joined there by Admiral Korniloff, commanding the Black Sea Fleet, and the chief of staff of the Russian force on the Danube. His orders from the Tsar were to insist on two things: maintenance of exclusive privileges for Orthodox Christians in the Holy Places, and the granting to Russia of a protectorate over Christians throughout the whole of the Ottoman Empire. At that time Turkish troops were suppressing a rebellion in Christian Montenegro and to show the Russians meant business, Menschikoff presented the Sultan with an ultimatum: these troops must withdraw immediately or Russia would go to war. With no real idea of what to do, the Sultan complied, said that he would reconsider the firmans to the Holy Places, but refused the protectorate. Meanwhile the British and French ambassadors had alerted their governments with urgent reports, suggesting that the situation was crucial and one which called for naval support for the Sultan. Negotiations continued until 21 May when Menschikoff and the entire Russian legation packed their bags and left Constantinople in high dudgeon. Mainly on the advice of the British Ambassador, Viscount Stratford de Redcliffe, who had long been an influence in Ottoman affairs, the Sultan rejected the Tsar's demands.

In spite of his fit of temper Menschikoff had left Constantinople expecting the Turks would change their minds. When this did not occur the Russian Chancellor, Count Nesselrode, wrote to the Sultan's Grand Vizier saying that if the Porte persisted in its attitude the Imperial troops would occupy the principalities of Moldavia and Wallachia – 'Not to make war upon a sovereign who has always been considered a faithful ally, but in order to secure a material guarantee' in further negotiations. This ultimatum was probably all part of the Tsar's brinkmanship. Nicholas himself was by nature averse to the use of force. He knew full well that neither Britain – because of her concern for the 'Avenues to India' – nor France – because of her proximity to the Balkans – would permit Russia to take Constantinople *en propriétaire*. What he aspired to was a large measure of Russian influence in the Porte and an arrangement by which Constantinople could be 'shared' with the other powers. This had been plain in January 1853 during his notorious colloquy with the British Ambassador in St Petersburg, Sir Hamilton Seymour. '. . . *we* [Russia and Britain] must come to some under-standing . . .' He, Nicholas, had abandoned 'the plans and dreams of Catharine', he had said; Turkey was 'falling to pieces . . . the sick man was dying . . .'

If Nicholas had thought that a policy of threat and bluff could succeed however, he was soon to see that he was mistaken. On 15 June, French and British fleets in the Black Sea concentrated at the entrance to the Dardanelles and the Turkish attitude stiffened.

Neither the Tsar nor Louis Napoleon could fail to comment about the dangerous situation which had developed ostensibly because of their efforts on behalf of the religious factions. Both made some attempt to pour oil on the troubled waters, whilst the Austrians urged a conference of interested parties in Vienna in order to try to arrange a settlement that would save the face of everybody. In a letter dated 11 June addressed to the ministers and agents of Russia at foreign courts the Tsar said that he 'did not aim at the ruin and destruction of the Ottoman empire, which he himself on two occasions has saved from dissolution'. On the contrary, he had always regarded the existing *status quo* as the best possible combination to interpose between European interests, 'and that as far as regards the Russo-Greek religion in Turkey, we have no necessity, in order to secure its interests, of any rights other than those which are already secured to us by our treaties'. However, the letter continued in a more sinister vein. 'After three months of laborious negotiations . . . the Emperor is now compelled peremptorily to insist on the un-conditional (*pur et simple*) acceptation of the draft of the note. But still influenced by those considerations of patience . . . he has granted the Porte a fresh reprieve of eight days in which to take its decision. That period passed, painful though it may be to his conciliatory disposition, he will be compelled to think of the means of obtaining by a more decisive attitude, the satisfaction which he has in vain sought by peaceful means.' Meanwhile a new French Ambassador, the one-armed quick-tempered General Achille

Baraguay d'Hilliers, had been sent to Constantinople with instructions to 'preach peace' and to seek a solution short of war.

At the Vienna conference a draft compromise formula which was agreed by the Russians, British and French was rejected by the Turks. But by this time Nicholas was furious and with the expiration of the time limit he had set the two army corps which had been waiting on the Russian side of the Prut River were ordered to advance and occupy the Danubian Principalities. On 3 July 1853 the Russians crossed the Prut and for all practical purposes the war had started although Turkey did not issue a formal declaration until 23 October.

The river Prut, a tributary of the Danube which it joins less than seventy miles from the Black Sea coast, then formed the southwestern boundary of Russia. The country on its right bank – which is Rumania today – consisted of a number of Principalities over which the Sultan exercised a nominal suzerainty. The Turks had never intended any defence of them; indeed, militarily, they had neither the resources nor determination to do so, although it was argued later that they might have done so if the Western Powers had not persuaded the Sultan that a policy of moderation and caution was in his best interest. Whether by ordering the occupation of Moldavia and Wallachia Nicholas had committed a strategic mistake, is debatable. Russian troops had not actually invaded Turkey proper, and as by treaty they could enter these provinces to preserve order, their occupation did not necessarily mean war. But to the Western Powers the move was indicative of the Tsar's intentions. In the Queen's speech at the close of the British parliamentary session in August 1853 hope was expressed that peace would prevail, and the high-minded British Prime Minister of the period, Lord Aberdeen, professed a proper horror of war. Perhaps the belief that Britain would avoid war at all costs had contributed to the Tsar's diplomatic brinkmanship, just as Redcliffe's influence over the Sultan was instrumental in the refusal of the Turks to accept the Vienna Conference's compromise.*

During the months of diplomatic skirmishing the Turks showed little enthusiasm for a war against their old enemies. But by the time the Russian troops crossed the Prut they were ready to fight. The Sultan's Christian subjects constituted a potential and sizeable fifth column, but the Moslem section of the population had come to believe that with the support of the Western Powers they had a

* Redcliffe's position when Russia marched into the Principalities was virtually that of a dictator. The 30-year-old Sultan, debilitated by sexual indulgence and hardly capable of coherent thought, relied on advisers – of whom Redcliffe became chief.

better chance of winning a new contest with Russia than in many of the other wars which they had fought single handed. Proclamations posted in the market places and fiery speeches stirred young Moslems and the Ottoman Empire began to organize itself for war in the usual atmosphere of Oriental demonstrations and disturbances. Above the Bosphorus an army began to assemble; the streets of Constantinople were thronged with ill-disciplined but colourful Bashi-Bazouks – cut-throats hastily recruited from the scum of towns as irregular Turkish infantry; at the arsenal, cannon balls destined for the front rumbled into trucks; and on the great Serazkierat Square, cavalry squadrons and infantry battalions wheeled and drilled. Omar Pasha was appointed commander-in-chief and in August his troops started to concentrate on the right bank of the Danube.*

In October 1853 the Russian and Turkish armies were still some hundreds of miles apart and with winter approaching immediate hostilities were not expected. Omar Pasha was supposed to have about 100,000 men, but sickness and desertions probably reduced this figure to about 70,000. Prince Mikhail Gorschakoff, the Russian commander, had an army of about 80,000 men in Wallachia and Moldavia but sickness had reduced its effective strength by about half. On 23 October the campaign opened when a Russian flotilla tried to force its way up the Danube. A few days later the Turks crossed the river on a wide front, and by 4 November they had established themselves at several places on the far bank. The operation was not accomplished without casualties and at Giurgevo, in the centre of the Turkish line, the Russians drove in the Turkish bridge-head. Nevertheless Omar Pasha had secured a tactical advantage. The Danube was a formidable obstacle preventing the Russians from incursion into his territory, yet Omar's troops could cross it at will to harry the Russians on both flanks. The Turks, because they either failed to appreciate their advantage or were incapable of exploiting it, did little throughout the winter months and the winter fighting along the marshy Danubian front degenerated into a series of indecisive minor actions. But it soon became

* Omar Pasha (Umar Pasha) was forty-seven years old at the time of his appointment. Born a Christian named Michael Lattas, in Austria, he had served as a regimental officer in the Austrian army until he deserted after a minor misdemeanour in 1828. He then became a Mohammedan and tried his hand at various jobs including that of teaching. Chance brought him the future Sultan as a pupil and by the latter's influence he gained rapid promotion in the Turkish army. In 1834 he was a captain in the War Ministry in Constantinople; in 1839, a colonel. Between 1840 and 1852 he was responsible for repressing a number of revolts and his actions were characterized by ruthless behaviour towards Christians.

evident to Gorschakoff that he had committed one of the most fatal errors in war: the passive occupation of the two Principalities had brought him all the disadvantages and none of the advantages that usually derive from aggression.

To regain the initiative the Russians would have to attack, and with permission from St Petersburg a spring offensive was planned. A bridge-head would be forced across the Lower Danube early in the spring; Silistria would be occupied by 1 May, and Gorschakoff's main force would advance south towards Schumla and the Balkans. Once across the Balkans its objective would be Adrianople and from there it would head for the Bosphorus. Before this projected invasion could get under way, however, an event which had far greater psychological impact in Europe than any of the reports about the fighting on the Danube had occurred.

In violation of the Straits Convention of 1841, the British and French fleets sailed through the Dardanelles into the Sea of Marmara, during November. Emotional reports to Paris from the French ambassador in Constantinople expressing his fears for the Christian population of the city – French subjects in particular – provoked this move. Redcliffe had been authorized to call on the British fleet to help out but he had not considered the situation had deteriorated to a point which required him to do so. When the French government told the British government that they were sending French warships through the Dardanelles, London – without reference to Redcliffe – ordered the British fleet to do the same. Russia indignantly demanded to know why the fleet had been moved up, and Britain replied to the effect that she would move her fleet anywhere she liked on the high seas, and to territorial waters also when asked by a friendly Power to do so. Presumably there could be no other answer.

Russian warships based on Sebastopol had been active in the Black Sea since Turkey had declared war. A few shots had been exchanged between Turkish and Russian cruisers, an Egyptian frigate had been captured, but the Turkish admiral, Osman Pasha, had kept his squadron of seven frigates and two corvettes at anchor in the bay of Sinope. Here on 30 November, it was suddenly attacked by six battleships, two frigates and three steamers under the command of Admiral Nakhimoff. Before the Turkish ships had even cleared for action all but two had been destroyed by a new gunnery technique employing time fuses and incendiary shells fired on low trajectories. Outclassed in every way, the Turks fought without hope but with great courage in this brief action. Three-quarters of them were killed, but as a state of war existed between Turkey and Russia a massacre of this nature was a perfectly legitimate act of war for which no doubt Nakhimoff was duly congratulated.

Europe recoiled with horror from the news of the holocaust at Sinope, and British newspapers described it inaccurately as a 'foul outrage' – a 'massacre'.* In Paris its impact was less violent although it was said to have produced on Louis Napoleon '*l'impression la plus vive*'.[3] Coming after nine months of blustering and bullying the Sinope affair aroused the greatest resentment both in Britain and France and from that moment the two countries marched in step. A joint demand that Russia withdraw from Moldavia and Wallachia by 30 April was ignored and on 27 and 28 March respectively France and Britain declared war, without offering any rational motive for their action.

Why Britain and France should ever have taken up arms against Russia would involve unravelling what the journalist W. H. Russell described as 'a mass of verbiage . . . wrapped up in endless coatings of manifestos, protocols and despatches'. The reasons were considerably more complex and deepseated than those which were pronounced as immediate – the defence of oppressed minorities, and resistance to the threat of territorial aggression. Britain's resolute determination to prevent Russia from dominating the land route to her proudest possession, the Indian Empire, was matched by the fact that in Louis Napoleon, France had a leader who was 'too much of a Bonaparte not to wish to revenge 1812 . . . too uncertain of his new throne not to welcome a successful war'. Whatever may be said for the claims of either side, it is probable that if a little more forbearance together with less greed, stiff-necked pride and patriotic hysteria had been shown by all parties in the negotiations which terminated in March 1854, there would have been no war. But these were considerations hardly to be expected from a deluded despot, a combination of feeble and aristocratic English gentry, and an upstart dictator apprehensive about the security of his regime. Neither Britain, France nor Russia really wanted war; none of them was propelled, they just drifted slowly into it. The British Prime Minister, Lord Aberdeen, hated the idea; the Queen, the Prince Consort, and even *The Times* (reviled by a belligerent contemporary as 'The Russian organ of Printing House Square'), were generally against it. After Sinope the British public was certainly pro-Turk and anti-Russian but it could not be said to have been spoiling for a fight. In Paris, where Louis Napoleon had recently declared '*L'Empire, c'est la paix*', no crowds thronged the

---

* Much was made of the allegations that the Russians had fired on Turkish seamen in the water.

boulevards shouting 'A St Petersburg'. In St Petersburg even Nicholas showed little enthusiasm. Perhaps Aberdeen came nearest to an explanation when he exclaimed sadly, 'Some fatal influence seems to have been at work'.

Fatal, but indefinable, there have been few situations in her history more ironical than Britain's determination to go to war with France in order to protect Turks. As 'Defender of the Faith', she found herself at the same time defender of the Faithful. And for the first time in centuries she was allied to France in a major war; that this should happen while France was under a Napoleon was perhaps the most remarkable feature of the whole sorry business.

1

THE BELLIGERENTS

By the middle of the nineteenth century the Russians were living under a tyranny harsher than they had ever known. Rebellion, fomented by young intellectuals who had watched the social upheavals in Western Europe, was already simmering. Nearly a hundred years were to elapse before it erupted in a great revolution. But a warning of what was to come came on 14 December 1825 – the day Nicholas I came to the throne – when one regiment of his army mutinied in St Petersburg, whilst another marched on Kiev. Quickly and relentlessly Nicholas smashed the insurrection and the insurgents, against whom he took terrible retribution, became the first martyrs of the Russian Revolution. Thus, from the very outset of his reign the Tsar adopted a policy of repression and for this purpose he maintained a standing army of three-quarters of a million men – an enormous force for any nation to support during the nineteenth century. With the passage of time, Nicholas's regime grew progressively more harsh and more repressive until by 1850 his people were living in a state of abject servitude. Almost every aspect of life in Russia was regimented, and the maintenance of law and order depended on a brutal punishment system. Brutal whipping for the most trivial offences was so common that the Russians themselves nicknamed the Tsar 'Nicholas the Flogger'.

In the Russian army conditions were such that those in the British or French armies were benevolent by comparison. In theory any Russian subject over the age of twenty was liable for military service, and those who were actually conscripted were compelled to serve for the whole of their working life. In 1850 the population of Russia was said to be about 80 million, of which about six million were reckoned to be men whose age qualified them for military service.[1] Physical incapacity or some other valid reason probably exempted a third of this number but even then there still remained about 4 million men in the Tsar's recruiting pool. Of those who were called up, few had seen a great town and nearly all were of low mental calibre. Not many contemporary British soldiers could read or write, but mentally most of them were better equipped than their Russian counterparts,* who were to show themselves incapable of fighting in anything other than column formation. There were few intelligent men in the army – those who had any sense invariably dodged the draft. Those who were unable to escape the conscription net inevitably found themselves swallowed up among the mass of ignorance. Nor were their officers much better. Few had any real interest in their profession and in the wild and remote regions in which most of the army was stationed they elected to 'quench themselves in strong drink and gross forms of sensuality'.

In 1850 the backbone of the Russian regular army consisted of 188 infantry regiments, most of which had three battalions, although some had four; additionally there were 32 rifle battalions and 48 frontier battalions, specifically organized to garrison Siberia with the Cossacks and fortresses in the Caucasus and Turkestan. Fifty-six regiments of cavalry, 310 batteries of artillery, 11 battalions of sappers, 6 half-battalions of *pontonniers* (bridging engineers) and various other ancillaries were all organized to support the infantry. Then there were the Cossacks, that extraordinary and peculiar Russian force of irregular cavalry. These wild horsemen were entitled to certain traditional privileges.† They were not regimental and organized like the rest of the army, and nearly all of them provided their own equipment and horses. Their dress was different, they rode horses which would be called ponies by most westerners, and they did not depend for their food on conventional methods of supply. Dressed in tunic, loose baggy trousers and fur cap, each of these feudal soldiers was armed with a pike, sword and carbine; on his horse he carried only a blanket, saddle, two leather wallets and a forage rope – nothing more. Unencumbered by baggage – unless it was the loot they were taking home to their savage wives – they could march incredible distances and harry the tail or flanks of an enemy army. Normally they operated only within their own territory, although between 1812 and 1814 Caucasian Cossacks formed a chain of posts from the Seine to the Don in order systematically to carry off works of art and other loot from Paris. Their horses were as intelligent as dogs; their pace was

---

* In 1858 approximately 12 per cent of the British army could neither read nor write, and a further 13 per cent barely could write their name.

† Although there were some Cossack infantry, interest in them has always been subordinate to the great force of cavalry.

the gallop and they would go on for miles over rough country with noses to the ground – picking their way like packs of hounds. British 'Heavy' cavalry of the period were known as big men on big horses, while the Cossacks were essentially small but strong men on little horses. But where the horse of a Scots Grey or Inniskilling would starve, the Cossack pony could flourish. They were of little use for the traditional charge which British and French cavalrymen believed was the ultimate reason for their existence but for reconnaissance duties they were superb.

Each regiment or *polk* of Cossacks of about 900 men at war establishment was divided into either four or six *sotnias*. Only Cossacks of the Don were liable for service outside their own region and in time of war 64 *polks* of Don Cossacks could be mobilized.* For this reason Don Cossack regiments had their own artillery consisting of a 12-gun horse battery and thirteen 8-gun field batteries. The real value of the Cossacks lay not so much in their own fighting ability as in the fact that the mobilization of the tribes committed only to home service quickly released other troops from garrison duties for the field army. At the same time the reserves of Don Cossacks enabled Russia to flood an enemy's country with almost savage horsemen possessing none of the mild traditions of civilized warfare who would act according to their untamed nature. They were not intended to stand against regular cavalry, and as they could move far and fast and were unconcerned about the ignominy of withdrawal the Cossacks were about as unmanageable as a horde of little boys under the charge of a solitary policeman. Had Britain been able to use her Indian cavalry in a similar fashion, the war in the Crimea might have gone very differently; certainly it would have been unlikely that there would have been a charge of the Light Brigade.

Apart from the Cossacks, the strength of the Russian army in 1853 could be said to lie solely in its numbers. The Tsar had used it repeatedly to suppress internal uprisings and he expected it to be just as effective in war.

In theory, Russia's military resources were matched by those of Turkey. Unfortunately a large proportion of the Turkish army

---

* To supplement the regular cavalry a total of 84 *polks* of Cossacks (including the 64 Don Cossack regiments) were mobilized – about 75,000 men – during the Crimean war.

existed only on paper, and her stores and military equipment existed only on the invoices presented to the Porte. Disregarding the seven million population belonging to other creeds and races whom they dominated, the Ottoman Empire could call on the services of about two million Moslems and the ranks of the Turkish army had always been filled by them since the days of the Janissaries. Divided into six corps districts each of which was supposed to contribute equally, the paper strength of the Ottoman Empire's standing army was about 700,000 men.* This consisted of 38 infantry regiments each of three battalions and 62 rifle and frontier police battalions, 22 cavalry regiments each of six squadrons and a dromedary corps, six regiments of artillery – usually made up of twelve 6-gun batteries. With no organized supply system or commissariat service the administration of the Turkish army was in a state of utter confusion. In Constantinople the garrison was dressed, equipped and fed liberally but in the provinces the troops were neglected. The fighting qualities of the troops themselves were as good as they had always been – although the officers, like their Russian counterparts, were sadly lacking in education, ability and professional interest. On the parade ground the poorly paid Turkish soldiers made a good showing and it was perhaps symptomatic that training for war was neglected in favour of ceremonial drill. The men, who were shortly to show that they were capable of enduring great hardship, who did not mutiny when they received no pay – an important matter in Turkey – had little training in the use of weapons.

As with the armies of the other belligerents, infantry was the predominant arm. Despite his lack of training in the use of firearms, the lasting qualities which have been described already made the Turkish infantryman a formidable opponent when he got to close quarters with his enemy. The cavalry were nowhere near so good. One hundred and forty squadrons of them, each with a nominal strength of 143 horses, were poorly equipped with old weapons, badly officered and inefficient. All the dash and enterprise which

* Designation and headquarters were as follows:
  1st Corps (Guards) Constantinople
  2nd   ,,   (Dambr) Shumla
  3rd   ,,   (Roumelia) Monastir
  4th   ,,   (Anatolia) Erzurum
  5th   ,,   (Syria) Damascus
  6th   ,,   (Mesopotamia) Baghdad

had made earlier generations of Turkish horsemen the terror of European armies and contributed so much to the march of the Crescent had been lost. During the nineteenth century they had been organized on French lines but they had gained none of the solidity and steadiness of their model and had succeeded only in copying the deficiencies of Napoleon's *arme blanche*.

As regards organization and instruction the Turkish artillery was superior to that of other armies. But as its equipment comprised cannons of all descriptions and calibres – with muzzle-loaders, breech-loaders, rifled and smooth bores often all confusedly mixed in a single battery – it could hardly be considered efficient. Lastly, there was a 2,000-strong corps of regular engineers, few of whose officers possessed any professional or technical knowledge and whose equipment was meagre and inadequate.

Mention has been made already of the Bashi-Bazouks. These colourful characters together with volunteer contingents of Spahis and Bedouins formed part of the Sultan's irregular forces. More often than not their predilection for plunder made them more of an encumbrance than a help to the regular troops, and they were raised primarily for employment against the unarmed or semi-armed occupants of a disaffected district. Most of the Spahis and Bedouins were embodied in irregular cavalry units under their own Arab chiefs and few of them were worth their rations. Ten thousand were raised during the Crimean war but because of their unreliability they were never used. Properly led and organized they were capable of relieving the regular troops – much as the Cossacks did in the Russian army.

To these forces of the Ottoman Empire proper could be added contingents from Egypt and Tunis. Egyptian troops, generally better trained and led than the Turks, had proved their worth in the campaigns of Ibrahim Pasha but because of financial reasons as well as his past differences with the Sultan, the Khedive was not anxious to associate himself with the failing fortunes of the Ottoman Empire. Finally, Tunis could provide only a token force to bolster the military resources of the state to which it was nominally subject.

Totalling all these resources it would appear that theoretically the Sultan could mobilize about two million men of whom less than 70 per cent would become effective. Furthermore the fact that the Russian threat extended from the Balkans to Asia diminished the number of troops available to defend Constantinople in an attack from the north. The Russian army in the Caucasus had an effective strength of about 50,000 men, and even if its strength had not been almost doubled and no invasion of Armenia contemplated, this was sufficient to tie down a large proportion of the Turkish army on the Armenian border. To maintain communications throughout Asia Minor large numbers of troops also had to be deployed so that the maximum number of Ottoman troops that could be available to oppose a Russian advance in Europe was about equal in strength to Gorchakoff's army. At the beginning of 1854 it was difficult to say whether the greatest danger from the Russians lay in Europe or Asia. Between the Armenian border and the Bosphorus there are no natural obstacles in Asia Minor which could be compared to the Danube and the Balkans. Constantinople was the goal but so far as the Balkans were concerned much depended on the attitude of Austria. To reach European Turkey, Russia had only the one road which ran through the gate formed by the south-east angle of the Carpathians and the mouth of the Danube. Austria's Hungarian territory west of this gate gave her some strategic advantage. Similarly the Lower Danube was controlled by Austria.*

It was nearly forty years since the last square of Napoleon's Guard had struggled off the field of Waterloo and during that time France and Britain had both forgotten a great deal. For some years, while memories of Waterloo were fresh, the bitter flavour of defeat lingered in French mouths. But, gradually, as the past receded the nightmare of defeat was forgotten and the French people recalled only the splendour of the Napoleonic years. By 1848 the brief Bourbon regime had been terminated, and the Napoleonic revival with its accompanying renaissance of military ambition had seen the creation of the Second Empire under Napoleon's sole surviving nephew.

As the memory of Waterloo had faded, the feeling that French military power was still supreme had steadily grown. And, unlike the British army, whose structure had remained virtually static, the French army had made considerable advances. In recent history there was not much to confirm a return to the standards of the old

* In 1854, before the war started, it was rumoured that Prince Paskewitch – one of Russia's best generals – told the Tsar that if Russia was going to fight Turkey, preparations should be made for war with Austria. The Eastern Question, he said, could be solved only at Vienna, not in Turkey. Events were to prove Paskewitch was right.

Imperial army, since French troops had scarcely been engaged in Europe since Waterloo. A military promenade had taken them to Spain to quell a revolution; there had been an uneventful siege at Antwerp; and outside Rome they had shown that they were capable of dislodging Italians from behind improvised defences. But in Africa a fresh generation of conscripts had helped to restore the military confidence of France.

French experience in Algeria was similar to that of the British in India, and in 1854 there was some reason to doubt that an enterprising but indifferently armed enemy would necessarily be successful against a well-equipped European adversary. But while British regiments remained in India unrelieved for twenty years or more, the conscription system and proximity of Algeria to metropolitan France kept French soldiers in the public eye. France was proud of its bronzed, decorated, exquisitely tailored heroes of the *jeune Afrique*, and demanded that they should be well looked after. In keeping with every other army of the period, discipline was harsh but democratization of the army was a continuing heritage of the Revolution. While the Bourbons reigned commissions could still be bought but under Louis-Philippe promotion from the ranks on the basis of merit became a regular practice. Consequently by 1840 France had an efficient army in which professionalism was regarded with pride. For the most part its officers were ambitious men and its generals who were all comparatively young had discarded most of the outmoded Napoleonic practices which still regulated British military thought. Unfortunately the new Emperor's *coup d'état* in 1848 brought less able men to senior ranks of the French officer corps – men whom Louis Napoleon could manipulate; men qualified less by their ability than by their pliability. St Arnaud, Canrobert, Forey and Pélissier were all names that were to become familiar in the Crimean war. St Arnaud – ex-Foreign Legion officer, once hounded out of Paris by creditors, prone to gambling, women and wine – commanded the French army. François Canrobert, St Arnaud's second-in-command, and Élie Frédéric Forey each led a division at the Battle of the Alma; Jean Jacques Pélissier – the only one of the new generals to prove himself to be of any worth – eventually succeeded to the command of the French army in the Crimea.

Like most other European armies, infantry was the basis of the French army. This was organized conventionally into regiments each of four battalions, and when war was declared many units were armed with old muzzle-loading percussion rifles. Like the British – who had recently adopted the Minié rifle, designed by a French-man – the French were re-equipping with Snider type breech-loading rifles. Of the cavalry little need be said since only the *Chasseurs d'Afrique* were involved in the campaign; it is sufficient to say that French Hussars were as elegant as British Hussars, Lancers and Dragoons equally as dashing. French artillery was no better and certainly no worse than that of the British. But when it came to administrative organization the French were years ahead. In Algeria they had learned that if troops were to fight well they had to live well. To do this every function necessary to an army's survival and maintenance had been incorporated into the army proper, and staffed by men who understood the business of war. As a result the pay, rations, medical services and supply arrangements for the French army in the Crimea were as good as those enjoyed by a garrison in France. Throughout the war ten hospitals handled their patients without any of the neglect and confusion charac-teristic of the British facilities and without the same mortality rate. Once aware of their own inefficiency the British could only boggle at their ally's equipment and methods – just as they were to boggle almost a hundred years later when an expeditionary Anglo-French force was raised for other ill-conceived operations in the Middle East. Early in 1845 Louis Napoleon saw the coming cam-paign as being little more than a colonial expedition, inexpensive in terms of men and *matériel* and of comparatively short duration. Initially the French contribution was to be a matter of only 10,000 men, and he expected to get these almost exclusively from Africa. Thinning out the Algerian garrisons would not affect the size of the garrisons in France and there was the added advantage of the troops being experienced fighters. Soon, however, it was not a question of 10,000 men, but of 40,000 and then 70,000 – with the possibility of still more being needed.

In Britain, the triumph of Waterloo had been followed by a strong feeling of revulsion from the military activities of the preceding twenty years. When the Napoleonic menace had been disposed of Britain was tired of war and sick of soldiers. Moreover there had been a marked aversion to professional standing armies in England ever since Cromwell and the Interregnum which had been reinforced by James II's manipulation of the army and his troop concentrations on Hounslow Heath. Forty years of peace brought a social revolution and an unprecedented expansion of wealth and this was not a climate to promote militarism. In those days Britain had no balance-of-payments problems; most of her people were prosperous and they had no interest in military adventure. England believed that so long as she maintained her navy her imperial status was unassailable. Other than to protect the outposts of her Empire from local dangers – inconsiderable by European standards – the need for an army was discounted by almost everyone. Parliament grew more and more parsimonious in sanctioning expenditure on the fighting services, and a bewildering number of civilian departments and military authorities kept a close check on the army's finances.

Within the army itself many causes contributed to the unpopularity of the soldier's calling. The severity and tedium of discipline, the squalor of barrack life and the deadly monotony of endless hours of 'square-bashing' all had their effect. Britain was not prepared to pay for anything more than the minimum needed to look after her expanding interests overseas, and the Duke of Wellington – although he was concerned – was afraid that any attempt to induce the British people to spend more on defence would start them questioning whether even the present cost of the army was justified. It was said that he tried to keep soldiers out of sight and deliberately hid the army away in foreign stations in order to disarm the animosity of Parliament. Such a suggestion is fallacious, because the army's tasks – well beyond its strength and means – necessitated the bulk of it having to serve abroad. However, it is certainly true that the Duke was opposed to any increase in the soldiers' pay because he sincerely believed that if the army became more costly the nation would resent the increased charges. In Parliament others were against better pay because they considered it would make the soldiers more drunken and licentious, necessitating greater severity in discipline.

Stirrings of conscience brought about the Reform Bill, the abolition of slavery and improvements in prisons, but little was done for the army. In the forty years of the long peace there were few changes in conditions of service, pay and the housing of the troops and in 1854 the troops were still 'infamously housed, abominably overcrowded and senselessly fed'. In such circumstances it is easy to understand that the only men who could be recruited were those unwanted elsewhere. And if a man was not an outcast from society before he enlisted as a soldier, be became one immediately afterwards. For a shilling a day, plus a penny a day beer money – from which was deducted sixpence for his rations, and various other stoppages in the way of fines, payments for uniform replacements and a host of regimental impositions – the recruit soon found that he had sold all but his soul to the Queen. When he was out serving in the monotonous surroundings of a foreign station, he lived – hugger-mugger – in the gaunt grim barracks which had been erected in haste at the beginning of the French wars. He was denied both comfort and social amenities. Even if he could read there were few books available to him. (The government feared that he might read some of the literature which emanated from the French Revolutionary or reactionary movements and so the only literature allowed into barracks were some twenty-eight volumes approved by a bench of bishops – issued specifically for the benefit of sick soldiers.)

Before the Crimean war education in the army was in the hands of its chaplains. Sixty per cent of the infantry were illiterates but nobody outside the army was particularly anxious to improve the system. Fear of revolutionary propaganda spreading in the ranks prevented any educational reform being undertaken. 'By Jove!', the old Duke of Wellington once exclaimed, 'if ever there is a mutiny in the army – and in all probability we shall have one – you'll see that these new fangled schoolmasters will be at the bottom of it!'

During the day most of the soldier's time was spent on the barrack square rehearsing repetitive drill-movements until he became a virtual automaton. Battles were still supposed to be fought in close formation and in theory all drill was based on the tactical movements. But ceremonial had become an end in itself and the need to relate drill to tactics was apt to be ignored. It was easier to move formations of troops backwards and forwards across the parade ground than take them into the fields and woods where war could be simulated. When he was not drilling the soldier was cleaning and polishing. With the passage of the years, uniforms had become steadily more exotic. Mounted men were loaded with fantastic headdresses, elaborate slung jackets, dolmans and pelisses; infantrymen had to wear huge shakos shaped like inverted bells; all officers were smothered in gold lace.* For the army tailors these were merry days. A soldier was expected to keep his uniform spotlessly clean, and to be smartly turned out. If he failed to do so or was guilty of any other minor misdemeanour he was flogged with a cat-o'-nine-tails – not as severely as when he mutinied or deserted, but flogged neverthe-less. With no clothes other than his uniform, treated with callous-ness and brutality that would have brought howls of protest from the public in any other context, it is hardly surprising that the soldier turned to tobacco, drink, and squalid assignations for solace.

Soldiers' drinking bouts were, in fact, accepted by the British public as an occupational disease. Little thought was given to the reason for such a besetting sin, but provision was often made to obviate its more serious consequences. Pay-days were 'staggered' in order to limit the nocturnal drinking that followed. Care was taken to see that neighbouring units were not paid on the same day, as standing feuds between men of different regiments were apt to end in brawls.

Of the officers, few except those serving in India and the colonies or who were old (sixty or over) enough to have fought in the Napoleonic wars had any experience of active service. Many of the younger ones had joined the army not because they were interested in soldiery as a career but because it was a fashionable place for young aristocrats with no aptitude for anything else. Matters varied from regiment to regiment, but – apart from an honourable few – the majority of the wealthier officers treated their regiments as 'a lounge they had taken on lease'. Wealthy men never needed to serve abroad, and even in England many of them habitually managed to stay away from their regiments for months on end. A rich man could command a regiment before the age of thirty, whilst his captains and subalterns grizzled in the lower ranks. The purchase of com-missions lay at the root of most of the ludicrous incongruities but it was a long time after the Crimean war before it was abolished.†

---

* Lancer regiments were arrayed in embroidered double-breasted scarlet jackets with two rows of buttons, and blue overalls with a double scarlet stripe. On their heads they wore a high 'cap' ten inches square at the top in which the officers carried a 16-inch-long plume of blackcock tail feathers. Large gold epaulettes and gold cap-lines with gold tassels completed the dress.

† The Army List printed a scale of regulations, 'Prices of Commission', according to which a lieutenant-colonelcy in a line regiment was worth £4,500, in a cavalry regiment £5,176, in the Foot Guards £9,000. But commissions were usually sold for prices considerably in excess of this scale and the cost of changing hands in some regiments was as much as £57,000.

In 1852, ensigns were paid four shillings and sixpence a day, and at a home station obligatory expenses invariably ate up the whole of this sum. Consequently the officer with small private means had little choice but to go and swelter in the West Indies or some other overseas station where the foreign allowance would stretch his pay further. For him there were few distractions and his chief hope of self-improvement depended on the professional progress which the system made so difficult to achieve.

Despite this appalling background, the British army which went to the Crimea was destined to astonish the world by its fortitude and endurance. The Crimean Army consisted largely of hardened soldiers, prematurely aged by a hard life and whose health was often undermined by drink. The majority were illiterate, yet stolid, shrewd and long-suffering. Their language was coarse and blasphemous; they suffered from a thirst which needed much slaking. But it was these men who defeated the Russians on the banks of the Alma, at Balaclava, on the heights of Inkerman and in the assault on Sebastopol. It is easy to attribute their behaviour to the insensitivity which derives from drink and debauchery and to fear of the lash. That was how those in authority defended the system under which the British army laboured. The truth was that the long-suffering and sorely tried sense of duty of the British soldier held good. 'For by nature they are so constituted,' wrote an eye-witness in the Crimea, 'that the ill fortune of their comrades does not commonly affect them with feelings of discouragement, but, on the contrary, is apt to heat their blood by rousing an emotion like anger; and when they have thus been wrought upon they are sterner men for a foe to have to deal with than they are when all has gone well.'

2

THE ARMIES
TAKE THE FIELD

The British and French Governments had been preparing their armies for the field since the beginning of 1854, when the prospects of intervention in the Near East were crystallizing. To ensure co-ordination of effort and understanding, conversations were held in Paris and on 23 February Louis Napoleon discussed with Lord Cowley, the British Ambassador, the question of the command of the allied armies in the coming war. The French view was that while the British were unquestionably superior at sea the land forces should be vested in a French supreme commander. To Louis Napoleon this seemed only reasonable and proper; after all, one of Napoleon Bonaparte's maxims was 'when war is carried on against a single power there should be only one army acting upon one base and conducted by one chief. . . . Long discussions and Councils of War . . . will terminate in the adoption of the worse course'.[1] But the British were not prepared to have their army serving under French command. Apart from any questions of pride, such an arrangement – as they saw it – would make the British commander-in-chief second-in-command to his own men. Better, they considered, to have a loose arrangement of simple co-operation both on land and sea.

Who was to command the British army had already been settled. It was to be Lord Raglan (Fitzroy Somerset) who was then sixty-five. During the Peninsula War Raglan had served on the staff of the Duke of Wellington, losing his right arm at Waterloo. For the next thirty years he had sat in an office in London, becoming Master-General of the Ordnance – an appointment for which he was not qualified by virtue of any technical knowledge – in 1832. A man of gallantry, breeding and tact, he was an able administrator but he had no experience of commanding troops in the field.

The 1st Division of Raglan's army was commanded by the Queen's cousin, the 35-year-old Duke of Cambridge. De Lacy Evans, another Peninsula veteran, who had been put on half pay in 1818, commanded the 2nd Division; he was a fretful, uncouth man, easily depressed. The 3rd Division was under the command of the 61-year-old Sir Richard England who had also fought against Bonaparte, and the 4th Division was under the orders of Sir George Cathcart, who had just returned from fighting Kaffirs in South Africa. The Light Division – perhaps the finest formation in the British army at that time – went to Sir George Brown, another Peninsula veteran, while the Cavalry Division was commanded by Lord Lucan, a mere fifty-four, but lacking in real military experience.* The Chief Engineer with the British army was the 72-year-old Sir John Fox Burgoyne, who had joined the army in the previous century and fought in the American War of 1812 as well as with Wellington. So far as senior officers were concerned it was Wellington's army without Wellington. The entire force under Lord Raglan consisted of about 30,000 men; as may be deduced from what has been said already it was in a sad condition and as a military instrument it was unquestionably defective.

In general the French Expeditionary Force was superior to the British. Not only was it better organized, none of its senior officers was more than 55 years old and many officers and men had had active service in Algeria. These facts alone were a powerful argument for the French being in command of the land forces — at least during battle.

Another contrast in the allied systems was that whereas the French Minister of War was always a soldier, his British counterpart was simply a Member of Parliament and political allegiances tended to lessen the efficiency of the British army. Duty to Britain seemed all that Tory Raglan and Whig Admiral Dundas had in common. Outwardly courteous, they treated each other with complete formality; but conversation followed only after a letter requesting a conference had been sent, as prescribed by protocol. The French, on the other hand, had a common bond in their experience in Algeria; and while differences did exist between them they were all on speaking terms with one another from the outset. One of their

---

* This was one of the biggest of Whitehall's mistakes. The story of the mordant family quarrel has been too well told in *The Reason Why* to need more than a passing reference. Some of its effects will be apparent when the reader reaches Chapter 11.

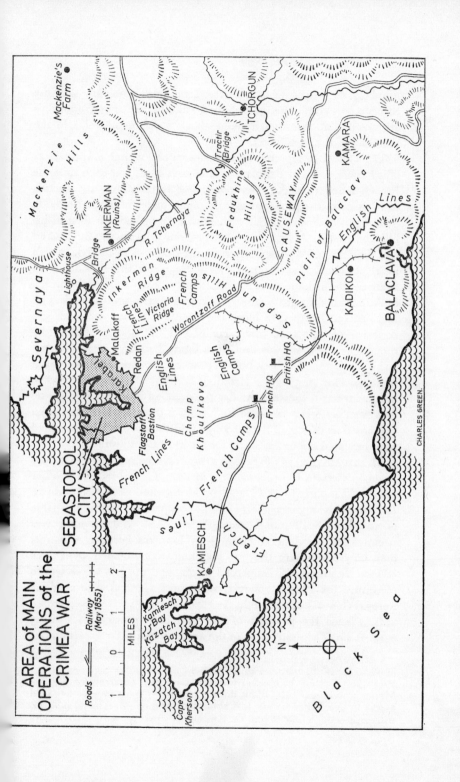

AREA of MAIN
OPERATIONS of the
CRIMEA WAR

Roads
Railway
(May 1855)

MILES
1   0   1   2

Mackenzie's
Farm

Mackenzie Hills

INKERMAN
(Ruins)

TCHORGUN

KAMARA

Tractir
Bridge

Fedukhine
Hills

CAUSEWAY

Plain of Balaclava

English
Lines

Lighthouse
Bridge

R. Tchernaya

Inkerman Ridge

French
Camps

Sapoune Hills

BALACLAVA

Severnaya

Malakoff

French
Lines

Victoria
Ridge

Worontzoff Road

KADIKOI

Redan

Karabel

English
Lines

English
Camps

British HQ

French HQ

SEBASTOPOL
CITY

Flagstaff
Bastion

Champ
Khoulikovo

French Camps

French Lines

French
Lines

KAMIESCH

N

CHARLES GREEN.

Kamiesch
Bay

Kazatch
Bay

Cape
Kherson

Black Sea

number, an officer who understood military problems, was the
Minister of War. This gave added validity to Louis Napoleon's
argument that the French should have a dominant voice in the
handling of the land forces.

The subject of supreme commander came up time and again at
allied conferences in February and March 1854, but each time the
French failed to make their point. For command of the French
contingent of the proposed expeditionary force, Marshal Leroy de
St Arnaud had been nominated. Born in 1789, he was then in his
fifty-third year. A vain and unscrupulous adventurer, St Arnaud
was the man largely responsible for the massacre of the boulevards
in 1851 which had brought Louis Napoleon the Presidency of
France – his first and most important step towards a French throne.
St Arnaud had fought against Turks and Arabs, and in Algiers he
had ordered his men to block the mouth of a cave in which 500
Arabs were entombed alive. He played the fiddle, occasionally
thought of God, and his taut, lean figure had once been athletic.
In his youth he had written poetry, practised a 'cynical debauchery',[2]
mastered four languages – including English – and had dabbled in
the theatre as a comedian under the name of Floridor. In 1854 he
had been suffering for some time from a disease which had been
diagnosed as cancer of the intestines and the doctors who attended
him disagreed about his fitness for a trip to Constantinople.*

The 1st Division of the French army was commanded by General
François Certain Canrobert. Born in 1809, Canrobert was another
who had supported Louis Napoleon in the affair of the boulevards.
In spite of his long unsoldierly hair he was perhaps the most capable
of the French divisional commanders. The 2nd Division was
commanded by General Pierre Jean François Bosquet, who was
then only forty-four; the 3rd nominally commanded by Prince
Jerome Napoleon, the Emperor's cousin, and the 4th, which was to
constitute the French reserves, was under General Élie Frédéric
Forey. When the armies embarked their strengths were about equal.

In France the prospect of war had been greeted with rising
enthusiasm. The destination of the armies was a little uncertain but

---

* His personal appearance was misleading. One day he would appear to
be close to death, the next to be perfectly fit. Nevertheless when he left
Paris the consensus of opinion was that he would never return alive. In
March he had asked one of his doctors how many more months he could
expect to live. When he was told about four or more, St Arnaud said this
was easily enough time to beat the Russians in Turkey.

some British units had already left England for Malta, where they were joined by French troops from Algeria. In the beginning the French Emperor had seen the coming campaign as being hardly more than a colonial expedition, comparatively short and inexpensive in terms of men and resources. Publicly the Emperor spoke of four armies of 60,000 men each and St Arnaud wrote about 600,000 and 1,200 guns. (France just did not have this number of men under arms, and such statements could only be interpreted as propaganda.) What Louis Napoelon hoped to do was to get most of the men he needed from Algeria and his early plans called for the bulk of the expedition to be made up of Zouave regiments. The Zouaves were veteran French colonial campaigners whose morale was high.

Along the Danube the Turks, already at war against the Russians, were anxiously waiting for help and a move in this direction was clearly indicated. But the French were already thinking of an attack on Sebastopol as the ultimate objective, and in January Baraguay D'Hilliers, the French Ambassador at Constantinople, had been told to investigate the possibility of a landing in the Crimea with a view to an attack on Sebastopol. In March, when Raglan had visited Paris, a plan to attack the Russian naval base had also been discussed. St Arnaud had been in favour of it but Raglan and his colleagues had cold-shouldered the idea. By April, however, it seemed that a campaign in the Principalities would be followed by a landing in the Crimea.

During April and May there was little military action. A British fleet in the Baltic cruised about, professing to establish an effective blockade, and on 22 April the allied fleets in the Black Sea bombarded Odessa. At the end of May the troublesome Christians of Epirus obliged the Allies to land soldiers at the Piraeus to induce King Otho to sign a declaration of neutrality. Finally the Turkish army at Silistria was attacked by the Russians. The Danube was crossed at several points, but the Russians made little headway south of the river as the garrisons at Varna and Schumla stood firm. By this time the allied armies had concentrated at Scutari and Constantinople and already the insalubrious Orient was having its effects on the troops. 'The amount of drunkenness,' one officer reported, 'is frightful. The other night 2,400 men were reported drunk . . . and we have not above 14,000 here [Scutari] altogether . . .' In the following month, also at Scutari, another wrote

'The army gets drunk I am sorry to say ... we have nothing to complain of in the conduct of our men when they are sober; when drunk they knock the Turks about; so we flogged a man the other day to make an example'. Other vices were accommodated in brothels; the process of debilitation which was to have such dire effects had begun.

A number of the wives of the soldiers had accompanied the British army and there were several hundred of them in the Crimean army. From ten to thirty women were allowed to accompany each regiment, authorized or chosen by the commanding officer. By the evidence of Lieutenant-Colonel Sparks given before the Select Committee in 1855, the 38th Regiment took about twenty women to Gallipoli. It appears that as they were not even entitled to a tent, they depended for shelter on the casual generosity of the officers. When Sparks was asked 'Can you give any opinion upon the condition of the women? Were they cared for in any way whatsoever?', he replied, 'No, it would have been better I think if they had not gone out'.[3] These women washed, cooked and mended clothes. Their morality seems to have been in accordance with the circumstances in which they lived; doubtless they were indulgent and often tempted. The Turks thought that they were members of the British generals' harems.[4] As few of them were sufficiently articulate to have recorded their experiences they have only a dim and scarcely verified existence, faintly appearing now and then on the bleak, ungenerous pages of an official report or as a casual reference in a regimental history.

Officers' wives lived in comfortable quarters in Pera or Malta. Madame St Arnaud and Lady Stratford, the wife of the British Ambassador in Pera, entertained with great elegance. A few of the more adventurous made their way to the Crimea and one of these, Mrs Duberly, was an eye-witness of practically the whole of the campaign.

While the armies waited for their orders to move towards the Danube, a chauvinistic spirit prevailed in Britain. 'As far as war depends upon finance,' declared *The Times* on 6 June 1854, 'we can override and cripple our adversary without the smallest difficulty; we shall overmatch him, we confidently trust, with equal certainty in the field and on the sea.' The writer was expressing the substance of the jingo's anthem: 'We've got the men, we've got the ships, we've got the money too'.

Orders for the advance of the armies had been prepared in the last week of April. They were to move up to Varna, the popular modern Bulgarian resort on the Black Sea, which Omar Pasha, the Turkish commander-in-chief, had assured the Allies was a 'salubrious' place.[5] Concentration at Varna began early in June, most of the troops going by sea although some of the French army marched up from Adrianople. Within a few weeks the allied camps covered the countryside to a distance of about twenty-five miles from the coast; a fleet was riding at anchor in the bay; and stores were being accumulated in the town.

Less than seventy miles away the Turks were fighting on the Danube, gradually forcing the Russians back. When on 23 June the Russians abandoned the siege of Silistria and started to withdraw, the object of the allied expedition would appear to have vanished. But soon it was to be apparent that the evacuation of the Principalities and the independence of Turkey were merely incidental considerations to the real purpose of the expedition. The aim of Britain and France was neither more nor less than the crushing of Russia as a power in the Black Sea.

On 28 June St Arnaud at Varna wrote to his wife, 'I cannot recover from the shock of the Russians' disgraceful retreat. I ... would have infallibly beaten them, flung them into the Danube'.[6] On the same day a drowsy English Cabinet was meeting at Richmond. The Secretary of State for War, the Duke of Newcastle, read a paper which disclosed the orders to Raglan for an invasion of the Crimea. 'It is very certain that before the reading had long continued all the members of the Cabinet except a small minority were overcome with sleep.'[7] The only excuse for somnolence on this occasion was that the plan had been fully discussed already.

Meantime an enemy far more terrible than all the armies of Russia was assailing the troops in their summery camps at Varna – an enemy for whom they were totally unprepared either by knowledge or provision. Symptoms of lack of provision and mismanagement had in fact already been seen. Some had been corrected but not many. William Howard Russell of *The Times*, who had accompanied the British Expeditionary Force from Malta and who is credited with being the first war correspondent, had already remarked on the deficiencies which he found at Varna.

'Where is the English post office? No one knows. Where does the English General live? No one knows. Where is the hospital to carry a sick soldier to? No one knows. Where are the field hospitals? At present, if a serious case of illness occurs in camp, the only conveyance for the sufferer is a bullock cart, and in that miserable, springless vehicle he has to perform the tedious journey into Varna – enough to destroy all chance of recovery.'

By July the armies already smitten by amoebic dysentery were struck by cholera; coming, it was alleged, in French ships from Marseilles by way of Piraeus, Gallipoli and Constantinople. On 4 July, St Arnaud was boasting of the excellent health of the French army: true, there were a few cases of cholera; but he declared confidently, 'I have prescribed precautions and the storm will pass'.[8] It was not long before his 'precautions' were seen to have been entirely useless and exactly a month after St Arnaud's prediction, Russell was writing of the British army:

'The cholera continues. The 50th Regiment . . . lost nine men last night . . . it is useless to alarm friends and relations at home by talking of the number of sick or by giving their names, but it is evident that we are in a very unsatisfactory state as regards health . . . At present the cholera has assumed a phase which baffles our best efforts, and throws all our past data to the winds. It is sometimes quite painless, there is little or no purging but the sufferer is seized with violent spasms in the stomach, which increase in intensity till collapse is established, and death then rapidly follows, attended with but little exhibition of agony.'

The British army suffered less than the French but the losses were heavy enough and the morale of the troops had suffered a severe blow. Rations were increased by half a pound of meat and a half-ration of rum because the time for embarkation for the Crimean operation was approaching.

OBJECTIVE SEBASTOPOL

In Britain a vociferous minority had been clamouring for the capture and destruction of the Russian naval base at Sebastopol. After the Turkish squadron was blown out of the water at Sinope, this focus of Russian power in the Black Sea had become a special object of execration, and within weeks the desire for its destruction had become almost a national aberration. British and French leaders had been discussing an invasion of the Crimea for some time. But practical expediency had ruled out such an operation while the Russians were south of the Danube. However, when the Russians evacuated the Principalities and retired behind the Prut, there were no plans for the future. Britain and France had committed themselves to the defence of Turkey but they had not thought of operations outside Europe. When the need for a definitive objective was forced upon them, the British Cabinet saw the destruction of Sebastopol and the Russian fleet as an excellent way of reducing a potential naval power in the Middle East. Louis Napoleon was not nearly so enthusiastic about such an operation, but he approved and was prepared to promote it.

By July the need to do something to improve morale was urgent. After the Russians had withdrawn from the Principalities there was little point in staying at Varna. Turkey might now be safe but the idea of sending the troops home was unthinkable. What was needed, St Arnaud told Louis Napoleon, was a 'beautiful climax' that would end the war. At a long conference in Varna the allied commanders reluctantly concluded that an invasion of the Crimea might provide just that sort of climax. None of them really liked the idea but they accepted the decision of their political masters in London and Paris. Admiral Sir James Dundas, the 69-year-old commander of the British Black Sea Fleet was the one who had most doubts about the venture. And he was considered to be an obstinate, over-cautious and difficult dodderer. 'Of the two admirals in command of the Black Sea and Baltic Fleets, one is always praying and the other always swearing,' a contemporary correspondent commented acidly, 'but they seem to agree on one point, namely, in not fighting.'[1]

Having decided that there should be an invasion, a commission was sent to reconnoitre the coast of the Crimea for suitable landing places. There was already evidence – supplied by a British officer, Captain James Drummond, who had visited Sebastopol in January – to the effect that 'the north side presented favourable points'[2] and the evidence of the commission confirmed Drummond's conclusion. The mouth of the Katcha, about six miles from Sebastopol, appeared to be a 'perfectly practical' landing place to Generals Brown and Canrobert, and with some hesitation Admiral Lyons, second-in-command to Dundas, agreed. Lyons, a man who saw himself as an embryo Nelson, had been one of the most outspoken and enthusiastic proponents of an attack on Sebastopol. But the realization of what the operation would involve as the event drew closer made him apprehensive of the outcome. The French admiral, Bruat, stressed every possible hazard and danger and then concluded calmly that the venture could be successfully carried through.[3]

While the commission was reconnoitring the Crimean coast, news reached the French to the effect that a force of about 10,000 Russians had been reported south of the Danube in the Dobrudja district about 150 miles from Varna. To St Arnaud this seemed to be a heaven-sent opportunity for provoking an alternative 'beautiful climax' to the war, and he suggested to Raglan that French troops should be sent up to engage the Russians. The realization that allied troops were in action against the Russians would improve morale, and fighting in the Dobrudja district ought to divert attention from the preparations for the projected operation in the Crimea. Reducing the numbers of men in Varna should benefit both those leaving and those staying behind, and it ought to be possible to cope with the cholera more effectively. Raglan, who had received specific orders from London instructing him not to go into the Dobrudja hunting for Russians, showed no enthusiasm for the venture. His staff cynically inclined to the idea that all St Arnaud was trying to show the world was that it was the French who were first into battle.

Despite Raglan's refusal to participate, the French commander-in-chief was set on a limited campaign in the bare and marshy Dobrudja. Apart from *la gloire* for France to which he aspired, there would be an opportunity to try out the newly organized

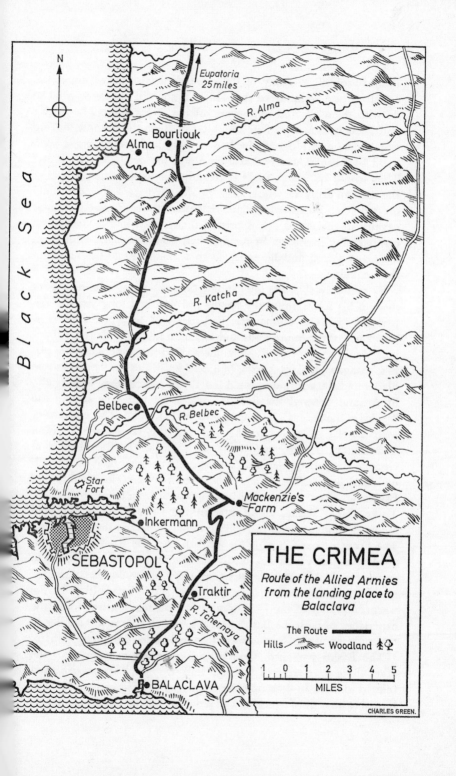

N

Black Sea

Eupatoria
25 miles

R. Alma

Bourliouk

Alma

R. Katcha

Belbec

R. Belbec

Star
Fort

Mackenzie's
Farm

Inkermann

SEBASTOPOL

Traktir

R. Tchernaya

BALACLAVA

THE CRIMEA

*Route of the Allied Armies
from the landing place to
Balaclava*

The Route ▬▬▬▬
Hills ⌢⌢⌢⌢ Woodland 🌲🍂

1 0 1 2 3 4 5
MILES

CHARLES GREEN.

Bashi-Bazouks. So many of these 'banditti who prowl about the country'[4] had volunteered that Omar Pasha did not know what to do with them all, and some were offered to his allies. The British and French each took four thousand of these picturesque-looking vagabonds, and although he had already had some trouble with them St Arnaud was enthusiastic about his new irregular army. They would be '. . . cossacks as redoubtable as the true cossacks of the Russian army' he wrote.[5] The 'Spahis of Africa' – the colourfully dressed Arab horsemen whom Frenchmen thought were the finest cavalry in the world – had proved their worth in two decades of campaigning in Africa. St Arnaud had been associated with them for many years, and he expected to turn the Bashi-Bazouks into their equals.

By mid-July 1854 the unfortunate General Yusef, who had spent most of his life training the Spahis and had had long years of experience as their commander, had managed to produce six regiments out of the 'murderous and inchoate rabble of Kurds, Albanians, Arabs, Negroes and every unclassified marauder carrying pistols, yatagans, kinjars, krisses, butchers' knives, or lovely damascene blades and rifles with decorated butts'.[6] As soon as they were ready, St Arnaud ordered the Bashis – whom he was now calling the 'Spahis of the Orient' – to lead the way to Dobrudja. The expedition, with Yusef's irregulars in the van and the 1st French Division immediately behind, moved off on 22 July. (In the absence of General Canrobert, General Espinasse was commanding the French division.) Bosquet's and Prince Napoleon's divisions followed that of Espinasse. There were no British troops, nor were there any regular Turks. Omar Pasha, knowing what the Dobrudja was like, had followed Raglan's lead in refusing to participate in the expedition. The French troops, hoping for a brush with the Russians, were in good heart but Varna was hardly out of sight when things started to go wrong. At Mangalia on the coast some of the Bashis contracted cholera and the disease spread among them like wildfire. In the warm humidity of the Dobrudja the pestilence flourished and the experience of both the Bashis and the French troops was similar to that suffered by the Russian corps that had pulled out ahead of them.

The Bashis panicked. One brigade deserted *en masse*, and the other three were reduced to about half strength. Those who stayed refused to listen to their officers; those who were fit enough to do so turned to an orgy of wrecking and plunder. And as Yusef's command

disintegrated, cholera was decimating the French infantry. Espinasse pressed on to his objective but by the time the French reached
Babadayh the main body of the Russians had crossed the Danube
and the sight of a couple of Cossack patrols was the only satisfaction
gained from the whole escapade. With the pestilence dogging their
steps the return to Varna was a 'veritable funeral march'.[7] Thousands perished *en route*, the 1st French Division losing six thousand
men, and the two others between 1,200 and 1,800 each.

Shortly before the remnants of his expedition staggered back into Varna, St Arnaud had been bragging 'If I disembark in the
Crimea, and if God will grant me a calm sea for a few hours, I am
master of Sebastopol . . . I will carry on this war with an activity, an
energy that will strike terror into the Russians.'[8] But with the arrival
of the troops from Dobrudja, St Arnaud's mood of elation turned
into one of abject dejection. While the cholera raged, he spent
much of his time among the sick, riding from unit to unit checking
personally the extent of the sickness. As he walked among the disheartened and demoralized men back from their fruitless expedition
into the Dobrudja, the Zouaves called out to him: 'Why have we
been brought here? . . . Take us back to Africa, if you will not lead
us against the Russians.'

What remained of the 'Spahis of the Orient' were disbanded and
ordered to return to their homes. France was satisfied with their
services, but had no further need of them. Most drifted away aim-
lessly, but some had to be forcibly driven out of the area. In the
long run their disbandment was the one beneficial product of
the Dobrudja disaster. The French were no longer bothered by the
Bashi-Bazouks. The British contingent – 'Beatson's Horse', so-called
after their commanding officer – still remained, to plague the British
throughout the war and to cause Colonel Beatson to wonder what he
could do with 'these disorderly rascals'. Only the wretched Yusef,
who tried to tell himself that his experiences with the Bashis were
nothing more than a bad dream,[9] continued to serve, and he was
given command of a division of Turkish infantry.

After Dobrudja the governments in both Paris and London
regarded the idea of an invasion of the Crimea as the next logical
step in their war against Russia. The British Cabinet had sanctioned
the operation immediately it was known that the Russians had
withdrawn from the Danube. According to their information the
allied armies in Turkey outnumbered the ill-equipped Russian

army in the Crimea and the fortifications protecting Sebastopol
were inadequate for a protracted defence. Not that there was any
suggestion it should be attacked from the sea. Even the most san-
guine agreed that Sebastopol was far too heavily defended for such
an attack even to be contemplated. But the considered opinion of
the armchair strategists was that the base would soon fall to a
determined land attack. Nobody seems to have considered quite
how the attack on Sebastopol was to be launched, or the more
immediate problem of how the Crimea was to be invaded. Not only
were the authorities in Britain confident of success, they were also
certain that the autumn would see the end as well as the beginning
of the campaign. Covered in glory, the troops should be home for
Christmas.

On the other side of the Channel, Louis Napoleon – exasperated
by the news of the demoralizing effects of the cholera – was ready to
fall in with any plan so long as it led to military glory. Turkey had
been saved and he wanted peace to be restored. But not before the
Tsar had been punished. For the French, the capture of Sebastopol
thus represented a face-saving formula, and in the long run it was
political rather than military factors which determined the invasion
of the Crimea. Between February and September 1854 most of the
leading British and French generals opposed the plan, and the
decision was taken not by military men but by politicians who had
little idea of the complex implications of their action. Both Raglan
and St Arnaud merely carried out orders. (As one of Raglan's
divisional commanders remarked, the government was clearly
determined on the invasion and if Raglan was not prepared to
undertake it he would be replaced by some other general.) Louis
Napoleon was optimistic. He had just heard that French troops
had captured the island of Bomarsund. Moreover he had been led
to understand that the newly invented rocket and iron-clad gunboats would quickly reduce fortresses like Sebastopol to impotency.
In such circumstances he instructed St Arnaud to take his army to
the Crimea if Raglan decided to go there.

Instructions that he should prepare for an attack on Sebastopol
reached Raglan early in July. The only discretion allowed in his
orders was that if *both* Raglan and St Arnaud felt the task was
beyond their capabilities the British and French governments would
reconsider the operation. In the event, both commanders agreed
that Sebastopol could be captured. Then the French dissented, and

finally the British were pessimistic. But as neither had agreed that the operation was *not* feasible, preparations for it went ahead.

Estimates of the strength of Russian troops in the Crimean peninsula varied from 45,000 to 140,000.* But as the Tsar was hardly likely to leave the pendant pearl of his empire in danger of being snatched away, most of Raglan's and St Arnaud's staff officers doubted if anything less than the higher figure was realistic. This was only one of their worries. Those who merited a professional rating were distinctly uneasy about the lack of information on almost every aspect of the operation, and some of this tension filtered down to the troops. Not without good reason the men began to feel that their commanders possibly lacked the ability to meet a crisis. Nor were the records of the notabilities inspiring. St Arnaud – said to have been a dashing colonel of cavalry at one time – was known to have won his marshal's baton not on the battlefield but as Minister of War in Paris. Furthermore he was an invalid. Canrobert, the French second-in-command, had gained imperial favour when his brigade stormed the barricades in the Faubourg St Martin, not by distinguished service in Africa. Except for an aura of reflected military glory, Raglan's name meant little, and the man himself visited the troops so rarely that few of them recognized him as commander-in-chief. When the operation got under way and health improved, the rumbling of disquiet was to vanish amid the cries of 'Hurrah for the Crimea'. But for most of August 1854 the British contingent of the allied expeditionary force was sick and sorry, and the French were not feeling very much better.

Although staff officers knew of it by late July, the troops who were to carry out the operation did not know that they were going to attack Sebastopol until 25 August, when St Arnaud told his men *'L'heure est venue de combattre et de vaincre.'* In London and Paris the public had known what was afoot a fortnight earlier, when on 9 August *The Times* announced that Sebastopol was the allied objective. The war in the Crimea was to be the last of the old-style wars but it was to be noteworthy for the introduction of two modern phenomena – the press correspondent and the war photographer. More often than not people in London, Paris and St Petersburg were better informed about the course of the war as a result of their

* In fact the Russians had about 70,000 men in or near Sebastopol. The field force comprised some 48 battalions, each about 800 strong; 3,500 cavalry; and about 100 field artillery pieces served by 2,500 gunners.

efforts than those in the field, and the despatches of William Howard Russell, correspondent of *The Times*, are among the most important records of the campaign. Similarly, the pictures of Roger Fenton were to provide clear evidence of what the new medium of photography could achieve in the vivid communication of major events. But journalists were not popular at the front. While some senior British officers were prepared to recognize that they had a duty to the general public and that 'recognized' correspondents performed their duties conscientiously, the majority wanted to banish them from the theatre of operations. 'Defects in war should be left to cure themselves, as they will do, by a slower and, perhaps, more salutary process . . .'[10] Nevertheless, those gentlemen of the Press who were socially acceptable – like Fenton – had ready access to the leading British personalities, while the French – not content with excluding correspondents from their camp – tongue-tied the press whenever possible.

The embarkation of the allied armies, originally fixed for 14 August, was delayed by the cholera which was still raging. Some regiments were reasonably fit, but most of the troops were pitifully weak. Even the Guards – by repute the strongest and toughest soldiers in the British army – were unable to carry their packs or to march in light order more than five miles a day. Not until the end of the month was it possible to start embarking the armies of invalids on the motley collection of fighting ships and transports that were awaiting them in the Bay of Varna. But once aboard the ships there was an immediate revival of spirits; discipline and energy and health began to improve. The troops were more than happy to leave behind the misery of their Bulgarian camps, and the prospect of action added to the excitement. Nobody expected the campaign to last very long; indeed a speedy victory was considered essential. 'It would never do', one British officer wrote, 'to have to stay here after the end of October.' Then it would be back to England and France, covered in glory; or, at worst, into comfortable winter quarters in Sebastopol.

Varna was the scene of feverish activity throughout the month of August. As the transports assembled in the harbour under the supervision of the British navy the troops were set to making gabions and fascines. The tiny harbour had none of the sort of facilities needed to embark an army and all its impedimenta and so wharves and landing stages had to be built, and vessels suitable for transporting the artillery wagons and horses had to be improvised. For the guns and their limbers flat-bottomed barges were lashed together and crude stages erected on top. As they swayed heavily in the swell of the bay the artillery officers noted that 'these great boats will make pretty targets if the fleet cannot silence the guns on shore'.

Ten battalions of Turkish troops which were to accompany the allied armies were the first to embark. Packed into Turkish warships every man carried five weeks' rations – a quantity considered sufficient to see him through the campaign, after which the allies had undertaken to be responsible for feeding the Turkish contingent. Conscripts, most of whom had had no more than three months' training, the Turks were almost in as bad a state as their British and French compatriots. To keep healthy it was generally accepted that the Turks needed less food than the Allies. But for months, owing to the monopoly established in Varna by the ready money of the British and French, few of them had tasted fresh meat or fresh vegetables. In less than four weeks one battalion, originally 900 strong, lost eighty men through sickness, most of which could be attributed to malnutrition. And those who did not die through lack of adequate food succumbed to that fatalistic nostalgia with which the Turkish conscript was often afflicted. Having no means of communicating with his family he would brood over their ignorance of his death – if he were to die. Or he would fret over the fact that bureaucracy might well prevent him ever receiving the arrears of pay to which he was entitled – if he were to live.

It took the best part of a week to embark the expeditionary force, and until the fleet was ready to sail those vessels which had been loaded first waited in the harbour.* Cholera still pegged away at the troops and those who suffered from it were kept in isolation on deck. (It was not known at this time that contact is harmless.) More closely packed into the ships than the British, it was the French who suffered most. Those who died were pitched overboard in shotted sacks, but 'the French buried theirs so badly that their dead rose again – heads uppermost, and they didn't look pretty floating about. In all this the men never grumbled . . .'[11] By the evening of

---

* The transport fleet, comprising 29 large steamers and 56 sailing ships, carried an approximate total of 59,600 officers and men, 7,100 horses, 128 field and 125 'siege' guns. (These figures do not include the Turkish contingent of 6,000.)

6 September, however, most of the men were aboard. So also were a number of women. The French *vivandières* were assured of passages as a matter of course; they were part and parcel of the French army's establishment. But orders had been given to cut down the quota of soldiers' wives accompanying the British regiments and as a battalion marched up the gangways it left pathetic knots of women on the quay. Some with help from the baggage parties managed to be smuggled aboard; others were taken on the transports at the last minute. But at least one hysterical group remained in Varna – to face a future more uncertain than that which would have been their lot if they had remained at home. In England the life of a soldier's wife who was not taken on service with her husband was bad enough. It might mean starvation; it certainly meant acute poverty and living on charity. Even so, conditions were better than those at Varna.

At dawn on 7 September, Admiral Dundas gave the signal for the British convoy to weigh anchor, and with bands playing and flags flying the long lines of sailing ships were towed out to sea by the steamers of the fleet. Once outside the harbour the ships shuffled into convoy formation, six parallel lines, with the steamers each towing a couple of the flat-bottomed gun barges or the slower sailing ships. St Arnaud, in the three-decker sailing ship *Ville de Paris*, had put to sea on 5 September and was waiting impatiently at the agreed rendezvous for the arrival of the British. The French and Turkish fleets, encumbered with troops and crammed with stores, had been at sea for nearly a week while the British struggled to embark the last of their men and more numerous horses. Fortunately for both fleets the Russians made no attempt to engage them. Only the British fleet was in any condition to fight and it had waited for Raglan's transports. Had the Tsar's fleet shown any initiative, St Arnaud's transports could have been decimated before the operation had even started.

On 8 September, the British fleet caught up. Leading the convoy was the steamship *Caradoc* in which Raglan had established his head-quarters; behind, 'as far as the visible horizon . . . the sea was covered with vessels, half obscured by the smoke of a hundred steamers . . . some with men-of-war, some with transports . . . a stirring spectacle – a novel exhibition of power . . .'[12] St Arnaud, too ill to leave his cabin, invited Raglan to come aboard the *Ville de Paris* for a conference. Because the sea was rough Raglan, with only

British troops being ferried ashore at Calamita Bay. The improvised landing craft were intended primarily for horses and heavy equipment.

A panoramic view of the British right flank at the Alma.

The principal commanders in the Crimean campaign.

one arm, did not feel that he could tackle the arduous climb up the side of the French ship and Colonel Steele, his military secretary, was deputed to take his place.

Steele, who was accompanied by Admiral Dundas, found St Arnaud sitting up in his bunk, but so ill that he could scarcely speak. Already almost at death's door the old Marshal was almost perpetually in pain. Narcotics helped but these were only a palliative and this was one of his bad spells. To speak for him there were Colonel Trochu and Admiral Hamelin, the French fleet commander, and a discussion took place as to a suitable landing-place on the Crimean coast. At the final allied conference in Varna it had been concluded that the north side of the peninsula and the Katcha Bay in particular were best suited for an assault landing. But during the voyage the French had changed their minds. A landing at Theodosia (Kaffa – the bay on which Yalta lies) was what they proposed now; there the wind would be more favourable.

When Dundas read the paper which was given to him in St Arnaud's cabin he found that it contained a summary of the French views against using the mouth of the Katcha as the landing area. Not only, the paper postulated, had the British press announced that this was the region the allies had fixed as the disembarkation port; its merits had also been discussed in Parliament. For this reason it was to be expected that the Russians would be prepared to oppose the landing there. Furthermore, the paper urged, the season of the year was too far advanced for a siege, the latest information indicated that Sebastopol's garrison was much stronger than had been anticipated, and that the Russians were now known to have a strong force of cavalry. For this reason it was advisable to reconsider the whole basis of the operation. A long and anxious debate between Steele and Dundas on the one side, and Trochu and Hamelin on the other, followed. St Arnaud took no part but listened wearily to the argument.

What about Theodosia, the French asked. It was true that it was over seventy miles from Sebastopol, but the bay was vast and safe and capable of holding all the ships of the invading force. A proper base could be established, and from here it would be possible to cut the road by which Russian reinforcements could be expected to come by way of the Sea of Azov and the Caucasus. From Theodosia the Allies could advance gradually towards the centre of the Peninsula, and Simpheropol, its strategic centre, would be occupied. An advance could then be made on Sebastopol and the decisive battle would be fought on the Simpheropol–Sebastopol road. If the Russians proved too strong nothing would be lost, since the Allies could fall back on Theodosia to re-form for another attack. If the Allies won the battle, they would go on to invest Sebastopol and its surrender would quickly follow as a matter of course.

This was not what the British had in mind at all. What the government in London, and Raglan, visualized was a short campaign, starting without any long-winded preliminaries – with a sudden *coup de main* – and ending with the fall of Sebastopol. So far as a landing at Theodosia was concerned, it was too far from Sebastopol and the troops were not fit enough to undertake a long march; the Allies had insufficient troops to undertake a campaign in the heart of the Crimea and neither army had enough land transport.

The argument continued until St Arnaud found sufficient strength to say that he would agree to whatever Lord Raglan thought best. Except for St Arnaud, the conference then moved over to see Raglan in the *Caradoc* where the two French officers reiterated their arguments to the effect that if a landing was made about 100 miles from Sebastopol it would be possible to postpone the forthcoming clash with the Russians until both armies had had time to reorganize. At this point Raglan sensibly proposed that there should be a proper reconnaissance of the coast all the way between Theodosia and Eupatoria. And so, at 4 a.m. on the morning of Sunday 10 September, escorted by the *Agamemnon*, the *Caradoc* steamed off towards Sebastopol, leaving the fleets anchored at the general rendezvous in Balchik Bay. With Raglan on the *Caradoc* were Canrobert, St Arnaud's second-in-command, Sir John Burgoyne the British Chief Engineer, and a collection of British and French staff officers.

By dawn the *Caradoc* had reached a point about three miles from the Russian base, and the ships in the harbour, the buildings of the town beyond, and great forts on the heights above were clearly visible. The sombre peals of church bells summoning the devout to prayer resounded across the water, and it seemed that Sebastopol's population was wholly unconcerned about the two British warships. But this was close enough, and the two ships now changed course, to steam south-west and east. Hugging the coast they reconnoitred as far as the Balaclava inlet, before turning back to make a wide sweep round Sebastopol. What Raglan had had in mind was an operation resembling that of Wolfe at Quebec. On the Chersonese Uplands, his troops would march out, colours flying, to give battle as their predecessors had done on the Heights of Abraham. Such a plan had much to offer, and it is possible that if it had been put into effect there and then Sebastopol might have fallen after a single bloody battle. But, after a brief glimpse of the cliffs on the east coast and the forbidding steppes behind, Raglan decided to abandon the idea of a landing on that side. In doing so he was to commit himself to complex operations which were to prove sterile. This was probably his greatest error of judgement in the whole campaign.

Steaming north, the mouth of the Katcha – which Canrobert and Sir George Brown had fancied for the landing – was the next place to be reconnoitred. It did not take long for Raglan's naval advisers to rule this out, however. In their opinion not only was there no beach suited to the disembarkation of large numbers of troops and great quantities of stores, but what appeared to be newly built defence works and some tents on the cliffs above Katcha Bay suggested the Russians had been alerted. The decision not to land there was also to prove unfortunate. But the *Caradoc* and *Agamemnon* sailed on up the western coast, towards the pretty little seaside town of Eupatoria, where there was a gap in the red sandstone cliffs and a long rolling beach. This, Raglan decided, was the place for the allied armies to land. It was a decision that should have been made before they left Bulgaria.

4

CALAMITA BAY

It was dusk when the *Caradoc* rejoined the allied armada in Balchik Bay, and as she steamed slowly past the lines of transports to her own anchorages the troops cheered lustily. Since they had been at sea they had been 'feeding like fighting cocks'[1] and as health improved their confidence had returned. Not even the regular splash of corpses, sewn into blankets and tipped into the sea, or the growing stink which polluted the atmosphere of the anchorage could dispel their rising spirits. They felt better, and they were looking forward to getting on with the war.

It was two days before the fleet got under way again. But within twenty-four hours 'a long range of barren low land'[2] came into sight, and that night the ships anchored in the Bay of Eupatoria. Next morning they moved slowly in towards the coast, to drop anchor again opposite the white-stuccoed, windmill-flanked sea front of Eupatoria. People ashore were plainly visible to the men crowding the decks of the troopships; some of them in the fields outside the town could be seen 'removing or making hay',[3] apparently completely uninterested in the invasion fleet. During the afternoon an Anglo-French party landed under a flag of truce and the mayor was handed a written summons to surrender. After fumigating the document, in accordance with Russian health regulations, the Mayor gracefully acknowledged that the surrender of the town was 'in order', and said that the troops could land – provided they observed strict quarantine. But Raglan had no intention of staying at Eupatoria and that night the fleet weighed anchor again and sailed south. By dawn on 14 September the transports had arrived off the landing place, and the troops had their first glimpse of enemy territory.* It was a sunny morning, the water was as smooth as glass, the view presented an idyllic picture. Beyond the long sandy beach were the unruffled waters of a lake, to the right of which was what appeared to be an old fort. Farther inland there was a vista of

* Coincidentally 14 September was the forty-second anniversary of the French entry into Moscow.

green pastures, yellow stubble and lilac patches suggestive of wild lavender. Except for a few cattle grazing peacefully and flocks of sheep browsing on the turf the only evidence of life was a child who appeared at the door of a cottage about a mile and a half inland.

But if the countryside seemed calm and inviting the situation at sea was anything but placid. During the night some of the ships had failed to keep their position in the convoy and this had resulted in the transports arriving off the landing beach in the wrong sequence. In itself this would have been bad enough, but to make matters worse the French ships had taken up more of the anchorage space than had been allotted to them. (In the words of one eye-witness 'The rules and regulations laid down for anchoring off the enemy's coast were upset and disregarded by all . . . The few conscientious men who tried to follow them only confused themselves and others more; and among such an immense number of ships confusion when it once commenced soon became irremediable . . .')[4] At the same time Admiral Dundas had kept the British warships of the covering force well out to sea in order to be ready to ward off any attempt by the Russian fleet to interfere with the landing operation. In view of the lack of initiative already shown by the Russians in Sebastopol and the information available to him, whether he was justified in doing so is conjectural. The point was that those who had planned the operation had relied on using his ships' boats in the disembarkation, and they were not available at the time they were needed most.

The selected landing places were about two miles apart. That of the British was opposite the lake and north of that of the French, who had been allotted the beach front of the old fort. Tactically the choice of the narrow spit of land – with the singularly forbidding name of 'Calamita' – which had been selected as the beach-head was certainly unique. During the disembarkation the lake would prove a formidable obstacle if the beach-head were attacked, and it was reckoned that the guns of the fleet would be more than adequate to protect the flanks. With some justification Raglan believed that the British and French naval armament could outrange and outgun such field artillery as could be mustered by the Russians, and he was confident that the fleet could cover an assault landing anywhere along the coast, so long as the landing place was not dominated by high ground – as it would have been at the mouth of the Katcha. Five hundred 32-pr guns from thirty ships of the line standing close into the shore could hurl a devastating barrage of $6\frac{1}{2}$-inch-diameter

cannon balls more than a thousand yards inland, while the range of
the Russian 18-pr and 12-pr field guns was less than a thousand
yards. Landing an invasion force against opposition is invariably a
difficult operation but even if the Russians could bring up all their
field artillery it was reasonable to suppose that they would not be
able to prevent the allied armies getting a foothold in the Crimea.
Raglan had settled on Calamita Bay because the terrain appeared
to offer a place at which any harassing operations would be reduced
to the minimum. He might well have chosen a hundred other places
along the Crimea's bleak coastline and his troops would still have
got ashore. Indeed, the problems associated with the Calamita Bay
beach-head were not those surrounding the actual disembarkation –
difficult as it proved to be. The main trouble was that the troops
faced a nine days' march to Sebastopol, through fairly open country,
along a route intersected by three rivers at any or all of which the
Russians could be expected to stand. In the event the Russians had
already decided that they would never be able to move fast enough
to contest a landing outside the immediate vicinity of Sebastopol.
Moreover, Menschikoff – little better fitted to command an army
than a diplomatic delegation – doubted whether such a hazardous
operation would ever be attempted. If it were, he reckoned that
the Allies would wait until the spring.

Soon after 7 a.m. on 14 September, the French started to disembark. Their transports were closer to the shore than those of the
British, and, judging by their zeal in erecting a flagpole on which to
hoist a tricolour, the Zouaves intended to leave no doubt as to who
was in the van. Within an hour several French regiments had landed
and outposts had been established four miles inland; by midday a
complete French division was ashore and by nightfall three divisions
(those of Canrobert, Bosquet and Prince Napoleon) had all disembarked. To begin with the weather was fine and sunny, but the
climate of the Crimea is notoriously variable and it was not long
before the sun disappeared, to be replaced by grey drizzling rain.
As the afternoon progressed the sea grew rougher and by evening
the rain was pelting down.

The landing was unopposed. Only the appearance of a troop of
Cossacks who trotted over the crest of a hill beyond the lake and
halted on the skyline, reminded the onlookers that this was more
than just a field exercise. Short, sturdy little men carrying fifteen-
foot-long lances and heavy sabres, the Russian soldiers in their

bulky coats, sheepskin caps and rough leather leggings were dressed in striking contrast to their officer in his lace-trimmed frock-coat and elegant boots. Until a patrol of the French headed towards them they sat mutely watching the disembarkation, while their officer took copious notes. Then, when the French troops began to get near, they turned and galloped off with the portentous news. This was not the last time they were seen. Right up to the time that the allied and Russian armies clashed at the Alma, troops of Cossack cavalry kept the allied armies under constant observation, making no attempt to interfere or harass the invaders but hovering round and keeping well out of range of small-arms fire.

Because of the worsening weather and the initial muddle over the anchorage – for which, not unnaturally, the French were blamed – the British were slower to start disembarking. Before the first troops swarmed down the rope ladders thrown over the sides of the transports into the landing craft below it was well after 9 a.m., and although the operation went ahead as fast as the rowing boats could ply between ships and shore it took nearly five days to complete. The French who had fewer horses to disembark were ready to move in three days, during which St Arnaud made little attempt to disguise his impatience at the slowness and disorganization of his allies.

Every French soldier landed with six days' supply of biscuits, meat for four days and water for one, and that night he slept under canvas oblivious to the heavy rain soaking his tentless British allies. Breakfasting and smoking in front of their gypsy-like bivouacs next morning they watched the British troops, unaccustomed to campaigning, trying to sort out the incredible confusion of the beach-head. Most of the men had been happy to get their feet back on to dry land, and by all accounts there was a good deal of light-hearted horse-play during initial stages of the disembarkation. But any gaiety and high spirits were short-lived; by the time the redcoats had struggled up to their regimental rallying posts on the hill beyond the beach many of their faces were drawn and haggard. The cholera was still with them and they were weighed down with a mass of cumbersome equipment. Packs had been left behind on the ships but every infantryman landed with a greatcoat, and – rolled up in a blanket on his back – a forage cap, a spare pair of socks, an extra pair of boots and three days' rations comprising 4½ lb. of biscuits and a similar quantity of pork, as well as his rifle and fifty rounds of ammunition. A haversack was slung over his right shoulder, and a water keg, similar to that which his predecessors had carried in the Peninsula War, over his left. Every officer wore full dress with epaulettes; his water bottle was filled with spirits, and instead of a rifle and ammunition he carried a sword and revolver and field glasses or telescope. In other respects his burden was similar to that of the rank and file. There was no transport, not even any of the rough and rickety ambulance wagons that had served them in Bulgaria.* Tents should have had a high priority, but there were none and it was a month before some of the regiments got any.

Struggling under the load of their equipment many of the British troops collapsed, and that evening several of them were interred in sandy graves hurriedly dug on the beach. There were no hospital ships as such and the one vessel to which the desperately sick were evacuated was soon overcrowded. Next morning its decks were strewn with dead and dying. When he heard of it Raglan is said to have expressed his displeasure but there was little he could do to improve a situation which thirty years of disinterest and drastic cuts in military expenditure had spawned. In 1846 Lord Palmerston had bluntly told his Cabinet colleagues that Britain's military weakness was such that England existed 'only by sufferance, and by the forbearance of other Powers'.[5] What had happened at Varna and now again at Calamita Bay was bad enough; worse was to come. Yet St Arnaud, who appeared to have made a sudden and miraculous – albeit temporary – recovery, was then writing with the fevered elation of a dying man. 'The troops are superb . . . We shall beat the Russians.'[6]

That night with the rain coming down in torrents, the British troops looked back disconsolately at the ships riding at anchor off the beach, and enviously at the *tentes-abris* of their French allies.

'Seldom' [wrote an officer of the 11th Hussars] 'have men suffered more than the British troops did on that night of rain and storm. Many of them had but recently recovered from cholera, dysentery or fever, they had but little food, no tents or shelter, officers and men incurred illness and disease from which many never

---

* In his despatch after the battle of the Alma Raglan explained:
'My anxiety to bring into the country every cavalry and infantry soldier who was available, prevented me from embarking their baggage animals, and officers have with them at this moment nothing but what they can carry and they equally with the men are without tents and covering of any kind.'

recovered. Men stood or lay drenched to the skin, for no ordinary covering could protect from that descending deluge.'[7]

Huddled together in the open or in the few places of shelter that were available, few of them got much sleep that night. Nor were the officers any better off. Raglan himself had decreed that they should land with nothing but what they could carry – exactly the same as the men. Under any circumstances resplendent full dress was wholly unsuited to campaigning; soaking wet and bedraggled, most of the officers lamented its expensive inadequacy. During the long peace uniforms had become little more than skin-tight long-sleeved vests – in bright-hued red or blue, except for the Rifle regiments who wore green – buttoned tightly at the throat or surmounted by the torturous stock.* Gaudy coloured trimmings sewn on the tunics; buttons, facings, cuirasses, epaulettes, cuffs; and striped trousers which also tended to be skin-tight – especially in the cavalry – contributed to the peacock appearance, which was rounded off by the multifarious assortment of helmets, shakos, busbies, highland bonnets, or glengarries worn on the head according to the regiments. Additionally, senior officers wore gaily plumed cocked hats, and the cavalry completed their dress ensemble with elaborate cuirasses and vivid pelisses slung over their shoulders. By comparison only the Zouaves with their bright cummerbunds worn over loose vests and baggy breeches were conspicuous in the French columns. For the rest, the French tunics and trousers were almost drab.

No careful and comprehensive plans for the British force had been drawn up. In effect, only one eventuality had really been considered – an assault landing in the face of the enemy – and no arrangements had been thought of for an unopposed landing on an undefended coast. In the event, cavalry should have been landed first because it was needed most. Moreover if the horses had had priority they would have got ashore when it was calm. But the plans called for the infantry to go first to seize the beach, and nobody ever considered changing the order.

Fortunately for the sodden troops ashore, the rain stopped before dawn, and the morning of 15 September was brilliantly fine. This was just as well, because it was now the turn of the cavalry to disembark. Yet despite the improvement in the weather, getting the

* The stock was made of thick string leather, three inches high all round, fastened at the back by an iron buckle.

horses ashore proved to be a most difficult business. Boats had been lashed together and a crude platform erected on top, to make rafts for the operation. Horses, guns and gun carriages were lowered on to these rafts, but in the swell many of them turned over, tipping their cargoes into the sea. Terrified animals floundered in the water and only with great difficulty were the guns salvaged. By the evening of the following day when the majority of the British army and its equipment had been landed, the troops were exhausted. Inevitably the effects of cold and damp exacerbated by extra exertion took their toll and the cholera claimed more than its usual number of victims that night.

Two problems now had to be faced. The massive piles of equipment, ammunition, tins of biscuits, and barrels of salt pork, which had been dumped on the beaches had to be moved. And no fresh water supply had been found near the beach-head. Most of the rain which had fallen soon dried up leaving only muddy pools, and wells hurriedly sunk by the sappers yielded only inadequate supplies of brackish, almost undrinkable water. Consequently on the 19th, when the armies began their march to meet the Russians the soldiers' water bottles were half-empty. To move the stores it had become obvious by the 16th, even to the most dull-witted staff officers, that wheeled transport would be needed.

Responsibility for the provision of land transport was supposed to rest with the civilian Commissariat Department, over which the military had no direct control – a fact about which Raglan regularly complained. When the Commissariat failed to supply what was wanted the deficiency had to be met by the time-honoured means, and some of the first British troops ashore – a detachment of the 23rd Foot – were sent off to 'liberate' some *arabas* [bullock carts] seen moving up a road nearby. The Tartar drivers made no attempt to escape and most of the wagons were found to be loaded with firewood. (One turned out to be full of pears and these were quickly eaten – with dire results afterwards.)

The French sent out foraging parties soon after the first waves of their troops had landed. Within twenty-four hours camels loaded with grain, and carts packed with vegetables were being driven into the French lines, together with herds of cattle and flocks of sheep. Having been ordered to pay for all requisitioned supplies many of the French soldiers merely handed over a uniform button for every consignment 'liberated', seized or 'hired', and the locals quickly learned to consider themselves lucky if any reasonable compensation was forthcoming from the French. French officers excused this behaviour with a shrug. Their army, they said, was 'revolutionary'; there was nothing they could do about it.

Raglan, anxious that the British should not emulate their allies, decreed that all supplies for his army would be paid for, and that looting would incur severe penalties. But as he urgently needed supplies and transport, his new Quartermaster-General, General Richard Airey, was told to get hold of as many wagons, baggage animals, drivers and supplies as he could lay his hands on. In two days 350 ramshackle carts with their accompanying bullocks and drivers had been seized or hired from the local peasants;* sixty-seven camels, 253 horses, forty-five wagon-loads of poultry, corn and flour together with 1,000 head of cattle and sheep had also been requisitioned. In the returns such figures looked impressive but to move and feed an army of 27,000 men the quantities were a good deal less than enough. When apportioned out to the army, each division got only nine carts – four for entrenching tools, two for the use of general officers, two for medical stores, and one for sick and wounded. Raglan told Airey that this was not enough. But between them the British and French armies had swept the area clean and no more were forthcoming.

Throughout the preparatory phase of the invasion, the Russians made no serious attempt to interfere with the allied beach-head. A determined night attack in the darkness and disorder of the 14th might have had far-reaching effects. But the Allies were allowed not only to land but then – while Menschikoff's army sat supine behind the river Alma – to organize their advance. Cossack patrols hovered around but only rarely did they venture to molest an allied detachment. Half a dozen lone Zouaves were captured during their foraging expeditions, but when allied patrols appeared in strength the Cossacks pulled back out of danger and out of range.

In the beach-head itself the troops grew restless as the days slipped by and no move was made. 'What are we waiting for?' one young British officer asked in angry frustration. 'Has the Tsar caved in?'[8] And St Arnaud wrote to his wife 'The English . . . have made me

---

* Crim Tartars. The drivers were compelled to accompany their carts, and nearly all those who did not desert died during the campaign. If the Russians had displayed the slightest initiative, neither the French nor the British would have been able to get hold of any transport whatsoever.

lose precious time.'[9] A tentative agreement between the two commanders-in-chief had set 17 September as the date on which the
allied armies would start their march on Sebastopol. By the 18th,
however, the British were still not ready to move and St Arnaud
could hardly contain his impatience. Knowing the condition was
critical he was anxious to get to Sebastopol, and to 'let the cannons
speak', before he was forced to give up his command. On 17 September, and again on the 18th, he rode across to Raglan's headquarters, with an escort of staff officers and spahis, to ask when the
British would be ready and to remind Raglan that his army and the
Turkish contingent were waiting to go.

Orders for the advance to begin were finally issued late in the
night of the 18th. The plan, so far as there was a plan, was to march
south along the coast straight for Sebastopol, thirty miles and five
river crossings distant. Allied information about the strength and
deployment of the Russian forces was anything but precise. However in an intercepted despatch the Governor of Sebastopol had
reported that the garrison of the naval base was in a 'desperate'
state and 'ravaged by fever'.[10] And because the Russians had not
tried to dispute the landing, most people, including some officers of
high rank, thought that the whole campaign was going to be easy.
Not even the generals, by the way they acted, appear to have considered the possibility that the Russians were hoping to draw the
invaders into a trap.

The material difficulties which now faced the Allies could hardly
have been worse. There was a shortage of almost everything necessary for the successful prosecution of a campaign, and although the
troops were in good spirits they were in a poor state of health. But
everybody looked forward with confidence to a speedy and glorious
conclusion to forthcoming operations and optimism prevailed.
All too soon this optimism was to have a rude shock.

THE MARCH TO THE ALMA

'The hardships of forced marches are often more painful than the dangers of battle.'
                                                                    Stonewall Jackson

At 6 a.m. on the morning of 20 September 1854, Bosquet's Zouaves marched out of their camp to take up their positions as the advance guard of the French Army. St Arnaud had told them that they had been assigned 'the post of danger', which would also be their 'post of glory',[1] and that they must be prepared to fight '*à l'Africaine*'. The rest of the French were ready to move off an hour later but at that time there were few signs of activity in the British camps, and as the plan for the advance depended on the two armies moving together the impatient French were compelled to wait. It was not that the British troops were asleep; since dawn the din created by French drummers and buglers had been enough to wake the dead. But they were tired and many had been up half the night lugging stores back to the boats, digging graves on the beach, and generally preparing for the advance. Because of the need to shake out into tactical formation before they actually started to march, their position on the left flank also contributed to the delay. By 9 a.m. however, Raglan's men were ready – although they had had no time to cook the raw meat of their rations and most of their water bottles were half-empty.

And so the Allies left the beach-head and tramped up to the high rolling plateau of which most of the Crimean peninsula consists. The combined force, under two separate commanders, totalled 65,000 men. Nearest the sea the four French divisions marched in diamond formation – the troops on the extreme right moving along the cliff edge from which the fleet could be seen sailing in formation parallel to the armies' line of march. The front apex of the diamond comprised Bosquet's 1st Division; behind and to the right came Canrobert's 2nd Division; Prince Napoleon's 3rd Division was on the left and Forey's 4th Division brought up the rear. The French artillery, followed by the baggage train, was in the centre of the diamond and Suleiman Pasha's Turks were sandwiched between the baggage and Forey. Leading the British force, and well out in front of it, were the 11th Hussars, the 13th Light Dragoons and a troop of Horse Artillery all under Lord Cardigan. Behind them the five divisions of British infantry marched with four divisions in square formation and the fifth bringing up the rear. De Lacy Evans's 2nd Division was on the left of Prince Napoleon. Behind him came Sir Richard England's 3rd Division; on his left was Sir George Brown's Light Division followed by the Duke of Cambridge's 1st Division. Farther left, to protect the inland flank, rode Lord Lucan with the 17th Lancers and 8th Hussars. Behind the Duke of Cambridge marched two-thirds of Sir George Cathcart's 4th Division,* and last of all came the 4th Light Dragoons under Lord George Paget. Unlike the French who marched in two separate brigade columns, each British division marched as one huge phalanx with a front and depth of about a mile, so that the effect was one of much greater concentration than the French. This difference in the formations of the two armies marked their distinctive tactical philosophies: British reliance on line and square and the French belief in the efficacy of the column. Should the enemy be encountered on the march the British could deploy quickly into line, facing front or flank, while the French would stand and fight in their columns. That was how they had fought each other in Europe, and separately that was how each army would fight together.

Despite their concentration, the two armies covered a four-mile front, and from van to rearguard the whole allied formation stretched back three miles. Cut off on three sides by the empty plain and on the fourth by the sea, this compact mass of twelve square miles of military might moved in lonely isolation. There was no base and no lines of communication and when Cathcart's troops rejoined their division the isolation of the allied armies would be complete. If anything went wrong only the fighting ships might bring succour.

A fresh breeze tempered the heat from the sun when the soldiers stepped out across the lovely undulating countryside. As the military machine eased forward, the bayonets glittered above the red coats of the British and blue of the French; regimental colours were uncased to flutter proudly at the head of the divisions, regimental bands struck up and the men were in high spirits. Familiar tunes, good weather,

* One brigade had been left behind to finish clearing the beach.

and above all the thrill of the anticipation of coming battle cheered them. The scene was one of inexpressible grandeur and the regular tramp of marching feet on the soft green turf produced a low audible rhythm, while the meticulous lines advancing so evenly had the appearance of an irresistible tide. As the morning wore on and the sun grew hotter however, bands stopped playing and with an infinite weariness the troops trudged on in foreboding silence. In less than three hours all the gaiety had gone and when stricken men began to stumble out of line and to discard equipment the straggling phalanx began to take on the appearance of a disconsolate and deflated army rather than of one about to engage the enemy for the first time. Everything not needed on the march – including, by Raglan's order, the restrictive leather stocks – had been left behind or reloaded on to the ships. Even so the unaccustomedly light loads were more than many of the men could bear. The worst ordeal was thirst. Water had been short since the landing, and what was found on the line of march was undrinkable. Lips turned blue, and by midday the British troops were about all in. The French columns fared better. 'The marching of our allies, laden as they were with all their packs was wonderful – the pace at which they went was really "killing".'[2] Unlike the British, the French infantry were accustomed to route marching as part of their training and their preparations for this particular march had been more thorough.

Fortunately for the British, the Russians did not try to harass the columns. In their wariness and restraint the Russian cavalry belied their reputation. But for the distant smoke of burning villages and the ubiquitous Cossack patrol hovering in front and on the left flank, there was no evidence of their existence. A few farmhouses were passed *en route*, but they were empty and silent. The furniture had been taken out of them and only a few bundles of dried herbs hanging from the ceiling beams, or gaudy pictures of saints hanging on the walls, showed that they had ever been occupied.[3]

The advance guard reached the first river crossing, the Bulganak, about two o'clock in the afternoon. From the plateau the ground sloped gently down to the sparkling waters of this slow-running stream, but on the far side it rose again in a series of stepped terraces to the undulating plain. On one of the lower terraces about 2,000 mounted Russians were drawn up in line; higher up, almost hidden by an intervening ridge, a force of about 6,000 infantry also waited and barred the way to the south. Out of sight of an observer down by the stream the latter were spotted from the plateau above the stream by the keen-sighted Airey who was riding with Raglan behind Cardigan's vanguard. Only the glint of the sun on bayonets revealed the hidden danger, and Cardigan was oblivious to it. Having crossed the stream with his four cavalry squadrons – less than 300 men in all – he had trotted up to the first terrace and was obviously getting ready to take on the Russians. When the troops began to edge into line it was obvious to the observers on the plateau that Cardigan was fully prepared to embark on a death or glory charge across the few hundred yards of empty grassland which separated him from the Russians. An exchange of shots in which four of Cardigan's horses were killed and four of his men wounded delayed the dressing drill rigmarole, and before the four squadrons were ready to attack the drama dissolved in an anticlimax.* Raglan was not prepared to lose the best part of two regiments of his precious cavalry so early in the campaign – even if they were spoiling for a fight. To cover their withdrawal he ordered the leading troops of the 2nd and Light Divisions to cross the stream and form line on the far bank, while two troops of artillery were called forward and Lucan ordered to take the 17th Lancers and 8th Hussars up to support Cardigan. When these moves had been completed Airey was sent to 'suggest' to Lucan that he should retire. In the circumstances one might have expected Raglan now to have issued a mandatory order couched in precise terms. But the British Commander-in-Chief had been brought up in a tradition where respect for the feelings of subordinates was all important, and he was unwilling to embarrass Lucan. Luckily the man Raglan had chosen to carry the message was less concerned about the niceties of etiquette and protocol. And the fact that Lucan was arguing heatedly with Cardigan about the way the projected charge would be conducted when Airey arrived probably made the latter's task easier. Raglan's 'wishes' were delivered in forthright and categoric terms and the two cavalry commanders agreed to pull back.

Unaware of the reasons why they had not been permitted their moment of glory Cardigan's squadron turned about and walked their horses back across the river. Russian jeers pursued them, and as they passed through the infantry screen there were a few ribald comments.

* *The Historical Records of the Eleventh Hussars* record that the first man in the British Army to be wounded in the Crimea was a Private Williamson of the Regiment. 'He rode out of the ranks, his leg shot off and hanging by his overall. Coming up to me [Cornet Roger Palmer] he said, quite calmly, "I am hit, may I fall out?" '

The cavalry was never popular with infantrymen and at the end of their gruelling march they recalled how the complacent horsemen had trotted along so comfortably. 'Silly peacock bastards', a private in the 41st wrote to his brother, 'serves them bloody right.'[4] In the eyes of the disgruntled troopers, their humiliation could only be due to Lucan's interference, and when an officer commented tartly that 'Lord Look-on' would be a more appropriate title for the commander of the cavalry division, the nickname stuck.

Under the covering fire of the two troops of artillery which Raglan had ordered up, the British cavalry was allowed to extricate itself without anything more than a few salvoes from the Russian gunners. Why the Russian cavalry did not charge Cardigan's four squadrons is difficult to understand. The explanation that the Russian commander was deterred by the steadiness and ceremonial precision of the British would be more convincing if similar hesitation to show initiative did not subsequently recur time and again. It may be that the Russians never had any intention of getting themselves involved at this stage. Certainly this would be more logical; only a few miles behind them was a position of enormous strength – a position which Menschikoff had told the Tsar could be held for at least three weeks while the defences of Sebastopol were perfected. Whatever the explanation, as the weary British infantry closed up to the river, the Russians left the ridges above the Bulganak and fell back to this position. The first concern of the marching men had been water, and when the Bulganak came into sight many of them broke their ranks and rushed forward to quench their thirst. If at any time during the campaign the British army's discipline appeared to be slackening, it was this occasion at the Bulganak and with some pride the regimental records of the 23rd Foot state that 'though sorely tempted', in General Codrington's brigade 'not a man moved until permission was given for the brigade to drink in comfort.'[5]

The Bulganak turned out to be little more than a shallow stream and the armies were able to cross it without difficulty. But for the sake of the water it was decided to bivouac for the night on the southern bank. The troops had only marched eight miles but it was clear to Raglan and St Arnaud that they had come far enough for one day. The French columns flopped down where they were but the British on the open flank were positioned in order of battle in case the Russians returned for a surprise attack. In the twilight the men collected dried grass which, with some staves of meat and rum barrels, provided the only fuel for cooking their evening meal. But many of them, too exhausted to eat, fell asleep as soon as they were permitted to pile arms and rest. An eerie silence descended over the allied lines on what was to be the last night for over 350 British and 60 French soldiers. But beyond the river on the ridges in the far distance, the allied sentries – and those too cold, too tired or too apprehensive of the impending slaughter – could see the glowing pinpoints of innumerable camp fires. Above the river Alma the Russian army was encamped, but not a single fighting patrol nor Cossack vedette came near the Bulganak that night where the invading armies slept.

Raglan's headquarters had been set up in a cottage near the wooden bridge over which the Eupatoria–Sebastopol road – the axis of the allied advance – crossed the Bulganak, and late that night St Arnaud rode across to discuss the plans for the following day. Accompanied as usual by the ubiquitous Colonel Trochu, he arrived in a state of querulous agitation and addressing himself to Raglan in a mixture of English and French launched into a passionate monologue. The theme was St Arnaud's *Projet pour la bataille de l'Alma*. Amiable and courteous as ever, Raglan allowed him to talk and because he appeared to be listening attentively, he may well have given the impression that he was agreeing to St Arnaud's views and suggestions. Both commanders knew that the Russians would be waiting for the Allies at the Alma and that the first and perhaps decisive battle of the campaign would be fought there. The possibility of the Russians attacking the bivouacked armies during the night could not be dismissed. But it was unlikely. So too was an attack the following morning, either before camp was struck or during the approach march to the Alma. To leave the dominating slopes above the Alma with their wide field of fire and prepared defences would be madness, besides being out of keeping with the Russian character.

Nor were these beliefs based wholly on speculation. Allied Intelligence had not been able to make any realistic assessment of the overall strength of Russian troops in the Crimea and nobody knew what proportion of them was defending the Alma. But it had been possible to form some idea of how this force was deployed. French ships had sailed along the coast past the mouth of the Alma, and from their mast-heads it had been possible to see some of the Russian positions on the south bank of the river. Distance combined with an oblique view and a bend in the river about three miles from its mouth made it difficult to scrutinize them in any detail and to conclude that the

Russians were all deployed above the south bank of the Alma. There could be a force on the north bank higher upstream, waiting to fall on the allied flank when they reached the river. But it seemed unlikely; every indication was that the Russians were deployed in a straight-forward line, stretching east to west.

One important fact which had emerged from the ships' reconnaissance was that the Russians were not occupying positions on the slopes above the south bank for at least a mile upriver. Nor did there appear to be any Russians on the cliffs overlooking its mouth. Because the Alma was not deep in September and could be forded at several places, the conclusion was that Menschikoff had deployed his men to block the crossing places and that he had reckoned the cliffs and slopes near the sea were unassailable. But the sailors had spotted a narrow path leading up the cliffs from the beach and had reported the presence of a sand-bar which suggested that the river was fordable near its mouth. St Arnaud's plan had been concocted on the basis of these facts. Like Raglan he had no idea of the terrain, but he had roughed out a sketch of how he considered the battle was likely to be fought. The course of the river was indicated by a wavy line – which showed none of the sharp bends and loops which were to be so important in the subsequent battle – and with no information on which to base his plans, the squares and lines which represented the Russian defences bore no resemblance to the actual positions they occupied. With an arrow pointing towards the supposed head of the Russian positions, St Arnaud had shown the French army and Turkish division facing them, and deployed in line – a formation completely out of French character. To the left of the French – where the British were equally uncharacteristically sketched in column formation – five curved arrowheaded lines suggested a turning movement; underneath there was a label *Armée anglaise tournant la droite ennemie* and an optimistic annotation *Départ à 5ʰ½*.

From this sketch it was clear what was in St Arnaud's mind.* The French divisions were to cross the Alma and attack the Russians near the river mouth while the British swept round to roll up the Russian right flank. The French would play the leading role and earn *la gloire* while the British would take on the lesser (in St Arnaud's view) but important secondary task. To Raglan the French army commander's proposals argued with such Gallic vehemence and pantomime were

* St Arnaud's sketch was published in the French press after the battle, and gave a completely false picture of what actually took place at the Alma.

too naïve to warrant much comment. At the same time he was not prepared to commit his army to a manoeuvre which might lead to its annihilation. The Allies knew nothing of the terrain across which the men would have to march, and the strengths and dispositions of the Russians on the left flank were matters of pure guesswork. But Raglan, always excessively conscious of the need to avoid Anglo-French friction and anxious not to appear impolite, assured St Arnaud that he could rely on the co-operation of the British. He had no intention of committing himself to the French plan, and if St Arnaud returned to his own lines believing that Raglan was arranging for the British army to be redeployed in five divisional columns ready to strike off on a semi-circular flank march by half-past five in the morning, he was incredibly ingenuous. Yet Raglan did not suggest any alternative plan. It might have been expected that his staff would have already drawn one up. But most of his staff had been appointed by virtue of their 'connections' rather than expertise. Little consideration had been given to the tactics to be employed; no proper reconnaissance had been undertaken, and it almost seems as if those in command were prepared to put their trust in a friendly providence, and hopes of the Minié rifle.

The key to St Arnaud's plan was the absence of Russians at the river mouth, and Bosquet's division was detailed to start scaling the heights there at 7 a.m.; Canrobert and Prince Napoleon would launch attacks farther left simultaneously with the start of this operation. Meantime, still farther left, the British would be well on their way round the flank – according to the plan anyway. But at 7 a.m. the British troops were breakfasting and their officers completing their toilets. Many were still tired, and in any case the British soldier of that time was not an early riser. In peace or war he liked to have his breakfast before he started the day, and the habits of the officers were conditioned by their peacetime social lives. Moreover the army had to re-form before it could start to march anywhere. The two divisions which had been moved across to guard the left flank during the night had to be brought back to the line of march and across the uneven ground the complicated wheeling and positioning of ten thousand men in close formation was a protracted and vexatious business. Old Sir George Brown, commanding the Light Division, knew that the march was supposed to start at 7 a.m. but he was not prepared to move off until his men were properly ready. He believed that his soldiers should be immaculate whatever the circumstances, and he had them flogged without compunction when they were not. Sixty-seven years old, Sir George de Lacy Evans, commanding the 2nd Division, had similar ideas and was just as averse to undignified haste as Brown. Other considerations also tended to delay the redeployment. At bullock speed the impressed Tartar transport had to be repositioned in the column, and rations had to be issued. 'Before marching, a spattering fire of musketry was heard in the rear . . . it was cattle being killed for the day's rations, each man getting his allowance of flesh warm and quivering' wrote Colour-Sergeant McSally of the 42nd Highlanders.*

By ten o'clock Raglan was becoming as impatient as St Arnaud. Quietly and efficiently the French divisions and the Turks had started to move at half-past five. Trumpeters sounding *'le réveil en musique'* and the rolling of drums were the usual prelude to a French move. However, on this occasion, St Arnaud had decreed that the advance would start without the usual accompaniment. Optimistically he hoped to surprise the Russians by a stealthy approach. As the movement of any large formation of troops unavoidably creates an uproar it is difficult to see how surprise could be possible, even if the more strident noises were suppressed. Waiting for the British to get into position, St Arnaud, in his full dress uniform and the plumed hat of a Marshal of France, had been forced to postpone Bosquet's order to attack three times before Raglan's army was ready to get under way.

The order for a general advance was finally given at 10.30 a.m. It was a beautiful morning and fifes preceded the Light Division on the left, a band played in front of the 2nd Division, and – not to be outdone – the French drums rolled a fitful tattoo in front of Prince Napoleon's division as the invaders moved forward across the turf. But the music did not last for long. In less than an hour it was apparent that the two armies were diverging and to close the gap between the French left and the British right the two forward British divisions had to close in. This involved more complicated wheeling and manoeuvring – almost beyond the capacity of officers who had little experience of moving anything bigger than a company of 150 men across a barrack square – and it was 11.30 a.m. before the two armies were in line again. A strange hush had now descended over the columns. Only the crunch of boots, the neighing of the horses, the rattle of equipment and the squeak of unoiled wheels of carts and limbers broke the silence.

* Extract from a text supplied to the author by The Black Watch.

Less than three miles from the Bulganak the marching columns came to a ridge from which the high ground of the plateau fell gently to sea level. The British reached this rise about noon and the two armies were ordered to halt. As they settled down to eat their mid-day meal the troops could see the silver streak of a river two miles ahead running between poplar trees to the sea. The valley – full of cypresses, willows, gardens and vineyards, and sheltering two colourful hamlets – was a belt of verdant green relieving the arid effect of the dusty plain and sombre background. This was the Alma river, a formidable natural obstacle to the progress of the Allies' march on Sebastopol; and on the far side of it a huge grey-coated Russian army was deployed.

Preceded by a trooper carrying his guidon, St Arnaud rode slowly across the front of his army towards the British lines. After his outburst the night before, the French army commander was feeling subdued; he was tired and the pallor of approaching death was already on his face. But he lifted his hat and called out 'Hurrah for Old England' when the British troops gave him a cheer as he rode past. And when he came to the 88th Regiment – the Connaught Rangers – he shouted 'I hope you will fight well today'. 'Shure, your honour, we will,' one of them shouted back. 'And don't we always fight well?'[6]

Raglan, in a *'costume de fantaisie'* – blue civilian coat with regulation buttons, open in front to show a white shirt and high cravat – accompanied by a crowd of hangers-on which eventually included the journalist-historian Kinglake, rode across to meet St Arnaud. Together the two army commanders rode forward to a low mound to get a better view of the Russian position. For several minutes they stayed there together. Raglan was seen to demonstrate the special support fitted to his saddle to enable him to manipulate his telescope with his one hand, and from their manner the two men appeared to be staring at the scene more like a couple of tourists than generals deciding on a course of action.[7] There is no record of what the two commanders said but by the end of the discussion it must have been clear to St Arnaud that his English colleague had no intention of following the plan he had outlined the previous night. The British army was deployed in line across the front, prolonging the French line, and there were no columns to be seen moving left to encircle the Russians. When General Airey rode forward, he heard St Arnaud's blunt enquiry as to whether Raglan intended to 'turn' the position or to attack in front. Looking towards the exposed flank on his left, Raglan was heard to reply 'With such a body of cavalry as the enemy has on the plain, I would not attempt to turn the position.'[8] All the evidence suggests that the British commander had never seriously entertained St Arnaud's proposals. If he had, then it was now clear that he had discarded them. Nothing was said about what he did intend to do, and no attempt was made to co-ordinate the tactics to be adopted by the two armies during the next few hours.

With a flushed look of bewilderment on his face the French Marshal took leave of Raglan and turned to ride back to his own lines. The time was just after 1 p.m., and under the brilliant blue of a cloudless sky it was intensely hot. Bugles sounded and the British army started to march forward again as St Arnaud cantered back. Then the Russian guns opened fire and low clouds of white smoke rolled out among the hills. The battle had begun.

THE BATTLE OF THE ALMA: THE FIRST PHASE

It is doubtful whether even the Russians would claim that Prince Menschikoff deserves to be remembered as one of the great captains. With complete lack of tactical perception he had decided that the only way to stop the allies reaching Sebastopol was to deploy his army across their path. If the fortifications guarding the north side of the naval base had been anything like adequate he would probably have settled down behind them. But no one had expected an attack from the north, and – like those of another great naval base at Singapore 80 years later – the guns of the forts only pointed out to sea. The wide reach of the harbour was a serious obstacle but it was not insurmountable and Menschikoff did not want to let the invaders get to the edge of the town. Yet he gave no consideration to striking the Allies in the flank; a war of movement was beyond him and his ideas centred on defence. He would wait to be attacked and his army would resist. The vulnerability of the allied armies never seems to have occurred to him. Lacking a base and communications to it they were dependent on the ships for their very existence. With a little imagination he could have seized the initiative, encircled the mass formation plodding up the coastal road, and trapped it between rivers. Cut off from the fleets and from fresh water, the Allies would have had to fight their way back to Calamita Bay, staged a Dunkirk, or surrendered. (And it is extremely doubtful whether they could have been successfully evacuated. When the invasion of the Crimea was first mooted Admiral Dundas told the British Government that he could take the army there but he could not undertake to bring it back again if it were forced to withdraw.)

Nevertheless, if Menschikoff had to choose a position to block the allied advance, he could not have selected anywhere better than the Alma Heights. Above the sluggish, winding river a range of hills rose from the plain, and through the ages the river had cut into their base to reproduce, on a gigantic scale, the classical military defences of military engineering. The river bank, steep and high above the water, formed a natural escarpment; bare slopes above it provided a naked smooth glacis, leading to a vast terrace from which a deadly fire could be poured on the ground below. At the mouth of the river were the sheer cliffs which Menschikoff – unaware of the path winding up them which the French ships had spotted – decided were unassailable. These ran inland for about a couple of miles; then, at the base of a high point known as Telegraph Hill from an unfinished telegraph station on its summit, the hills curled back – receding from the river in a horseshoe curve about a mile across and half a mile deep. On the far side of this amphitheatre another hill, 450 feet high, topped a series of terraces above the river's southern bank. This was the famous Kourgane, destined to become the key of the battle.

From Sebastopol Menschikoff had brought an army of 39,000 men and 106 guns. Forty infantry battalions were supported by 3,400 cavalry and 2,600 artillerymen manned the guns. Numerically strong, this army's weakness was its lack of a proper chain of command, since the commanders of its battalions – each about 800 strong – were directly responsible to Menschikoff; unlike the British and French armies, there was no formal divisional or brigade structure. The system reflected the Russian partiality to static warfare, and in a battle where tactical movement was important it broke down. Lacking cohesion, units tended to act according to the whim of the individual battalion commander – or did not act at all. Menschikoff could not possibly hope to cope with the co-ordination of so many units; indeed he was too inexperienced and much too volatile a personality to be entrusted with the central direction of an army of this size. When battle was joined he tackled every tactical problem pragmatically, with no consideration, and often no knowledge, of what was going on outside the sector in which he found himself. Under his direction, groups of battalions were marched and countermarched from one position to another, with disastrous results.

The Kourgane Hill was selected as the centre of the Russian position and most of Menschikoff's troops were disposed around it. On its slopes, about half-way down towards the river, was a ridge on which the only prepared fieldwork was dug. Emplaced behind a three-foot-high breastwork were fourteen of the heavier guns which had been brought from Sebastopol, and on either side of this position – which British writers invariably refer to as 'Great Redoubt' – a protective ditch accommodated some of the infantry. Between the guns shallow trenches were dug for marksmen sharpshooters. Higher up the hill and a mile to the east, a smaller 'Lesser Redoubt' of similar design, held a battery of field guns. No other trenches were dug, no sangars built. Elsewhere the Russian infantry stood, or lay down, like herded cattle in compact columns on the bare hillsides where they had been deployed – dense masses of close-packed, grey-coated figures retaining a formation in which allied bullets found not one mark but sometimes six. Even when they moved these drab columns remained concentrated, marching not with brisk military precision but with the ponderous deliberation of an irresistible tide of mud.

The Great Redoubt dominated all the ground between itself and the grassy slopes beyond the vineyards on the opposite bank of the Alma while the Lesser Redoubt – on the Russian right – positioned at right angles to the river line – commanded the valley up which any flanking attack would have to be made. On the other side of the Great Redoubt a battery of guns straddled the road which was the allied axis of advance and covered the bridge where it crossed the Alma. Around the Kourgane Hill sixteen infantry battalions were deployed – four from each of the Kazan, Vladimir, Sousdal, and Uglitz Regiments – together with two battalions made up of sailors from the ships marooned in Sebastopol harbour. (The latter were not expected to be of much use in the battle; Russian sailors were not highly thought of by the army – or even Russian civilians for that matter.) Four of the sixteen battalions were positioned in two long oblique lines behind the Kourgane, about two miles from the river where its southerly slopes levelled out on to the plateau. The other twelve battalions were haphazardly grouped around the Hill itself. In the most forward position were the four Kazan battalions, echeloned on each side of the Great Redoubt to channel an enemy assault towards its guns. Four of the eight were on the rising slopes directly behind the Great Redoubt, two behind the Lesser Redoubt and two hidden behind the hill – from which they were to emerge at a critical stage of the battle. The two battalions of sailors were on their own, half-way between the hill and the battalions on the rear edge of the plateau; here they were to remain throughout the battle.

Of the remaining twenty-four battalions, eight were deployed in the vineyards on the south bank of the river, on the ledge at the foot of Telegraph Hill.* Those on the left were the nearest Russian troops to

---

* Four of these battalions were of the Taroutine Regiment; the other four were Russian 'reserve' battalions – made up of mobilized conscripts and not belonging to any regular regiment.

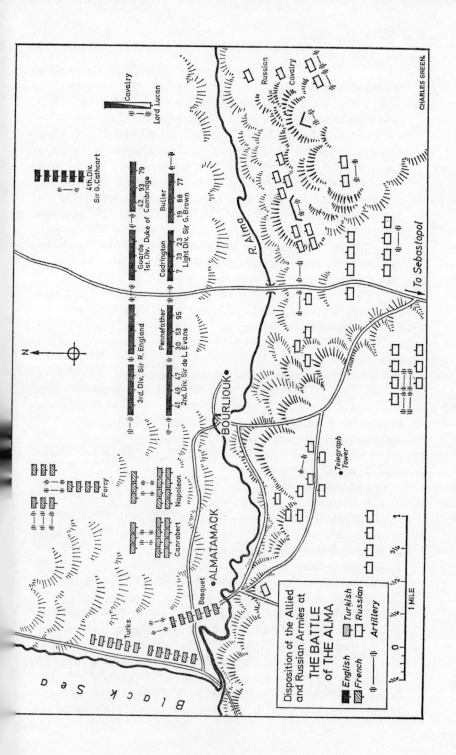

Disposition of the Allied
and Russian Armies at
THE BATTLE
of THE ALMA

English
French
Turkish
Russian
Artillery

Black Sea

R. Alma

To Sebastopol

BOURLIOUK

•ALMATAMACK

Telegraph
Tower

Russian
Cavalry

Cavalry
Lord Lucan

4th.Div.
Sir G.Cathcart

Guards
1st.Div. Duke of Cambridge   42 93 79

Butler

Codrington
7 33 23   19 88 77
Light Div. Sir G. Brown

3rd.Div. Sir R. England

Pennefather
30 53 95

41 49 47
2nd.Div. Sir de L. Evans

Forcy

Napoleon

Canrobert

Bosquet

Turks

N

CHARLES GREEN.

1 MILE
0   ½   ¾   1

the sea, and they were at least two and a half miles from the river mouth. This was potentially the most dangerous position, and as these were Menschikoff's weakest troops the Russian commander-in-chief cannot be said to have shown particularly sound judgement. Above these eight battalions, four others of the Moscow Regiments in square formation and supported by a battery of artillery on each flank were well placed to support them. But before the battle started the deployment in this sector suffered a fundamental change. Appreciating that they had been put in what might well become a suicidal location the four 'reserve' battalions moved back up the hill. Not relishing the prospect of being left alone, the four Taroutine battalions followed. The move was made unobtrusively and without any authorization; Menschikoff knew nothing of it, and when it was completed the eight battalions were positioned just below the crest of Telegraph Hill – a mile and a half from where he had put them.

Further towards the centre four battalions of the Borodino Regiment with a rifle battalion and sixteen field guns (two field batteries) were deployed astride the road, overlooking the bridge. Behind them also astride the road but farther up the hill, Menschikoff located his tactical reserve – four battalions of the Volhynia Regiment, three battalions of the Minsk Regiment, and two more batteries of guns. Finally, the cavalry – a Brigade of Hussars and two regiments of Cossacks of the Don with three batteries of horse artillery were positioned on the eastern slope of Kourgane Hill, covering Menschikoff's right flank.

To make control easier Menschikoff divided the Alma defences into three sectors, each containing about 10,000 infantry, and a major-general was put in command of each. General Kiriakoff was given the Telegraph Hill and the twelve battalions and twenty guns on the left; Prince Gorschakoff was given the twelve battalions and sixteen guns astride the road, and General Kvetsinski the sixteen battalions and cavalry force deployed round the Kourgane Hill. (Kvetsinski had about 70 guns in his sector, including the fourteen heavies in the Great Redoubt.) By French standards Kiriakoff and Kvetsinski would be described as *généraulx ordinaires*, since neither had shown till then – nor were to show subsequently – any professional merit. But Prince Gorschakoff had made a name for himself by suppressing a near revolution in the Caucasus in 1820; later he had been made Governor of Eastern Siberia – a job which was no sinecure. He had retired in 1851, but at sixty-four he had volunteered his services at the beginning of the war and the Tsar had given him command of an army. Unfortunately for Gorschakoff this army, of 60,000 men, had behaved badly when it was attacked by the Turks at Giurgevo on the Danube, with the result that Gorschakoff had lost his command and been demoted to become Menschikoff's second-in-command.

Although Menschikoff had concentrated his defences on a comparatively narrow three-mile front he believed that he had created a formidable obstacle against which the British and French must fling themselves and be destroyed. The first two miles of the Alma Heights had been left undefended, but he assumed that his left flank was in no danger. Indeed, he was so confident of the impregnability of the Russian position that he invited a party of spectators from Sebastopol to watch the annihilation of those who had the temerity to invade Holy Russia. Thus it was that on the morning of 20 September, thirty gaily-dressed young ladies assembled on Telegraph Hill. There, from specially constructed stands, they were able to watch the allied armies march down to the Alma. With Colours flying and drums beating Raglan's army in its colourful uniforms must have presented a magnificent sight – the like of which was never to be seen again.

The British started to advance at one o'clock, and within minutes the thin line of riflemen preceding the main columns of the Light and 1st Divisions were exchanging shots with Russian skirmishers positioned above the bridge. Soon afterwards the Russian batteries on the slopes of Kourgane Hill opened fire, and cannon balls started falling on the north bank of the river. Drawing out his watch with a flourish, one of the only two officers of the Scots Fusilier Guards to have seen active service, announced 'The battle begins at 1 o'clock'. His watch must have been nearly half an hour slow because the British army was halted again shortly afterwards.[1] The time was then 1.30 p.m.; the leading troops had reached the verge of the grassy slopes leading down to the river and the cannon balls were now ripping through their lines. 'Great ponderous shot, they came bounding along the ground like cricket balls. As the men saw them approaching they opened their ranks and the balls went hissing past.'[2] Some 'caused not a little fright and uneasiness amongst the horses' of the cavalry on the British left flank.[3] When a sergeant of the Light Division was killed, it was clear that the time had come to deploy the leading divisions into line.

Inevitably the deploying of 10,000 men into line was an evolution of some magnitude. Under the nagging supervision of their senior non-commissioned officers individual regiments had practised its ceremonial version on the parade ground time and again. But there had never been an opportunity, let alone occasion, on which to practise with a formation as big as a division, and sheer inexperience had put the Light Division too close to the 2nd Division.* Such an error is corrected by shuffling across to the flank when only a few men are involved, but with 5,000 men this is not easy. The result was that the 2nd Division had to move forward so that its left could extend across the front of the Light Division's right, and when the deployment was completed the two divisions overlapped each other. The aim of the deployment drill was a continuous line of soldiers; in this instance the 7th Regiment on the extreme right of the Light Division with the two flanking field guns of the Light Division, found itself behind the 95th of the 2nd Division whose own field guns were in front of the Light Division line. Raglan watching the wheeling, marching and dressing from a vantage point near the road saw that the broken line and misplaced guns might well lead to complications when the advance was resumed.

Obviously Sir George Brown would have to move the whole of his Light Division over to the left and then forward to bring it into line. But old Sir George was nowhere to be found. (He had in fact ridden over to the left of the line, and being short-sighted— a fact which he obstinately refused to recognize – he had not seen the chaotic situation at the junction of his division with that of de Lacy Evans. And if any of his staff noticed that things were going awry in the centre they kept quiet; Sir George was not a man in whose company subordinates were at ease.) Raglan, not wishing to cause unpleasantness decided to let things sort themselves out, and when Brown saw the congestion it was too late; the lines were moving forward again.†

By this time the extended British lines were coming under considerable fire and Raglan must have begun to regret that he had failed to agree on a concerted plan with St Arnaud. On the right, he

---

* A division in line – two ranks of 2,500 men each – would extend across a front of more than a mile.

† Usually, when dealing with subordinates Raglan punctiliously respected the chain of command. But there were exceptions. At Varna he aroused resentment when he disregarded Lord Lucan and dealt directly with Lord Cardigan, Lucan's subordinate commander, brother-in-law and implacable personal enemy.

could see Bosquet's division moving down towards the river and the tiny village of Almatamack on its north bank – presumably in accordance with the French plan to cross at its mouth and climb the cliffs. But he had no more idea of what the rest of the French army intended to do than St Arnaud had of Raglan's intentions. In the event it was the relative positions of the armies which determined the tactics of the battle. Besides Almatamack there was another little village called Bourliouk on the north bank of the river about a quarter of a mile below the bridge. (Directly opposite, on the far bank were the vineyards in which the men of the Borodino battalions waited. Later that afternoon they were to set fire to Bourliouk because it offered cover to the advancing British troops. But at that time Bourliouk marked the right of the British front.)

The British lines were still a mile from the river when it became evident to Raglan that he must hold up his men's advance until the French had crossed the river and diverted the attention of the Russians on their left flank. It was not that the British commander was reverting to St Arnaud's plan, merely that he now saw that the way the battle was developing the sequence would be Bosquet's outflanking hook, followed by a French assault on the Russian left, and finally a frontal attack straight across the river by the British. And so, following their imperfect deployment, the two leading divisions were ordered to halt and lie down. Behind them, but out of effective range of the Russian guns, the men of the 1st and 3rd Divisions – still in their columns – were also halted and told to stand easy. To their cheers some of the British 9-pounder field batteries raced up to the front, unlimbered and tried to hit back at the Russian artillery. But the Russian guns were at too great an elevation and after a short time they gave up and withdrew.

For an hour and a half the men on the ground were shelled with impunity. There was nothing they could do but suffer in silence. Few of the rank and file and not many of the officers had been in action before, and this was their first experience of unexpected death. Sergeant Gowing of the 7th 'felt horribly sick, a cold shivering running through my veins' and Captain Montgomery of the 42nd was 'afraid for the first time in my life'.[4] At first it seemed simple to avoid a hit. A man could follow the trajectory of a round shot fired from one of the heavy Russian guns and move out of the way when it started to descend. (Most of the Russian heavy guns fired plain round shot which was lethal only if it scored a direct hit.) Not that moving out of line was encouraged, but to dodge decapitation was worth the rebuke of a sergeant. Fortunately General Shrapnel's Peninsula War invention had not been developed by the Russians. Nevertheless the grapeshot fired by some of their field guns, which was not so easy to avoid, inflicted ghastly wounds. So too did the elementary shells – hollow iron spheres stuffed with gunpowder detonated by means of a crude fuse. Skilful gunners could gauge the timing of these missiles so that they burst with an effect similar to that of today's sophisticated airburst missile.

There was nothing skilful about the arrangements for those who were hit during this scarifying ordeal. The casualty would be pulled out of the ranks, forward or backward, according to his position, by the men on either side. He was then left untended to writhe in agony, for it was against orders for combatant British soldiers in action to move a stricken man. In the 1st Division Sir Colin Campbell rode up and down the lines of the Highland Brigade, telling them, 'Whoever is wounded must lie where he is until a bandsman comes to attend to him – I don't care what his rank is. No soldier must go carrying off wounded men. If any soldier does such a thing, his name shall be stuck up in his parish church.'[5] Thus nobody could escape by pretending he was braving enemy fire to carry a wounded comrade out of danger.

Under this ordeal the discipline of the British army was put to the test for the first time in 40 years. By the way the troops reacted it was evident that they had been imbued with a spirit which could not have derived solely from the lash. Every man behaved according to character but discipline held. Some appeared to accept the situation unconcernedly: others, feeling less brave, covered their fear with a veneer of nervous humour – chaffing one another, giving the Russian guns girls' names and passing bawdy comments on their respective performances. To maintain morale, senior officers ostentatiously rode up and down the lines in full view of the Russians, purposely advertising themselves to draw fire. Conspicuous in his blue frock coat and white-plumed cocked hat, Raglan was amongst them – enjoying every moment, it was said. So too was General Codrington, commanding the Light Brigade of the Light Division; whose white Arab pony provided the Russian gunners with a prominent target. In Raglan's case it was not just that he was exhilarated by a whiff of powder or the whistle of a bullet – though this was said of him afterwards. He was intent on setting his troops an example of absolute

Lord Lucan.

Sir Colin Campbell.

Prince Napoleon, Commander of the French 3rd Division.

General Canrobert.

calm and when he sent an aide-de-camp with an order to one of
the divisional generals he told him 'Go quietly; don't gallop!' Without doubt this attitude paid dividends and Raglan's bearing, together with that of the other generals, contributed much to the
steadiness with which the British troops waited that afternoon by the
Alma.

While the British waited, Bosquet's troops were climbing up on to
the plateau on top of the cliffs. In Algeria, Bosquet had had plenty of
experience in moving troops up steep hills and through narrow
passes so that the operation to which he had been assigned was not a
novel experience. Full of energy and enterprise – in marked contrast to the other French generals – Bosquet was probably more
qualified than any of the other generals, British or French, to
command troops in a commando-type assault. His division comprised two brigades of 3,000 infantrymen each, and the Turks,
9,000 of them, had been put under his command. His briga-
diers were Generals Bruat and d'Autemarre and the Turks were
allotted to Bruat's brigade. This tremendous force was sent to cross
the river by the sand bar at its mouth while d'Autemarre's brigade
was directed towards the village of Almatamack. But before they set
off, the troops were ordered to take off their packs – containing their
rations and spare clothing – and dump them on the ground where
they had halted. (When two more French divisions dumped theirs
in the same area a little later, 18,000 packs were to litter the ground
that sloped down to the river.) This was a perfectly normal preliminary to battle but the need to recover the packs after the battle
was to have serious repercussions.

Crossing the river at the sand bar proved to be more difficult
than had been anticipated. Whilst the river was fordable at this
point the surf breaking on the bar compelled men to move slowly.
Then when they got to the far side the cliff path proved to be so
narrow and winding that it took the first files half an hour to struggle
up to the top of the cliffs. And in that time some of Bruat's Zouaves
had swarmed up the steep face of the ravine. What was quite evident
was that to drag Bruat's artillery across the sand bar and up the
cliff path was quite out of the question. Meantime d'Autemarre,
accompanied by Bosquet, had splashed across the shallow ford at
Almatamack, followed by the 3,000 men and 12 guns of his
brigade. Once across the river the brigade marched straight up
the road which led to the plateau, its progress being marked by

bursts of prophylactic firing. And when the Zouaves reached the plateau the nearest Russians to be seen were Kiriakoff's battalions on Telegraph Hill, a mile and a half away. When, in turn, they were seen by the Russians, Kiriakoff started to move a couple of the Moscow battalions in their direction and four guns deployed near Ulokol Touiets – a little village about two miles south of the river – were moved up to within range of the river mouth and brought into action. When shots from these guns started to fall on the cliff top the Zouaves dropped back to take cover in the ravine. Before Bosquet could go any farther he had to wait for his guns; it was contrary to French training and tradition to advance without artillery cover. As it took over two hours to drag the guns up, the French 2nd Division played no further part in the battle.

With his staff St Arnaud had taken up a position from which he could best observe the course of the battle. The old Marshal was anxious for news which would tell him that Bosquet's operation had succeeded. When he saw a flutter of movement below the cliffs on the far bank he turned to his aides and cried enthusiastically 'He is established on the heights; I see the red pantaloons. Ah! I easily recognize my old Bosquet from Africa.'[6] Turning to Canrobert and Prince Napoleon he then issued an order that was as singularly simple as it was sweepingly vague. 'With men such as you,' he said, 'I have no orders to give. I have but to point to the enemy.' In effect the arrangements for the French assault had been finalized the night before as part of the concerted plan put to Raglan and, when Bosquet was presumed to have successfully completed the first phase of the operation probably nothing more than a grandiloquent *envos* was necessary. The French divisions were to cross, in their columns*i* at the recognized crossing places. (To the French commanders the British method of advancing in line and for every individual to wade through the river at whatever point he approached it – still in formation – would be to court disaster. Traditionally the French moved in columns; equally traditionally the British covered their front with one extended line.) Having decided that Canrobert's 1st Division would cross at a ford below Telegraph Hill and Prince Napoleon's 3rd Division at the ford below the village of Bourliouk the Marshal believed that all that he was required to do was to point to the enemy; the rest was up to his generals.

It was now nearly half-past two as the second phase of St Arnaud's operation was about to begin. Despite the lack of an overall plan the battle had seemed to be following a logical sequence so far. But from this point things began to go awry. Preceded by a line of skirmishers Canrobert led his column down towards the river and his troops negotiated the river without difficulty. But the road up the ravine on the far side turned out to be too narrow for his guns. Hearing that Bosquet had got his artillery up to the plateau by way of the road from Almatamack, he sent them off to his right to follow in the wake of d'Autemarre's – with orders that they should rejoin him at the top of the cliffs. In consequence Canrobert's division reached the edge of the plateau less its guns and so, like Bruat's brigade, was unable to go any farther. In the French army the generals believed that infantry could not operate in any circumstances without artillery support, that without field guns they were useless.

Meantime Prince Napoleon had taken his division down the slope towards the Bourliouk ford in eight battalion columns. In the vineyards on the left, the troops were not screened from the Russian guns by the cliffs on the south bank like the troops farther downstream and the Russians were now reacting sharply to the French threat. It was not long before both Canrobert's troops on the edge of the plateau and those of Napoleon's division in the vineyards found themselves under heavy fire from the Russian batteries on Telegraph Hill. A crisis, as perilous as it was unanticipated, had developed. Canrobert was pinned to the edge of the slopes and the 3rd Division's advance had been halted before it even reached the river. Casualties were mounting, and Prince Napoleon's battalions broke formation to scurry for cover in the vineyards on the northern bank.[*] St Arnaud and his staff who had moved with the 3rd Division found themselves isolated in one of the gardens by the river. The French operation had ground to a halt and the Marshal could no longer exert influence on the battle. Everything now depended on the British.

If Menschikoff had had any tactical ability, this was the time to have gone over to the offensive. But the significance of the situation escaped him and the opportunity was let slip. Angered by the report that a large enemy force had suddenly appeared on the plateau near the mouth of the river, the Russian commander rode across to see

---

[*] As a child Prince Napoleon was known as Plon Plon, but undeservedly after this action his nickname became 'plon plomb' – a distortion of the French phrase *plomb plomb* which suggested fear of a lead bullet.

for himself. None of his section commanders was told where he had gone; two batteries of guns, three battalions of the Minsk Regiment from the reserve near the road, and the four battalions of the Moscow Regiment on Telegraph Hill were ordered to move to the threatened area without losing any time. When they arrived Menschikoff's confidence had been deflated and his anger had lapsed into dismay; the solemn grey squares were ordered to turn round and march back to their original positions – as quickly as possible. By the time they did get back the battle was not over but its outcome was almost certain.

It was just after three o'clock when an urgent message reached Raglan from the French headquarters. The British commander had just ridden to the right of the British line and was looking to see what the French were doing when a young French aide-de-camp cantered up to him. It was not clear whether he had come from St Arnaud or from Bosquet but he was in an agitated state. Prince Napoleon's troops were being 'massacred' he said and Bosquet's troops were being 'compromised'. Unsure of what the verb *compromettre* meant in a military context, Raglan asked the young officer what would happen if Bosquet were 'compromised'. Despairingly the Frenchman replied '*Il battra en retraite*'. [He will beat a retreat].[7] Whether this message to Raglan had any authoritative origin is doubtful. Unlike Canrobert and Prince Napoleon, Bosquet was known to have plenty of self-reliance and unlikely to be deterred by a mere bombardment. But whether or not the message gave a false picture of the French army's predicament it had the effect of making up Raglan's mind. It had been his intention to attack as soon as the French were on the Heights and the Russian left was committed to battle. From what he could see, the Russians had not yet been committed and what the French had done so far had done little to suggest that they would be able to withstand a Russian counter-attack. If the British advanced and the Russians decided to set about Canrobert and Prince Napoleon's divisions, it was possible that they would be able to swing round the right flank of the British line just as it was crossing the river. It was also possible that the Russian cavalry on Kourgane Hill might well ride round the other flank to attack the British left and Raglan's army would be caught in the river between two gigantic pincers.

Yet there was another major consideration which weighed heavily with Raglan. The sight of his men suffering for so long under fire had become almost unendurable. Supremely brave himself he could not fail to be affected by the ordeal the British soldiers were undergoing, and there is little doubt that the French *cri du coeur* anticipated Raglan's orders by a very few moments. Turning to General Airey he issued the last executive order that he was to give in the battle. 'The infantry will advance' he said. No objective was defined; the command was based on no tactical reasoning and the inference was that the line would advance until it was told to stop somewhere beyond the Alma. If Raglan had any other plan in his head, he kept it to himself.

With this order the British army was now committed.

7

THE BATTLE OF THE ALMA: THE SECOND PHASE

The Infantry Will Advance . . . 'I shall never forget the excited look of delight on every face when I repeated the order' wrote David Lysons, one of De Lacy Evans' staff officers.[1] Leaping to their feet, the men of the two forward divisions dressed ranks with ceremonial precision. Sergeant-majors shouted for a file to edge forward here or drop back there, while every few seconds cannon balls punched gaps in the two impeccably aligned ranks. Only in the middle of the line, where the left flank of the 2nd Division overlapped the right of the Light Division was there a flaw; otherwise nearly 10,000 British soldiers faced the Russians in a line two miles long and two men deep. Both De Lacy Evans and Sir George Brown were sticklers for discipline and it was not until the regimental officers were completely satisfied with the dressing of the ranks that the executive order to move forward was given. But when the final 'Eyes Front' was called, a bugle sounded and the British line in perfect step set off down the slope towards the river. Mrs Evans, one of the three women who had managed to accompany their husbands from Varna with the King's Own Regiment, and who had 'got on somehow' as far as the Bulganak was watching from behind the 3rd Division and she recorded later that one of the regimental officers standing beside her turned and said, 'Look well at that Mrs Evans, for the Queen of England would give her eyes to see it.'*[2]

At this moment the village of Bourliouk went up in flames. Its inhabitants had been forcibly evacuated the day before, and the Russians had stuffed the houses with straw. A small rear party with orders to fire the village as soon as the British got anywhere near the river did so as the long line of redcoats started to advance. Burning

* Mrs Elizabeth Evans, who died in January 1900, went right through the Crimean campaign with her husband. So too did Mrs Rebecca ('Becky' to the troops) Box. The third woman, whose husband was killed at Alma, was sent back to England.

Bourliouk was a cunning and well-timed stroke and it took the British by surprise. Soon 'the dogs of the village ran about, scared at this novel change in their affairs, and pigeons darted and dived on the wing through the smoke in evident terror of their lives.'[3] With less disciplined troops the Russian ruse could have had serious consequences. The Light Division was unaffected because the smoke drifted across the front towards the sea. But the brigade commanded by Brigadier-General Adams on the right of the 2nd Division – confronted by a seemingly impassable obstacle – faltered and came to a halt. On their left, the other brigade of the 2nd Division – that of Brigadier-General Pennefather – pressed on; but inevitably it was compelled to veer over towards its left, and this tended to increase the confusion where the 95th Regiment overlapped the 7th Regiment of the Light Division's right. Under fire an advance in line is difficult enough; and, when part of the line is deflected by an obstacle, forward movement becomes even more difficult. Troops moving in loose formations will make their own adjustments to pass round something in their way. But it is almost impossible to compress extra men into a line in which men have been drilled to maintain their positions in a set geometrical pattern. At the overlapping junction of the two divisions, the line rippled and the 7th Regiment (the Royal Fusiliers) shouldered their way through the 95th. As the 95th were also being pushed to the left by the regiment on their right – the 55th – the confusion was chaotic and heavy fire from the Russian batteries served to make matters worse. Impelled by some common impulse half the 95th followed the 7th, while the other half moved across the front of the Light Division.

Meantime, still farther left the pace of the Light Division's advance had been too swift for the Russian artillery to be really effective. But as soon as Brown's men reached the vineyards it was a different matter. Not only was their progress slowed down by the undergrowth but the Russians had erected white posts topped with straw bundles among the vines to give them exact ranges. To the intense cannonade was added the small arms fire of the Russian skirmishers who had retired across the river to line the southern bank and were now picking off the British as they struggled through the vineyards. Because of a shortage of timber for poles, the vines were planted in holes, four or five feet wide and about three feet deep, and such obstacles could not fail to disrupt the lines of men who had been disciplined 'to march like a wall and wheel like a gate.'

With the breaking of the line went some of the discipline. With that thriftlessness which still often characterizes the British soldier on active service, shakos and bits of equipment which impeded movement were tossed away. Some of the troops paused to pluck the green grapes, while others decided to shelter behind the wall in front of the vineyard. Above them all, wrote Colour-Sergeant McSally, 'Russian shells whirred through the trees like . . . innumerable partridges taking flight'.[4] In the event, all trace of alignment had been lost by the time the men reached the river.

At the Alma, the Light Division was in more respectable order than the 2nd Division. To all intents and purposes the 7th Regiment, after elbowing its way through the 95th and veering off to the right, was lost to Brown's division. But the half of the 95th which had inclined to the right found itself in the line of Brigadier-General Codrington's brigade, which now had three battalions – comprising the 33rd (Duke of Wellington's), the 23rd, and 95th; and Brigadier-General Buller's brigade – on the left of that of Codrington – still consisted of the 19th, 88th and 77th Regiments. Both brigades marched straight down to the river behind Sir George Brown, and as they were on the extreme left of the allied line and Russian attention was concentrated on the road axis and the bridge, neither were shelled to the same extent as the two brigades of the 2nd Division. However, when they reached the vineyards they were assailed by a hail of musketry from sharpshooters lying out in front of the Russian columns on the opposite bank. Fortunately for the men concerned, musket fire – and even rifle fire at that stage of its development – was remarkably inaccurate. If only because the powder charges varied so much, the likelihood of being hit depended more on chance than marksmanship, even though the long ranks presented such a wide target. Nevertheless some of the shots found their victims.

Going through the vineyards the soldiers of the Light Division faced the same hazards and obstacles as their comrades in the 2nd – walls to be climbed, vines to be avoided, ditches to be jumped – but Brown's men suffered fewer casualties than did those of De Lacy Evans. To pass the obstacles the line had to be broken but when the men reached the river bank they regrouped to reassume their correct formation. With orders *not* to pick their way most of the troops dutifully leapt into the Alma, holding their rifles and ammunition pouches above their heads. The more fortunate had to wade only up to their ankles; a few found themselves waist-deep. But a few, who stumbled and fell into deep holes, were borne down by the weight of their equipment. Floundering and struggling, some of them drowned; others, who were wounded, slumped forward and were also drowned. Some hurried across; others, in whom the salt pork of their rations had raised a thirst, paused to fill their water bottles.

Luckily for the men of the Light Division the south bank of the Alma lay a little way back from the actual river, and rose to a height of about ten to fifteen feet; without this natural cover there might have been no British victory, or victory only at a hideous cost. Above the bank the ground sloped upwards, quite gently, towards the Great Redoubt – no more than 400 yards away – and as soon as the troops climbed to the top they found themselves in the direct line of almost point-blank cannon fire. But so long as they remained on the ledge in the shelter of the bank they were almost entirely screened. The only casualties inflicted were by some of the more adventurous Russian sharpshooters, who crept up to the lip of the bank in order to take pot shots at the mass of British infantry crowding below.

The bank started to drop away in front of where General Buller's brigade crossed the river, until – in front of the 77th, on the extreme left flank of the allied armies – it vanished. There the British troops faced a rising stretch of ground running up towards the eastern slopes of the Kourgane Hill. As there was nothing between the 77th and any Russians who might try to roll up their flank, Buller ordered the 77th to face left and the men to lie down and wait. Buller – Gentleman George – was not overgifted with imagination, and having complied with the command not to stop until the river was crossed, he was at a loss what to do next. Appreciating that the guarding of the left of the allied line was his responsibility, Buller preferred to play safe.

Hardly had the 77th swung into position when Buller saw, or thought he saw, some of Menschikoff's cavalry forming up round the side of Kourgane Hill, and he ordered the 88th (with whom he was moving) to form a hollow square with its front facing up the hill. With reluctance and some indifference, the turbulent Irishmen of the 88th complied, but a similar order passed on to the 19th on Buller's right was ignored. Believing that the Russian cavalry were about to attack, Buller's precautions were justified. But to the commanding officer of the 19th the situation looked different. He could see no danger from the left, where the 77th and 88th were deployed, and he was very close to the Russian guns in the Great Redoubt. Moreover, whilst a square was the approved method of resisting a cavalry charge, forming a square within range of a battery of heavy guns would be to invite disaster. And so, with commendable indiscipline the 19th swung off to the right, to attach itself to Codrington's brigade whose 23rd, 33rd and half of the 95th Regiments were shaking themselves out preparatory to an advance on the Great Redoubt.

On the narrow ledge where Codrington's troops had collected, officers and N.C.O.s of the three regiments involved had been trying to collect their men together and to get their companies and platoons into a semblance of order. The divisional commander, who had been one of the first across the river, was in a tearing rage. To Sir George, drill and discipline were the ultimate objects of soldiering, and he was determined to see that his division was properly aligned before it moved on. Amid the confusion on the ledge he found a place where the bank had crumbled away and spurred his horse to the top; from there he shouted orders to the milling mass below. No one could really hear, and it is surprising that the Russians failed to shoot him for it was clear that the infuriated figure in a cocked hat who was gesticulating in full view of their position was a character of considerable importance. However, as Sir George instilled the fear of God in his own troops maybe he deterred the Russian sharpshooters.

Codrington had never been in action before, nor had he been long with the Light Division. A Coldstream Guardsman and a man of considerable means, he had been disappointed when he was not given a command with the Guards battalions that had been sent to Turkey. Determined not to be left out, he had travelled out at his own expense and presented himself to Raglan at Varna to ask for an appointment. And when Raglan gave him a brigade of the Line, Codrington became something of a rarity. In the British army the Guards and the regiments of the Line existed in separate worlds, and for a Guardsman to command anything but Guards was almost unheard of; indeed some of his brother officers would consider that he had demeaned himself by accepting the appointment. Nevertheless, for all his ostensibly 'superior' background Codrington was a dedicated soldier and despite a lack of experience he saw that his brigade could not stay down on the narrow river ledge. In theory he had attained his objective. His orders had been to take his battalions across the river; this he had accomplished, and it was reasonable to suppose he would receive new orders soon. Presumably they would come from the divisional commander. However, as the river twisted and turned Codrington had no idea of the whereabouts of the irate Sir George (who, in fact, at that very moment was haranguing some of Codrington's men a few hundred yards away.) In the confinement and confusion of the ledge, Codrington could see that it was not feasible to re-establish the formation for which the troops had trained – the unbroken, outflanking line which, gradually advancing, they had been taught to believe would have a shattering moral and physical effect on the enemy. The only commands the men would heed were 'Fix bayonets' and 'Come on!'. So, like Sir George, he found a place where his charger could scramble to a vantage point above the ledge and from there he shouted for the men below to get up the bank and advance.

It was a little time before the command was acted on. The troops were accustomed to obeying only their own regimental officers and they were hesitant about following someone whom few recognized as their brigadier. Codrington had never expected to be given a brigade and consequently he had no cocked hat with flowing plumes; what he was wearing was a simple regimental forage cap – Guards pattern at that. To the rank and file a cocked hat demanded respect and spontaneous obedience but orders from an 'ordinary' officer of some regiment other than their own were treated with some suspicion. Nevertheless, Codrington eventually succeeded in collecting a few men together, and when they scrambled up the bank more followed. Soon the 33rd, the 23rd and the 19th from Buller's brigade were all following him in a series of short forward rushes up the deadly glacis towards the Great Redoubt. There was no line; that had gone long ago, and it was a great ragged horde that surged forward. Shouting and cursing, officers and sergeants alike tried to get the mob into a semblance of order, and many of the soldiers realized that they were not going into action as they had been trained to fight. But once on the slope there was only one purpose – to reach the Russian strong point.

Almost at the same time that Codrington had given a lead, Colonel Lacy Yea (he pronounced it Yaw) had rallied the Fusiliers. Passing through the 95th his companies of the 7th had inevitably become disorganized and Yea quickly appreciated that it was fruitless to try to sort out the confusion on the narrow ledge below the bank. 'Never mind forming,' he shouted, 'Come along anyhow'. It was an unprecedented order but the men of Yea's own regiment hastened to obey. They had little love for their commanding officer but they respected his authority. (Yea knew this. Writing to his sister on the eve of the battle he said 'The Russians are before me and my own men behind me, so I don't think you'll ever see me again.') And so – except for Buller's two battalions watching the left flank – all the men of the Light Division who had survived the river crossing were soon scrambling up the long slope which led to the Great Redoubt. In front of them the Russian skirmishers hastily made for the shelter of the redoubt, and as they cleared the slope, the Russian gunners were seen to be lowering the muzzles of their cannon and getting ready to blast the oncoming British infantry into eternity. At a range of less than 600 yards, reducing every minute, they could hardly miss.

So far as the Russians were concerned, the attacking force was less of a shapeless mass of soldiery than the apoplectic Sir George Brown believed it to be. They had been trained to resist dense columns similar to their own, so perhaps a concentrated mass would have been less frightening than the irregular knotted line which stretched out before them, way beyond their flanks. 'We did not think it possible,' wrote one eye-witness, 'for men to be found with such firmness of morale to be able to attack in this apparently weak formation our massive columns . . .'[5] The Russian columns – each of 1,500 men – drawn up in eight ranks – were deployed behind the earthworks and behind the guns. 'Their strange drab coats and ugly heavy looking helmets looked anything but sightly, though perhaps martial . . . The strength of the enemy seemed enormous, and, having advanced close, looked like the dense crowd as you see it at Epsom on the Derby Day.'[6] The Russians in the front ranks raised their muskets and fired but their fire was uncontrolled and virtually unaimed. Their tight packed formation did not permit the inner ranks of the column doing anything more than firing into the air, and so although there was a lot of noise, the shooting was not very effective. Nearly all the casualties suffered by the British were inflicted by the Russian artillery. Codrington's men advancing into a searing hail of shot, shell and grape suffered more than those of Yea who came in on the flank; and, as might be expected, casualties were most severe where the ranks were thickest. At short range a single shot could mow down half a dozen men if they were bunched together in its path, and a single discharge of grape is credited with killing no less than fourteen.

If credit for the capture of the Great Redoubt is to go to any particular individual and regiment, it must be to Yea and his Royal Fusiliers. Somehow or other, as soon as Yea had got his men up the slope he managed to get them into two ranks facing two battalions of the Kazan Regiment at a distance of less than a hundred yards. How this was done amid the din and disarray is difficult to picture. But Yea's cursing and pushing coupled with the Fusiliers' discipline and concern with what would happen to them if they hesitated to obey eventually brought the battalion into a formation capable of bringing the maximum firepower on to the Russians' close packed columns.* At point-blank range the Fusiliers and the men of the Kazan Regiment poured fire into each other's rank. The Fusiliers were hopelessly outnumbered but they presented a less vulnerable target, and only the two front ranks in the dense columns of their enemies could shoot back. Moreover the Russians were equipped with an 1832 smooth-bore musket – recently altered from flintlock to percussion and hardly lethal at 100 yards – while the Fusiliers were armed with Minié rifles of infinitely greater range and penetrating power. At 100 yards a single Minie bullet would tear through seven or eight men, so that in this short-range duel difference in numbers was not a limiting factor. The line formation had been developed from Wellington's theory that the longer the line the greater the firepower that could be brought to bear. A battalion of a thousand men drawn up in two long ranks presented a front of 500 rifles while a column of the same number advancing eight men abreast could only bring eight rifles to bear; and from 500 rifles a devastating cone of concentrated fire could be poured on to the narrow column. As small-arms fire was painfully slow this was an important consideration.

The fight between Yea's battalion and the Kazan columns lasted for about half an hour, and as a detached action it was an epic on its own. Its effect was to draw the attention of the Russians in the

---

* During the action Yea found he was getting short of men so an officer was sent to see if anybody was skulking down by the river. A dozen or so frightened men were rounded up and brought before Yea. Punishment was deferred and the defaulters hurried into line. As musket balls whistled round their ears no doubt each of them hoped that a wound would save him from the flogging which Yea had promised.

Great Redoubt to their left flank, and this helped Codrington's men to get up the hill. The Russian columns had been deliberately deployed at an angle in order to funnel the attackers in towards the centre and this is what happened. At the river Codrington's four battalions (19th, 23rd, 33rd and 95th) had covered a front of nearly three-quarters of a mile, but by the time they reached the Russian defences they had been compressed into a seething mass whose front was no more than 400 yards wide – hardly longer than the Redoubt itself. With more determination the Russians could have held on. Suddenly, however, after a final withering volley the guns fell silent and when the pall of thick smoke which hung over the forward edge of the redoubt rolled away the Russians could be seen to be limbering them up, hitching them to teams of cavalry horses, and dragging them off to the rear. The leading British troops were still a hundred yards from their objective and many of them were feeling the effect of their exertions. But the sight of the Russians pulling out stimulated final effort. Shouts of 'He's carrying off his guns' brought a frantic rush to the Russian parapet. A young ensign of the 23rd, carrying the Queen's Colours of his regiment, was the first to reach it; Codrington, miraculously unscathed despite his conspicuousness, was close behind.

The battle was almost won. But not quite; Russian infantrymen still held the rear of the redoubt and as he thrust the Colour pike into the ground on top of the parapet the ensign of the 23rd received a bullet in the heart.* Within minutes, however, two thousand British soldiers were milling about and around the Great Redoubt; they arrived just in time to prevent the removal of the last two guns. (With the point of his sword Captain Bell of the 23rd scratched '23' on the barrel of one, while Captain Heyland of the 95th – who had lost an arm on the way up – laid claim to the other.) [7]

At least one contemporary historian has recorded that the 'discreditable' withdrawal of the Russian guns was the turning point of the Battle of the Alma. [8] But it was not fear which was the cause of the guns being dragged out of the redoubt. Believing that Wellington had never lost a gun,† the Tsar had decided that none of his would ever be taken and Menschikoff had issued an uncompromising

---

* Epaulettes, gold braid and drawn swords, as well as their position in the forefront of the battle made all regimental officers conspicuous. Subalterns carrying the colours risked almost certain death – the 95th lost every ensign in quick succession.

† In fact Wellington lost four, although they were Portuguese.

order to that effect. The physical bravery of the Russian troops was never in doubt; it was just that they were badly led. (As a Russian officer cynically explained: 'No wonder our soldiers are brave! They have so little to lose that they lose nothing when they lose their life. The way to make a good soldier is to make him careless about his existence.') The fact remains that Codrington's capture of the Great Redoubt was a spectacular success, not achieved without a sizeable butcher's bill. Three hundred dead and wounded lay on the glacis below the redoubt before the battle in this sector could be said to have been anywhere near over. Yea and his Fusiliers were still engaged with the two Kazan battalions on the right of the redoubt, while on the other side – the British left – the two battalions that had been driven back by the 19th and 23rd were still intact. They and the massed Russian cavalry remained a hazard to Codrington's own flank, 400 yards forward of where Buller was sitting by the river with the 77th and 88th Regiments.

In the redoubt itself the four battalions that had converged on it had merged into a chaotic hugger-mugger. In this shallow pocket, 300 yards long, 10 yards wide, at the foot of Kourgane Hill, 2,000 men now sought shelter from the fire of the Russian guns that had been repositioned further back, and around them well-ordered columns totalling 14,000 Russian infantrymen were still deployed. In the circumstances it was to be expected that the Russians would counter-attack. Codrington realized that the lull which followed his success could be critical. With the survivors tired and the regiments intermixed, he knew that it would not be easy to recapture the *élan* that had carried the men up the glacis to the redoubt. However, he was sure that the British 1st Division would soon be coming up to reinforce the position, and he was determined to hang on until this happened. But, as yet, there was no sign of the 1st Division, and while Codrington was considering what to do a great column appeared round a spur of Kourgane Hill. Four battalions of the Vladimir Regiment, carrying in their midst the image of the blessed St Sergius, had been sent to recover the redoubt and as they tramped towards it the men sang a sorrowful, wailing tune. To Codrington it was obvious that he was witnessing the precursor to a desperate venture, and he did not have to wait long to learn its significance. After the battle, Prince Gorschakoff and General Kvetsinski both claimed to have led the Vladimir column in person. The action was in Kvetsinski's sector but it appears that Gorschakoff – in his role of second-in-command to Menschikoff, who had gone off without saying where – had decided to take over and direct the battle. From the centre he could see that the critical area was in Kvetsinski's sector, and so he had ridden over to the Vladimir Regiment and ordered it to march round the eastern end of Kourgane Hill to attack the British left flank; Kvetsinski, unaware that Gorschakoff had taken over, claimed that he did the same. Irrespective of who was responsible, the result was that 3,000 Russian infantrymen, in a column eight files wide, were sent round the Kourgane to attack the redoubt. The column moved in a great phalanx, the outside files marching with fixed bayonets and muskets lowered. This was a charge, Russian style, in slow tempo: an automaton advance which was intended to act like a ploughshare to rip out the mass of British soldiers in the redoubt, whose effectiveness was never tested, because by the time it reached its objective the British had gone.

The actual circumstances of Codrington's withdrawal were based on a misunderstanding that has never been resolved. The men in the redoubt were tired and short of ammunition. But there was still plenty of fight in them and the fire from their Miniés could have inflicted heavy casualties in the dense Vladimir column – perhaps even enabled them to hold back the Russians until the 1st Division arrived on the scene. Nor was there any immediate panic when the column was sighted. But this was a moment when perception was easily blunted and credulity stretched, and when someone shouted 'Don't fire! Don't fire – the column's French!' the order was obeyed.

How anyone could mistake the long grey coats of the Russians for the blue uniforms of the French is difficult to understand; nor is it easy to explain how anyone should believe that the French could have moved so far across the front. But in the stress of the moment the cry was sufficient to implant doubt and to cause a check, and as if to confirm the order, a bugler sounded the 'Cease Fire'. Then the monotonous 'Not one shot more; not one shot more' was taken up by others, and as the bugle call passed from left to right the troops stopped shooting. To some of the officers it was obvious that a mistake had been made. Colonel Chester of the 23rd shouted 'No! No!; it's a Russian column. Fire! Fire!' and Major Lidwill of the 19th, 'utterly dumbfounded'*[9], dropped back to try to find out why and by whom the order had been given. But for its tragic sequel its

---

* According to him it was a mounted officer . . . a distracted looking maniac . . . whose name I never could obtain.'

immediate consequences were almost humorous. Surprised by the cessation of fire the Russians suspected a trap and a halt was called to their ponderous advance. This served to confirm doubts about the nationality of the column and when a bugler sounded the 'Retire', Codrington's troops started to scramble over the parapet. Under a hail of fire they were soon scurrying down the slope towards the river. In their disorganized state most of the men accepted the orders relayed by the bugle; they had been trained that this was how orders would be given in the fog of war, and theirs was not to reason why. Officers of the 23rd, who realized something had gone wrong and who tried to rally their men were shot down by Russian snipers as they stood on the parapet. Codrington sent an aide-de-camp to Brigadier-General Bentinck telling him to hurry on his brigade of Guards which was at that moment approaching the Alma. But before the guns could cross the river the Great Redoubt was back in Russian hands.

While the battle for the Great Redoubt was being fought out, the French army made no move. At the river mouth Bruat's brigade assembled in its columns on the plateau at the top of the cliffs. But Bruat's guns had been sent round to Bosquet and although the nearest Russians were still two and a half miles away he was not prepared to move without artillery. Behind him St Arnaud had moved up a brigade from General Forey's 4th Division, and when the battle of the Alma was over part of this brigade was still queuing up to cross the sand bar. A mile up-river, overlooking Almatamack, Bosquet also waited with the d'Autemarre brigade. Bosquet had four batteries of guns with him, and the nearest Russians were a mile and a half from him. A mile higher up Canrobert's division had also crossed the river but it was also waiting for the guns which Canrobert had sent round via Almatamack. Still further left Prince Napoleon was busily acquiring the military reputation for inactivity which was to dog him for the rest of his life. By three o'clock, four of his battalions had crossed the river – the 19th Chasseurs, a battalion of the Marine Corps, and two battalions of the 2nd Zouave Regiment. Of these only the Zouaves showed any initiative. Once across the river they moved along the river ledge to their right and took up a position on Canrobert's left, alongside their comrades of the 1st Zouaves. Meanwhile the remainder of Prince Napoleon's division had halted on the north bank of the river, seeking cover from Russian artillery fire. St Arnaud, believing that the only way to get things moving was to throw in more men, had ordered Forey's other brigade under General d'Aurelle to join the Prince. With this move the French commander-in-chief dissipated his reserve and, if it had been obeyed, would have congested the Prince's crossing place in the same way as Forey's other brigade had increased the confusion at the sand bar. In the event d'Aurelle's brigade did not join the queue at Prince Napoleon's ford, for as soon as he saw the situation in the vineyards he marched his men downstream until he found a place where he could get his brigade across without difficulty and with little interference from Russian fire. When they were across the river he marched back to the point where Prince Napoleon's men were supposed to be crossing and waited for orders. But the Prince was unaware of d'Aurelle's presence and as no orders were forthcoming d'Aurelle assumed that he had to remain where he was.

Raglan had been on the extreme of the British line when he gave the order to advance and when his army moved forward he advanced with it. His intention had been to move at the junction of the British and French front. But as De Lacy Evans's men advanced while Prince Napoleon's remained static the continuous Anglo-French front ceased to exist and the gap between the British right and the French left steadily widened. To avoid the burning Bourliouk, Adams's brigade had to incline right and for a time this narrowed the gap. Nevertheless the weakest part of the whole front remained this central junction and if it had been exploited by the Russians the outcome of the battle could have been disastrous.

Unlike St Arnaud, Raglan and his headquarters moved independently of his divisions and, when the British troops moved forward, he and his staff rode down to the Alma on a course parallel to the end of the advancing line. At the river his little party found an easy crossing and Raglan himself probably reached the far bank even before any of his infantry had crossed upstream. French skirmishers operating on the left of Prince Napoleon's division were busily exchanging shots with Russian snipers at the bottom of Telegraph Hill when Raglan crossed and the Frenchmen were astounded by the sight of a posse of staff officers in cocked hats nonchalantly riding in front of their own front line. Two of Raglan's staff were hit by the Russian snipers but the rest of the party followed their commander-in-chief up a path which eventually joined the main Sebastopol road at a point where Menschikoff's reserves were stationed. Where it emerged above the main road on one of the lower spurs of Telegraph Hill was a semi-circular knoll which Raglan recognized was an ideal vantage point from which he could see the whole of the British sector of the battlefield. Straight ahead were the Great Redoubt and the Russian positions on Kourgane Hill; almost immediately below, and less than 500 yards away were some of the Russian battalions and batteries astride the road.

Virtually inside the Russian lines, far in advance of his army and quite isolated, the British commander coolly sat on his horse Shadrach watching the fighting. In a day and age when it is considered better that generals should dress and move on the battlefields as inconspicuously as possible, Raglan's behaviour will be judged foolhardy. And it is true that he ought to have stationed himself somewhere near the centre of his army where he could more easily have influenced the battle. As it was he could do nothing to speed up the move of the 1st Division to Kourgane Hill where the battle of the Alma was being decided. 'Oh! for a couple of guns up here!'[10] he is reputed to have said when he saw the Russian batteries in action just below the knoll on his immediate front. Raglan sent one of his staff scurrying down the hill back across the river to General Adams, and in due course two 9-pounders were dragged up to the hillock. They arrived just as Codrington's brigade was working its way up towards the Great Redoubt and, thanks to their elevated position, there is no doubt that they caused havoc in the redoubt and possibly influenced the Russian commander's decision to remove his artillery. After that, these two pieces under the direct orders of the commander-in-chief were turned on to Borodin's battalions 900 yards away.

The French skirmishers through whom Raglan had passed on his way up to the knoll had been quick to report the presence of the British commander-in-chief, and just as Codrington was making his final assault on the Great Redoubt a French aide-de-camp ran up the path to Raglan. Cap in hand, excited and breathless from his climb, this young officer blurted out, 'My Lord, my Lord! We have before us eight battalions!' He did not say who it was that was faced by eight battalions or why the fact should be so critical. Raglan might have retorted that his troops had sixteen battalions in front of them. But bending down from his great brown horse he said soothingly: 'I could spare you a battalion.' Seeming to be satisfied, the Frenchman hurried away and that was the end of the matter. Raglan did not follow up his offer; he could hardly have done so anyway, since he had not been told where the battalion was supposed to go.

In fact the eight battalions disturbing the French were the force which Menschikoff had marched across towards Bosquet and then sent marching back again. When they returned to Telegraph Hill they had been handed over to Kiriakoff who in turn marched them in a wide arc down towards the ravine in which Canrobert's men were waiting for their artillery prior to an advance. There the Russians had halted while Kiriakoff waited for Canrobert to make the first move. But Canrobert was not prepared to fight without his guns and he withdrew the whole of his division, including Prince Napoleon's Zouaves, down to the river ledge without firing a shot. Menaced by what appeared to be a formidable force it was Canrobert who had sent the messenger to Raglan. But Raglan had already decided that the French battle had fizzled out and his sole concern now was with Kourgane Hill.

THE BATTLE OF THE ALMA: THE THIRD PHASE

When the two forward divisions had started to advance, the 1st Division, deployed in line behind the Light Division, had waited. Raglan's orders to the divisional commander, His Royal Highness the Duke of Cambridge, had been that the latter should 'support the front line', and the Duke had no clear idea as to just when and where he should act. First cousin to Queen Victoria and the youngest lieutenant-general in the British army, the Duke was a good academic soldier but he had seen no active service. Moreover the weight of responsibility for five thousand of Britain's most highly regarded troops pressed heavily on him. The 1st Division consisted of two brigades, the Guards Brigade and the Highland Brigade, and the regiments of both saw themselves as the élite of the British army. The Guards had proud battle histories, although they were best known then, as now, for their superb ceremonial performances in London. But no Guards regiment had served overseas since Waterloo; their role had been to protect the Sovereign and only a few of the older men in the ranks of the brigade that stood before the Alma had seen any active service. Socially the regiments of the Highland Brigade were not in the same class as the Guards. In theory they were part of the Line; but to Scotsmen the Highland regiments were every bit as distinguished as the Guards. Full of fighting soldiers the three regiments from which battalions had been drawn for service in the Crimea had all seen recent active service.

Under Brigadier-General Bentinck, the Guards Brigade was made up of the 3rd Grenadiers, the 1st Coldstream, and the 1st Scots Fusilier Guards. The Highland Brigade, under Brigadier-General Sir Colin Campbell, consisted of the 42nd Regiment (The Black Watch), the 79th (The Queen's Own Cameron Highlanders), and the 93rd Regiment (The Argyll and Sutherland Highlanders), and their brigadier was probably the most able and experienced officer in the field that day. A contemporary of Raglan, he had fought at

Corunna, served in the American war of 1812, and seen service in China and the West Indies. He had been wounded four times in action, but – in a social atmosphere which favoured those with influence in high places – promotion had come to him slowly. Having learned his profession on active service however, Campbell understood his men in a way that was unusual for officers of that period. In modern times an understanding between officers and men has become part of the art in which good officers are trained, and its development has been accelerated by the social revolution which removed so many of the old class distinctions. However, a century ago the social gulf between an officer and a private soldier of the British Army was so wide that it was virtually impossible for one to understand the other. Colin Campbell was an exception; he had fought beside his men in situations where artificial distinctions counted for little, and the practical affection that he showed towards his troops was demonstrably returned.

When the divisions leading the advance started to pick their way through the vineyards the Duke ordered the 1st Division to move down to the river behind them, and the move was effected with even more ceremonial deliberation than that of the divisions ahead. At the extreme right of the line the Grenadiers just overlapped the road, and on the far left the Camerons were about a mile upriver from the bridge. Behind the Duke's divisional line the 3rd and 4th Divisions, waiting in battalion columns, moved outwards to take up positions on the flank – Sir Richard England's 3rd Division on the right; Sir George Cathcart with part of the 4th Division on the left. Beyond the 4th Division – and even further off to the left – the two brigades of British cavalry, under Lord Lucan, formed up in column and prepared to withstand the onslaught of a force three times their numerical strength which would come if the Russians decided to swing round the British left.

For all his ability to handle a division of five thousand men in line, the Duke of Cambridge found himself at a loss as it approached the vineyards. Clearly an advance into the undergrowth would mean that his line would be broken – a contingency he did not relish. The two forward divisions were already across the river trying to sort themselves out on the ledge, and Codrington and Yea were collecting their troops preparatory to their assault. Undecided as to what to do for the best, the Duke ordered a pause just short of the vineyards. Realizing that the Duke was hesitating, Airey – acting as

Raglan's chief of staff* – rode across to Bentinck when he saw the lines of the 1st Division come to a halt. In the open, on the edge of the vineyards, the Grenadiers and Scots Fusilier Guards now came under heavy fire from the Russian artillery and Bentinck, who could see Codrington's brigade moving up towards the Great Redoubt, was already impatient. Asked what he was waiting for, Bentinck told Airey that the Duke had ordered that a wide gap should be preserved between the two divisional lines. Airey replied that this was not necessary, and said that the 1st Division's task was to close up and support the Light Division; Bentinck was to get the line moving straight away and to send a message to the Duke to the effect that Raglan wanted the division to press on. Resuming their advance the Guards Brigade and the Highlanders entered the vineyards, where inevitably they came up against the same obstructions that had been met by their predecessors in the forward line.

On the right the Grenadiers staged an almost unbelievable spectacle. During their whole passage down to the river – and even through the river itself – they maintained perfect formation for the full length of their line. Under continual bombardment from the Russian guns they moved forward in two ranks, 400 men in each, and as any section of the line met an obstacle it hurried round and the rest of the line was brought up to be re-formed. As a military movement in the middle of a battle it is doubtful if this intricate and laborious process was really necessary. But the battalion had been sent forward in line formation to cross the river and, in the tradition of the Guards, as long as the formation had to be maintained it would be maintained to perfection. Every few yards the line was halted and dressed before the order was given to march forward again. When the Grenadiers came to the river the same perfection was maintained and the men marched forward in step, shoulder to shoulder, into the water. Some found the river so shallow that they could keep on marching; others had to break step and wade through deeper parts of the stream; some had to swim; some, of course, were shot down in the water and drowned. But still the battalion moved forward in one line, each man advancing straight

---

* The title 'chief of staff' is not quite correct, but it is used to avoid confusion which will arise if constant reference is made to Airey's real title of Quartermaster General. In the Crimea, the Q.M.G.'s duties were mainly 'G'. Many 'Q' duties fell to the Commissary-General. 'M.G.G.S' is the nearest modern approximation to the position held by Airey; but as there was no General Staff in the Crimea it is inadvisable to use this abbreviation.

ahead, and when it emerged on the far bank the regimental sergeant-major called for the company right markers and the whole battalion fell in, took up its dressing, and stood rigidly to attention as if the regiment was on the Horseguards Parade in London.

Next in line the Scots Fusilier Guards followed the example of the Grenadiers, but with less precision. Compared with the performance of the Line Regiments in the two forward divisions – few of which had kept any real formation – they maintained a high degree of order, but they hardly emulated the superb performance of the Grenadiers. On the left of the brigade the Coldstream, jealous of their own reputation for precise movement, made no attempt to pass through the vineyards in line. Taking his own initiative, their colonel broke the line into columns of platoons and marched his battalion across the river in that formation. The river twisted in a sharp 'S' bend at the point where he had chosen to cross and the column actually marched through the water three times because of his determination to adhere to the chosen course. But, when the battalion finally reached the far bank – where Pennefather's brigade had assembled earlier – the platoons and companies were reassembled in line with as much formality and ceremony as the Grenadiers. The entire Guards Brigade had now crossed the Alma almost as formally as if it had been Trooping the Colour before the Queen.

While the Guards were negotiating the Alma the 2nd Division, which had passed on each side of the burning Bourliouk, was pinned down on the river bank. This was the sector on which Menschikoff had concentrated the bulk of his artillery, and the constant hail of fire from the heavy guns – particularly those only two or three hundred yards ahead alongside the Sebastopol road – made it suicidal for anyone to try to climb the bank in the way that Codrington and Yea had done higher up the river where the artillery fire was less heavy. But when the Russian guns in the Great Redoubt had stopped firing the two British cannon on Raglan's knoll turned their fire on to these batteries. To the Russians it seemed as if they were being shot up almost from overhead and the Russian gunners could not get sufficient elevation on their cannons to be able to shoot back. Unable to cope with this situation their commander decided to withdraw all sixteen guns to a less vulnerable position further up the hill, and so for the time being the 2nd Division had a respite.

When the fire slackened De Lacy Evans ordered his division up on to the bank and the line was extended. The broken ground precluded any rapid advance, but the 2nd Division started to edge forward. By this time it was half-past three and Colonel Yea and his Fusiliers were still heavily engaged with the Kazan battalion on the left of the 2nd Division's new position. In so far as the participants interfered with nobody else and nobody interfered with them this fight was quite detached from the rest of the battle. Facing each other in parallel formations – the Fusiliers in line and the Kazan Regiment in column – the opponents blazed away at each other at a distance of only fifty yards for over half an hour. No British soldier had seen the Russians at such close range before, but although they were so close there was no actual hand to hand fighting. On one occasion a young British officer did run across to the enemy column to push his sword through a man in the front rank and hit another with his fist, but he was soon killed. On another occasion a Russian stepped out and took careful and obvious aim at Yea but a Fusilier ran out from the British line and shot him down.

The turning point of the engagement came when the Russian commander was shot. Spotting who was the commander was not easy since the Russian uniforms, unlike those of the British, were all the same – with no distinctive badges of rank. But Yea had noted that there was one man moving among the Russian ranks who was clearly exercising a controlling influence, especially where the casualties were heavy and the men tended to get out of formation. Some of the Fusiliers were ordered to concentrate their fire on this particular individual and when he was shot down the Russian column started to lose its cohesion. Men in the rear ranks, out of sight of the Fusiliers, began to break away; gradually the rot set in and the Kazan Regiment simply melted away. The superiority of line over column had been patently demonstrated, but by the time the fight was over the Fusiliers had suffered more than 200 casualties – a heavy cost.

When the battalions of the Guards and Highland Brigades had been drawn up in line on the bank above the river, Codrington's troops were beginning their precipitate retreat down the slope from the Great Redoubt. The survivors, morale gone, retired in a disordered mass which bore down on the Scots Fusilier Guards whose rigid line could do nothing to withstand it. After two thousand men had rushed through it on their way to the safety of the river bank, the Scots Fusilier Guards were left sprawling – the line was shattered, and to add to the mêlée the area came under heavy artillery fire. The range of the Russian guns had progressively lengthened as they followed the fleeing mob, and when cannon balls started to reach the disordered Scots Fusilier Guards the whole battalion was forced back into the shelter of the river ledge. On the right the Grenadiers were also in the path of some of Codrington's retreating survivors. But they parted their ranks with ceremonial precision to allow the fugitives through, and although they were also incurring casualties from the Russian cannon the Grenadiers' line stood fast. The Coldstream on the left also maintained their formation, and the net result was that the Guards Brigade were now facing the Russians with a gap in the centre of their line caused by the temporary disorder of the Scots Fusilier Guards.

By this time the Highland Brigade had also reached the bottom of the long slope up to the redoubt, and as each of its battalions climbed the bank it formed line and moved forward. On the right the Black Watch was the first battalion up, the Argylls were in the centre and behind them, on the left, were the Camerons. Campbell moved with the Black Watch having got the line moving with a shout of 'Come on the 42nd'. And so the 1st Division line moved up the slope towards the Great Redoubt and Kourgane Hill with the Guards on the right and the Highland Brigade in echelon on the left rear. Behind them remained Buller's two battalions, the 88th and 77th – the two left-most battalions of the Light Division – which had taken up their positions before Codrington made his attack: the 77th in line facing the left flank and the 88th in hollow square facing the front. Passing the Highland Brigade through these two battalions caused a certain amount of confusion and Campbell rode over to see what was happening. As he did not know that Buller had stayed back with these battalions he sent orders to their two colonels to move up the slope with his brigade; Sir Colin could not see that they were fulfilling any purpose on the river bank and he was one who believed that every man should be in the forefront of the battle. Buller waiting with the 88th in their hollow square might have felt affronted when Campbell's order came to his battalion, but – like so many of the other generals on the field that day – Buller was an indecisive commander and it now seemed to him that Campbell was right. Now that the supporting line of the 1st Division had come up he felt that the two battalions which were really part of the Light Division line should move up to their proper place, and he sent an order to that effect to Colonel Egerton, the commanding officer of the 77th.

Egerton had been watching the left of the army for nearly half an hour and he had his own views. The Russian cavalry could still be seen higher up the eastern slopes of Kourgane Hill and he was sure that sooner or later it would move down to attack the British left flank. (This was a reasonable expectation and the fact that the Russians never actually made such a move does not necessarily invalidate Egerton's belief that they might have done so. At Inkerman, some weeks later, Egerton and the 77th exhibited a forcefulness and enterprise that virtually saved the day.) Egerton was in a difficult position. Buller had ordered him to move; so too had the brigadier commanding the support line troops moving through them. Yet he was convinced that if he were to comply with this order he would be exposing the British flank to serious danger. It was not a question of timidity; Egerton felt that he might well find his battalion in a worse position if he kept it where it was. Nevertheless he felt it was his duty to remain *in situ* and sent a reply to Buller to say that he did not feel that he should carry out his brigadier's order. Receipt of this message caused Buller to change his mind and he reverted to his belief that the duty of the two battalions was to stay where they were. Campbell was not too pleased but he had no authority over Buller's men, so the Camerons on the left of the Highlanders marched past the 88th square to the accompaniment of an exchange of uncomplimentary, soldierly epithets.

Once clear of Buller's battalions, Campbell ordered the Highland Brigade to fix bayonets and incline to the left, so that there would be none of the convergence and consequent confusion which had brought disaster to the Light Division.* Fully extended the 1st Division line now stretched for nearly a mile and a half. Guards on the right, Highlanders on the left; it advanced in perfect step, impeccably aligned, with the men shoulder to shoulder – front ranks with fixed bayonets at the high port, rear ranks with their muskets sloped at the correct angle on their shoulders – a ceremonial

---

* When the order to fix bayonets was given to the 42nd, one young soldier dropped his. When he turned back to recover it his company commander shouted 'Shoot that man. Shoot the bloody coward'. He would have been shot too if he had not been seen to pick up his bayonet. Doubling back to his position in line he passed the colonel to whom he said naively 'I was na rinnin awa, Sir'.

spectacle designed for battle and conducted on a scale and at a
standard of perfection that had never been seen before and was
certainly never to be seen again.

Led by General Kiriakoff the eight battalions that had driven
Canrobert's division back down the road towards the river had
hesitated to follow it into the ravine. Kiriakoff may have decided
that his purpose was limited to keeping the plateau clear of allied
troops and as long as his eight battalions stood at the exit to the
ravine no French force was likely to challenge it. In time, if they did
not break out on to the plateau, Canrobert's troops would have to
withdraw back across the river where they would again be bombarded by Russian artillery. It was obvious that Bosquet and his
two brigades seemed likely to stay where they were – far enough
away to be of no real threat to the Russians. Of Prince Napoleon
and the 3rd Division down by the river at the foot of the narrow
road Kiriakoff had no knowledge. But shortly after Canrobert had
withdrawn, the guns which he had sent round by Almatamack
moved on to a road along the crest of the cliff which would take
them to the head of the ravine. The gunners had no knowledge of
Canrobert's withdrawal and the presence of a Russian column near
the ravine. Their road ran along a hollow trough so that neither the
plateau nor Canrobert's ravine could be seen from it. In order to
take his bearings the major in command halted his guns and climbed
the bank of the road; there, to his surprise, he was greeted by what
can only be described as an artilleryman's dream target. Not more
than a hundred yards away stood a solid mass of Russian soldiery.
The Frenchman did not hesitate, his guns were unlimbered in the
roadway and as soon as they opened fire the effect on the Russian
battalion was altogether predictable. With no artillery of their own
to counter the hidden menace and with shot and canister cutting
deadly swathes through the packed ranks of their crowded formation the Russians turned about and made off towards Telegraph
Hill. To their credit must be recorded that they withdrew in perfect
order. As they did so the French guns were shifted to the plateau to a
more advantageous position at the head of the ravine; from there
they were able to bombard the whole area near the telegraph tower.
    Led by the two Zouave regiments – one of which it will be remem-
bered was from Prince Napoleon's division – Canrobert's men
streamed up the ravine to take up positions on the edge of the

plateau. At a stage in the battle which was rather later than St Arnaud had planned, the French were about to attack the Russian left with some effect, and almost within minutes the whole situation on Telegraph Hill was completely reversed. Up to this time the Russians had been in full possession of the plateau. Their very presence and the menace of their guns had kept the French from venturing out into the open – except in the case of Bosquet who was so far away that he and his men had little influence on the situation. At long last the French were in a position to dominate the whole plateau as far as the Sebastopol road. How this startling and rapid transformation actually came about is a matter of some conjecture. The French subsequently claimed that they had driven the Russians back in a heroic infantry engagement. Russian accounts of this particular piece of the battle however, could be expected to have emphasized the resistance put up by their soldiers before they were compelled to withdraw. But they make no reference to any battle with the French, and Kiriakoff's explanation was simply that when he realized it would be suicidal to remain within range of Canrobert's guns, he marched his eight battalions back towards the telegraph tower where they would be safely out of range. There his column was joined by more Russian battalions converging on the road from the other side as they were pulling back in front of the British 1st Division. To Kiriakoff the only solution was to collect all these battalions together, withdraw to a new position higher up the road, and re-form on a new defensive line; he did not say anything about any battle with the French. Other than Kiriakoff's column, the only other Russian infantry formation on the plateau were the four Taroutine and four militia battalions which had withdrawn without orders from the positions in which they had been placed down by the river before the battle started. A certain Major Chodasevitch of the Taroutine Regiment later wrote an account of what he saw of the battle of the Alma, and it could be expected that he would almost certainly have mentioned an engagement with the French at this stage – particularly as there is no other action during the battle with which his own regiment or the militia battalions could be credited. But as Chodasevitch said nothing except that his battalion was forced to withdraw when the French guns came out on to the plateau, his account implies that it was solely the French artillery which drove the Russians back.

French accounts paint a very different picture of the situation at this stage, and according to them Canrobert's and d'Aurelle's troops subjected the Russians to such an overwhelming defeat that the battle of the Alma could be said to have been won on the plateau, while the British assaults on the Great Redoubt and Kourgane Hill were but secondary engagements. The fact is that when Kiriakoff withdrew under Canrobert's guns the French 1st Division hurriedly retraced its steps up the ravine and d'Aurelle's brigade followed. All these troops were still comparatively fresh – having been standing or sitting about most of the day – and when they emerged on to the plateau and saw the massive Russian column retreating it appears that their Gallic exuberance knew no bounds. Surging forward with uncharacteristic abandon, they pressed forward *en masse*. The Zouave regiments were in the van and within a few minutes their colours were hoisted on the incomplete brick pillar of the telegraph tower. Half an hour later 10,000 men had converged on the tower, milling around and excitedly firing their muskets in the general direction of the retreating Russians. With all this musketry fire and Canrobert's guns still hammering away at the receding Russian columns anyone viewing what was going on from a distance might well imagine that a lively battle was in progress on Telegraph Hill. The British, of course, could see nothing of what was happening because their view was cut off by the intervening hills. The chief witnesses to what really went on were Bosquet and his men on the cliffs and the crews of some of the French ships lying off the mouth of the Alma about two miles distant. Not unnaturally these witnesses preferred to believe that they were watching an epic battle and it is probable that their evidence is the main basis on which was founded the circumstantial story of this great feat of French arms.

A few months after the battle the French Ministre d'Instruction Publique sent a certain Baron de Bazancourt to the Crimea to write up the story of the part played by the French at the Alma. What he produced and what was accepted in Paris was a highly dramatic account of how the Zouave Regiments and Chasseurs d'Afrique attacked the Russians under heavy fire and how finally a French colonel of Zouaves galloped forward – in the best Algerian tradition – to lead his troops in a bloody hand to hand engagement. (To paraphrase the record the dead and dying were heaped together, trampled on and smothered by the other combatants, while the men who were fortunate enough to escape this unhappy fate, lunged

at the Russians with their bayonets and drove them from the field.)
St Arnaud's report to the Emperor lent credence to Bazancourt's
story. Hailing the Zouaves as the finest soldiers in the world he had
reassured Napoleon III, 'Your Majesty can be proud of his soldiers;
they have not degenerated; these are the soldiers of Austerlitz and
Jena'.[1] This was an exaggerated view: most of the Zouaves faced
artillery for the first time that day and many were stupefied by it.
Furthermore, as only three officers and fifty other ranks were killed
in the whole battle and the total number of wounded did not exceed
500, it hardly seems as if there was much of an engagement. During
the battle there were no other active fights in which French infantrymen were engaged, and as both Canrobert's and Prince Napoleon's
divisions suffered considerable casualties from Russian artillery fire
at the river crossing Bazancourt's report about the dead and dying
lying about in heaps seems to bear little relation to the truth. The
Russian left flank was broken between 4 and 4.30 p.m. that afternoon, and the plain fact is that the break came too late for St
Arnaud to be able to claim that the outcome of the battle was
decided by the French turning off the Russian left flank.

In effect, the battle was won on Kourgane Hill – in an entirely
separate area of operations to that in which the French were involved. The ravine which carries the Sebastopol road divided the
battlefield into two distinct parts – the high plateau on the west and
the hill-studded ground running down to the river on the east – and
so the very nature of the ground, more than anything else, kept the
operations of the French and British armies entirely disconnected.
Neither could see how the other was faring during the fighting, and –
as there was no proper communication link between the two – their
commanders were equally disconnected. Raglan was able to watch
the British army but he had no idea what the French were doing;
St Arnaud down by the river did not even know what his own troops
were doing. However, when the French were supposedly driving the
Russian battalions off the plateau, the British 1st Division line was
forming up on the river bank; Yea's battalion was licking its wounds
forward and to the left of the 2nd Division, and the Kazan column,
which it had driven off, was reassembling a quarter of a mile away
on the Russian left of the Great Redoubt. In the gap between the
two Guards battalions, left by the Scots Fusilier Guards, Codrington
had managed to rally about 300 men from the survivors of his

brigade. Forming them into a line two deep, he asked Colonel Hood of the Grenadiers if these 300 men could take position on the left of the Grenadiers in the gap left by the Scots Fusilier Guards. Codrington was a brigadier, and a guardsman to boot. But even he would never have put men of Line regiments alongside a battalion of the Guards without asking permission.

In the event Hood curtly refused. Maybe he was concerned with protocol and did not consider that there was any place in the Guards line for rag tag and bobtail; possibly he hoped that the Scots Fusilier Guards would rally and retake their position between his own battalion and the Coldstream. As he issued a spontaneous invitation to eight survivors of the 95th, who were still carrying their regimental colours, to take their place on the left of the Grenadiers, it seems that the latter consideration might have been foremost in his mind. In any case, as the Grenadiers were moving forward, the first company of Scots Fusilier Guards did actually climb the bank and stationed themselves in their proper position, so that the gap in the line was partially filled. Then in immaculate order, the Grenadiers and Coldstream with this solitary company of Scots Fusilier Guards marched forward up the slope.

When Codrington's men had left the redoubt the Russians had repositioned themselves to meet the advancing British battalions. Part of the column which had been mistaken for a French unit had formed up in front of the redoubt under the command of Prince Gorschakoff, while the rest of it – under General Kvetsinski – had taken up a position in the redoubt itself. On the left of the redoubt stood the residue of the two Kazan battalions which had been engaged with Yea's Fusiliers; to the right rear two other battalions of the Kazan Regiment, and spread across the extreme right of the Russian line were the eight battalions that had marched round Kourgane Hill. The latter were standing in three columns – one column comprising four battalions of the Uglitz Regiments, and the other two each of two battalions of the Sousdal Regiment. All in all 15,000 Russians now faced no more than 5,000 Guards and Highlanders.

As soon as he saw the Guards starting to advance, Gorschakoff directed his two battalions straight down the slope towards the gap in the Guards Brigade. The Russians moved like a great grey tortoise and if both sides had held their course the Russians would have passed between the Coldstream and Grenadiers – engulfing the solitary company of Scots Fusilier Guards in the process. When the distance between the Grenadiers and the Vladimir column had closed to less than 100 yards, however, Hood halted his men. Wheeling the left platoon of his battalion with a precise parade ground movement the Grenadiers' line hinged back so that it faced directly towards the Russian column. The front thus presented to the Russians was no more than twenty men but when the front rank of the Grenadiers' platoon opened fire the Russians were halted in their tracks. The Russians returned the fire as best they could, but they were in an awkward position. The British line stood diagonally across one of the corners of their column, so that neither the front nor the side ranks had a proper field of fire. Consequently while the Grenadiers were able to inflict casualties at a rate which was dictated only by the speed of muzzle loading, their own lines were hardly touched. When the Coldstream, who had halted in line with the Grenadiers also opened fire, the Russians suffered further discomfiture. The Vladimir battalions held their ground but they were soon suffering heavy casualties and these increased when Hood pivoted the whole line of Grenadiers on the point where the left platoon had swung back, in order to bring forward the companies on his right – so that the whole front of his battalion had a clear field of fire at the Vladimir column.

Gorschakoff bravely rode up and down the front of his troops, exhorting his men to hold their positions and keep up their fire. But in their column formation the Russians were at a distinct disadvantage and the British superiority in fire power soon began to tell. One of the early casualties was Gorschakoff's horse and when it was hit and killed its rider fell to the ground, to stagger away from the column in a dazed condition. Kvetsinski, who had been sitting on his horse by the parapet of the redoubt, rode over to speak to him, and before he stumbled away round the end of Kourgane Hill Gorschakoff gabbled something about the officers of the Vladimir Regiment all having been killed. This was not true, in fact. But when Gorschakoff left them it was not long before the Vladimir battalions started to falter. Soon their fire started to slacken, and Hood now gave the command 'The line will advance on the centre! The line will advance firing!'[2] The air was filled with thick smoke generated by the continuous fire of the muskets of both sides so that it was difficult to see quite where they were advancing to. There were also some tragic gaps in the ranks where men had fallen. Despite this the

Grenadiers wheeled back to their proper front, and moved forward in a well dressed line. As they advanced the men brought their muskets up to their shoulders, fired, and reloaded on the march. This was too much for the Russians; suddenly the column disintegrated as the survivors scurried away, back towards the Kazan battalions on the Russian left of the redoubt. When they got there the Kazans joined the fugitives and the whole unruly mob made for the Sebastopol road, where Kiriakoff was shepherding the battalions retreating from the French. Here, for the first time Russian units from the two separate sectors of the battlefield joined in the same move to the rear.

Kvetsinski seeing the dissolution of Gorschakoff's half of the Vladimir Regiment could think only of getting the remainder of the Vladimir battalions out of the way of the approaching lines of Bentinck's guardsmen. Round the west of the hill his line of retreat had already been cut by the Grenadiers, so he led them straight across the Coldstream front. Almost as soon as he left the shelter of the redoubt his horse was shot from under him and a wound in the leg left him unable to walk. When he was carried off the battlefield, Kvetsinski – like Gorschakoff – was out of the battle. Command of the Vladimir column now devolved on a colonel who, it seems, was not prepared to retire so precipitously. Two battalions of the Kazan Regiment – the ones that had been driven back by the 19th earlier in the engagement, when Codrington's men first assaulted – stood on the Russian right of the redoubt, and when the Vladimir battalions drew alongside, the colonel quickly amalgamated the four battalions and turned to face the British. By marching across the Coldstream front, the Vladimir column had taken itself out of the line of advance of the Guards Brigade and the newly combined Vladimir and Kazan column now stood in the direct path of the Black Watch, the right-hand regiment of the Highland Brigade advancing up the slope slightly in rear of the Guards.

The rocky ground on the eastern slopes of Kourgane Hill was steeper than that in front of the Great Redoubt and it was broken by gullies, so that when advancing over it the line of the 42nd had lost its dressing. Campbell had no intention of allowing one of his battalions to engage the enemy in this state and the Black Watch were halted while the ranks were straightened. Then, firing as they advanced, the two imposing lines of men in dark tartan – their height accentuated by the long plumes that stood up proudly from their highland bonnets – moved forward again. Within minutes the Highlanders had broken yet another Russian column. 'In ascending the hill the Russians stooped very much forward with a view to present as small a mark as possible, but from the way their great-coats spread out, they looked twice as big as before. When hit they lay quietly forward on the ground without a kick or struggle, not at all filling up one's preconceived idea of how men fell on the field of battle. Most of the wounded retained hold of their muskets when they fell and word went along our line that they fired at us when we passed them. On passing any of them after that our men took the arms from them and smashed them. Some of the Russians could only be induced to give up their muskets by a threat of knocking out their brains.'[3]

In turn each of the two other Highland battalions – the Argylls and Camerons – engaged a Russian column in the same way; in their case two battalions of the Sousdal Regiment. Twice more the same action was repeated although in both instances the Russians put up a stiff fight before they were broken. And by the time they had had enough, the superstitious Russians had come to believe that the angel of light had departed and the demon of death had come. At a distance the white waving sporrans above the bare knees of the Highlanders were taken for the heads of stunted horses, pro-vided by the devil himself and as the grey-coated blocks of Mus-covite infantry broke a wail of despair was drowned by a Highland cheer.

But for what are usually termed 'mopping-up' operations the Battle of the Alma might be considered over. However there was still a chance that the Russians might rally behind Kourgane Hill. Seven thousand five hundred men had been driven in that direction and there were another four battalions – 3,000 men – who had not yet been engaged, waiting there. These were four battalions of the Uglitz Regiment and their colonel had drawn them up so that they blocked the path of the retreating battalions. Fortunately for the British he never got a chance to prove the worth of the Uglitz Regiment, because Lucan, on whose meagre force Raglan was relying to hold off the massed cavalry of the Russians, had decided to take his squadrons across the river. He had been given no auth-ority to do so but Raglan never objected to his generals' initiative, so long as their enterprise led to success, since it enabled him to get on with his own duties. As it did not seem that Mens-

chikoff was going to use his cavalry – and it was too late to
do so now, with the Russian infantry in retreat – Lucan crossed
the river on the left of the British front where Buller's battalions were still waiting. Accompanied by a battery of horse
artillery, the cavalry crossed the river, climbed the bank and joined
the battle at a moment so opportune that it is a pity to have to
record that his action was unplanned. Lucan arrived just as the
Uglitz colonel was rallying the retreating Russians and consolidating
a new defensive position. Ten thousand five hundred men might
not have broken so easily if they had been allowed to establish
themselves. But when the six guns which Lucan had brought across
the river began to fire into the middle of the Russian column, it
broke. This really was the end of the battle for by now the Russians
were in full retreat.

When Prince Gorschakoff staggered away from the battle round the
west end of Kourgane Hill he reached the Sebastopol road without
quite knowing where he was or what he was doing. Quite by chance,
Menschikoff – who was still darting mercurially from one sector of
the battlefield to another without effecting any real control over
what was going on – met him on the road. For the first time that
afternoon the Russian commander-in-chief and his second-in-
command faced each other. The battle was at a critical stage and
plainly there was need for a quick review of the situation. But the
exchange which followed between the two generals was hardly on an
executive level. ' . . . Why are you on foot?' Menschikoff demanded
sharply. 'Why are you alone?' Plaintively the dazed and dog-tired
Gorschakoff replied, 'My horse was killed near the river. I am alone
because all my aides and staff officers have been killed or wounded.
I myself,' he added, 'have received six shots.' As he spoke he pointed
to the sorry state of his uniform.[4] The Russian commander-in-chief
rode off angrily and Gorschakoff stumbled on up the road. Lower
down the hill Menschikoff met the retreating battalions of the
Vladimir Regiment which he sought vainly to turn back to face
the British. But the fire had gone out of their bellies – if it had ever
existed – and for the first time Menschikoff heard murmurs of
defiance of authority. Even he realized that the battle was now over
and the Russians were being driven from the Alma. Only Kiriakoff
seemed to keep his head; as they converged on the Sebastopol road

he regrouped the battalions driven off from the French and British sectors and directed the withdrawal of thirty guns into a position where they could cover the retreat.

By this time Prince Napoleon had got his division on to the plateau, and his men were drawn up with Canrobert's troops in some semblance of massed formation on the open plain between the Sebastopol road and the telegraph tower. (A British aide-de-camp who rode over with a message for St Arnaud from Raglan reported that the excitement among the French was positively tumultuous, and that in his estimation 20,000 French soldiers were all talking at once.)

Like the French the British were assembling on the ground they had won from the Russians. The lines were redeployed in columns of companies and repositioned until the whole British army stood on a wide arc that covered the lower slopes of Kourgane Hill. The divisional generals gathered near the Great Redoubt and Raglan rode down from his knoll to talk to them. As he made his way through their positions his soldiers cheered him as if he were the fountain of their success. Reining his horse in front of the Highland Brigade he shook hands with Campbell and said 'I left you on the plain Sir Colin, and I could not believe my eyes when I saw you riding up the hill followed by your brigade . . .' Flushing, Campbell replied – more for the benefit of the troops who stood behind than himself – 'Gentlemen, I have known the commander-in-chief a long time. In fact ever since I was a boy he has been kind to me, and I trust he will do me one kindness more.' Raglan nodded his head and Campbell continued 'I trust that henceforth he will give me leave to wear the Highland bonnet.' When Raglan inclined his head in acquiescence the Highlanders cheered and roared their applause with shouts of 'Scotland forever'. (Followed by 'Ireland for longer' and a hurroo, bawled by an enthusiastic Irishman.)

Apart from relief that the battle was over there was little cause for elation. When the last shot was fired about 8,000 scarlet, blue or grey-coated bodies littered the green slopes of the Alma valley. A quarter of these had been killed in action; many of the others were in mortal agony. The Russians had suffered the heaviest casualties – officially put at 5,709 killed and wounded; the British lost 362 killed and 1,640 wounded; and the French produced an ingeniously concocted casualty list of 1,600 which was subsequently reduced by an indignant Raglan to a maximum of 560.* Nineteen British soldiers were posted as missing – presumably drowned in the river. Relatively few prisoners were taken. The Russians did not capture any British or French, but the Allies did round up a few Russians, apart from the wounded who had been left on the battlefield.

It was wounded – allied and Russian alike – who suffered most; for neither side had the proper facilities for coping with casualties. In the British Army a handful of buglers and drummers put aside their instruments after a battle to become the regimental stretcher bearers and medical orderlies. They had no special equipment, and few – if any – had had any training for the job they were supposed to do. The French were better served by their women *vivandières* whose role included tending the wounded. But a severely wounded Frenchman had not much better chance of survival than his British counterpart. Russian arrangements were even worse than those of the Allies. Medical supplies were about non-existent, and when any man was unable to fend for himself he could expect little help. More often than not he would be left to die where he had fallen. At the battle of Schumla in 1828 the blood and disease had so disgusted Nicholas that he had simply packed up and returned to St Petersburg.

The Alma was the decisive battle of the Crimean war, and one which Raglan believed had been won by the British with very little help from the French. For both commanders-in-chief it was a first and last success. In their despatches neither said much about their allies, but St Arnaud saw the Alma as a personal triumph as well as a victory for the French. To his wife he wrote 'Victory! Victory! my well-beloved Louise: yesterday the 20th of September, I beat the Russians completely. I took their formidable positions which were defended by 40,000 men who fought bravely; but nothing could resist the impetuosity of the French, the order and the solidarity of the English ... The whole army loves me.'[5] And in his despatch to the Emperor, he said: 'We have gained a complete victory. At half past four the French army was everywhere victorious. All the positions had been taken with the bayonet ... The English broke up the Russian lines in admirable order under fire... Lord Raglan is like an ancient hero.'

---

* The figures quoted for British casualties do not take into account those who succumbed during the journey from Alma to the infamous hospital at Scutari.

Yet three hours of fiery conflict did not bring the glorious victory which St Arnaud proclaimed, and which the newspapers in London and Paris reported. The battle was not so much won by the British and French as not lost. If it had been lost the war would certainly have been finished because there can be little doubt that the Allies would have been driven off the Crimean Peninsula. Unfortunately the frail success was never turned to account and the Allies gained no direct advantage from it in the subsequent campaign. Had the cavalry force been stronger and used properly, the Russian losses might have been greater; as it was Menschikoff was able to recover from the shock.

THE FLANK MARCH

As soon as the battle of the Alma was over and Raglan and St Arnaud had congratulated each other, the British commander-in-chief suggested that a combined Anglo-French force should pursue the retreating Russians. St Arnaud refused. 'Quite enough has been done', he said, and it was 'impossible' for his soldiers to go until they had retrieved the packs which they had discarded before going into battle; furthermore, the wounded needed attention, and in the course of the battle the artillery had expended nearly all its ammunition. In the French view the idea of a soldier being without his pack except when he was actually fighting was wholly unacceptable, and all but Bosquet's troops had dumped them before they crossed the river. Bosquet's division was an exception. His troops had faced the Russians not while scaling the heights as the others had done but afterwards, and their packs were fairly accessible. As Bosquet had already issued an order for their recovery it seems that he at least was expecting to pursue the Russians. But this was before he knew of St Arnaud's decision.

Raglan, who had already told Sir Richard England to stand by with the 3rd Division, the cavalry and the horse artillery, appears to have been irritated by St Arnaud's lack of co-operation. He did not believe that the reasons the French marshal gave for not going on were really important, and probably suspected it was the Marshal's own lassitude that was behind his decision to keep the French on the battlefield. (At his age and in his state of health St Arnaud probably did feel in need of a rest. That day he had spent twelve hours in the saddle. Nor was he alone; many other senior officers – sexagenarian generals and quinquagenarian colonels – also felt in need of a respite. 'In the morning I am forty,' one of them said, 'In the evening I am eighty'[1]) Raglan deferred to St Arnaud's view, and as it appears that Raglan never seriously considered a pursuit in which the French did not share, the 3rd Division was told to stand down. Disappointed and dissatisfied, his smouldering irritation was expressed at supper two days later, when the sounds of trumpet calls

from the direction of the French camp provoked the petulant comment, 'Ah, there they go with their *too-too-tooing*; that's the only
thing they ever do.'[2] Whether, in fact, the British could have
mounted a follow-up operation so soon after the battle is debatable.
Judging by the events of the next forty-eight hours Raglan's suggestion, which was made before he appreciated how many
casualties his army had suffered, may seem irresponsible.

When St Arnaud said that his men were not ready Raglan rode
into the still smoking village of Bourliouk where a primitive field
hospital had been set up in the ruins. Surgeons, still wearing their
full dress uniform, were at work among the wounded and one of
Raglan's aides-de-camp wrote home in horror of the surgeons'
'arms covered with blood, the floors strewn with limbs just amputated and slippery with gore'.[3] And a surgeon wrote 'I cannot liken
the battle to anything better than an abattoir'. The slopes of
Kourgane Hill and the banks on both sides of the river were
littered with bodies, and it took two full days to clear the battlefield of dead, sick and wounded.* (Apart from those who were
struck down in battle, the casualties included some who had been
stricken by cholera during the course of the battle.) In pain, and
tortured with thirst, many of the non-walking wounded spent at
least one bitterly cold night lying where they had fallen. Individuals
in the different regiments sought out their friends to give them water
and to try to make them comfortable where they lay, but in the
absence of drugs there was nothing that could be done to relieve
their pain. A subaltern wrote 'I am willing to believe that our
surgeons did their best but still some poor fellows unseen or un-
sought passed the night in sleepless groans on the field of battle'.
Because there were no stretchers the casualties had to be picked up
and dragged to collecting points where the surgeons operated on the
bare ground or on doors wrenched from barns and cottages. The
dead were piled in separate national heaps – Russian and British.
French arrangements were more efficient, and one of the British
surgeons recalled 'there were no means of carrying the wounded
off the field . . . and whilst on the day following the battle there was
not a wounded Frenchman on the ground, it was disgraceful to the

---

* On the eastern slopes of the hill the retreating Sousdal Regiment
was raked by the batteries behind the Highlanders. There the Russian
dead lay in ranks, many of them decapitated.

British nation to see ... many of its brave defenders suffering
without human aid, where they fell.'[4]

From the collection points the casualties were taken to the mouth
of the river – the British being carried, the French in mule drawn
ambulance wagons. There they were lifted into boats and taken
through the unquiet surf to ships lying off-shore. Painfully they
were hoisted aboard and because it was impossible to take them
below down the companion-ways they were left on deck with no
protection from the weather and no guarantee that when the ship
rolled they would not roll helplessly with it. The destination of the
British wounded was the hospital in the Turkish army barracks at
Scutari, and their chances of survival were limited. More wounded
men died in Scutari than were healed, and they died in most
instances of diseases contracted in the hospital itself. Several months
were still to pass before the miracle that was Florence Nightingale
came to Scutari and few of the casualties from the Alma lived long
enough to benefit from her ministrations.

In the attention so inadequately rendered to the casualties it is
pleasant to record that no distinction was made between British or
Russian. Any inhumanity was not deliberate. But initially the British
were too occupied with their own wounded to give more than super-
ficial attention to their enemies, and what these abandoned men
must have suffered is indescribable. The sun was not hot, but for
stricken men tortured by appalling thirst it was painful enough. On
the third day 750 Russian survivors were collected, carried down to
the river and laid out in rows in a shady grove. Unfortunately a few
incidents of Russians shooting the men who had given them a drink
marred the succouring operation and provoked bitterness. Most of
the Russians showed a pathetic gratitude, kissing the hand that held
the water bottle. But news of the outrages – often committed by
frightened Russians temporarily deranged by their agony – spread
fast and hope that the war might be conducted with chivalrous
respect disappeared overnight.

The dead were interred in communal pits on the hillside, and
when the armies marched away some twenty-four gigantic mounds
remained to mark the last resting place of those who fell in the battle
or died of wounds. For the most part the burials were conducted
haphazardly and without any pretence of ceremony. The Zouaves,
hardened by years of savage warfare in Algeria, displayed a grisly
humour as they shovelled the corpses into the mass graves.

'Midshipman Wood wrote home to say that he was shocked to see a
Zouave tip a body into a grave and then pick up a loose leg and
stick it in the corpse's crutch.'[5] British soldiers, for most of whom the
battle had been the first horrifying foretaste of war, were less
callous. Many had lost too many friends to feel anything but
sadness and sickness at the sight of the dead and wounded.

Because of the lesser number of casualties involved – a firm indication of the ratio of fighting – clearing their sector of the battlefield was less of a problem to the French than it was to the British.
By the morning of 21 September they had picked up their packs,
evacuated their wounded and replenished their ammunition supply;
St Arnaud then announced that he was ready to go. This time
Raglan demurred. It was necessary now, he insisted, to bury the dead
and embark the British wounded. This was an excuse which would
preclude any victory ever being followed up, and in the light of
Raglan's professed anxiety to press on the evening before such a
reply seems inconsistent. Whether the inconsistency arose from his
sudden appreciation of the casualties – for Raglan was a humane
and sensitive man – or from St Arnaud's excuses having awakened
Raglan's only lightly dormant francophobia, is difficult to assess.
It may be that during his tour of the battlefield after leaving St
Arnaud the night before he had come to realize that if the allied
armies had rushed off in pursuit of the Russians the wounded would
have been left to die on the hillside. Or it may be that having
started to clear the battlefield he was glad to have an excuse for
paying back St Arnaud in kind. According to Lord George Paget,
Raglan's staff officers were 'eloquent with hate against the French'
and Raglan's own comment at dinner on the 22nd about the '*too-
too-tooing*' of the French trumpets implies that he was not exactly
pleased with his allies.

Whenever any decision, tactical or administrative, had to be
taken Raglan was prone to ask himself what the Duke of Wellington
would have done in similar circumstances. After a battle, the Duke's
rule had always been, whenever possible, to pursue the defeated
enemy. Raglan had a well-balanced military sense of proportion
and he knew that clearing the battlefield was not the first purpose of
a victorious army. And while the men of the 1st, 2nd and Light
Divisions were in no condition to go any further until they had
rested, the 3rd and 4th Divisions and the cavalry – although they
had been on the march or in the saddle since early morning – were

still comparatively fresh. In retrospect, however, tactical considerations suggest that an immediate pursuit might have been more hazardous than some contemporary historians have credited and it is possible that when St Arnaud said that he was not prepared to go on, a review of these considerations caused Raglan to have second thoughts. It was true that the Russian army was in retreat, and moving in an uncertain direction, and it was not unreasonable to suppose that the morale of Sebastopol's depleted garrison would be affected by news of Menschikoff's defeat. But Sebastopol was still a long march and two river crossings' distance away, and when Raglan made his initial suggestion to St Arnaud the sun would have started to set in less than an hour and a half and in that latitude the twilight is comparatively short. And if the Russians had stood at the next river, the Katcha – as was quite possible – the performance at the Alma would have had to be repeated.

With an effective cavalry force, properly and aggressively used, the situation might have been different; without it a rapid pursuit was just not practicable. Lucan's two brigades might have been able to inflict some damage or take prisoners if the Russians were fleeing with complete abandon and lack of discipline. But when the Allies did move they found that 'the Russian retreat must have been in better order than most had imagined, for there were not many traces of a beaten army. A good many helmets and knapsacks were to be met with, and occasionally a ghastly corpse but altogether it did not give one the idea of a disorganized force.'[6]

Whether or not the Russians retired in good order, many of those who had seen them abandon the battlefield believed that their retreat might have been turned into a rout which would have brought the destruction of Menschikoff's army and possibly the end of the campaign. 'The more I think of the battle, the more convinced I am that it might have ended the campaign' wrote Charles Windham. But 'we have no Wellington here'.[7] Some of the French also thought that an opportunity had been missed. In November 1855 Marshal de Castellane told the Emperor that the French would have gone after the Russians if it had not been that the packs had been left behind. It was St Arnaud, he said, who 'wrecked the day's work from beginning to end'. And in Algeria, when General Aimable Jean-Jacques Pélissier, the man who would eventually step into St Arnaud's shoes, heard about the battle, he was sceptical about it being the great victory which had been proclaimed in Paris.

'Where were the trophies'? he asked; the fact that there were none, or very few, suggested that the Allies had not been able to pursue their enemy. And that meant that the victory was incomplete.

The question of trophies had already caused friction. Soon after the battle a French detachment was caught trying to haul off a gun captured by the British, and in the discussion which followed this incident St Arnaud suggested to Raglan that all captured trophies should be equally divided between the Allies. As nearly everything that had been captured had fallen to the British, Raglan categorically refused. He was already seething about the losses declared by the French, as he had learned that they had included 300 cholera victims in the battle casualty list. (Although when this fact was disclosed it dramatized the proportionately large losses suffered by the British.) Despite his growing irritation Raglan remained outwardly calm and polite, reasonable and accommodating, in his relations with the French: he did not wish to disrupt an alliance for which he believed the British government held him personally responsible. Because of this it may well be that his apparent willingness to accept the French point of view misled St Arnaud. Similarly, because he did not say much about his differences with the French Marshal in official communications to Whitehall the French were subsequently able to present themselves as held back from following up the battle on the Alma by Raglan's *lenteur*. A few months later Raglan was to confess that the preservation of the alliance troubled him more than the actual conduct of the campaign, and he regretted that he had always conformed to French ideas. But in September 1854, he believed that the maintenance of the *Entente Cordiale* was essential.

Mention of the fact that Raglan rejected the idea of an immediate pursuit by a British force alone has already been made. It has been suggested that if he had really been convinced of its value the 3rd Division and Lucan's cavalry could have gone on alone, leaving the French to follow up as and when they were willing. Once the British got started, the French – anxious to see that they did not miss their share of *gloire*, would probably have been quick to resume the march. Raglan was not prepared to take the risk. He was convinced that the British should never move without the French, and those who have criticized him on this score have underestimated the emphasis which the British government had put on the necessity for joint action. 'It is not intended,' his original direction read, 'that in every operation of a minor character an equal number of the two armies must be jointly employed. This might sometimes be inconvenient, but you will take care that even in such cases previous concert shall be secured.'[8] Acting alone might in any case prove a military as well as a political disaster; Raglan had lost 2,000 killed and wounded in the battle and although St Arnaud had told him that his army had suffered 1,600 casualties the British commander-in-chief knew full well that the French were in a better state than the British. Twenty-four hours after the battle, when the Russians had had time to recover from their initial setback, a resumption of the advance was a vastly different proposition to the pursuit he had advocated on the evening of the 20th. Even if Menschikoff had lost over 5,000 men the Russian army was still over 40,000 strong and reinforcements would undoubtedly be marching to the Crimea from all over the south of Russia. Nothing had been decided by the 22nd but by the evening of that day Raglan had cleared the battlefield and was ready to move on. By this time, of course, the French were again complaining 'The English are not ready'.

But at last both armies were ready, and they moved from the battlefield on the morning of 23 September. One reason why the advance did not move faster than it did may be attributed to St Arnaud suffering a serious relapse during the night of the 22nd. Raglan had already decided that the old marshal was as good as dead, and said so to one of his aides after the advance began. Ironically enough St Arnaud rode across to discuss the disposition of the troops soon afterwards, and he appeared to be more interested in the question of reinforcements than in his own condition.

The advance began two hours after sunrise on 23 September. Up and down steep hills under a hot sun it was a tiring march, and morale was not high. Cholera was still in the ranks and in the British column there were no means of coping with those who were suddenly contorted by the now familiar cramps and spasms. Their arms were taken from them and they were left on the parched plain – to die. A few recovered and managed to rejoin the column but many more succumbed. As the troops descended into the valley of the Katcha, however, spirits began to improve. The Sebastopol road now ran through fruit-filled vineyards, where there was an abundance of melons, apricots and pears for the picking, and past deserted hamlets where there were chickens to be 'liberated'. The road itself was littered with equipment abandoned by Menschikoff's troops; broken wagons, packs, blankets, headgear, ammunition and even part of Menschikoff's sumptuously appointed field kitchen marked the path of the retreating Russians. But of the Russian army itself there was no sign. Neither the Katcha, where the armies settled down for the night of the 23rd, nor the next river, the Belbec, was defended and both rivers were crossed without opposition. Information to the effect that there was a battery of Russian guns at the mouth of the Belbec brought the armies to a halt, but after a couple of hours the area was reported to be clear of Russian troops and they moved on again. In their hurry to get back to Sebastopol the Russians had not demolished the bridges over the river or attempted any of their usual scorched earth routine; the houses and farms were intact and even the buckets still hung at their well-heads.

Several cases of cholera had to be evacuated to the fleet at the Belbec. Despite the fact that the fever still lingered in the ranks and the diarrhoea brought on by exposure to hot days and cold damp nights – and exacerbated by the vast quantities of fruit, much of it unripe, which it was impossible to prevent the men from eating – the health of the troops was improving. After the depression which had set in on the night of the 20th, morale was also improving. The war it seemed was as good as won. Rumour had it that Menschikoff had cut his throat and that Sebastopol would not be defended, and the troops marched up from the Belbec in a mood of renewed confidence. From the crest of the ridge above the river they caught their first glimpse of their objective. Below them the white buildings, onion-shaped towers topped by green copper domes, and the steep streets of Sebastopol shimmered in the sunlight. It was a scene of peace and quiet which belied the feverish activity in the town.

A long arm of the sea divided Sebastopol into two parts. This inlet, which formed the anchorage, separated the city proper on the south side from the naval barracks and supply depots on the north. The south side was itself divided by the inner harbour – the residential quarter being on the west and the barracks, arsenals and dockyards on the east. On the sparkling blue water of the harbour the Russian Black Sea fleet rode at anchor; above it – on the side nearest the Allies – stood an imposing star-shaped fort, whose gun embrasures faced north as well as out to sea. Numerous other gun emplacements could also be seen on the steep hill which guarded the entrance to the harbour. As the troops looked down on the massive solidity of the Star Fort and the packed harbour the sounds of muffled explosions drifted up to them. Expecting that the allied fleets would try to finish off what the armies had begun on shore, the Russians had blocked the harbour entrance with a barrier of sunken ships.*

In retrospect, why the two commanders-in-chief now felt that they should reconsider their strategy may seem puzzling. The facts had been known from the first. The original *coup de main* had been planned with open eyes and none of the hazards were new. To attack the north side of the base had been the object of the landing and the chances of success had materially improved after Alma. At this time Raglan still favoured an attack from the north, supported by a bombardment by the fleet. He believed that once the Star Fort had been captured Sebastopol would fall, and Todleben – the young Russian engineer who had been charged with the town's defence – also subscribed to this view; so did Prince Gorschakoff.[9] Subsequent intelligence information revealed that there were only 11,000 men on the north side of the harbour at this time. At this particular moment even a determined naval assault without any further land operation might have brought the surrender of the town. Alternatively if foul weather or unforeseen circumstances had compelled the allied fleets to abandon the armies after the battle of the Alma, Raglan and St Arnaud would have been compelled to act quickly and directly if their troops were to survive. As it was the sense of dependence on the sea predominated and the indecision which was shown suggests that the two commanders-in-chief had forgotten the original aim of the Crimean expedition. Undertaken late in the season, without any preparation for a winter campaign, its object – less military than political – had been to administer a sharp blow to Russia which would compel her to cut short the war and leave Turkey alone. And no doubt if Sebastopol had been captured in October 1854 that might well have been the effect. As it was a protracted defence of their Crimean base gave the Russians' prestige a welcome boost and provoked in Central Asia a new respect for Russia's innate vitality.

St Arnaud, told that the Russians had blocked the harbour mouth, commented: 'This deed, which is a parody of Moscow, will cause me some embarrassment. I must think to find some ports for

---

* Four warships (not seven as many contemporary accounts have recorded), chained together in line, were sunk across the harbour mouth leaving a narrow channel near the north shore.

wintering my fleet. This will perhaps change my plan of attack. I will probably go to the south.'[10] Meantime Sir John Burgoyne, Raglan's engineer adviser, had suggested that an attack on the city from the south would find that approach defenceless.* Arguing that an attack from the north would be expected, he claimed that by attacking from the south the Allies would enjoy not only the advantage of surprise but also that of assaulting what were likely to be still imperfectly prepared defences. With insufficient troops to invest the whole perimeter of the town and at the same time repel possible attacks from the interior the attack had to be launched from one side or the other. The terrain on the south side afforded much better cover than on the north, and if anything went wrong and a protracted siege operation became necessary, the harbour at Balaclava provided a better base for the fleet than anywhere within reasonable distance of where the Allies now stood.

Having listened to Burgoyne's advice, Raglan said that he still preferred a direct assault from the north side. (Before the Russian army had time to re-form, he added – although it had already had four clear days to do so.) Attacking the south side of Sebastopol meant a march round the town through unknown and wooded country without adequate maps. During the march he would be out of contact with the fleets and when it was over his line of communication to the sea would have to be switched from the western to the southern coast of the peninsula. Moreover the march and redeployment on the south side of the town would mean that an attack could not be mounted for at least another week. On the other hand he felt that a delayed attack might suit the French and Burgoyne was told to go and put his (Burgoyne's) point of view to St Arnaud. At the French headquarters nearly all the staff were against the plan. Prince Napoleon particularly objected to it, cogently pointing out that the Russians were probably demoralized from their defeat and that any defence works erected on the north were not yet ready to withstand an attack. But decisions still rested

---

* Burgoyne's advice was considered invaluable. Seventy-two years old, the illegitimate son of the popular singer Susan Caulfield and the General Burgoyne who had been surrounded by the Americans at Saratoga, he enjoyed an international reputation as an engineer. He had joined Raglan's staff on 25 August to advise on the best method of attacking Sebastopol, but with instructions not to interfere with General Tylden who commanded the Royal Engineers in the field and 'merely to give his valuable advice and opinion on engineering matters'. (Calthorpe I, p. 117.)

with St Arnaud who had been sitting rigidly in his chair with his hands gripping the armrests while Burgoyne propounded his theory. Since leaving the Alma the old marshal's health had been rapidly deteriorating and he had not long to live. His interest in the campaign was waning; however, he had followed the arguments and listened to the objections, and when asked if he was prepared to commit the French to Burgoyne's plan, he nodded. The conference then broke up. As Raglan left he turned to one of his staff and asked, 'Didn't you see, he's dying?'[11] It was true; St Arnaud was in the agonies of cholera a few hours later and next morning he was too ill to see Raglan when the latter rode over to see him.

Raglan, swayed by Burgoyne, abandoned the idea of a direct attack on the north side of Sebastopol against his better judgment. It proved to be a fatal decision. Yet it was understandable. Definite information to the effect that a determined attack on the north side would have been successful – even two days after the Alma – became available later. This fact has obscured some of the most important problems which the British and French were up against at the time. Foremost in the minds of both Raglan and St Arnaud was the need for a port which could serve as a base. North of Sebastopol both armies were exposed to an attack both from the rear and from their left flank; there was no decent harbour within easy distance and the relatively calm weather could not be expected to last forever. If the initial attack on the north side were repulsed or if a storm were to disrupt the flow of supplies from the ships to the shore, disaster could easily follow. Marching round Sebastopol was a risky business but on the information then available it seemed to present relatively fewer risks than a direct assault. And, with so many lives at stake, needless risks could hardly have been condoned. By marching south the Allies would be able to bypass the Star Fort, and when they had seized a harbour on the south coast the safety of the two armies would be assured for the winter – if this should be necessary. To St Arnaud the prospect of an attack from the rear appeared to be 'a beautiful manoeuvre';[12] almost to a man the British generals approved, and Admiral Lyons – who had not heard of the change in plan until it was actually under way – congratulated Raglan for 'one of the most brilliant movements ever made by an army'.[13]

With the British in the van the allied armies set off on their march round Sebastopol at half-past eight on the morning of 25 September.

Shouldering their way round the head of Sebastopol harbour, crossing the river Tchernaya which runs into it, and marching to Balaclava involved a journey of about thirteen miles. The axis of advance was a forest track, and in order to leave this clear for the artillery and cavalry the infantry were sent off on a compass bearing. The route between the Belbec and the Tchernaya led through dense oak forest and there the heat was overpowering. Thick brushwood made it impossible to keep the brigades together, and even regiments were split into small parties as each man scrambled forward, his arms uplifted to protect his face from the lacerating briars and swinging backhanders dealt by the boughs. Sometimes they resembled beaters pushing through a thick covert, sometimes – threading their way along narrow woodland paths – a tribe of Indians. Here a shako would be knocked off, there some briar would lay its tenacious hold on a soldier's knapsack or cling to the tails of his coat. Many more collapsed through exhaustion and as nothing could be done for them they were left where they fell. Haunted by the constant fear of running into the Russians while in this irregular formation, the infantry pushed blindly forward.

Meanwhile the cavalry and horse artillery were moving up the track. Lord Lucan had been ordered to reconnoitre a group of buildings once the home of a Scottish admiral who had supervised the construction of the Sebastopol dockyard at the end of the eighteenth century, and which were now marked on the map with the friendly-sounding name of Mackenzie's Farm. Just beyond these buildings the track joined the main Sebastopol–Simpheropol road. The cavalry was not to leave the wood but when it reached Mackenzie's Farm patrols were to keep a watchful eye on the main road and report on its condition. Accompanying the first squadron was the officer of Airey's staff responsible for planning the route, and when the track forked in the middle of the wood this individual led the cavalry up what appeared to be the larger of the two paths. It was an unfortunate choice. Gradually the path degenerated and finally, within a mile of the fork, it petered out altogether. When the leading files were compelled to halt there came the realization that the cavalry were lost. With the column pressing up behind there could be no question of turning back and so after a hurried consultation a compass course was set in a south-easterly direction.

Behind the cavalry, the horse artillery had not been able to move

so fast, and when the gunners reached the track junction they halted.
A hussar had been left at the fork to direct them up the path Lucan
and his squadrons had taken, but the leading gunner officer
hesitated. Apart from the fact that it would be well nigh impossible
to get the guns up the path which the guide indicated, it seemed to
him that something was awry. Word was passed back to the battery
commander and while the latter was trying to make up his mind
what to do for the best, Raglan and his escort trotted up.

At the sight of the gunners making what appeared to be an un-
authorized halt Raglan was inclined to be tetchy. But when the
situation was explained to him he agreed that the gunners were
right in assuming the cavalry had taken the wrong track; spurring
his horse he led the way up the other path.

With the cavalry struggling to force a passage through the wood
Raglan was now the point of the vanguard. Oblivious or not to this
fact it was the sort of situation he accepted and probably relished.
Airey cantered up a little further on and the two generals rode
forward together. It was not far to the end of the wood and just
before they came to it Airey saw a gap in the trees. Having asked if
he might ride on to investigate, he galloped up to the clearing where
he was seen to pull up his horse abruptly and hold his hand above
his head. There was no mistaking the urgency of his gesture; the
column was warned to halt and keep quiet. Strolling about the
road, talking, smoking and leaning against the sides of a long column
of wagons, stretching down the hill in front of Mackenzie's Farm,
were scores of Russian soldiers. Airey had stopped just in time, and
for a few brief moments he sat and watched. Clearly the British
advance guard had blundered into the rear of a considerable
Russian column, marching across the front of the allied line of
advance. The really interesting fact, Airey noticed, was that the
Russian transport was facing away from Sebastopol and that
Mackenzie's Farm was a charred and smoking ruin. He could not
know that Menschikoff had marched his army out of Sebastopol,
intending to fall on the flank of the Allies when they attacked from
the north – as he was sure they were about to do. With the Allies
marching round Sebastopol to capture it and the Russians marching
away from the town in order to defend it, the conduct of both
sides was so unlikely that it was bound to cause surprise.

In this sort of situation Raglan was superb. Realizing that something was amiss he turned in his saddle, and in a 'low tranquil voice'

ordered one of his staff to find the cavalry and another to tell the gunners to hurry forward.[14] Slowly he then moved up to join Airey, reined, and sat looking down on the Russians. By this time the cocked hats of the two generals had been spotted, and the Russians were at a complete loss. No doubt some of them realized they were being watched by senior British officers. But surely, they reasoned, no allied officers would remain quite so placid unless they felt secure; probably an attack was brewing. By failing to give the alarm, a rare opportunity was missed, for if Russian infantry had mounted a quick attack Raglan might have been captured and a large part of his disorganized column would have been at their mercy.

When nothing happened, it seemed that the bulk of the Russian column was unaware of the impending danger. Its ignorance now was short-lived. With a rumble the first troop of horse artillery raced up and deployed for action on the edge of the wood; minutes later a breathless and red-faced Lucan galloped up with some of the cavalry. As he passed Raglan, the latter – controlling his anger with evident difficulty – shouted 'Lord Lucan, you're late!'

By this time the guns of the horse artillery were blasting round shot down the hill and the Russians were running for cover. The cavalry galloped on in pursuit but they had not gone very far before they were called back. True to his often-expressed idea Raglan waited to keep them 'in hand' for an emergency or when real danger threatened. They must at all costs, he had told one of their commanding officers some days previously, be kept back until they were really needed. The men, unappreciative of what seemed to be excessive caution, were furious with disappointment which the discovery of some rich booty in the abandoned wagons only parti- ally alleviated. Fur coats, silk shirts, food and drink, and porno- graphic literature were all found in the Russian wagons. In one also was a befuddled Russian officer, the only one who appears to have been with the rearguard. Greeting his captors with a champagne bottle, he pressed them to have a drink. When his offer was accepted, however, the bottle was found to be empty. Hauled in front of Raglan to explain why the column was moving out of Sebastopol and how much of the Russian army was involved, the Russian was scarcely able to stand on his feet and wholly incapable of giving any intelligible information; Raglan, disgusted by the sight of a drunken officer, turned his back on him.

At this moment Cardigan rode up and to him Raglan said sharply: 'The cavalry were out of their proper place.' 'I am, my Lord,' Cardigan replied in a smug tone, 'no longer in command of the cavalry.' The inference was that anything which had gone wrong was Lucan's fault and not his. Lucan was not present. Resentful at being blamed for the cavalry getting lost while one of Airey's staff was leading it, he was furious at the rebuke which had been shouted when he had galloped past Raglan at the head of the leading squadron, and after this episode Lucan had no social and little official contact with the commander-in-chief. Lucan did not consider he was being fairly treated, while Raglan for his part considered he could not rely on Lucan, 'It was common gossip,' wrote one of the Light Brigade officers, 'that Lord Raglan thought the cavalry were being wretchedly handled.'[15]

The first infantry struggled out of the wood near the still smoking ruins of Mackenzie's Farm in the early afternoon.* Tired and thirsty, their faces and hands scratched by briars, they were fed up with the march and even more frustrated when they found that the well at Mackenzie's Farm had been filled in by the Russians. Considering the shortness of the march and the fact that no enemy had been encountered, the casualties were extraordinarily high. (At an inquiry months later the commanding officer of the 21st Fusiliers stated that forty-seven men of his regiment were 'unaccounted for' after the march.[16] Presumably most of these succumbed to heat, exhaustion and cholera.)

That night the troops bivouacked on the Fedukhine Hills above the south bank of the Tchernaya and Raglan established his headquarters in a stone hut where the Traktir bridge crossed the river. Somewhat bewildered by the events of the day and apprehensive: 'We were', he wrote afterwards, 'in a dangerous situation.' In the heart of unreconnoitred hill country and cut off from the fleet – which was still anchored at the mouth of the Katcha – his army was an ideal object for attack, and if Menschikoff had attacked the result would almost certainly have been disastrous. But by any standards the unimaginative Russian commander was an inferior general, and his troops were not imbued with an aggressive spirit. Yet Raglan was not to know this and – as he told his wife a few

* The British Light and 1st Division were first in the order of march. The 3rd Division, followed by the French and British 2nd Division, were two hours behind.

weeks later – he was never more relieved than when he saw the sun come up on the morning of 26 September, to shine on an army that was rested and which had not been attacked. Soon after dawn he was up, in the saddle and across the Tchernaya. A message had been sent back through the forest to the Katcha with instructions for the fleet to sail round to Balaclava, and Raglan wanted to lose no time in getting there himself. Four miles from the Traktir bridge he came to the little village of Kadiköi which stands on the plateau above Balaclava. Its inhabitants seemed friendly and Raglan was told that Balaclava was undefended. Raglan rode on down the track, and near the bottom of the slope where it made a sharp turn he had a picturesque view of Balaclava Bay. Seemingly enclosed on all sides by high cliffs, the narrow inlet which formed the harbour had the appearance of an inland lake. The surrounding heights were reflected in its green depths, and the town on its eastern side appeared to be a place of great beauty. A mediaeval castle crowned one of the lofty heights and as Raglan surveyed the scene a mortar bomb crashed down in front of him. Balaclava, it seemed, was defended after all. The Light Division was ordered up, but as it deployed to occupy the cliffs the boom of heavy guns announced the approach of the allied fleet.

The show of resistance appears to have been only a formality; a flag of truce was soon fluttering from the castle and the commandant came down to surrender his force of seventy militiamen – most of them were Greeks of the Balaclava district – and four brass mortars. As Raglan rode down into the village the locals knelt and held up trays of fruit and flowers together with pieces of bread sprinkled with salt as a sign of hospitality and friendship. At the other end of the town Her Majesty's ship *Agamemnon*, flying the flag of Admiral Lyons, rode majestically into the harbour. Soon she had tied up opposite the house which was to serve as Raglan's base headquarters.

In normal times Balaclava was a little fishing village, which served as Sebastopol's summer playground. At a distance its green-tiled, white-walled cottages clustering below the steep sandstone cliffs, its rose-filled gardens, and the castellated ruins of two Genoese forts which dominated the heights above, made it seem a picturesque and restful place. But a closer inspection quickly revealed several objectionable features. To begin with the charming cottages were squalid and insanitary. Moreover most of them were occupied by undesirable Greeks who required no provocation to shoot or stab strangers if there was an opportunity to profit by it. The harbour was deep and well protected – both desirable factors when considering the establishment of a military base. But a sharp curve at its mouth and a bottle-neck approach made it difficult for a long or heavy ship to negotiate the entrance. Fortunately the depth of water at the edges made it possible for almost any ship to moor with her bow or stern overhanging the road below the village. Even so it did not take long for the allied staffs to agree that the harbour capacity of Balaclava was not enough for both armies.

Before the campaign had started there had been a tacit understanding that the French would fight on the right of the line. The British had reached Balaclava first but when the two armies turned about to face Sebastopol they would be on the right and it could be assumed that Balaclava would fall in their sector. Canrobert, acting for St Arnaud, told Raglan that he could choose between keeping it and staying on the exposed right flank – which the British were best fitted to protect because they had nearly all the cavalry – or moving over to the left and using the bays at Kamiesch and Kazatch, east of Cape Kherson. Admiral Lyons' advice to Raglan was that the British should keep Balaclava, as he maintained that it was the best place for maintaining communications between the army and its sea base. When Raglan complied and accepted responsibility for the exposed flank he made the greatest mistake in his career. Both Kamiesch and Kazatch proved more adequate bases than Balaclava and while the French enjoyed the protection of the sea on their left flank and that of the British army on their right, the British right flank was open to attack. Finding enough men to protect this flank while laying siege to Sebastopol was a problem which was to remain with Raglan throughout the rest of his campaign. At the time, however, all the generals were optimistic. In Raglan's opinion there was now certainly no serious need to spend the winter in the Crimea. No one supposed that the capacities of Balaclava would ever be fully tested; it was expected Sebastopol would be stormed within a week or so and Raglan and his staff confidently expected to be in London in time for Christmas.

It was now a case of the hopeful mind failing to appreciate the difference between the possible and the inevitable. Raglan, supported by Lyons, was all for an immediate assault before the Russian

defences could be strengthened. And the Russian commanders
believed that if such an assault had been pressed home with the
same sort of determination that the British had shown at the Alma,
Sebastopol would have fallen. But once more the French did not
agree. This time it was not St Arnaud, for he had been relieved by
Canrobert. From the Belbec the old marshal had travelled in a
Russian carriage – said to be that of Menschikoff – which had been
captured at the Alma; behind him his staff had ridden 'like
mourners following a hearse'.[17] By 25 September, even St Arnaud
recognized that he was sinking fast and too sick to continue in
command. 'I have become so weak that the command has become
impossible for me. In this situation . . . I deem it a duty of honour
and conscience to tender it to the hands of General Canrobert, whom
the special orders of His Majesty designated my successor.'[18] He
had no illusions about the gravity of his condition. With the hand
of death in his vitals, he did not expect to see France again but he
was hoping to reach Therapia where he had left his wife at the
French embassy. In the event even this limited wish proved to be
too much.

Canrobert assumed command of the French army, while preparations were made for the Marshal's departure for Balaclava
where the French ship *Berthollet* had come to take him to Constantinople. Before he left St Arnaud confided to his doctor: 'I only
wanted one thing, to enter Sebastopol. Perhaps I could have done
it if I had been able to carry out in time my first plan, but I have
been master neither of myself nor of events. I am leaving the army
in good hands . . . I hope His Majesty will be satisfied with what I
have done.'[19] To Raglan, who went to say goodbye to him on 29
September and who left him with tears in his eyes, he said 'I am
better, my Lord; the sea air, the care of my wife will make me well
again soon, and I'll always be thinking of you.'[20] He died on the
voyage, soon after saying goodbye to his noble colleague.

St Arnaud's successor had absolute confidence in a rapid success.
Forty years later he said that he was seized at the time with an
imposing vision of triumph. The fall of Sebastopol was virtually a
certainty; the adventurous part of the undertaking had been accomplished successfully, and the Russians could surely have no better
opportunity to check the Anglo-French force. But he rejected the
idea of an immediate assault. He was not prepared, he told Raglan,

to ask his men – whose obedience to such orders was not so unquestioning as that of British troops – to attack across open ground in the teeth of guns firing at them from both the redoubt and the ships in the harbour. Besides, there was the danger of a flank attack to be considered. Menschikoff had obviously taken his army out of Sebastopol to deploy it for an attack on the besieging armies from the hills on the Allies' right flank. Storming Sebastopol without the support of heavy guns, he said, would be a crime. Burgoyne agreed with him, and in less dramatic terms than those used by the Frenchman told Raglan that an unsupported assault before siege guns had smashed the enemy's artillery would be 'utterly unjustifiable'.[21]

SEBASTOPOL AND THE FIRST BOMBARDMENT

'A fortress that is not attacked has no need of defence.'

French proverb

Five days after the occupation of Balaclava a plan of Sebastopol's fortifications was discovered in the house of a certain Mr Upton, whose grandfather had built the dockyards. From a study of what appeared to exist on the ground, it seemed that few changes had been made to the defences on the south side of the base since Upton's map was drawn. The main obstacles to an attack from this direction centred on a fortified mound topped by a martello tower and what the commander of the 4th Division, General Cathcart, airily dismissed as 'a low park wall, not in good repair'.[1] Six months were to elapse before the Allies came to realize that the strongpoint on this mound – known by then as the Malakoff – was the key to the Russian defences. If it had been occupied in September 1854 there would have been no need to dig forty miles of trenches nor for the costly assaults which became necessary after it had grown into a fortress. While the British and French delayed their assault, the Russians in Sebastopol were building up a powerful line of defences.

When the allied armies reached the Belbec the Governor of Sebastopol appeared to have only two alternatives – to see his town reduced to ruins or to capitulate on disastrous terms. After the battle of the Alma, Prince Menschikoff had led his army back into Sebastopol only to lead it out again. The move was not just to make sure that it was not cut off from the supplies and reinforcements which were already on their way from Kertch and Odessa; he wanted to redeploy it in a position where it could hover on the allied flank, lay siege to the besiegers and attack them at their weakest points. According to Burgoyne, the Russian commander had done 'exactly what was right'. Whether or not he did what was right to

begin with Menschikoff certainly took no advantage of his opportunities. When Raglan's straggling army brushed his rearguard,
on the flank march, Menschikoff had an opportunity to turn and
fight the Allies when they were at a severe disadvantage. But he
continued his march, left the way open to Balaclava, and did not
even bother to find out where the Allies were, let alone attack them.
He 'seemed lost', one of his officers wrote, 'and he was certainly
no help to the garrison.'[2]

'Of the Prince', Vice-Admiral Korniloff, Menschikoff's chief-of-
staff, wrote in his diary on 26 September, 'nothing is to be heard'.
There was still no news of him next day and 'the evening passed in
gloomy thoughts about the future of Russia.'[3] Menschikoff had
left Sebastopol in Korniloff's charge with four battalions and instructions that he 'must maintain the place at any cost, and even make
use of the sailors and marines to defend it.' Any other man might
have despaired. But Korniloff and at least two of his assistants
were remarkable men. Deeply religious and sincerely patriotic,
Korniloff possessed the melancholy fortitude of Russian heroes.
'Let the troops be first reminded of the word of God', he told the
priests, 'and then I will impart the word of the Tsar.'[4] Korniloff
himself was prepared to die if need be in defence of the base – and
did, in fact, do so. Vice-Admiral Nakhimoff, who was supposed to
share the command with Korniloff was the Russian hero of the
Sinope action and the idol of the sailors. Like Korniloff, he had the
same contempt for death but was less sure of himself.

At a conference summoned by Korniloff on 22 September, the
Russian commandant had outlined the apparent hopelessness of
the situation and asked the naval and military commanders
whether the Russian fleet should be destroyed or whether 'it would
not be better that it should put to sea and carry terror into Constantinople at the risk of encountering the overpowering armada of
England and fighting a battle of life and death.'[5] While protesting
that they were not averse to a death or glory venture, the naval
captains suggested that it would be stupid to sacrifice the fleet in
'some futile expedition, which would have neither object nor
advantage'. They preferred, they said, to make the sacrifice in the
'home' of the fleet, and to show their courage in the defence of
Sebastopol. Korniloff agreed and it was then that it was decided to
scuttle the oldest and least valuable ships in the harbour mouth and
to release guns and ships' crews for the defence of the town. At the

time this may have seemed a wise move. Immediate security was required and Admiral Nakhimoff may have had visions of the magnificent spectacle of the allied fleets sailing into Sebastopol harbour in battle array. With the harbour mouth blocked this would be impossible. But locking the allied fleet out meant locking the Russian fleet in and giving up its deterrent advantage. If the Russian fleet had been able to sail out of Sebastopol the French base at Kamiesch would have been untenable unless the allied fleets were prepared to sit outside Sebastopol throughout the siege.

'Let no mention', said Korniloff when the meeting broke up, 'be henceforth made of surrender, none of retreat. Let us consider the town as our ship, and perish rather than surrender. I empower everyone to cut down on the spot any man – be he general or private soldier, myself included – who speaks of negotiation or retreat.' These were brave words, but Sebastopol needed more than rhetoric, faith and courage if it was to withstand an allied assault, and fortunately for the Russians there was in Sebastopol a man who was capable of translating Korniloff's sentiments into practical terms.

Franz Eduard Ivanovitch Todleben was the only man in the Crimean campaign to acquire the reputation of a military genius. And it was he who now decided the destiny of Sebastopol. Born in the Baltic provinces of Russia, Todleben was in appearance, origin and temperament a Prussian. Tall and broad-shouldered, with penetrating eyes, a long beaked nose and determined mouth, he had a commanding presence. He also had a reputation for 'plain though courteous manners, a merry disposition . . . cool judgement . . . and a marked aversion to plotters and rogues . . .'[6] Commissioned as an ensign of Engineers at the age of eighteen, he was only thirty-six when he undertook to organize the land defences of Sebastopol. Less than a year before he had been walking the streets of St Petersburg conscious of his own ability and burning for employment. His opportunity almost came too late. When war broke out between Turkey and Russia in 1853 Todleben had been chiefly responsible for the construction of the trench system at the siege of Silistria – a siege terminated by a purely strategic withdrawal. For this work he had been promoted to lieutenant-colonel, and Gorschakoff had introduced him to Menschikoff as a man who would be useful in Sebastopol. When he arrived in the Crimea, Menschikoff had instructed him to study the defences of the base

but his report on them had been so unflattering that Menschikoff
had coldly advised him to return to regimental duty. But Todleben
had not left Sebastopol when the allies landed at Calamita Bay
and within a few days the danger that Menschikoff had dismissed
as unfounded was real and urgent. Todleben was expected in a few
days to complete the work of months, and it is to the credit of this
remarkable man that he was able to do so.

Todleben knew that it was not possible to make Sebastopol
impregnable overnight. His prayer was for three weeks respite and
this the Allies accorded him. As the days and nights passed,
and the expected assault did not come, the defences grew stronger
and every Russian in Sebastopol must have crossed himself in
thanksgiving. To build up the defences the whole of the effective
population was mobilized and work went on twenty-four hours a
day. Encouraged by the priests with Gregorian chants and the
sprinkling of holy water, the Russians toiled to dig trenches and
build redoubts. Children pushed wheelbarrows, women carried
earth in their aprons, and dragged wash-tubs filled with ammunition. In consequence Todleben was able to say on 29 September
'Our works [have] advanced with surprising rapidity; several
batteries are already finished and armed with naval guns of heavy
calibre.'[7] Slowly the 'thing like a low park wall' of which Cathcart
had spoken with such disdain became a formidable defence line
four miles long. Six strongpoints, all designed for mutual support,
were arranged in a semi-circle round the southern half of the town.
Guns were trundled out and emplaced in them and cannon balls
stacked beside them. On the west, nearest the sea, was Fort Quarantine; next to it the Central Bastion; forward and in the centre –
pointing to the allied armies like a blunted arrow – were the Flagstaff Bastion and the Redan; behind and to the east of the Redan,
the Malakoff; and farther to the east the Little Redan.

On October 2, Menschikoff came to inspect the defences and
was duly impressed. Korniloff, pointing out that the fortress would
have to rely solely on its bastioned '*enceinte*' if the Allies attacked,
asked for the garrison to be reinforced. More men was what
Sebastopol needed, he told the Prince. Menschikoff, whose army
had just been joined by 10,000 men from Odessa, demurred. He
had lost so many officers at the Alma, the allied armies were very
strong, he was preparing to attack their right flank. Korniloff was
furious, and when it appeared that he was prepared to write to the

Tsar about the Prince's lack of co-operation, Menschikoff gave way. Four battalions of the Minsk Regiment moved into Sebastopol immediately and by 9 October they had been joined by another ten battalions.[8] Korniloff could now feel secure. 'Notwithstanding the number of our enemies . . . on the south side of the bay,' he confided to his diary, 'we have no fear of not repelling them. Unless', he added with humility, 'our God forsakes us; and in that case His Holy Will be done. It is the duty of men to submit to Him in resignation as He is always just.'[9] Todleben also felt more relieved. It was obvious that the situation could not continue much longer but with every day that passed the Russian defences were more secure than the day before.

One thousand yards away from the most advanced point of Todleben's defences the Allies worked leisurely and routinely at their own lines. After the Battle of the Alma some of the officers had grown contemptuous of the Russians. 'Let them do what they like', was the general feeling, 'in due course we shall level their works: that will strike terror; and the place will then fall without bloodshed.'[10] In this belief the allied commanders were reconciled to the delay in opening fire. Their troops had demonstrated their mettle and won their spurs at the Alma; now they just wanted to go home. If Sebastopol had to be stormed then it would be stormed, but with any luck the place could be taken without further loss of life and limb. Many of the troops felt the same way. Serving an abstract cause, which appealed to the hearts and minds of only a few, they considered that they had fulfilled their duty; the fall of Sebastopol would not add to the glory they had won at the Alma. Moreover the weather was warm and sunny and everyone had been struck by the unexpected charm of the countryside.

After Bulgaria what the British troops were now experiencing came as a welcome relief to everyone. Little of the baggage had arrived and most officers and men had no other clothes than those in which they had landed. But the knapsacks were brought ashore on 3 October, blankets were distributed and from that day daily rum rations were issued – one ration at dinner time, another at sunset, and a third to the men in the trenches or on guard duty. The infantry drew field pay of sixpence a day, and a further eight-pence a day working pay by day or tenpence by night. Most of their time was spent on fatigues, fetching provisions from Balaclava in the afternoons. But in their spare time they were able to make fascines and gabions for which they were paid sevenpence and a halfpenny respectively. Shakos, the repulsive leather stocks, and epaulettes had all been discarded.

No roads were made, since none were needed; the troops cut their own firewood; vegetables were a matter of regimental supply. Mrs Evans – still with the King's Own – sat in the tent she shared at night with her husband and six other men, sewing the regimental colours which had been torn at the Alma. If the situation was unreal, life was not unpleasant and against such a background it is not difficult to appreciate the cheery confidence of the allied armies at the beginning of October 1854. The prevalent belief was that when the time came the Russian redoubts would not stop them occupying Sebastopol. Only a few sceptical individuals felt uneasy and no doubt if they had expressed their views, they would have been answered in the words of Henry v before Agincourt.

Soon after Balaclava had been taken, Burgoyne had declared that Sebastopol could have been captured or would have capitulated on 26 September if a determined enough attack were launched against it. But such an attack might mean heavy casualties – 500 men was forecast – and Raglan was not prepared to accept the cost. Once a full-scale siege had been agreed, Burgoyne maintained that the town's batteries must be silenced by artillery fire, and this required a massive build-up of material. Up to 13 October not a single round had been fired towards the town, and it was the Russians who opened the next stage of the war on 16 October. Even then 'we returned not a single shot, nor budged an inch.'[11] According to Bosquet's aide-de-camp, the delay was much regretted by the French and St Arnaud would never have condoned it.[12] Not only the French regretted the delay when the time came to test the Russian strength, for both British and French were to find that the Russians' fire was far superior to their own and they were able to respond to each of the allied field pieces with three or four guns of a higher calibre.[13]

Since 26 September both armies had busied themselves with the work of disembarking supplies of food, ammunition and engineering equipment. In his Balaclava headquarters Raglan went about his duties as composedly as if he had been seated in the Horse Guards. In the cool of the evening he and Admiral Lyons would ride up to the front line to see what progress had been made by the engineers and then return to a late dinner. Whether the feeling which

An allegorical painting of Bosquet's Zouaves crossing the Alma.

'Night after the Battle'. A popular and typical post-war artistic theme depicting the macabre situation after the Battle of the Alma.

The objective Sebastopol. As seen from the Redan in September 1855.

This scene depicts the first Allied bombardment of Sebastopol harbour in September 1854. Fort Constantine is on the left of the picture, Quarantine Fort on the right.

predominated was one of satisfaction for the past or confidence in the future is difficult to decide. In the first fortnight there was an ample and cheap supply of locally grown fresh vegetables, tomatoes, plums, grapes and even poultry, with which to supplement the troops' rations. But the demand for them was such that there was soon a shortage and the falling sickness rate was reversed. By 4 October, British troops were dying at the rate of about twenty-five a day.

At Kamiesch the French quickly established their base. The bay, which was soon seen to be superior to Balaclava, was found to be more than adequate for their needs and was appropriately dubbed 'the bay of Providence'. Under their new commander, Canrobert, they began to set up their camps and reconnoitre the ground in front of them on the left of the allied line. It did not take them long to find out that the task of digging trenches and setting up batteries in the rocky soil of the Chersonese would be hard work, and that they would be exposed to bitter winds if they were still there when winter came. By this time there was no longer any talk of the immediate storming of Sebastopol; it was accepted that there was going to be a siege, and to prosecute it effectively Canrobert reorganized the French Army. Work associated with the siege was handed over to the 3rd and 4th Divisions under Forey and the two remaining divisions were formed into a *'corps d'observation'* under Bosquet. When Menschikoff's army disappeared in the direction of Simpheropol the Allies were compelled to consider the possibility of an attack from the rear. Bosquet's task was simply to prevent Menschikoff from giving effective aid to the Sebastopol garrison. To do this and to protect the plateau his two divisions were deployed along the ridge of the Sapoune hills.

On the French right the British were in a less happy position. Dependent on a single road running up from the harbour to the plateau through the 'Col de Balaclava', they faced the constant possibility of an attack from the north-east. Raglan's prime concern was with the siege operations, but as the insecurity of Balaclava became evident a defence of the town was organized and Sir Colin Campbell made responsible for it. In the harbour, which was already degenerating into a sink of filth, supplies and stores were trundled, hauled or slung ashore in insanitary disorder from a crowd of ships. As no one was anticipating a sojourn in the Crimea little thought was given to organizing Balaclava as a base. Confusion and waste abounded: streets became sewers; the harbour a receptacle for offal; houses were looted, and doors, windows and rafters were taken for firewood.

Detached a little from the common ships was Lord Cardigan's elegant yacht, the *Dryad*. With Raglan's permission the commander of the Light Brigade dined and slept aboard, while his brigade suffered the discomfort of camp life three miles away. His Lordship was constantly late for the dawn 'stand to', and there was a good deal of criticism by those who resented his escape from the discomforts of the field.* But in such matters Cardigan was a thick-skinned individual, and he was not prepared either to change his way of life or to relinquish his command. Other senior officers were also affected by the spirit of unreality that existed alongside the harsh practicalities that governed the existence of most of the soldiers in the Crimea. And not only were the armies affected. Admiral Dundas was accompanied by his wife and her maids, and he kept cows on his ship for their benefit.

Allied patrolling during the three weeks of preparation for the siege assault was almost negligible, and outside the immediate vicinity of Balaclava the Cossacks began to reassert their former grip on the local Tartars. Russian cavalry approached the town itself one day but retired when a party of Scots Greys and Horse Artillery went out to meet them. On the other hand the Allies sent some steamers to Yalta to get some wine. None was to be found, but some coal was taken from Prince Woronzoff's empty mansion and the caretaker given a receipt for it. This was probably one of the few occasions during the war when respect was shown for private property. Balaclava itself had become a haven for speculative individuals seeking to profit from the British army's requirements. The original Greek population was expelled in order to ease the feeding problem and eradicate a possible fifth column. But most of the pariahs managed to hide among the primitive undesigning Tartars.

On 2 October, the British Naval Brigade landed at Balaclava

---

* On the morning of Balaclava the Light Brigade was taken into action by another officer. At Inkerman Cardigan was so late that, in order to avoid unnecessary publicity of the fact, the part played by the Light Brigade was practically ignored in despatches.

sensibly dosed with quinine, and to the music of a fife or fiddle, teams of sailors hauled 8- and 10-inch naval guns and ammunition up the Balaclava road to the plateau. Two great elliptically-bored Lancaster guns, which were expected to throw their erratic missiles, 4,500 yards were also manoeuvred on to the plain. Except for the latter, the average distance of the British guns from the Russian lines was about 1,200 yards – their range being (quite wrongly) considered compensated for by their calibre as compared with that of guns used in previous sieges. The French batteries, of smaller calibre brass cannon, faced the western side of the town and were closer. By 16 October, when the Allies considered they were ready to give battle, the British had 73 guns in their batteries – 29 of them with naval crews; the French had 53. (On the Russian side there were about 240 guns but of these only 118 would be capable of being used in a counter-battery role.)

The bombardment, which was to open on the morning of 17 October, was expected to wreck the defences of the town and open the way to victory. A council of war was held on the evening of the 16th when the plan for the operation was finalized. Fire orders were issued and arrangements made for an assault after the bombardment had smashed Todleben's line. Prince Napoleon had already asked Canrobert for the command of the French force designated for the assault and the French commander-in-chief – remembering the Prince's performance at the Alma – had agreed. As Russian deserters had reported that the Sebastopol garrison was demoralized and that terror reigned in the town the allied commanders felt that a concerted bombardment of both armies with such naval fire as could be brought to bear would be enough to ensure the success of the operation. But as so often happens, things did not go according to plan.

Disinterestedly – anticipating success whether joined by them or not – Raglan and Canrobert had not invited the fleets to share in the honour of the attack until 14 October. Taken by surprise, Admiral Dundas met Admiral Hamelin on board the French ship *Mogador* off Kazatch to consider the proposal. With the armies wholly dependent on sea power for their maintenance both were averse to risking the fleets. But neither wanted to reject the general's invitation and they agreed that a diversion which would compel the Russians to man their coast defence batteries would help the assault. They left it to the generals to decide whether the fleets should be used on the first or second day of the bombardment, or on the third – the day provisionally agreed for the assault. The original plan was for a two-day bombardment, followed by an assault on the morning of the third day. But confidence increased as the hour approached, and the two commanders-in-chief decided that the first day should be a combined land and sea attack.

Throughout the night of 16 October, the allied gunners completed their preparations for the sudden and colossal bombardment that was to finish the war. An air of tense excitement hung over the allied lines as ammunition was laid out and the muzzles of the guns aligned on their targets. The barrage was scheduled to begin at half-past six in the morning when shells were fired from three French mortars. But before the signal was given the Russian gunners opened fire, and from then on everything seemed to go wrong. The Russians had been watching the allied preparations and had decided that their moment had arrived. The psychological advantage of a surprise bombardment from the allied batteries was lost; when they started to return the fire it was with a disappointing lack of co-ordination which was unable to match that of the Russians.

In the naval battery the 68-pounders, firing at a range of more than 2,000 yards, were soon obscured by a thick sulphurous cloud which shut out the view of the gunners. Men worked their pieces in a murky obscurity, using a chalked line on the gun platforms to lay their aim. The noise was deafening, as the sailors loosed off great shattering salvoes in broadsides as if they were aboard ship. Distinct above this bursting uproar came the crack of the big Lancasters, followed by a peculiar *swoosh* as their erratic missiles flew towards the Malakoff.* Casualties among the sailors were

---

* The allied fire plan allotted individual targets to each battery. By modern standards it may seem over simple.

British Batteries		Target
Right attack	7 32-prs 6 24-prs 8 8-in. guns 5 10-in. mortars	Directed against the Malakoff 'Round' Tower, the Redan, Barrack batteries and ships in the dockyard
Left attack	24 24-prs 12 8-in. guns 5 10-in. mortars	
Lancaster Battery	4 68-prs 1 Lancaster	The Malakoff
Picket House Battery	1 Lancaster	Ships in the Dockyard Creek

heavy because they would jump up on the parapet of the protective earthwork surrounding their battery in order to see what had happened after each salvo. Todleben had deployed snipers in the front line and they took a heavy toll of the exuberant British gunners.

The fleets, which had been expected to join the battle at ten o'clock, did not appear until 1 p.m. During the night Admiral Dundas on board the *Britannia* had received a message from Admiral Hamelin to say that he did not intend to open fire at 10 a.m. 'as his shot would not last long and, if expended early, the enemy might think he was beaten off.' Dundas considered this excuse to be 'a fair one' and sent Admiral Lyons a note to say that he intended to arrange for the British fleet to comply with Hamelin's arrangements.[14] At 7 a.m. however, after the land bombardment had already started, Hamelin himself arrived at the *Britannia*, where he told Dundas that the whole plan, on Canrobert's instructions, was to be altered again. Instead of the ships being able to manoeuvre while they delivered their broadsides as had been previously arranged, they were now to be anchored in line. And, moreover, anchored in line at a considerable distance from the forts which would be their main targets. When Dundas refused to agree, Hamelin said that the French navy would have to act alone. Realizing that the French admiral meant what he said, Dundas gave way.

As a result of these changes in plan it was 10 a.m. before the fleets started to get under way, and well after midday before they were in their allotted positions. The French led and were first into action. Admiral Hamelin remembered that his predecessor had lost command of the fleet for arriving at Basika Bay behind the British and he was determined not to repeat the mistake. As the great men-of-war without engines were propelled into position by a steamer lashed alongside, a signal fluttered from the masthead of his flagship: 'France observes you.'

From their positions on the right of the harbour entrance the French ships engaged Fort Quarantine and batteries on the

(Total of 73 guns of which 42 were manned by the Royal Artillery and 30 by the Naval Brigade.)
French Batteries
43 guns   ⎰Directed mainly against the Flagstaff Bastion and works in
10 mortars ⎱the Russian western sector
See Appendix 6 for a description of Sebastopol, its environs and defences.

southern side of the harbour, while Lyons in the *Agamemnon* directed the guns of his ships, the *Sanspareil* and the *London*, towards Fort Constantine on the north side of the harbour. There was a terrific cannonade and much noise, but at the end of the action the forts had suffered very little damage. After a few rounds the stationary ships were wrapped in smoke and as the gunners could not see their targets, and were in any case shooting at extreme range, their skill was never really tested. In the fog created by their own powder, they might just as well have been firing *feux de joie*. Fortunately the same fog obscured the ships and the Russians, who tended to give their own guns too much elevation, could only see their masts. Even so, when the action was terminated at sunset and the allied fleets returned to the anchorage off the Katcha the ships had taken more punishment than they had handed out.

Seven hundred tons of shot discharged through 500 guns had been fired at the casemated granite works of the Russians, and at the end of the day all the forts, towers, bastions and redoubts were still in action. A few guns had been blown off the mountings but by the morning of 18 October they had been replaced, and the only evidence of the cannonade were marks in the walls of the forts. The battleships *Albion* and *Arethusa* were completely crippled; the *Retribution* had had her mainmast shot away; the *Firebrand* had scarcely a whole spar left and the *Rodney* had nearly been lost when she ran ashore during the action. Forty-four British and thirty-two French sailors had been killed and 266 British and 180 French wounded. As a supporting operation or even as a diversion, the naval action could be considered an abject failure. By this exhibition the Allies had degraded the deterrent effect of their navy and the Russians ceased to worry about the threat. The fleets had learned their lesson too and, except for occasional nocturnal visitations by a single raider to loose off a couple of broadsides and then sail quickly away, no further attempt was made to bombard the harbour fortifications.

On shore the land artillery had little better success. When the British guns silenced Russian fire from the Redan and Malakoff, an assault might have succeeded. But the French were unable to breach the Russian defences and until they did so, no attack was possible. A supreme commander might well have poured assaulting troops of both armies through the gap in front of the British. But there was no supreme commander and Raglan 'wrung by the yoke of the alliance' was not prepared to act alone. The French, already discouraged by the number of guns which had concentrated on them rather than on the more distant British batteries, received a shattering blow to their morale about half-past ten. With a thunderous roar one of their powder magazines blew up when it received a direct hit. Sixteen men were killed instantly and thirty-seven others wounded as further explosions were touched off. For all his military experience Canrobert was shocked by this event and General Thiry, his artillery commander, was told that he should decide whether or not the French batteries should continue to fire. Thiry decided against continuing and at half-past ten the French batteries were silent. Word was sent to Raglan – who with everyone else could see the smoke billowing up from the scene of the disaster – that it was *not* one of the French magazines which had blown up but a new sort of shell which the Russians had thrown into their trenches. Raglan was not fooled and Canrobert's aide-de-camp, Major Vico, who had brought the news was told that he refused to believe 'such humbug'. Vico left, full of indignation, but soon returned with an apology from Canrobert for trying to misinform the British commander-in-chief, and a message to the effect that the French 'hoped' to open fire again next morning. 'Nobody, however, believed him'.[15] Canrobert's duplicity was regarded as being in poor taste and in the eyes of the British officers with whom he still had to deal for a long time, his word and reputation suffered.

Inside Sebastopol the land bombardment on the south of the town had a greater effect than the Allies realized, and if the French gunners had kept firing – or if Canrobert had agreed to a combined assault on the British front – Sebastopol might well have fallen. In Todleben's hastily constructed defence line there had been no time to revet the trenches and embrasures properly, no time to make fascines or dig the guns in properly. Under the ceaseless cannonade gabions were set on fire and even some of the emplacements began to crumple under the blast of their own cannon. Trying to repair them the defenders incurred many casualties. With the whole semi-circular line of defences covered in smoke it was impossible to see across the plateau to where the allied infantry was waiting. Russian columns, drawn up to withstand the expected attack were showered with flying earth and sometimes shattered as cannon balls shot over the ramparts into the ranks.

Admiral Korniloff, unconcerned about the cannon balls crashing down on the front line or oblivious to them, rode round the batteries encouraging the defenders. Coming back to the town for a late breakfast after visiting the Central Bastion he sent his watch to his wife by a courier, saying he was afraid it might get broken. It was a prophetic utterance. At the Malakoff an hour later a cannon ball shattered his left leg, and he died that night praying that God would 'bless Russia and the Emperor' and 'save Sebastopol and the fleet.'[16] There was no one to take his place. Menschikoff should have taken over at this critical juncture but he had left the town soon after his tour of inspection and was back with the field army. In consequence the garrison command was divided – Admiral Nakhimoff, who had also been wounded, being in charge of the sailors, while General Moller took over the land troops. Colonel Todleben – wearing his medals so that his body could be identified if he was killed in the bombardment – continued to act as an adviser, but he had no recognized authority.

By the middle of the afternoon the bombardment had reached a peak of violence, despite the fact that the batteries in the French sector had stopped firing. Todleben's defences in the vicinity of the Malakoff and the Redan were crumbling, and after nine hours waiting under fire the infantry columns had withdrawn to the shelter of the town. Soon after three o'clock, a shell exploded in one of the magazines in the Redan – killing over 100 men, dismounting the guns and smashing their carriages in a battery nearby – and the defences in that part of the line were completely paralysed.[17] The Russians' need for a leader capable of giving a boost to flagging morale was never more necessary. None was forthcoming, so in the circumstances it was lucky that the Allies lacked the resolve to see the operation through to its conclusion. Had an assault been launched soon after the Redan disaster Todleben considered it might well have succeeded.[18]

The only people to make a sortie that day were, in fact, the Russians themselves. Late that afternoon two hundred of them sallied forth against the French left flank, but they could not penetrate the devastating curtain of small-arms fire with which they were greeted. When they retired the Allies did not attempt to follow up and by the evening, when the guns fell silent, the operation was over. Twenty days' preparation had ended in a dismal failure. Canrobert decided to resume the bombardment two days later when his guns and magazines had been relocated in more secure positions and the confidence of the troops restored. But by this time the Russians had also recovered. The respite had enabled Todleben to repair and regroup his resources and although the new bombardment went on for six days it accomplished nothing. At the end of it the Allies had not gained a yard of ground, and the Russians were no worse off.

In effect – although the fact was not appreciated at the time – the Crimean expedition had now shown itself unequal to the task which it had been set six weeks before. And when its object was achieved nearly a year later few of those who had embarked in Bulgaria were there to share the triumph. A corrupted telegram told Europe that Sebastopol had fallen and that night – when the sun had set on the disappointed armies – salutes were being fired, bells rung and toasts drunk in London and Paris. When it was learned that the news was false, the reaction was that the celebration had merely anticipated the event by a few days. Those in the Crimea knew better. Officers who had been talking of a siege lasting no more than three days now discussed not how soon Sebastopol might fall but how on earth they would get away if it was not taken. In the Naval Brigade officers who had accepted bets that Sebastopol would not be captured by 19 October collected their winnings and offered the same odds against it falling within a month. Despondency took the place of careless optimism. Everybody recognized that the town would only be taken after a difficult and determined campaign. Tattered, wasted and sick, the troops now faced the grim possibility of a winter in the campaign. Whatever glamour there had been was gone. Few of the officers had a shirt to their backs and their red dress coats – they had no others – were black and ragged.

On the imminent horizon another cause for anxiety now appeared. Prince Menschikoff's army was reported to be hovering near the Tchernaya valley, within six miles of Balaclava.

BALACLAVA:
THE BATTLE OF THE SABRES

'The speed of the horse and the impetuous spirit that the constant habit
of riding seems to impart to the horseman, have in all ages caused the
cavalry service to be noted for its dashing and chivalrous temperament.
While steadiness and solidity have marked the infantry and artillery
arms, boldness and vigour have characterised the cavalry.'

A History of Cavalry, G. T. Denison, 1877

During the progress of the bombardment both sides received reinforcements. Shipping troops to the Middle East from Europe
raised a number of administrative snags and at this stage ships and
troops rarely appeared at appropriate ports at the same time. In
September the French had 10,000 men waiting in idleness at
Marseilles while the British had another 4,000 ready to sail but
only enough ships to take 700. Eventually however, after the British
had managed to collect enough steamships for themselves and had
loaned a few to the Emperor, 4,000 British troops and 7,700 French
were disembarked in dribs and drabs in the Crimea. On the Russian
side General Liprandi's 12th Division and a few reserve battalions
had joined Menschikoff's field army before the bombardment and
the rest of General Dannenberg's 4th Corps was on its way by forced
march from Odessa.

Pressed by Todleben to do something to ease the pressure on the
town and by the Tsar for some demonstrative action against the
insolent invaders, Menschikoff decided to seize the initiative. By
18 October he had assembled a force of about 25,000 men near the
village of Tchorgun on the north side of the Tchernaya valley, six
miles in a direct line north-east of Balaclava. As the occupation
of Tchorgun put the Russians within striking distance of his all-
important supply and communication centre, it may seem odd
that Raglan did not think it worth while to watch their movements
more closely. But in the absence of any method of aerial

reconnaissance, his information must necessarily have been derived from close daily observation and spies; his intelligence system was weak, and Raglan himself felt that the use of spies or information gained from deserters was strangely repugnant.*

Raglan's attention was riveted on Sebastopol and the preparations for another bombardment that would end in its capture and a speedy evacuation before winter set in. Insufficient thought appears to have been given to the security of the base. With his army on the heights above, Balaclava itself lay well outside the allied perimeter and although some provision had been made for it to have its own defensive system the inadequacy of these arrangements was soon to be apparent. Balaclava had powerful internal defences. But once through the narrow gorge, the Col de Balaclava, which connected the land-locked harbour to the north, the route to the allied armies ran across a plain extending three miles east to west. Closed to the west by the Sapoune Heights it was completely open on the eastern side. To the north, the plain was bounded by a bow-shaped cluster of hills called the Fedukhines over which ran the road to the Mackenzie Heights down which the allied armies had marched. Between the Fedukhine Hills and the gorge, a low ridge running due east and west divided the plain into two. Along this ridge, from the Sapoune Heights, ran the Woronzoff road, by-passing Balaclava and connecting Sebastopol with the extensive estates of Count Woronzoff to the south-east. These Causeway Heights, as they were called, were sufficiently lofty to conceal what was happening in the north valley from anyone in the south. Thus an enemy sweeping into the north valley from the east or over the Fedukhines could reach the top of the Causeway Heights and be within two miles of the harbour before being seen. To meet this threat, rather than to protect the road, five redoubts – roughly half a mile from each other – had been

---

* Raglan's staff officers took their lead from the commander-in-chief, and scorned the use of spies. The Russians had no such scruples, and Russian officers wearing British uniforms were discovered inspecting the French defences, while men in French uniforms – who scampered off in the direction of Sebastopol when challenged – frequently wandered through the British lines. British intelligence relied primarily on information supplied by Russian deserters (nearly all Poles) which was usually conflicting and unreliable, and on misleading reports supplied by the Turks. In fact on 24 October a message from a Turkish spy had been passed by way of Campbell and Lucan to Raglan to the effect that the Russian General Liprandi was going to attack Balaclava with 25,000 men the next morning. Raglan, believing it was a false alarm merely said politely, 'Very well'.

built along the causeway and a sixth on what was called Canrobert's Hill slightly to the south and on the extreme right of the British defences.

The tiny forts had been hastily constructed – one was built in a day – and their defences reflected careless optimism. Nobody seriously believed the Russians would attack Balaclava and the wide intervals between the forts, the fact that they were incapable of mutual support, lacked any effective support line and were a comparatively long way from Balaclava, were signs of a faulty disposition. To conserve his own manpower Raglan had entrusted the keeping of these exposed and dangerous posts to *esnan* – Turkish militia: one battalion in the Canrobert Redoubt and a half in the other three. Short of officers, the Turks had not been long in the army and never in action; ignorant and suspicious of their foreign masters there is some excuse for them believing that they had been put into the position by 'infidels' who were prepared to see them sacrificed. Because Raglan probably appreciated their latent un-reliability nine 12-pounder naval guns from H.M.S. *Diamond* were also deployed along this forward line – three on Canrobert's Hill and two in the next three redoubts running west, each gun being in the charge of a single British gunner.

For the immediate defence of Balaclava, Campbell had one infantry battalion and a field battery (Barker's) which were stationed at the village of Kadiköi near the northern entrance of the gorge. In the event of an attack it was obvious that the forts could expect little assistance from that direction. Only by withdrawing troops from the plateau could the redoubts be reinforced and by the time they had marched down to the plain it would almost certainly be too late. However, Lucan's cavalry division, neatly encamped in some orchards below the plateau – about a mile south of the Cause-way Heights at the extreme western end of the gorge – were considered to be admirably placed to take any attack on Balaclava in the flank. Under the muzzles of Bosquet's guns their orderly collections of tents and row upon row of picketed horses could plainly be seen from the heights above. Theoretically the cavalry might have been expected to have been vigorously reconnoitring and patrolling, as well as providing a mobile support to the Balaclava garrison. But as the Russian attack which was launched on 25 October, the anniversary of Agincourt, came as something of a surprise, Lucan's men seem to have been singularly ineffective in the reconnaissance role. Yet between the 17th and 25th there was a growing uneasiness – possibly because of the distant sound of military music in the Tchernaya valley and persistent reports from the local inhabitants to the effect that the Russians were concentrating less than six miles away. Even so there was no systematic reconnaissance, no careful posting of advanced pickets or vedettes, and the cavalry contented itself with standing to every morning an hour before dawn and picketing the ridge about a mile in front of Canrobert's Hill.

The night of 24 October 1854 was raw and cold, and although a chilly dawn brought a prospect of bright unclouded weather a feathery mist lay light on the hill tops. Conditions were ideal for a Russian attack and it seems that Lucan may have had a premonition of trouble brewing since he and his staff were out in the saddle riding towards Canrobert's Hill before daybreak – well before Cardigan had come up from his yacht in Balaclava harbour. Any premonition Lucan may have had was confirmed when he saw two flags fluttering over the forward redoubt (No. 2) in the early light; this was the pre-arranged signal indicating that the Russians were approaching. The alarm was given at 6 a.m. but it was over an hour later before the news reached Raglan at his headquarters and by the time the commander-in-chief had ridden to the edge of the plateau the Russians were storming the redoubt on Canrobert's Hill.

Under the direction of General Liprandi, four columns of Russian infantry had crossed the Tchernaya one hour before sunrise. On the left General Gribbe with three battalions had seized the village of Kamara; General Semiakin with another five battalions had advanced to assault Canrobert's Hill; on his right General Levontski's three battalions had been given the No. 2 Redoubt as his objective, and on Levontski's right Colonel Scuderi – advancing from the Traktir bridge with four battalions, a field battery and three squadrons of Cossacks – had been ordered to seize No. 3 Redoubt. Following these columns and ready to support them when the occasion arose was the main body of Russian cavalry.

Raglan's headquarters was in a farmhouse by the roadside not far above the Col de Balaclava, with Canrobert's headquarters a little farther up the same road. Half way between his administrative base and the front line, tactically it was a sensible location. From here it was easy for Raglan and his officers to ride along the bluff overlooking the Balaclava plain and observe what was going on. Thus, when the news reached him that the Russians were attacking the redoubts, he was able to ride to a vantage point which gave a panoramic view of the battlefield, from which he and his staff could watch the battle develop. But by the time Raglan reached his vantage point it was nearly eight o'clock and Canrobert's Hill had fallen. Outnumbered twelve to one, the Turks in this particular redoubt had resisted stubbornly and with great gallantry. When their positions were overrun the retreating survivors left more than a third of their number dead. The Russians now turned their artillery on to the other redoubts, and the Turks – demoralized by what they had seen happen to their compatriots – seized their blankets and personal kit and fled. Pursued by the Russian cavalry they surged across the valley and made for the road leading to Balaclava. To the few British soldiers they passed *en route* they shouted plaintively 'Ship! ... Ship!' and that they were being pursued by 'too many' Russians. Condemned as cowards and curs by all who watched from afar, the panicking Turks had gained a valuable hour of breathing space for their allies. In that hour Raglan had been told what was happening, orders issued for counter-action, and troops were deploying to meet the Russians. Outnumbered, outgunned, and in a precarious position where they would undoubtedly have been slaughtered the Turks, acceptance of their *khismet* is understandable. Without immediate reinforcements it is unlikely that any troops would have stood up to the Russian attack. As it was the 12-pounders were spiked by the lone British gunners, and the British cavalry took up a position across the valley, between Redoubts 4 and 5. But they were not able to prevent the Russians occupying the first four redoubts.

When Raglan gazed down at the panorama of the battlefield shortly after 7 a.m. the Russians could clearly be discerned closing in on Canrobert's Hill, and a troop of horse artillery was in action between No. 3 and 4 Redoubts. But only Lucan's 1,500 sabres and lances, and Campbell's meagre garrison stood between the Russians and the crowded confusion of Balaclava, and if Liprandi's marching battalions and jingling masses of cavalry had swept on over the plain the British base would almost certainly have fallen. (In the event the great blue and grey Russian squares halted, and when the advance was resumed, the offensive had lost its impetus and resolve. The allied commanders rarely displayed much capacity for original thought, but the Russian commanders easily surpassed them in this respect.) Thoroughly alarmed, Raglan ordered the 1st Division, under the Duke of Cambridge, and Cathcart's 4th Division to march down to the plain straight away. At the same time he sent a message to Lucan telling him to pull the cavalry back and closer in under the heights on which the commander-in-chief was standing, and another to alert the French. Canrobert, for whom the siege operations took precedence, saw the Russian threat as little more than a diversion. Reluctant to take it as seriously as Raglan, he was obliged to act. Bosquet was told to stand by, and 200 of the Chasseurs d'Afrique were ordered into the plain. (Subsequently Bosquet was to claim that the Light Brigade would have perished to a man if it had not been for the French. In fact very few French troops were ever engaged at Balaclava.)

At that moment the great mass of Russian cavalry could be seen moving slowly up the valley, parallel to, and north of, the Causeway Heights; and from this mass four squadrons were seen to break off, turn south and climb the Heights between Redoubts No. 3 and 4. Topping the rise these squadrons dropped into the south valley and stolidly resumed their march towards Kadiköi and Balaclava. Clearly this was a critical juncture in the battle. In the direct line between the Russians and Balaclava harbour there was now only Campbell's small force of infantry – 550 Highlanders of the 93rd, 40 Guardsmen who happened to be in Balaclava on fatigue duties that day, 100 convalescents waiting to return to their regiments, and two battalions of Turks. Deployed on the rear slopes overlooking a hillock at the north end of the approach road to Balaclava, the troops had been ordered to lie down when the Russians started to bombard the position. But as soon as the four squadrons were seen to wheel towards Balaclava, Campbell ordered them up on to the crest. Riding along the 'thin red line' of history he told them sternly that there must be no retreat, that they must die where they stood.

For a few brief moments the line waited in silence, and observers on the escarpment above have claimed that they could hear the heavy breathing of the horses and the tinkle of bits as the Russians jogged towards it. In the ranks the troops waited impatiently: rifles trained, waiting for the command 'Fire'. Then with a great shout the cavalry thundered up the hill, and at 600 yards a volley rang out from the 'thin red line topped with steel'. The range was too great; no one was hit and the Russians continued to advance. But when the second volley was delivered at 350 yards and supplemented by fire from the guns of Barker's battery the Russians wheeled to their left. Taking this as an attempt to cut in on his right, Campbell ordered the line to hold steady. 'Ninety-third, damn all that eagerness' he shouted, as he ordered the company on the right to swing out. Finally a third volley, delivered at 150 yards, visibly shook the Russians. Wheeling in the smoke, their formation broke and soon they were galloping back across the Causeway. From the safety of the Sapoune Heights the spectators surrounding Raglan, Canrobert and Bosquet – the staff officers, the 'hangers-on' and newspaper correspondents – shouted 'Bravo Highlanders' with misguided impetuosity. The Russians had been driven off, but they were certainly not beaten. Indeed, as they had left no dead on the ground when they galloped off, it might well appear that it was noise rather than the actual fire effect of the volleys which had caused the four squadrons to break.*

Whether the physical damage inflicted on the Russians was great or small however was of little consequence compared with the moral effect. Unbeknown to Raglan the Russian objective had not been Balaclava but the destruction of Barker's battery which they failed to achieve. The refusal of Campbell's infantry to be intimidated by the flourish and thunder of a powerful force of cavalry was something on which the Russians had not reckoned and it was altogether disconcerting. A worse humiliation was to come, however.

The main body of the Russian cavalry – about 3,000 men in blue and silver uniforms, commanded by General Rykoff – had been steadily advancing up the valley, unseen as yet by Lucan's two brigades. Level with the 4th Redoubt the Russians came under heavy fire from French guns on the escarpment, and their casualties accelerated their move across the causeway. Wheeling sharply to their left across the ridge they were now about half a mile ahead of the eight squadrons of Lucan's Heavy Brigade under command

---

* Whether or not the shooting caused casualties was the subject of much argument. Years later a Russian officer who took part in the charge said that the second and third volleys had hit very many men and horses but that they all reached the shelter of the Causeway before collapsing.

of Brigadier-General Scarlett,* which Lucan had sent to help Campbell. Both forces saw each other about the same time, and both appreciated that a clash was inevitable.

Fifty-five year old Brigadier-General the Honourable James Yorke Scarlett was caught both unprepared and at a disadvantage. Because he was a capable and courageous man, however, he was able to turn the situation to his advantage and to perform one of the few remarkable deeds of the war. Prior to this campaign he had seen no active service; indeed he had been on the point of retiring in 1853. But, unlike his colleague Cardigan, he did not discount the value of active service and for this reason he had selected as his aide-de-camp a certain Captain Alexander Elliot, late of the 8th Bengal Cavalry, who had seen some fighting in India. In the circumstances the 'Heavies' could not have had two better men to lead them.

Because of the nature of the terrain Scarlett's Brigade was moving towards the gorge in two irregularly spaced columns. A squadron of Inniskilling Dragoons, and two squadrons of Scots Greys were leading; another Inniskilling squadron was coming up on the right, and behind them were the 5th Dragoons. In the rear, but halted because they were not included in the force Scarlett was taking to Kadiköi, were the 4th Dragoons. Thus the total force immediately available to Scarlett mustered only about 300 sabres. Nor was the Russian numerical superiority the only factor with which the Heavy Brigade commander had to contend. He was also at a tactical disadvantage, as the Russians were on higher ground, and there was a vineyard limiting movement on his left flank. (Beyond this vineyard was the old Light Brigade camp – hurriedly struck that morning, then ravaged by Turks fleeing from No. 4 Redoubt, and now a cluttered mess of tent poles, guy ropes and abandoned equipment.)

When the great blue and silver block of Russian cavalry first came into view on the skyline it had been moving in a slow orderly fashion. But then it had halted, and while Scarlett was moving his

* With the Light Brigade only a few hundred yards away, about 4,000 horsemen were concentrated in an area not much bigger than a racecourse. But as neither side had any scout or flank guards out and fortuitous folds in the ground concealed them, Rykoff's troops and those of Lucan remained blissfully unaware of each other's presence. To those watching from the plateau, sipping sherry and eating sandwiches, the atmosphere was more like that of a field-day than war.

leading squadrons into line it had waited. Meanwhile Lucan, having seen the Russians cross the Causeway, had galloped up and ordered Scarlett to charge without any further delay. Scarlett was not to be hurried, and he insisted on aligning his troopers as if they were on parade. Only when he was satisfied with the dressing did he ride to the front of the three squadrons which were about to engage a force numerically ten times as strong.

Throughout the ceremonial ritual Rykoff's cavalrymen had simply sat and stared down the slope at the impudent performance of the red-coated troopers three hundred and fifty yards away. By all the accepted rules of cavalry warfare they should have charged down and engulfed the Heavies. Yet they waited, fascinated perhaps by the imperturbability and confidence of their enemies. They had heard of the terrible Foot Guards at the Alma and no doubt the tall black bearskins of the Scots Greys made them wonder whether the same troops had been put on horses. But then, as Scarlett completed his unhurried preparations, the front of the Russian phalanx began to curve outwards with slow methodical precision and the whole mass began to advance. Up on the Sapoune Ridge the spectators waited breathlessly; by comparison Campbell's fight was less exciting than this.

Turning to his trumpeter Scarlett said curtly: 'Sound the charge,' and as the notes rang out, the Heavy Brigade tore off in a thunderous gallop up the hill, with the brigadier fifty yards in the lead. There were now less than three hundred yards to go before the brigade smashed into the Russian ranks. Soon the two sides were inextricably mixed and pandemonium broke out as Scarlett's troopers cut and slashed their way through. As they carved their way forward inside the mass the Russians edged in from the flanks to close their broken ranks, and it was now that Lucan showed a momentary and, for him, unusual flash of insight. Ordering the 4th Dragoons to attack the right flank of the Russian column, as the Royals charged the pivoting front, he hurled the 5th Dragoons at the centre. In less than five minutes it was over; as the flank attack came in the Greys and Inniskillings emerged from the chaos and the Russians reeled, broke up and turned to scatter in complete disorder.

The action was all over in eight minutes and casualties on both sides were surprisingly light. The British suffered about 80, of whom most were wounded; the Russians lost about 200 of whom again the majority were wounded. The congestion in the packed ranks, blunt sabres and the thick greatcoats worn by the Russians all contributed to this result. The British trooper had been trained to slash rather than to use the point of his sabre and Russian uniforms were exceptionally thick. But the moral effect was great. Throughout the remainder of the war there was scarcely a Russian squadron that could be trusted to hold its ground on the approach of the British Cavalry. Despite its limited results there can be no question that the Heavy Brigade won a neat, clean-cut and important success, and it was no fault of theirs that this success was not expanded into one of the greatest cavalry exploits in history. To grasp how incomplete was Scarlett's triumph it is only necessary to ask what the Light Brigade was doing when Rykoff's squadrons wheeled across its front and crossed the causeway. Drawn up not more than a quarter of a mile from the Russian right flank with its first line of three regiments mounted, it was ideally placed for a dash into the demoralized Russians. Such a dash by this well-trained, eager brigade should have converted a hurried retirement into headlong flight, and this is what the spectators in the 'gallery' were expecting. But to the amazement of the observers and the fury of the cavalrymen concerned, the Light Brigade remained glued to the ground.

To explain its inactivity it is necessary to glance briefly at the character of its commander, Cardigan. Inexperienced in war and a soldier by drill-book only, he was one who believed that under no circumstances is a soldier who receives an order from his superior officer justified in disobeying it. And before Lucan had ridden off to join Scarlett he had told Cardigan that Raglan had ordered the Light Brigade to occupy the ground on which he was now standing, and to defend it; the brigade was not to move away or get involved in anything beyond the confines of its immediate surroundings. To Cardigan such orders permitted only a literal interpretation. Moreover, consumed as he was with jealousy of Lucan, he was not prepared to give his detested brother-in-law the slightest excuse for complaint about his actions. If he worked 'to rule' Lucan, not he, would take the blame for anything that went wrong. Had the locations and roles of the two brigades been reversed there is little doubt that Scarlett – either on his own initiative or on Alexander Elliot's advice – would have launched an immediate attack against the compelling target which now presented itself. But Cardigan was immovable. Scarlett's success irked him, and as he rode up and down in front of his squadrons he was heard to mutter sulkily, 'Damn those Heavies, they've the laugh of us today.' Captain Morris commanding the 17th Lancers, and an officer of much experience acquired in the Sikh wars, pleaded with Cardigan for an attack by the Brigade, or, if not, by his own two squadrons. But Cardigan was adamant; once possessed of an idea no argument would ever make him change his mind. To Morris's appeals the response was '. . . My orders are explicit; we must remain here'. When at length the angry Morris wheeled his horse and rode back to his regiment, slapping his leg with his drawn sword, he was heard to exclaim, 'My God, my God, what a chance we are losing!'

No statement could have been more true. After five frustrating weeks the magnificent Light Brigade had a real chance to prove its worth. There were no obstacles, no vineyards or camps, between itself and the retreating Russians. Within a matter of minutes the Light Brigade could have smashed into their enemy's flank and rear; drawing the Russians off the causeway, past the redoubts and across the Tchernaya. There need never have been another charge that day and Balaclava might well have become the classic example in military literature of the superiority of the *armes blanches* when properly and aggressively used. But the golden opportunity which Napoleon said 'comes but once' was allowed to slip away, and the disorganized and shaken Russians soon gained the shelter of the guns from which the Light Brigade was soon to take such terrible punishment. Once they had reached the redoubts they were safe, and so far as General Liprandi was concerned the battle of Balaclava was as good as over. He had failed to achieve his objective, and when he brought his infantry and artillery up through the Fedukhine Hills it was to cover his retirement and not to resume the offensive. The morale of his troops had suffered as a result of the stand made by Campbell's garrison and the charge of the 'Heavies'. Nor was the effect confined solely to the Russian cavalry. The sight of their horsemen being driven back by a third of their number had had an unsettling effect on the infantry and those occupying the captured redoubts on the causeway were in no mood to remain in the isolated position in which they found themselves when the cavalry streamed past. If Raglan had but held his hand the chances are that the redoubts would have been evacuated by the following morning. Admittedly the nine spiked naval 12-pounders would probably have been lost but – as Canrobert had pointed out – the prosecution of the siege while the fine weather lasted was far more important than diversionary engagements.*

From Raglan's point of view, however, the Russians appeared to have won the battle – despite the success of the Heavy Brigade. They were still in possession of three of the redoubts and in control of the Woronzoff road along the causeway; their cavalry was now rallying and regrouping; in the jumble of hills to the left front their infantry could be seen advancing and there appeared a good deal of activity in and around the redoubts. From his vantage point the situation did not look at all healthy, and at this juncture Raglan's chagrin may well have been affected by his customary concern about what the French would think. Why he should conclude that the Russian column stretching towards him along the line of redoubts might prove 'soft to the touch' is not clear, but in the event he issued orders for a combined cavalry and infantry operation. To Lucan, an urgent written message was sent: 'Cavalry to advance and take advantage of any opportunity to recover the heights. They will be supported by the Infantry, which have been ordered to advance on two fronts'. Clearly the essence of this order was that the operation should be a joint one and when he received it Lucan shifted the Heavy Brigade to the opposite side of the ridge to await the arrival of the infantry. Before the infantry had had time to get down to the battlefield, however, Raglan had decided that the Russians would have to be evicted from the redoubts. This decision to initiate more aggressive measures was based on movements which seemed to indicate the immediate withdrawal of the captured guns. (According to Lucan's evidence in the House of Lords, Raglan misjudged what he saw through his glasses because the guns were not in fact being withdrawn.)[1] Lucan, waiting for the infantry to arrive did not consider that the 'opportunity to recapture the heights' had yet arrived. Like Cardigan, Lucan was another drill-book soldier. Nevertheless his decision to wait seems both logical and justifiable. To attack – with cavalry alone – an unknown force in a position containing three strong points which the Russians had had three hours to consolidate would be nothing short of madness. But as the minutes drifted by – 30, 40 – some who were present said 50 – and

---

* The Russians claimed later that this action *was* intended only as a diversion. Menschikoff was waiting for the rest of Dannenberg's 4th Corps before he mounted the full-scale attack which took place on 5 November.

the cavalry remained motionless Raglan was growing increasingly impatient. If the captured guns were being pulled out, it would seem that the situation had changed. Removing the guns would indicate that the Russians were voluntarily abandoning the redoubts and so the question of 'recovering the heights' would no longer be a question of cavalry charging strongly defended localities. No commander likes to see some of his artillery being carried away before his eyes and probably his chagrin was exacerbated by the presence of Canrobert and his staff who were with him on the edge of the escarpment. The question 'What will the French think' was never far from Raglan's mind. At the same time there can be no doubt that he was specially moved by what he thought he could see, and possibly the significant phrase from the Duke of Wellington's funeral ode: 'Nor ever lost a gun', was ringing in his ears.

Whether Raglan was justified in his decision to order the cavalry to act is a matter for conjecture. From the point of view of trophies the guns could be considered to have been handed over to the Turks, and it was the Turks who had lost them. Furthermore, if the Russians wanted to carry them off it seems logical to suppose that they would withdraw them ahead of their infantry, and it would be most unlikely that the British cavalry would ever get near them. Or if the Russians could not do this they would certainly make them unfit for further action. This is not to suggest that Raglan could watch complacently while the guns were being removed, but there can be no question that if it had not been for this display of chivalry the disaster to the Light Brigade would never have occurred. Thus it may be concluded that the generous emotion of the soldier got the better of the prudent calculations of the commander-in-chief.

Of the British officers watching the scene with Raglan at least two were aides-de-camp. An aide-de-camp, though technically on the staff is not a staff officer in the sense that he shares in the deliberations of his superiors, is consulted by them or entitled to offer an opinion or advice. His job is to see to the personal administrative needs of his general, and – when required – to act as a messenger. But one of these aides-de-camp, Captain Nolan, was no ordinary officer. Although only thirty-five, this son of an Irish father and Italian mother had served in a regiment of Hungarian cavalry before buying a commission in the British army. Before becoming a captain in the 15th Hussars he had seen active service in India and he was a fluent linguist, a brilliant swordsman and a fine horseman.

Nolan had also studied his profession, but because he was the author of a little book on *Cavalry*, which had attracted considerable attention, fellow cavalry officers – especially senior ones – tended to regard him with suspicion. A passionate believer in the power of cavalry as an arm, outspoken in his criticism and impatient of the performance of the mounted arm in the campaign so far, Nolan was to become the key figure in the action that ensued.

In the discussion in which Raglan was involved Nolan took no part. But he was able to survey the field for himself, had seen the Russian cavalry escape wholesale disaster after the charge of the 'Heavies', and it is possible that he overheard scraps of the excited conversation – phrases such as 'The Russians are off', 'They're removing the guns', 'Now's Lucan's chance . . .'. With his boundless enthusiasm for the power of cavalry boldly used, and his opinion of Lucan and Cardigan as incompetent bunglers, Nolan was bound to speculate on the possibilities of what might be done to retrieve what he considered to be the shame of the morning. His speculations were cut short when – much to his own surprise and that of others nearby – Raglan called for him to take a message to Lord Lucan. In the event it was a disastrous choice. But as Nolan was not 'next for duty', the reason why he was selected to ride down to the plain appears to have been his well-known skill as a rider. Raglan wanted the message to reach Lucan as quickly as possible, and no one could get down the hill quicker than Nolan. Because of its urgency, when the message was handed over at about a quarter to eleven, no detailed explanation of what it contained was given to Nolan. But it was believed that Raglan said something like 'Tell Lord Lucan the cavalry is to attack immediately'.

And so the order which for many years was to become the subject of acrimonious and inconclusive debate was despatched. It had been written – badly written – in pencil on a light blue leaf torn from a pocket book, not by Raglan himself but by Airey. How exactly the order was composed is obscure. It is possible that it was dictated by Raglan to Airey and then handed by the latter to Nolan; according to Lucan (who was obviously not present), it was first delivered orally to Nolan by Airey, who then called him back and scribbled the gist of it on paper. What was actually written reads as follows.

'Lord Raglan wishes the cavalry to advance rapidly to the front, and try to prevent the enemy carrying away the guns. Troop of Horse Artillery may accompany. French cavalry is on your left. Immediate,

R. Airey.

Into such an ambiguous order – oddly expressed as a 'wish' – it is possible to read several meanings. The cavalry had been ordered to advance to 'the front'. As the Light Brigade was in the North Valley looking down it and the Heavy Brigade on the slopes forming the southern edge of the same valley, it is not clear where an advance on the front would lead: down the valley, or up on to the Causeway Heights. 'Try to prevent the enemy carrying away the guns' could be little short of baffling. From where Lucan was sitting neither enemy nor guns were visible; Raglan had forgotten that what he could see from a vantage point 800 feet above the battlefield was not necessarily visible to an officer on the ground below. Similarly, vague reference to 'the guns' introduced another inexcusable uncertainty, since it was not clear whether these guns were the British pieces lost by the Turks or the Russians' own artillery. If it was the latter that were being limbered up preparatory to a Russian retreat against which the cavalry were expected to act, the order did make some sense since guns out of action were recognized to be a notoriously vulnerable objective. Finally the allusion to French cavalry 'on your left' was also incomprehensible. The Chasseurs d'Afrique who had taken up a position behind the Light Brigade had not been given any orders to do anything and the message did not imply any movement, position or direction. The only thing that can be said in excuse of the ambiguity of the message is that Raglan and Airey might well have thought it unnecessary to weigh words nicely. Time being the all-important factor it was not unreasonable to expect that any obscurities could be explained by its bearer – if he knew what was expected. But even if Nolan had had matters explained to him in simple terms it is unlikely that he would have interpreted the message dispassionately. Excited by and furious at Cardigan's apparent indolence, his own concern was to give the cavalry a chance to show its mettle.

Nolan galloped down by the road and over the plain to find Lucan in the saddle, half-way between his two brigades. In the time he had taken to deliver the message, the observers on the hill had concluded that their first impressions of the Russians pulling out the guns from the redoubts had been wrong. Not that this made any difference. Lucan, who had been in the saddle since before dawn – who was tired and possibly hungry – was frankly bewildered by the order which Nolan brought. All he could make out was that he was to attack 'rapidly' an unknown battery in some position not revealed to him. It seemed absurd to suppose that Raglan expected him to send the cavalry down the North Valley to attack artillery at the far end, while both sides of it were held in strength. In such circumstances his men would be advancing into a positive death-trap; clearly the order was impracticable. Nor did Nolan's attitude help. Neither man liked the other. Not only did the irascible Lucan share the common antipathy of regimental officers towards the staff, he was also well aware of Nolan's opinions about his management of the cavalry brigade. In Lucan's eyes Nolan was as much an insufferable arrogant and ambitious prig as in Nolan's view Lucan was an exasperating and incompetent nincompoop. Had only a moderate degree of affability existed between Lucan and Raglan's messenger it is possible – though by no means certain – that Lucan might have questioned Nolan and interpreted his message in a different way. As it was Lucan reacted just as a sensitive but stupid man might react. To Nolan's curtly delivered and peremptory words 'Lord Raglan's orders are that the cavalry shall attack immediately', he snarled petulantly, 'Attack, sir! Attack what . . . ? Guns . . . what guns?' At this both men lost their tempers – Lucan because of the ambiguity of his orders, Nolan because of Lucan's hesitation – and, what was quickly developing into an unseemly squabble between a captain and a lieutenant-general was cut short by Nolan's hot, angry and insubordinate reply: '*There*, my Lord, is your enemy; *there* are your guns.' As he spoke the impetuous aide-de-camp waved his arm in a rebellious gesture towards the rolling skyline of the Causeway.

Stung by the taunt, Lucan felt that the last word had been delivered; the Light Brigade would advance down the valley and he would follow on with the 'Heavies'. Trotting off alone, he made for the ground in front of the 13th Light Dragoons where Cardigan had positioned himself, while Nolan rode into the interval between the 13th and 17th Lancers to tell his friend Captain Morris that he proposed to ride with the Light Brigade. In front of the troops, Lucan then held a brief conference with Cardigan. The two brothers-in-law regarded each other contemptuously but observed the customary military punctilio. According to Lucan,[2] Cardigan was not shown the written order, but told to advance at a steady pace with four squadrons, keeping the rest in hand. 'My idea was that he was to use his discretion . . . it was clearly his duty to have handled his brigade as I did the Heavy Brigade.'[3] Cardigan's version was that he was given orders to attack the Russians in the valley and that he pointed out that an advance down the valley between batteries of guns and riflemen to attack a battery of guns at the far end was a lunatic operation.* To this Lucan gave some sign of consent, but shrugged his shoulders and said that it was Raglan's positive orders. Some discussion on the arrangement of Cardigan's brigade† followed and then Cardigan brought down his sword in salute before riding to speak with Lord George Paget, commanding the 4th Light Dragoons. As he turned away from Lucan he is reputed to have muttered 'Well, here goes the last of the Brudenells'. To Paget, he said 'Lord George, we are ordered to make an attack to the front . . . and I expect your best support; mind, your best support'.[4] Then at about ten minutes past eleven, when the three lines were dressed and steady, Cardigan placed himself in front of the leading squadrons and speaking quietly, gave the fatal order: 'The brigade will advance. Walk. March. Trot.'

The first line went off at an easy trot and the others followed at drill-book intervals; Paget, at the head of his Dragoons in the third line, was smoking a cigar as he jogged along. Trotting down the valley the brigade of rather more than six hundred men must have seemed a brave sight. Cardigan himself was wearing the distinctive uniform of his old regiment, the 11th Hussars, and riding a chestnut charger 'Ronald'‡ with white 'stockings' on the near fore- and hind-

---

* At the Mansion House in February 1855, following an official lunch, Cardigan delivered a long-winded and egotistical speech: 'It was late in the afternoon when I received an order to attack the Russian forces posted in the valley, which consisted of a long line of guns drawn up in the form of batteries. I received that order, my Lord Mayor, and I obeyed it. I delivered that order myself to the brigade under my command. I ordered them to attack the Russians in the valley, but my Lord, I must say that on that occasion, it being my duty to give the order to my men, I did give it, though I deeply regretted it at the time . . .'

† The 13th Light Dragoons and the 17th Lancers were drawn up in the first line, then came the 11th Hussars; and in a third line the 4th Light Dragoons and 8th Hussars.

‡ Ronald has taken his place in history with 'Bucephalus', 'Copenhagen' and 'Marengo', the horses of Alexander the Great, Wellington and Napoleon. He died on 23 June 1872, eighteen years after the charge. His head

legs – facts which should be borne in mind. To begin with the pace
was a trot, for with horses in poor condition and with nearly a mile
and a half to go, a steady advance was essential. Actually, and
contrary to a legend that has been perpetuated, the 'Charge' was
never sounded. Nor did Cardigan, once his brigade was in action,
issue any order or command by voice, trumpet or signal. Erect
on his charger, without speaking, without gesture and without ever
turning in the saddle, 'the rigid hussar' picked out the central flash
of the Russian battery, steered on it as his mark and showed his
troops '. . . the straight, honest way – the way down to the enemy's
guns.'[5]

As the first line, consisting of the 13th Light Dragoons and 17th
Lancers gathered speed an incident occurred around which controversy still rages. Nolan, riding in the front line, spurred his horse
and galloped obliquely across the front from left to right. As he
crossed the path of the brigade commander he turned in his saddle,
pointed frantically with his sword, and shouted something which
could not be heard above the thunder of hooves and clatter of
accoutrements. At that moment a Russian shell from one of the
Causeway batteries burst near Cardigan and a fragment of jagged
iron tore into Nolan's chest. Nolan's sword dropped and his horse
turned back towards the advancing line. Nolan remained erect in
the saddle and as it passed through the line of Dragoons a fearful
agonizing cry burst from his lips. A few yards farther Nolan dropped
from the saddle, dead. Cardigan rode on angrily. He had seen Nolan
pass him – 'riding to the rear', he thought, 'screaming like a woman'.
To him it was a clear case of insubordination; and he made a mental
note to put Nolan under close arrest after the action – with a view to
a court martial. For the moment his attention was fully occupied
with more pressing considerations. From the hills to the right and
left of the line of advance, guns and rifles were now opening fire.
The Russians at the far end of the Causeway who were beginning
to withdraw, now stood firm – watching the incomprehensible
British cavalry with astonishment.

What had Nolan meant to do? Three explanations have been

was stuffed and is preserved at Deene Hall, Cardigan's seat, with his tail,
and one hoof mounted as an inkstand. Two other hooves are known to be
in existence: one in the Regimental Officers' Mess of the 11th Hussars and
the other in the Guard Room of Windsor Castle. Wearing his full regalia,
Ronald followed the coffin of his master on 6 April 1868.

suggested. Of these the first is rather hinted at than definitely expressed. It is that Nolan had galloped down with no knowledge of the contents of the message he carried; that he was exasperated by its confusing contents and by Lucan's apparent hesitation, and was determined that the cavalry should do something quickly; that he gave the guns in the valley as the objective because they were the first thing he could think of; and that, the advance once started, he had decided to 'take charge' and force Cardigan's hand should there be any sign of checking the advance. As has been said, this theory has merely been hinted at and it has several obviously weak points. The second suggestion is that Nolan was convinced that Raglan meant the cavalry to charge the guns in the valley, but that he (Nolan) – brooding over the inactivity of the Light Brigade during the morning – was afraid that Cardigan might not have the determination to 'go all out' and that the steady trot might degenerate into a halt rather than accelerate into a gallop and a charge. In this case Nolan wanted – contrary to all the rules of discipline and etiquette – to get the brigade into a gallop and then let the rest take care of itself. If this suggestion appears absurd it is quite clear that some such theory occurred to Cardigan and, quite naturally, he was furious at the insult he conceived had been directed at him in front of his brigade. The third suggestion – and the one most commonly accepted – is that Nolan never had any idea of a charge down the valley; that he understood Lucan interpreted Raglan's order as one to prevent the Russians removing the naval guns from the redoubts and that now, seeing Cardigan heading straight down the valley, he rushed out to try to turn the brigade and get it to make for the Causeway Heights. The theory is plausible, but leaves unanswered the question: Why did Nolan point towards the valley when saying '*There* are your guns'? Kinglake, the contemporary historian, answers it with an airy statement to the effect that the difference was after all little more than 20 degrees. But 20 degrees are a great deal in direction and it makes all the difference in the world when in the one case it means pointing down a valley and in the other pointing to the top of a ridge which bounds it.*

Another possible solution not previously considered is that Nolan rode down to Lucan convinced that the Russian guns down the

---

* As the angle between valley and ridge was in fact 30 – not 20 – degrees, the theory is correspondingly weakened.

valley were the objective Raglan intended, but that when the advance began his attention was caught by guns firing from the Causeway Heights. That scraps of the conversation heard in the 'gallery' above now came back to him, but with a different meaning. That possibly the words 'the guns' which he remembered in conjunction with other scraps of conversation now took on the significance not of the Russian guns at the end of the valley, but of the naval guns captured from the Turks. That in a flash he realized the possibility that he had been preoccupied with thoughts of Russian guns and failed to make the correct deduction. And that now, *for the first time*, he realized his error. He had induced Lucan to send the Light Brigade to destruction. What was to be done? It would be useless to try to explain to the long-winded and pompous Cardigan. He would probably halt the brigade, exposed in the open, and demand a full explanation. The only course open seemed to be to dash to the front and try to head the brigade in the right direction, and explain when it was racing for the Causeway. And so he hurled himself to the front – frantically waving his sword towards the Causeway Heights.

'Someone had blundered'.[6] Nolan certainly committed some blunder, but if he did so it was because of a series of blunders on the part of his superiors. On the Causeway some of the headquarters staff, looking through their fieldglasses, *thought* they could see horses being brought forward with lassoo tackle; they *thought* that this must mean that the Russians were about to take away the captured naval guns; and this made them *think* that the Russians were about to retreat. Thus, although these theories were wrong Raglan blundered in deciding to send the cavalry to act. (There was, of course, no question of recovering the Heights if – as supposed at the time – the Russians were voluntarily abandoning them.) Raglan blundered again in forgetting – as he obviously did – that Lucan's range of view was something quite different from what he could see from the heights above; and the fact that he sent an order to Lucan about the guns and the recipient had to ask, 'What guns?' is sufficient evidence of the fact that the order was a confusing one. Lucan blundered in not making any real attempt to get the meaning of Raglan's orders clear and Cardigan blundered in 'attacking' when he had merely been given the order to 'advance'. (At the subsequent inquiry Lucan expressly put his opinion on record that Cardigan 'should have halted his squadrons as soon as he found there was no useful object to be gained, but great risk to be incurred.'

Automatically, as the advance progressed the pace increased, and in spite of Cardigan's desire to keep the Light Brigade under his control until the very last minute it swept forward at an ever increasing rate. Before half the distance had been crossed heavy casualties were being suffered and those on the plateau watching the brigade receding could see that on the course it was following it was riding to annihilation. Cardigan, plainly discernible in his red overalls on the white-stockinged Ronald, was expected to wheel to the right and lead his squadrons on to the Causeway. Soon it was seen that not only was he not going to divert the line of advance but that it was too late to do so. There was no checking of the pace and as horses and men were knocked over the survivors closed in and the line contracted – their movements having all the precision of a piece of machinery. The spirit of the men who rode in the charge may be gauged by the words of a trooper of the 13th Light Dragoons who shouted to another, 'Come on! Don't let those bastards [the 17th Lancers] get in front of us.'

In the front of the charging brigade was a line of twelve brass cannon which became the objective. With an echoing roar these guns were firing simultaneous salvoes, while at the same time infantry and other guns on the hills were pouring deadly converging streams of shot or canister and bullets into the flanks of the brigade at a range of less than a quarter of a mile. Above the pealing crash of the artillery the chatter of musketry fire sounded like the irregular tapping of great drumsticks. Riders and men fell, some dead, some wounded, to lie still or drag themselves painfully away from the carnage. But still the brigade kept on, so perfect was their discipline. (And even as the charge proper got under way Cardigan remembered his drill-book – stretching out his level sword across the chest of Captain White of the Lancers to warn him not to draw ahead of the brigade commander.)

After about eight minutes from the time the advance had begun, the first line – or what remained of it – had almost reached the objective. A mass of cavalry and infantry was drawn up behind the guns and across the end of the valley. At a range of about eighty yards these guns now fired a final salvo which blasted most of what was left of the first line to destruction. Yet Cardigan was untouched – although the wind of one shot was so fierce that he thought he had lost a leg. Ronald swerved violently but his rider regained control, jammed in his spurs, and forced a way through the gap between two of the Russian guns. He was the first man to get inside the enemy's battery.* The din and confusion were indescribable. A pall of smoke hung over everything; guns were roaring; there was a continuous crackle of musketry, shouts and screams of men and horses together with the sound of blows as the cavalry lunged at the Russians with their sabres. Cardigan himself sped on past guns and limbers and soon found himself almost isolated facing a large body of Russian cavalry standing at the halt about a hundred yards away. Before he could check his course this distance had been reduced to a mere twenty yards or so. The thickest of the smoke was now behind and in the comparative clearness a Russian officer recognized in the gorgeously caparisoned hussar a former acquaintance of a London drawing-room. Some Cossacks were ordered to capture the Englishman and a scuffle ensued in which Cardigan was slightly wounded by one Cossack and nearly un-horsed by the lance of another. But he got away, and – somewhat bewildered – decided that the only thing left for him to do was to get out of the position as quickly as possible. Turning his horse he galloped back towards the Russian guns and then through them to follow the wreck of his first line retreating up the valley. The ground was littered with men and horses but the brigade itself had disintegrated and Cardigan could not see what had happened to the second and third lines.

When he started on the advance Cardigan does not seem to have had any definite scheme in mind or, if he had, he did not explain it to his subordinates. Beyond directing Paget to render his 'best support' with the third line there is no evidence to show that he told any of the other commanding officers what to do. Indeed the whole episode was so unreal that Lucan said afterwards that it was completely beyond his comprehension. Cardigan had never tried to interpret Lucan's order to advance as anything other than a command to proceed to his own martyrdom, and no doubt it was this belief which minimized in his mind the necessity of entering

* That is to say of the charge proper. Actually the first appears to have been Captain Oldham of the 13th Light Dragoons. He was riding his second charger, a white mare, which bolted with her rider early in the charge and Oldham was last seen vanishing in the whirl of smoke of the last salvo.

into a brief explanation of what the Light Brigade was to do if and when they reached the guns at the end of the valley. Cardigan considered that for some reason or other his brigade was to be sacrificed, and that it was most unlikely that either he or any useful fragment of it would ever reach its undefined objective. Consequently, while galloping back from the abortive charge, he was probably the most astonished man in the Crimea – astonished to find himself in the enemy's position on a sound charger and practically unscathed himself.

Probably to him the disconcerting fact was that he was alone. But his isolation was due to the fact that of his first line of four weak squadrons the greater part had been practically blown to pieces or knocked over in the advance. (Some survivors had forced a passage through the guns on either side of Cardigan, and a small residuum had got past them round the flanks.) Of the second and third lines, the bulk had swept round the guns or were at that moment just doing so and had passed out of sight. Cardigan could therefore see nothing of his brigade but swarms of wounded men, mounted and on foot, slowly making their way back up the valley. One thing that would be clear to him at that moment was that the Heavy Brigade was not coming down in support and he may even have thought it possible that his own third line (the 4th Light Dragoons and 8th Hussars) might have been held back by Lucan so as to avoid a useless sacrifice of it. He had himself rigidly refrained from turning in his saddle during the advance and thus he was unable to tell with certainty how much of his brigade had actually followed him. So numerous were the wounded stragglers moving up the valley that Cardigan concluded they must all be survivors of the complete brigade and not just of the first line. In these circumstances he decided the best thing to do was to follow up the stream of retiring wounded. Thus, when Paget got back to the start line with the mounted remnants of the brigade some twenty minutes later, the first person to greet him was Cardigan. Utterly surprised, Lord George involuntarily exclaimed 'Why, Lord Cardigan, were you not there?' There was a titter from the bystanders, but Cardigan answered at once, 'Wasn't I though? Here Jenyns, did you not see me at the guns?' (The individual called to corroborate his statement was a Captain Jenyns of the 13th Light Dragoons, one of the survivors of the first line.)

So ended one of the most unaccountable episodes in British

Balaclava Town.

Balaclava's land-locked harbour.

The 'Thin Red line'
of history; the 93rd
Highlanders at Bala-
clava.

THE CARDIGAN GALOP.
BY
CARL HÖCHST.

A contemporary
cartoon of the Earl
of Cardigan.

military history. It only remained for the survivors to crawl or walk, struggle, trot or run up the valley. The 4th Chasseurs d'Afrique had succeeded in silencing the batteries and driving away the infantry on the Fedukhine Hills. This made the return of the fugitives less perilous and secured one flank from which they could not be harried. If this move had been supported on the opposite side of valley by an attack on the Causeway Heights it is possible that the outcome of the day might have been different. But it was not to be. Neither Cathcart nor Campbell made any move of importance and Lucan withdrew the Heavy Brigade when they came under fire. He was not going to risk what remained of the Cavalry Division. '*They* have sacrificed the Light Brigade,' he said. 'They shall not the "Heavy" if I can help it.'

Meantime at the site of their old camp where they had collected together, the survivors of the charge are reputed to have given three cheers for Cardigan when he joined them. He spoke to them saying that the charge had been a foolish one but that he was not responsible for it. 'Never mind my Lord, we'd do it again' shouted some of the men. 'No, no' replied Cardigan, 'You have done enough.'

Of the 673 men who had charged down the valley less than 200 returned. 113 were killed and 134 wounded; 475 horses were either killed in the fight or were shot immediately afterwards. Welcome reinforcements of horses were provided by the Russians when some of their horses stampeded that night and found their way to the British lines. As only 195 mounted men answered the roll call after the charge the Light Brigade could no longer be considered to be in existence. Asked by Raglan to explain what he meant by attacking a battery in front 'contrary to all the usages of warfare and the customs of the service,' Cardigan replied, 'My Lord, I hope you will not blame me for I received the order to attack from the superior officer in front of the troops.' Turning to Lucan the commander-in-chief then observed briefly 'You have lost the Light Brigade'. Lucan defended himself by referring to his orders but Raglan retorted that he should have used his discretion.

When it came to apportioning responsibility for the disaster Raglan, Airey (who had transcribed Raglan's orders, or composed them in terms of his own), Lucan and Cardigan were all cited. Among the cavalry the general feeling was that Cardigan had done everything that was expected of him – and more. His return from the charge had been in the nature of an anti-climax but that could not obliterate the fact that he had shown the way to the guns in first-class style. Invalided home at the end of November, he found himself the idol of the people and the lion of London society and was wined and dined in royal style. Always a vain, arrogant and unscrupulous man Cardigan allowed his head to be turned by the adulation and flattery poured out on him. Worse still, in his speeches, he ignored the services of others and left his audience under the impression that the greater part of the glory of the charge was due to himself alone. As a result he spent the rest of his life in argument and litigation.

Tennyson's account of the charge and two films have done a good deal towards making the general facts of the charge common knowledge. Indeed the publicity given to this single action has created the impression that the war in the Crimea was a cavalry campaign. During the action Bosquet, watching from the gallery on the plateau, expressed something of the hour of the occasion and a truncation of his famous phrase '*C'est magnifique mais ce n'est pas la guerre. C'est de la folie*' has become the stock expression for brave and stupid acts. What the Light Brigade did was certainly magnificent in so far as it was a sublime example of obedience, discipline, self-sacrifice and devotion. But it was not war in that what happened was due to an error of judgement. The Russians as well as the Allies were deeply moved by the show of heroism. At first General Liprandi could not believe that the men of the Light Brigade had not all been drunk. 'You are noble fellows,' he told a group of prisoners, 'and I am sincerely sorry for you'.[7]

The British and French had need of sympathy. Whatever feats of courage had been displayed the action could not be considered as a success. Admittedly Balaclava had not been taken, but the Russians remained in possession of the three captured redoubts and in control of the Woronzoff Road.

INKERMAN:
THE 'SOLDIERS'' BATTLE

The heroic disaster of 25 October was but a foretaste of the bloody battle which was to come. And, from the allied point of view, it was just as well that when Raglan consulted Canrobert at the end of the day they decided not to counter-attack Liprandi's forces on the Causeway. After the Balaclava action, during which the Duke of Cambridge's 1st and Cathcart's 4th Division had marched down to the scene of the battle, the 1st Division returned to its trenches on the plateau leaving Cathcart's division on the plain. Believing that the ring round Sebastopol had been weakened by this withdrawal of a division the Russians decided to attack. Early on the morning of 26 October about 6,000 Russian infantry with four field guns sallied from the fortress, marched up the Careening Ravine and attacked the left of the 2nd Division. The guns moved up to Shell Hill and opened fire as the British pickets fell back fighting, and until the divisional batteries were brought into action the 2nd Division camp was pounded with shot. The Guards Brigade and some units of the 4th Division had come up by this time and De Lacy Evans led his division in a counter-attack against the columns of Russian 'Muffin Caps' – so called because of their headgear – stolidly climbing up from the ravine. The counter-attack was successful and the Russians retired in good order back into Sebastopol. This affair came to be known as the 'Little Inkerman' and Mrs Duberly noted that there was a great stir in Balaclava that day. Even two days later she could write of 'steamers getting up their steam, anchors being weighed, and all made ready for departure'. Raglan had given orders for the partial withdrawal of ships and stores.

To the French this action signified the end of a phase of Russian offensive action, and, with the north and east temporarily secured, Canrobert believed that the time was ripe for an assault on Sebastopol. The French had suffered considerable casualties from the Russian response to the allied bombardment, and – so far – there was little, if anything to show for their sacrifices. Canrobert was an easy-going tactician, a moody considerate man who hated losing troops in battle. He never devised or contemplated a bold offensive although it was clear to him that the basic concern of the Allies must be Sebastopol not Liprandi – especially now that Liprandi's offensive had been checked. Raglan, all too keen to get the campaign over, was more than ready to agree with this view. The weather was still good but it was getting quite cold at night. Indeed on the night of 2 November there was a severe frost, and the approach of winter which this heralded made the logic of an assault even more imperative. The attack was scheduled for the night of 7 November 1854, and Forey – charged with its overall direction – made his preparations carefully, selecting the pick of the Zouave units. All was virtually in readiness when the chain of events leading to the battle of Inkerman forced Raglan and Canrobert to abandon all thoughts of an immediate assault.

The Russian plan for an offensive had been carefully worked out for weeks. Menschikoff was only waiting for the arrival of the reinforcements of which Liprandi's 12th Division had been first instalment. When the other two divisions (10th and 11th) of Dannenberg's 4th Corps arrived from Odessa on November 3, everything was set for the plan to be put into operation. The Grand Dukes Nicholas and Michael had even travelled to Sebastopol to watch the battle and see the Russian triumph. That matters did not turn out the way they expected was not due to any inherent defect in calculations of allied strength or lack of Russian valour. Menschikoff's men fought well and in St Petersburg the Tsar himself had helped to draw up the prospective lines of battle and he was anticipating a brilliant success. To the Prussian military attaché, Count Munster, Nicholas spoke enthusiastically about the prospects of the impending attack, and the Count promptly relayed the information to Berlin. From there the information leaked back to London and Paris – where it might have been expected to have been sent on to Raglan and Canrobert, who would just have had time to make the necessary changes in the dispositions of their troops. No such message seems to have been sent to either commander and what information their Intelligence gleaned about Russian preparations for an offensive came from prisoners and deserters.

To appreciate what happened and to make what developed into a series of isolated conflicts comprehensible it is necessary to say something about the terrain over which the battle of Inkerman was fought. Happily this geography is easily describable. At Inkerman, in contrast with the Alma, it was the Russians who attacked from the plain the Allies on the heights. The name Inkerman (In-Kerman), which is Turkish, was given to the massive spur of wooded hills which towers above the right bank of the Tchernaya. Rising to an average height of about 400 feet this spur thrust forward at the north-east end of the plateau beyond the Sapoune ridge, while its rear end lay parallel with the harbour. Along its base, connecting the town with the interior ran a military road. On its eastern side the ground fell sharply into the Tchernaya valley and on the west it was bounded by the Careening Ravine (which divided it from the parallel Victoria ridge). Out of the long rocky fissure of the Careening Ravine ran two gullies, the Miriakoff and the Wellway. From the Tchernaya valley on the other side there were three similar approaches by way of the Volovia, Quarry and St Clements Ravines. Of these the most important – and for the British the most dangerous – was the Quarry Ravine along which ran the main road from the interior to Sebastopol. In the centre of the broad south-eastern end of the Inkerman Ridge there was the hump known as Shell Hill – which has already been referred to in connection with 'Little Inkerman'; south of Shell Hill were the camps of De Lacy Evans's 2nd Division.

Inkerman Ridge was in the British zone of responsibility but Raglan had not occupied it. Bosquet had been saying since 10 October that it ought to have been occupied in strength. Not only did it threaten the entire northern portion of the allied siege positions he maintained, so long as it remained unoccupied the Russians could take men and supplies in and out of Sebastopol by this route. Inkerman's vulnerability had also been pointed out to Raglan by De Lacy Evans and Burgoyne had said that this sector of the British front needed to be strengthened. Canrobert had said that he would be prepared to spare some French troops for the area, but although Raglan wanted help he does not appear to have been specific about his request.[1] The French commander thus assumed that Raglan had found a defence from within his own resources. Learning later that 'so important and so exposed a position' had been left 'totally unprotected by fortifications' Canrobert professed that he was amazed.[2] Raglan, it seems, had chosen virtually to ignore danger from this quarter.

At this time Canrobert and Raglan could muster only about 65,000 effective combatants between them. There were about 11,000 other troops – mostly Turks – in the battle area at the beginning of November, but as nearly all of these were employed in and around Balaclava they could not be considered 'effective'. The Turks, in any case, were reckoned to be useless – fat, idle, un-trained – and the British had too few men for the siege operations let alone the garrisoning of Inkerman. Had simultaneous attacks been launched against several points of their line they would have been incapable of repulsing them all. Nevertheless by 3 November Raglan's staff knew that a Russian attack was pending and that the Inkerman Ridge was one of the exposed positions where an assault might come. Russian strength in the Crimea had been estimated to be about 120,000 and reinforcements could actually be seen march-ing in to Sebastopol. Obviously something was afoot and on 4 November when the Russian guns facing the siege positions opened a furious cannonade – which the French batteries answered but which the British chose to ignore – no further evidence that an assault was impending should have been necessary. The British view was that the Russians would not have 'determination and courage enough to overcome British firmness and French gallantry' and no changes were made in their dispositions.*³

In seizing the initiative Menschikoff's intention was to inflict a crippling blow on the Allies which – even if it did not represent a decisive defeat – would ensure that an attack on Sebastopol would be out of the question for a long period; a period in which the bitterness of winter would favour the Russians. Three alternatives had been considered before it was decided to settle for an attack on Inkerman Ridge. To some of the Russian staff there was a good case for attack-ing the centre of the allied siege defences, at the junction of the French and English lines. The junction was bound to be weak they argued, and Napoleon had twice shown that if allies were first divided they could be destroyed singly. (Napoleon had, of course failed to do this at Quatrebras in 1815 and perhaps a reminder of this fact silenced those who supported a plan for a similar attack in front of Sebastopol.) The second alternative was another attack on Balaclava, and it was rejected because of Liprandi's failure on 25

---

* Despite the fact that Menschikoff had sent a message to Raglan on 2 November saying that he regretted that he would be compelled to destroy the whole allied army in the course of the next few days.

October. The British would be expecting another attack here, it was reasoned, and would be ready for it. Besides, Balaclava was only an appendage to the allied position which was concentrated on the plateau. Raglan might lose his base and base stores but with the French established at Kamiesch this would not necessarily be the fatal blow that was needed. To effect the latter an attack must be made on the plateau where the allied troops could be assailed '*corps à corps*' and then driven into the sea.

The object of the plan that had been settled upon was the complete destruction of the British army. To do this it would be necessary to launch diversionary attacks to pin down the French and stop them coming to the aid of their allies. But the main attack would come from a pincer movement on the Inkerman Ridge. To immobilize the French, General Timofief on the Russian right would attack Forey's division, while Prince Gorschakoff would keep Bosquet's *Corps d'Observation* busy on the Sapoune Heights and try to entice them into the Tchernaya valley. For the main attack, under the direction of General Dannenberg, Pauloff's 11th Division would cross the Tchernaya and assault the British right flank, while General Soimonoff – who had been sent into Sebastopol with his 10th Division – would sally out from the town's Karabel suburb on the left of the Malakoff Hill, climb the western side of the Careening Ravine and throw himself on the British left flank. To make sure that the main attack was synchronized with the feints by Timofief and Gorschakoff, a telegraph station was set up on the Mackenzie Heights which could transmit orders simultaneously to Sebastopol and Gorschakoff's headquarters at Tchorgun. During the battle Menschikoff stationed himself near this telegraph station but as he was unable to see very much of what was going on, and as Dannenberg – who should have been co-ordinating the closing of the Pauloff and Soimonoff pincer arms – had moved with Pauloff, the station proved to be of little value as a command post.

Menschikoff issued his orders for the following day's battle on Saturday 4 November, and the Tsar in St Petersburg spent three hours in his chapel praying for the success of his army. A grey dismal rain started to fall that afternoon, softening the ground and obscuring the outline of the hills.

Throughout the night it continued to fall, and the cold and wet tended to make the British outposts less attentive than usual. But in the early hours of the morning of the 5th a few quick ears could distinguish a distant tramping and the rumbling of wheels in the Inkerman valley. As nobody expected an attack in such a black downpour the sentries paid little attention to these noises; a sound of wheels in the night was neither unusual nor inexplicable and it was assumed that they were Tartar wagons carrying ammunition and supplies to the Sebastopol garrison. Towards morning the rain eased up, and a thin drizzle was followed by a misty haze. Day came slowly: cold, humid and obscure. At four o'clock – as the streaming blackness of the night gave place to a visible grey gloom – the deep tones of the church bells in Sebastopol quavered in the damp air. Being a Sunday it was presumed that they were sounding for early matins. In fact the ringing of the bells signified that the first prayer for the success of the offensive that was now under way had been offered up to Heaven. But the Russian troops were not in church. Many of them had been standing to or on the march since 3 a.m., and in the whitening obscurity thousands of men were tramping over the sodden earth – advancing in great grey columns towards their objectives. And through the slush on the roads and tracks, batteries of guns were being laboriously dragged into positions from which they could shell the allied positions.

At 5 a.m. General Codrington – one of the few British generals who was up and about at that time of the morning – visited the outposts of his brigade. As was his usual practice he had been on his horse since before dawn and on this particular morning he was riding in the mist hoping to find his way along the ridge (Victoria Ridge) which ran parallel to the Inkerman Ridge. Whenever he pulled up he must have been aware of the vague noises emanating from the valleys and the folded hills but at his outposts he got the usual 'All's well' reports.* However, as he turned his horse's head back towards the brigade camp, a sudden burst of musketry fire stabbed out of the fog. It appeared to come from the foot of the hill on the left of the Light Division's outposts. Codrington did not

---

* Outpost duty was still but little understood in the allied armies and a monotonous repetition of the formula 'Halt! who goes there?' 'Rounds.' 'What rounds?' 'Visiting Rounds'. 'Visiting Rounds advance. All's well' – or its French equivalent – had not yet taught them the practical duty of advanced posts. Kinglake's opinion was that 'When these words have been reiterated by the same men a few thousand times they are as lulling as the monotonous waves that beat and still beat on the shore.' 'A man's wits may easily be deadened, they can hardly be sharpened by formula.' (*The Invasion of the Crimea*, Kinglake II, pp. 77–80 and p. 407.

hesitate; it was clear that the British army had been taken by surprise and he galloped back to turn out the division.

Down on the forward slopes of Inkerman Ridge the British pickets could now hear the tramp of approaching columns, and see dimly in the mist the great grey masses of the Russian infantry, looming towards them. The pickets exchanged a brisk fire with the heads of these columns, in some places checking them and in others giving way before the advance. On one side it was Soimonoff's column approaching from Sebastopol; on the other that of Pauloff. The battle began with a grim series of isolated fights among the brushwood in the misty hollows – bloody, swaying conflicts between men who never had any view or sense of the general action and who were unaware of the strength and resource of those opposing them. For the mist and drizzle, which gave to the opening of this sinister battle its peculiar ghostliness, was an advantage and also a disadvantage to both sides. It enabled the Russians to approach unseen and covered the whole movement of their main attack; but it prevented them from seeing precisely where they were going, hindered Menschikoff's control of his battalions, and obliged him to guess the positions and manoeuvres of his opponents.

Soimonoff had led his men out of the Karabelnaya at five o'clock, after they had received a pontifical benediction. Crossing the ravine near the seaward end, his columns moved on steadily in the chill mist over the spurs and hollows of the Inkerman Ridge. Dannenberg, who was with Pauloff's column, had altered the plan at the last minute and ordered Soimonoff to march up the Victoria Ridge. Had he done so the outcome of the battle might have been different. But Soimonoff had ideas of his own, and he stuck resolutely to the original plan. His men first encountered a roving patrol of Guards, and it was the sharp firing of this patrol which was heard on the downs by Codrington. Meanwhile – as Soimonoff's troops climbed up the western side of the Inkerman Ridge – Pauloff, coming up from the other side, was feeling his way to Shell Hill and a flanking column, turning sharply to the left after crossing the river, was advancing southwards towards Quarry Ravine – below Shell Hill on the eastern side.

By this time a steely cold rain was again falling through the fog, in some cases rendering weapons ineffective. Few had thought to cover the muzzles of their rifles or muskets. Arms had been piled in the ordinary way, sloping upwards, and the water had run into the barrels, damping the powder of cap or cartridge, and obliging the soldier to rely upon his bayonet – or else to pick up stones and other handy missiles. The fire of the mortars and guns was also affected by the rain. Waterproof cartridges, or propelling charges enclosed in metal, were unknown; and frequently it was no easy matter to keep the powder dry. Russian guns were hauled up to Shell Hill. These guns began to fire through the curtain of mist and rain, pitching their iron balls into the camp of the 2nd Division under the Home Ridge nearly a mile away. A great deal of damage was done to the camp and many horses were killed, but most of the men were out of their tents and were now moving forward.

As the greyness of the morning faded and visibility increased, the numbers and intentions of the Russians were more clearly realized. But the main phase of the battle was fought under the shroud or fickle drifting of mist, in rain and a white obscurity. Indeed, it was not in the military sense a battle at all; it was a series of undirected encounters, fought by groups of men who met each other by hazard and who struggled over the wet grass or down in scrubby dells, fighting body to body, thrusting or clubbing, bayoneting or crushing with masses of rock. Others were killed, unseen, by unseen enemies. Musketry and artillery fired into the fog, pushing out into the chill white air enormous banks or volumes of coiling smoke. Many were killed as they walked or rode forward, uncomprehending, into the noise, the rolling vapour and the ghostly incoherence. To them it must have seemed like a fight in a dream.

In the actual fighting it is doubtful whether any unit larger than a regiment was ever under complete control. Inkerman was the grand total of as many encounters as there were detachments of British soldiers – and individuals – and for this reason alone it was a battle which is without comparison. In its earlier stages the main fight was carried on between the unsupported British army and Dannenberg's troops. Gorschakoff's artillery, opening fire on the Sapoune Ridge from the south-east was answered by Bosquet's guns: with little effect on either side. At the first sound of heavy firing – about 6 a.m. – Bosquet had ordered his troops to stand to, leaped into the saddle and galloped across to Cathcart's headquarters. Believing that his men had successfully repelled what he then thought was a minor assault, Cathcart declined Bosquet's proffered aid. So too, in turn, did Sir George Brown and the Duke of Cambridge. Bosquet returned to his camp, but sensing that danger was at hand,

kept his regiments ready to move towards either Inkerman or
Balaclava. Events were to show that it was just as well he did.

Gorschakoff's force, which was supposed to have put in a feint
attack on the Sapoune Heights, did not attempt any really aggressive action and it had practically no effect on the course of events.
Similarly, although some of Timofief's troops succeeded in reaching
the French batteries and in spiking some guns his sortie was equally
without effect on the general action.

During the fighting the fact that on both sides the men were
wearing grey overcoats often led to confusion, loss of advantage and,
sometimes, to mistaken killing. When battle had been joined and
there was no longer any question of surprise some of the Russian
regiments in the rear went into action to the accompaniment of
music – to the strident sounds of brass bands or the chanting of
Russian voices in harmony. Others marched up to the beat of a
drum and as the heads had been slackened by the damp air, their
muffled notes sounded like the drums of a phantom brigade.

Raglan, with Burgoyne, Strangways, the artillery commander,
and the rest of his staff rode up to the edge of the battle scene
shortly before 7 a.m. During the course of the action Raglan himself did not issue a single effective order; nor did Canrobert, who
joined him on the plateau, exercise any general control over the
movements of the French army. On the other side, however,
Menschikoff – nominally in supreme command – appears to have
been equally powerless, while the orders of Dannenberg, when they
did reach his divisional commanders, were not infrequently disregarded. With limited visibility and obvious difficulty in getting a
message from one part of the field to another there can be little
doubt that the mist and rain largely accounted for the grim
uncertainties of the action.

Temporarily in command of the British 2nd Division was the
54-year-old brigadier, General Pennefather. De Lacy Evans, in-
capacitated by a fall from his horse a few days before, insisted on
being carried up to his divisional headquarters; but he did not
interfere with Pennefather. And it was Pennefather's early decision
to reinforce the outposts which gave the action much of its peculiar
character. This 'feeding the pickets' broke the Russians' front, and
by keeping them engaged in a series of scattered encounters checked
their advance. Soimonoff, appreciating that his advance was slowing
down and that Pauloff's column was getting near to the other side

of the ridge, urged his grey columns on. Shell Hill had now been occupied and a column was pressing forward under its eastern slopes. At the same time some of Soimonoff's men began to edge away towards the lower ground on the right while one of his battalions wheeled off across the hill to link up with Pauloff. Every movement, Russian and British alike, was made in confusion and obscurity; there was none of the regularity of a set-piece battle. But the fighting was more bitter, more primitive and more exhausting than in any previous conflict – and infinitely more deadly. From Shell Hill, the Russian batteries firing salvoes through the mist were exacting a heavy toll. (One eye-witness reported seeing a team of six gun-horses knocked out by a single shell. To those who have witnessed the devastating effects of a modern air-burst shell or the direct hit of a 500 lb. bomb, casualties of this order will seem small. But the soldier's mind of 1854 was not attuned to the horrors of the Somme, Verdun, Stalingrad or Korea of six and nine decades later.) By now, however, the British artillery was feeling its way into the action, firing into the mist at the flash or rumble of the guns on the other side.

Overrunning a portion of the British line the Tomsk and Koliwan Regiments spiked a couple of guns and hacked their carriages to pieces; other men of a Katherineburg battalion succeeded in spiking another four field guns – albeit ineffectively with bits of wood – before they were driven back. But every foot of the British position was obstinately defended. And in the Light Division's sector George Brown's troops – all expert shots, equipped with Miniés – did terrible execution wounding or killing nearly all the officers of the Tomsk, Koliwan and Katherineburg regiments.

The numbers on both sides were of course hidden by the fog, and everything depended on the result of a narrow contact on a partly visible front. In a raging little battle of his own, Egerton of the 77th fought against an overwhelming mass of Russians. In a fierce tumult of clubbing, stabbing, firing, punching and wrestling, Egerton's men broke the advancing mass of grey battalions and chased them down into the brushwood of the lower slopes of the valley. In this fight Soimonoff himself was wounded, and soon afterwards four of the spiked guns were recovered.

Despite their gallant resistance the British front was beginning to yield. Pauloff's battalions were approaching on their objective and Dannenberg's pincers were ready to snap shut. The British pickets, out in front, had fallen back by this time, leaving the British guns a clear field of fire over open sights and at point-blank range. Charging with 183 men of the 49th Regiment, Colonel Bellairs repulsed a whole battalion of Russians as they marched ponderously up the hill. But the sheer weight of Russian numerical superiority was now beginning to tell, as Pauloff's battalions – working round across the head of the Quarry Ravine – attacked the incomplete two-gun battery to which had been given the name Sandbag Battery. (More simply 'Sandbag' to the British troops, and after the battle, known as *l'abattoir* by the French.) There were no guns in this battery and it was not provided with a banquette or firestep. Located on the slope overlooking the Tchernaya valley, on a slight rounded extension of the main ridge known as the Kitspur, men could fire through its narrow embrasures, or over the sloping shoulders of the battery proper, but they could not fire over the central parapet. The work was therefore of no practical use to either side, but it stood in the direct line of a flank attack and so became the pivot and obstacle in a bloody, passionate, swaying fight.

Between the Kitspur battery and the ascending line of the main road many confused actions were now taking place. So far as any actual times are ascertainable, it was not long after seven o'clock in the morning when a few hundred men of the 2nd Division came down towards the road and the battery. Rain was falling on the misty, smoking hills, drenching the soggy earth and the heavy grey overcoats. A viscous whitish mud was oozing through the trampled grass, churned or spattered by the cannon balls. Cold and exhaustion were adding to the grimness and misery of the battle. Men who had been on duty all night were now desperately fighting, and very few managed to get any breakfast.

At a stone rampart on the road Colonel Mauleverer with 200 men faced the advance of at least four battalions of the Borodino infantry. Unable to fire their rifles because the barrels were full of water, his men clambered over the low wall and ran forward with lowered bayonets. The shock of the charge broke the head of the leading battalion, and its furious impact shivered down through all the close ranks behind it to scatter the whole of the advancing mass. Many similar actions were in progress. But by now, the British losses had been heavy, and the men in the front of the fight were running short of ammunition or were unable to use it in their damaged rifles. At the same time a double tide was flowing over the Inkerman Ridge and undulating across the long ravines: an ebbing tide of Soimonoff's defeated or discouraged army pouring into the Careening valley on the left, and a rout of Borodino or Taroutine men crowding towards the Tchernaya on the right; while an advancing tide of about 10,000 was coming over Shell Hill in the centre.

Meantime the Guards Brigade was tramping forward through the mist – Grenadiers leading, Scots Fusilier Guards in support, Coldstream following in the rear. Their camp was more than a mile from the scene of action; and the men of the 4th Division under Cathcart were even farther away. These men, led by Cathcart himself, were also coming up towards the battle. Although a large number of demoralized Russians were leaving the field, it still seemed as though the British would eventually be swept away. Perhaps the mist and rain were now an advantage to the weaker side, hiding their positions or movement and allowing them to advance without coming under a specially directed fire of artillery. The men of the 2nd Division were fighting down towards the Kitspur and the Sandbag Battery; Adams on a great horse towering above the rest, lifting his cocked hat with its heavy mass of sodden feathers as he cheered his Welshmen; Pennefather boisterously cursing as he trotted about, urging his men on with ribald comments. Soon they were a line no longer, but scattered in groups, and fighting in a blind agony of desperation.

The Kitspur Battery was taken by the Russians, retaken, and taken again. All around this grim mound clusters of dead or wounded men lay on the ground, on the slippery muddy grass now darkening with blood or filth and awful pools of bloody water. Repeatedly the Russians rose up from the hollow misty ravine, and were again driven back by swinging rifle butts, stones and a spattering uncertain fire. And then again the British were forced slowly up the hill behind them, while the Russians flowed in grey waves round and over the battery and over the dead and writhing men who lay so thickly on the ground.

Then, emerging dimly out of the drizzle or the sheets of driving mist, a line of tall Grenadiers came into the battle. They could not fire, so they charged the battery impetuously and perhaps without orders. Again the Russians were pushed over the edge of the hill – to a great deal of excited confusion among the leading officers. 'Where the devil are you going?' shouted the Duke of Cambridge to the colonel of the Scots Fusilier Guards. 'Form up on the left, sir, immediately!' This was followed by a counter-order from Bentinck to the opposite effect, and the Scots Fusilier Guards were wheeled into position on the right.

So the battle swayed in broken unrecorded combats about the fearful battery. All formation was lost, the Guards were scattered among the men of the Line, and the fight degenerated into a furious clash of opposing mobs. Two French battalions had come up the slope of the Home Ridge, but they refused to advance, even when implored and insulted. Even more inexplicable, the men of Cathcart's division were only being sent forward in driblets; Cathcart himself does not seem to have realized the desperate position on the Kitspur. Still the Russian battalions came up in line after line, and the Grenadiers eventually fell back leaving the Sandbag to them. But another line of Guards in tall bearskins loomed up in the fog; it was the Coldstream advancing. Rivalry stirred the men in front of them and a shout of 'Charge again Grenadiers!' drove the retreating mass back over the earthwork. The Coldstream, after drying their rifles by snapping off numbers of caps, were soon firing volleys and the fight continued to sway back and forth.

Against the advice of the Duke of Cambridge and Lord Raglan's orders, Cathcart now decided to move one of his brigades along the slope to the right of the Guards. It was unfortunate that he did so as the Russians were pushing round on the left of the Sandbag, and it was here if anywhere that immediate support was needed. Cathcart himself went down over the slope of the hill and on to the brushwood. Coming under fire from his left rear, where the Russians had come forward on the high ground above him, he was killed by a musket ball, and the last recorded words of this man who had been designated as Raglan's successor were: 'I fear we are in a mess. We must try the bayonet.'[4]

The Russians were now on the left flank and in rear of the Guards, who began to retreat along the hill. The horse of the Duke of Cambridge was killed under him, and the Duke retired as quickly as he could with a grazed arm. A regiment of French infantry came charging down the Kitspur and impetuously drove the Russians back from the battery. For a time the position on the right flank was more hopeful, but the main attack of Dannenberg was now developing on the Home Ridge, where 6,000 men were advancing in echelon. The Allies were only able to command, in this part of the field, a force of about 3,000 in all.

By this time (towards nine o'clock) the mist was beginning to rise or drift in dissolving shreds of white vapour among the hills; and the rain was no longer falling. The Russian attack in mass was at least partly visible to the allies, and it was controlled and orderly – the first advance of a large number of troops in regular formation. A battery of three guns, captured by the Russians in this advance, was soon retaken by a dashing party of 'truant' Zouaves. But the grey lines came on steadily passing in wave after wave through a curtain of drifting smoke. It seemed as though a Russian victory was now probable, for Dannenberg still had in hand a large reserve; and Gorschakoff, with 22,000 men under the hills was ready to play a decisive part in the battle. A temperamental battalion of French light infantry, after firing a volley or two, fell back with noisy chatterings of alarm and it is said that Raglan allowed himself to express 'astonishment and annoyance'. However the French troops rallied quickly and were soon back in the fight.

It was about this time that Raglan and his staff came under the fire of the Russian guns. A shell plunged into the body of Captain Somerset's horse, where it exploded; not leaving much of the horse but without injuring Captain Somerset. Another shell – or it may have been a fragment of the same one – took off one of General Strangway's legs. A veteran of Waterloo, the old gunner showed no trace of fear or alarm. 'Will anyone be kind enough to lift me off my horse?' he said gently. In two hours he was dead.

The battle was now at its height. Among the tents of the 2nd Division's camp Pennefather was bellowing and raging, urging his troops to greater efforts. Inkerman was Pennefather's battle. In the smoke and mist the lines of soldiers surged backwards and forwards. But the situation was becoming critical in the centre and on the extreme right of the British position. The British troops were beginning to tire and as Raglan had no reinforcements to call on, while the Russians still had four regiments that had not yet joined the battle, the odds in favour of the Russians were beginning to lengthen. Up the winding road along the Quarry Ravine fresh columns of Russian infantry could be seen approaching the ragged rampart of earth and stones that blocked the road near the original front line. The road block, known as 'The Barrier', now became another focal point in the fighting. Deployed on the left of the Home Ridge was the 63rd Regiment under Colonel Swyny. Swyny's men, who had suffered heavy casualties from the Russian artillery,

rallied round their colours and charged forward in line to drive the
Russians back. But the disparity in numbers was now beginning to
tell, and the 63rd's attack achieved little. Meantime the Russian
gunners, who were now able to see their targets in the clearing air
were beginning to gain a deadly ascendancy. On the bloody slopes
of the Kitspur the fight swayed backwards and forwards. The Guards
were still there, disputing every step of the Russian advance, but
losing heavily. The time was almost eleven o'clock and Raglan,
seeing the companies of Russians continuing to come on, was beginning to expect the worst. Turning to Canrobert who was with
him he used an uncharacteristic phrase: '*Nous sommes . . . nous
sommes foutus.*'

The decision to ask for the proffered help that had been rejected
earlier had already been taken. Colonel Steele, of Raglan's staff
had ridden over to Bosquet's headquarters to give him a frank
outline of the precariousness of the situation. 'Ah!' said Bosquet,
'I knew it', and his troops were ordered to move in support of the
British.

When physical strength has been exhausted, troops often continue to fight with that dogged determination which derives from
that undefinable factor *esprit de corps*. It is then that the appearance
of fresh troops can give a decisive turn to the battle. The morale of
one side is boosted, and their opponents become dispirited. On this
occasion the shrill sound of bugles playing 'Père Casquette'
announcing the approach of the French put new life into the
British and filled the Russians with dismay. On the Kitspur the
beleaguered Guards raised a cheer for the three battalions of
Zouaves and Algerians which came up at a run. Above the din, as
bugles blew and drums rattled, Bosquet was heard shouting in
Arabic 'Prove yourselves, Children of fire!'

Like the Prussians at Waterloo, the French arrived at the
critical moment, and as their numbers increased the tide of battle
slowly began to turn in favour of the Allies. On the Kitspur the
Coldstream and Zouaves charged forward together, forcing the
Russians out of the battery and down the hill. Behind them they
left a grisly heap of bodies; 'My God!' Bosquet commented when
he saw them, '*Quel abattoir* (what a slaughterhouse)!' From
Shell Hill Russian guns were keeping up a steady well-directed fire,
and as Bosquet's attack got under way two 18-pounder guns were
hauled over the Home Ridge to deal with them. Laid by British

officers, nearly every shot from these guns scored a direct hit on the Russian batteries and shortly after eleven o'clock they had been silenced.

This marked the turning point in the battle. In terms of numbers the British now had about 8,000 men left to continue the fight, and Bosquet committed another 6,000. These 14,000 were probably equally matched by the Russians. But as the three regiments of the 10th Division in Soimonoff's column had been disorganized by the loss of all its senior officers and many of the subalterns they took no part in the fighting. Nor did the Borodino and Taroutine regiments who had already abandoned the field. There were still four other regiments in Soimonoff's column but these were held back at a time when they might have decided the issue. Consequently the whole weight of the Anglo-French counter-attack fell on Pauloff's main force of the Ochotzk, Yakutzk and Selensk Regiments, which had gone into battle with 8,500 men but had been reduced in three hours of fighting to something less than 6,000. Between twelve and one o'clock General Dannenberg – without consulting Menschikoff – decided to give up the battle.

An orderly withdrawal was not easy and it is to the credit of the Russians that they were able to get their guns away down the steep inclines from the Inkerman Ridge without leaving any as trophies for the allies. According to the Russians it was only Pauloff's three depleted regiments that made this possible. The French, striving to smash through the Russian infantry and stop the guns getting away, were driven back three times. In one of these attacks their 6th Regiment lost their colours and these were recovered only by the most desperate efforts of the regiment's commanding officer, Colonel Camas, who lost his life in the process. Charges by the four squadrons of Chasseurs d'Afrique that Bosquet had thrown into the action failed to accelerate the Russian retirement and they suffered heavy casualties. (Lucan's cavalry did not play any part in this battle, although what remained of the Light Brigade suffered three casualties while trying to create a diversion. The ground was not suited to cavalry action, and – like the British – the Russian cavalry also stayed outside the fighting arena.)

Covered by the Vladimir Regiment the Russians retired in good order back across the Tchernaya, and by two in the afternoon the battle ended. Dannenberg excused his retreat by blaming Gorschakoff who he said had not been sufficiently aggressive, and

Gorschakoff's excuse was that it had been useless for him to try to advance when Dannenberg's attack on the ridges failed. There was no pursuit. Raglan urged Canrobert to follow Dannenberg's columns with French troops but the French commander-in-chief – who had been wounded in the arm during the action – refused. Raglan considered that the French troops, who had joined the battle for its final phase, were fresher than his own men who were now too few and too tired to go on. But Canrobert would not entertain the idea of the French undertaking a pursuit on their own. Unless sizeable units of the British army accompanied his units, he said, there would be no 'follow-up'. Nor was there.

On the Inkerman Ridge there was the usual aftermath of battle. Arms and equipment were being collected, boots being pulled from the feet of the dead and medical officers were busy doing what they could with a lamentable scarcity of drugs and surgical equipment. 'There was not a single angular splint' a surgeon with the Coldstream recorded.[5] Amputated arms in sleeves, and legs in trousers were collected in pathetic little heaps outside the tents hastily erected as operating theatres. 'Chloroform was but seldom used because it occupied so much time.'[6] It was not that the surgeons were inhumane: 'The smart use of the knife is a powerful stimulant, and it is much better to hear a man bawl lustily than to see him sink silently into the grave.'[7] The battlefield was strewn with dead and wounded men from both sides, British red, French blue and Russian grey all intermingled. Down in the tangles of brushwood or huddled under the rocks in the Quarry Ravine where they had crawled were hundreds of Russians. It took days for some of them to die and for more than a year their grim tattered skeletons awaited burial. Throughout the appalling winter which followed men who needed a pair of boots, a coat or a blanket, would look for them in the Inkerman area. In and around the Kitspur over 1,100 corpses were counted. Those who had died as a result of gun-shot wounds lay with calm brows, glassy eyes and half-open lips. And as the distorted features of many showed that they had been bayonetted to death, a letter was sent to Menschikoff complaining of the atrocities. During the battle the Russians had given no quarter and there were rumours of many instances where men lying on the ground, wounded and out of action, had been stabbed repeatedly. Even Cathcart who had died from a head wound had been bayonetted. Ironically, the Russian conduct was if anything more restrained than that of many

Turks – especially the Bashi-Bazouks. Asking for an explanation, however, the allied letter inquired if the war was really to be carried on 'in such an inhuman and barbarous manner as would disgrace any civilized nation'.[8] Menschikoff's reply pointed out that atrocities happened in all armies, but that he doubted there were many cases of Russian troops behaving as the British and French claimed and he suggested that the allied commanders were probably misinformed. His letter concluded with a complaint about the French burning a church at the head of Chersonese Bay. (Subsequently, an allied Court of Inquiry investigating the original charges and Menschikoff's counter complaint found 52 witnesses who testified to the inhumane slaughter of six officers and twice as many other ranks, while the burning of the church was found to be 'accidental.')[9] The British losses amounted to 632 killed – of whom 43 were officers and of these eight were from the Coldstream Guards; 1,873 were wounded, many of whom died on board ship or in the wards of Scutari. French casualties totalled 1,726 killed and wounded, and the Russians are said to have lost no fewer than 12,000.*

Speaking to the Princesse de Beauvea in August 1855, Canrobert said of the battle of Inkerman: 'They [the British] would have been slaughtered where they stood, if we had not come up to hurl back the Russians who were crushing them under their masses'.[10] Canrobert considered that it was *he* who had won the battle – or rather that without him it would have been lost. Ironically this was also the personal outlook of both Raglan and Bosquet who both felt that they individually were responsible for its outcome. Actually the laurels belonged to Bosquet. The battle was decided on the Kitspur and there is no question but that the Russians would have overwhelmed it had it not been for the timely arrival of Bosquet's Zouaves and Algerians. In his report to Whitehall, Raglan acknowledged that Bosquet deserved some credit. Observing that his own army had 'effectually repulsed and defeated a most vigorous and determined attack of the enemy' he added graciously that it had

---

* No exact return of Russian casualties has ever been published. Menschikoff reported 2,969 killed – of whom 42 were officers; 5,791 wounded. Todleben's figures were 3,288 killed, 11,664 wounded and out of action. By these figures the Russians must have had every third man disabled, the British about one in five. Both the Russians and the British were suspicious of Canrobert's return of 1,726, as it was known that all reports of French activities in the Crimea were 'rectified' in Paris.

been 'powerfully aided by Bosquet's troops'.*[11] Of the commanders in the field, only Pennefather seems to have understood the nature of the battle, and he saw it as a series of emergencies.

The results of the battle were that the Russians gave up hope of driving the Allies out of the Crimea before winter. But, true to Russian expectations, the siege operations were interrupted and the Allies postponed indefinitely any ideas of a direct assault on Sebastopol. Inkerman was a victory for the Allies but its cost soberly impressed them with Russia's strength and the enormity of the task that lay ahead.

Details of the battle reached London and Paris on 15 November. Raglan's despatch was a long, formal and misleading document which even he admitted gave only an 'imperfect description' of the conflict; that of Canrobert was no better. The public in both allied capitals were delighted by the news of a victory, however, and congratulations were showered on both commanders. Raglan was made a Field-Marshal, and there was speculation – albeit some of it sarcastic – that he would be created Duke of Inkerman; Bosquet was promoted in the Legion of Honour and for everybody who had been on the battlefield the award of an Inkerman clasp to the promised Crimean medal was announced. But in the midst of the congratulations a subtle change of atmosphere became noticeable. In both Britain and France the buoyant optimism was disappearing. In Paris comparisons were being drawn between Inkerman and Eylau – the indecisive Franco-Russian battle which had been fought in 1807; and from London the Earl of Clarendon, the British Foreign Minister, was writing to Lord Cowley in Paris saying that the dubious victory had fostered despair and the apprehension that the army really might not be able to sustain another such 'triumph'.[12]

---

* When the French joined the battle, a Russian general said to his staff 'The French are saving the English at Inkerman as the Prussians did at Waterloo.' *With Lord Stratford in the Crimean War*, Skene, p. 155.

13

WINTER 1854-55

At Raglan's suggestion, the artillery of both armies bombarded the Russian positions on the morning after Inkerman. During that morning also a council of war met at the British headquarters to discuss whether the assault planned before the battle should be attempted. Opinions differed. The fine weather had returned and those in favour of an attack suggested that it stood a good chance of success because the Russians would be demoralized by the failure of their offensive. But most of the generals present argued that the allies were not strong enough, particularly while Menschikoff still had such a large mobile force in the field capable of another attack on Balaclava. Some were so disheartened that they advised abandoning the siege completely – even evacuating the Crimea. The Duke of Cambridge favoured a withdrawal of the British forces to positions on the heights above Balaclava; De Lacy Evans was for getting out of the Crimea altogether. Raglan rejected this idea out of hand. The French and Turks, he said, relied upon the British for transport and he was not prepared to leave his allies 'in the lurch'.[1] In the event it was decided to await reinforcements which were on the way; and, as it was obvious that the armies would not be going home for Christmas, plans had to be made for wintering on the plateau. As such a contingency had not so far been seriously contemplated no provision had been made for it. It was rather late in the day to make proper arrangements – though not too late, as the French were to show.

The variability of the winter climate of the Crimea was well known and that of the 1854-5 winter was to be no exception. It was to be cold in the Crimea – so cold that ink froze in bottles, tooth-brushes had to be thawed out before use and one private soldier who put his shirts in to soak overnight found them next morning so embedded in ice that he had to show his frozen wash-tub at the daily kit inspection. Fortunately the spells of cold weather were rarely prolonged, and even in January there were mild and sunny days. But for the most part it was a period of cold, rain, sleet and snow. Provided the authorities had taken reasonable measures, however, the sufferings which the British army was called upon to endure could have been very much reduced, and the troops might have wintered on the heights above Sebastopol almost as comfortably as in England. Naturally conditions varied according to location, regiment and individual resources. Those who had the means to keep themselves warm and comfortable probably suffered some discomfort but little hardship. Generally, however, lack of foresight, ignorance, neglect, and officialdom combined to make the life of the infantry one of appalling miseries. The chaos in Balaclava, where food rotted and accumulating stores of almost every mentionable commodity went to waste, where bales of clothing, bags of biscuits and trusses of hay were flung into the harbour to serve as the additional landing stages which no one had thought to build before January, all stemmed from these shortcomings. Departmental barriers and the traditional British governmental red tape clogged the administrative machine. Problems were tackled on an *ad hoc* basis – not always with success; they were rarely anticipated.

No doubt it was the combined stupidity of many men which was responsible for the breakdown of the sea transport system. One of the most stupid appears to have been Admiral Boxer, the man who was given the job of organizing the shipping arrangements at Constantinople. There was no doubting his gallantry; he was the hero of a number of actions at sea. But as a staff officer where tact and competence were the prime requirements he was an absolute failure. Introducing himself as 'bloody old Boxer' – an appropriate description in which he appears to have taken particular pride – he would tell those who applied to him for coal 'to go and look for it'.[2] That he was largely responsible for the failure of the sea transport arrangements became apparent when the eventual and inevitable inquiry was held.[3]

This failure was incredibly, disastrously complete. Stores were ferried backwards and forwards across the Black Sea; empty ships were kept idle at a time when every seaworthy vessel was urgently required. No proper records were ever kept and everything in Boxer's office was in confusion. Some cargoes disappeared entirely and it was impossible to forecast when any specific consignment would reach its proper destination. Of those that did actually reach Balaclava there were many scandals. Apathy and ignorance in the army departments undoubtedly assisted the professional fraudulence of some of the less scrupulous contractors. Boots and greatcoats were found to be too small and one large consignment consisted of boots for the left foot only; 10,000 pairs of stockings were found to be in sizes intended only for children.[4] Throughout the whole Commissariat there was apathy and neglect, and Mr Commissary-General Filder was blamed – unfairly in fact – for the breakdown of a department in which nearly every subordinate appears to have been unreliable.

On 14 November nature brought a catastrophic addition to the manmade problems. After five days of torrential rain which had filled the trenches knee deep with slush and mud, the climax came as a terrible storm. The greatest damage was to ships in the Black Sea, especially those just outside Balaclava harbour. As the naval authorities had had ample evidence of the approach of this storm critics were quick to point out that the heavy losses which were incurred were quite unnecessary. Not only had Admiral Dundas had three good months in which to establish a naval base in the Crimea or Black Sea region in which vessels could have sheltered, but there was plenty of room in Balaclava harbour on 14 November. Ships' captains reported that they had made urgent and repeated requests for admission. But the Balaclava port authority denied them entry, and apart from a few who ignored their order and crashed their way in without permission, most of the vessels had to face the hurricane in a deep and dangerous anchorage outside the harbour. The *Prince*, one of the finest steamers of her day, went to the bottom laden with stores; so too did the *Henri IV*, the most imposing vessel in the French navy, and of the ships near Balaclava alone twenty-one were dashed to pieces and eight others severely damaged. Others ran ashore or sank near Katcha Bay and five transports were wrecked off Eupatoria. A great many people were drowned, and on board the steamer *Retribution* the Duke of Cambridge was said to have nearly gone out of his mind with anxiety. The value and quantity of the lost cargoes were exaggerated by the authorities so that God – rather than the supply system – might be held responsible for the shortages that were now prevalent. But there can be no doubt that what did go to the bottom of the sea included stocks of 'everything that was most wanted – warlike stores of every description, surgical instruments, guernsey coats, flannel drawers, woollen stockings, and socks, boots, shoes'. Furthermore 'Our principal ammunition ship was also cast away, and each of the others bore with it to the deep, part of that which we depended on for existence'.[5]

The storm caused as much chaos on land as at sea. In Balaclava houses had their roofs lifted off but it was on the plateau that the worst damage occurred. There, tents were torn down, blankets blown away and hospital marquees ripped to ribbons – leaving scores of helpless sick and wounded exposed to the storm. Clothing and even heavier articles such as chairs and tables were carried off in the ferocious wind. (The 4th Regiment deeply regretted the loss of their band's big drum which was blown across to the Russian lines. After Alma regimental bands had ceased to exist when the bandsmen were issued with stretchers and deprived of their instruments. But the instruments were retained in the camps, ready for the victory march through Sebastopol.) Large quantities of food and forage were spoiled and thousands of tired and hungry men returning from their disagreeable duty in the trenches found neither food nor shelter waiting for them. Surprisingly enough it was the Turkish army which came through the storm in best condition. Pitched by men who knew what to expect, the Turks' tents were little the worse for wear at the end of the blizzard. The storm ended with the rain turning to sleet and snow, against which – with their tents and clothes gone – the drenched and frozen men had no protection. Traffic to and from Balaclava, which had stopped during the storm because no progress could be made against the wind, was now hardly possible as a blanket of snow settled over the rain-drenched road of mud. Below the cliffs outside Balaclava harbour, which was choked with floating debris, the sea daily cast up more bodies of those who had perished. At long last the armies began to realize that they were faced with problems of supply and nutrition rivalling the Russians' attention. They were faced, in fact, with a grim test of administrative efficiency, which the French barely passed and which the British failed.

Of course it was to be expected that the storm would be quoted as an excuse for the breakdown of the supply system. In Balaclava the harbour-master, the elderly Captain Christie, was suspended and told that he would be court-martialled. (He died – allegedly of a broken heart – before the trial could take place. Subsequently Christie's name appeared in the *London Gazette* of July 1855, having been posthumously awarded a C.B.) Russian occupation of the old Turkish redoubts was also avidly seized upon as a reason excusing inefficiency. Deprived of the use of the only metalled road up the Sapoune ridge the army was confined to the rough country road through the Col and in the worst of winter this became impassable, the authorities claimed. How this excuse could be condoned by any, including contemporary historians, who looked at a map of the Crimea, is difficult to understand. The Woronzoff Road, running three miles to the north of Balaclava, bypassed the port and to get to it meant a trek across the mud of the open country. The road over the Col was used because it was the most convenient and most direct, and the invalidity of the official excuse was shown on 6 December when the Russians abandoned their forward positions and retired across the Tchernaya. Men and horses continued to stumble and slither up the muddy road over the Col and the opening of the Woronzoff road made no difference.

Canrobert worried constantly about the French food stocks. At the beginning of October these stocks were down to a bare three days supply, with only enough meat for a single day. Only the arrival of supplies from Varna had avoided the necessity of going on to half-rations. But from then on Canrobert kept a personal eye on the situation, and French rations were precariously balanced with the stocks. The snow, sleet and days of continuous rain which followed the storm of 14 November and precluded replenishment resulted in the French eating further into their reserve stocks than Canrobert considered safe. And it was this factor rather than the weather which led to plans being cancelled for an attack on 2 December – marking the anniversary of Austerlitz. According to Canrobert's despatch of 3 December no assault was possible because the 'rain was falling in torrents, the roads were cut up, the trenches filled with water, and the siege operations . . . in a state of suspense'.[6] In London Karl Marx quipped '. . . the sun of Austerlitz has melted in water'.[7]

In the case of the British there should have been no lack of food, clothing or stores; in Balaclava there was an abundance of everything. Moving goods up to the plateau was the task of the overworked mules and ponies of the Commissariat responsible for providing the British army's needs, and the failure to provide sufficient forage for these animals was the crux of the breakdown of the British supply system. Regiments were ordered to hand over their pack animals to the Commissariat and mounted officers invited to sell their chargers – for which they had no use in the trenches even if forage had been available nearer than Balaclava. Even when every horse, mule and pony had been mobilized there was a shortage of transport animals, which tended to get worse as their casualties exceeded the numbers of their replacements. Critics in England raved about the numbers of horses easily available in the Black Sea area. But they had nothing to say about how they were to be fed or looked after because they could not understand the exact cause of the army's misery. With an abundance of hay and corn the Commissariat's transport corps could have fed the troops, sheltered them in huts, provided them with all the ammunition they needed for the siege, and coped with any emergency.[8]

After Inkerman, Canrobert persistently urged Raglan to move what was left of the British Cavalry Division to a position on the right where it could cover the weak and extended flank of the allied line. Equally persistently, Lucan had objected – pointing out that it would be extremely difficult and probably impossible to feed the horses so far from Balaclava. Raglan supported him, not because of the forage problem but because he reckoned that the cavalry force was too weak to be of any real military worth. To Canrobert the mere presence of cavalry – no matter how weak – would be enough to deter the Russians from attacking the right flank and that was all that was required of it. Moreover if the cavalry were shifted to a more protected area the Russians would hear of it and interpret the move as an act of weakness – which indeed it would be. Therefore, Canrobert concluded, the practical thing to do was to move the cavalry up to the Inkerman Ridge and supply it as well as possible. Because he 'hardly liked to thwart General Canrobert's wishes, as he had lately rendered us so much assistance on the right',[9] Raglan finally assented.

In the event, Lucan's gravest forebodings about the problems of feeding his horses proved to be optimistic in relation to what actually happened. When the transport system broke down the horses became unmanageable. They ate each others' tails and manes and there were confused and chaotic scenes of horror as frenzied, starving cavalry chargers stampeded through the camps after the food of the artillery horses. Lucan had forbidden the killing of horses except those with glanders or broken limbs, and they died in the slush of the lines – their bodies lying where they had fallen, to become the food of prowling dogs. On 1 December Lucan reported that his division was practically extinct and Raglan, relaying this information to Canrobert, agreed to the horses being moved down to Kadiköi. Here they were stabled in dark caves which were soon overrun with rats. ('Rat-hunts' were popular – the French hunting for the fun of it and their larder; the British merely for the fun.) Better arrangements might have been made – from ships' sails and timber which were to spare in Balaclava, more hygienic shelters might have been run up and there was plenty of ready-made horse clothing to be had in Constantinople. But the staff did not know how to harness the ample resources it had at its finger-tips. Nobody thought of portable shelters and although a requisition for two thousand suits of horse clothing was sent to Constantinople towards the end of November, it stipulated a pattern which needed tailoring. In fact the requisition was fulfilled within a month but by that time most of the horses for whom it was intended were dead.

The other animals, overworked on the daily trips to Balaclava, grew weaker and less fit with each successive journey. As they fell and died, men were required to take over much of their work – in addition to the regular trench and guard duty. Through the quagmire and back, the trek to Balaclava for rations or ammunition or clothing took twelve hours – twelve hours without food, shelter or rest. No labour – not even Turkish labour – could be spared to bury the dead carcasses that littered the route. And as road conditions deteriorated the rations at the front grew more limited – down to a quarter on two occasions and on one day there was no food at all. For over six weeks British soldiers went without their rice or vegetables, and the lack of green food inevitably brought epidemics of scurvy and jaundice.* But what made their lives most miserable, and what sent more men to the hospital or the grave – frequently they were synonymous – than Russian bullets, was the lack of firewood. Without it men could not only never get warm or cook their ration of 'cold grunter', they were never dry. After a spell in the trenches men would return wet and hungry, report to the hospital tent still wet and hungry, die that night and be buried in their wet blankets the following morning. Two or three ships sent across the Black Sea could have collected enough wood from the forests of Anatolia to last the British through the winter. Instead, men already exhausted by a long spell of sentry-go or the digging of

---

* Their monotonous ration was supposed to consist of salt pork, biscuit, rice, rum, sugar and raw coffee beans; fresh meat was nominally issued twice a week but in practice once only.

new trenches and soaked to the skin, were compelled to go farther and farther afield to grub up first the brushwood and then when that petered out, its sodden roots.

On several occasions the road between Balaclava and Kadiköi was impassable to both man and beast. Attempts to macadamize it late in the year failed and supply came virtually to a standstill.[10] In England the critics said that Raglan's first consideration should have been a suitable road from the Balaclava base to the front and that his failure to provide one was indicative of his leadership. To Raglan the reasons why he had not ordered the existing road to be improved or for a new one to be built were obvious, but in London they seemed unconvincing. In late September and early October the soil had been firm, and horses and vehicles had been able to cross the open country without needing a road. Rations for men and horses had been supplied regularly, and it was not until the beginning of November that things started to go wrong. Up to then everything was all set for the assault which was going to end the necessity for supplies to come via Balaclava. But the battle of Inkerman had put a different complexion on the campaign. It was obvious now that the road was vital but the estimate was that it would take a thousand men two or three months to put it into proper shape. In the event the Turks who were hired for the task died by the hundreds and the survivors were kept busy burying those who had perished. Soon it was officially admitted that 'hired labour could not be obtained'.

With supply at a standstill, extremes of sickness and hardship could not be avoided. Morale in the British army deteriorated, and some of the officers sent in their resignations. Most were told that they would not be allowed home until their successors arrived to replace them. But one or two, described as belonging to 'the wealthier class'[11] were permitted to leave. Among these was Lord George Paget who had commanded the 4th Dragoons in the Light Brigade's charge. He had been less than two months in the Crimea but he gave as his reasons for retiring that he had only recently married, and that as the cavalry were not likely to be actively employed during the winter he wanted to settle down. His brigadier saw no objection; Lucan, the divisional commander, warmly approved; and Raglan not only saw nothing odd in the request but wrote the grant of leave in his own hand, asked Lord George to stop to dinner and wished 'George' the best of luck. (In England, where the public was becoming aware of the sufferings of the troops on the Chersonese, Paget got a frigid reception. Stung to the quick, he endeavoured to live things down and then – to his credit – applied to go back to the Crimea, and his application was granted.) Imagination boggles when one attempts to strike a modern parallel with this transaction. Yet it was not unique. Mrs Duberly's extended stay in Balaclava; Cardigan's sleeping on his yacht and enjoying a French cuisine are perhaps the best known examples of British officers availing themselves of privileges which would now be considered extraordinary. There were also cases of families travelling out to Balaclava to visit their officer relatives. In general therefore the situation of the officers was one of discomfort rather than suffering, although in relation to their former mode of life they probably felt that they were being denied just as much as their men. Private soldiers were rarely given leave and there were bitter complaints about officers who were able to pay for passages back to Britain. Campbell wrote indignantly that officers who could not put up with their lot without grumbling did not deserve to have commissions, and branded stories of their privations as nonsense. At the very worst after twelve hours in snow and sleet officers in the front line would be in a dry bed and enjoying hot tea with ham and biscuit, while their men – who rarely had a change of dry clothing – slept on damp mud.

Cases of desertion and of suicide – of men blowing out their brains after spells in the trenches – are recorded, and it would be easy to make sweeping generalizations about the army which had stagnated after the Wellingtonian era. Individual characters, background and experiences varied, as they always do. One man's hardship could be another's luxury. Many of the old campaigners accepted the situation with sang-froid and remained cheerful; men who had lived through the Irish potato famine were not disposed to grumble even when their rations were halved. Circumstances also varied according to the location, and to the resourcefulness and energy of commanding officers. Because they were nearer the source of supplies, had no trench duty and suffered less from the weather, the Highland Brigade near Balaclava lived better than regiments on the plateau. Because they had more horses to make the journey down to Balaclava, the gunners tended to be better off than the infantry. Because in Lacy Yea the Royal Fusiliers had a commanding officer devoted to his regiment, their lot was made easier. Guards and cavalry officers were better off than officers of Line regiments, and of course the generals lived better than regimental officers. (Colonel Darby Griffith of the Scots Greys arrived in the Crimea with a French cook and hampers containing a magnificent stock of provisions, tastefully organized by Fortnum and Mason. Lord Rokeby, who took over the Guards Brigade from Bentinck in February 1855, arrived with a patent water closet which was promptly stolen by the Zouaves for use as a soup boiler.)

In contrast with the British the attitude of the French stood out in sharp relief. So far as the officers were concerned there was no question of privileges such as those tacitly approved by Raglan. When General Bazaine spent a night with his wife, Forey reported to Canrobert that he had deserted his post and his troops.[12] In the field British officers grudgingly admitted that the French were better organized and many blamed Raglan for the poor showing of the British army. 'I wonder what Lord Raglan thinks when he contrasts the two armies', noted an officer of the 63rd. '. . . Things are going on very badly here, and I can hardly imagine what will be the end . . . the regiments are gradually dwindling down to nothing . . . the 63rd had only *seven* men fit for duty the day I left . . . There is a very prevalent impression that Lord Raglan does not hear the truth . . . Our only stand-by is the French; they are still an army and in first rate order'.[13] Another hoped that all the Peninsula heroes would be sacked before it was too late.

Until the news of Inkerman had been digested the British press had been full of glowing accounts of the campaign, of the great guns and batteries that were being hauled up to the plateau and of the impending fall of Sebastopol. But with the blizzard the tone of the newspapers changed. The squalor and disease, the lack of food and shortage of transport were now all described in such detail that there was a storm of protest. *The Times* organized a *Comfort Fund*; and there was a flush of *Gift Funds* and *Hospital Funds*, all of which were well supported by public subscription. A witch hunt was inevitable and it was inevitable that Raglan should come in for a major part of the criticism. 'What remains of more than 50,000 men, the best blood of this country?' queried *The Times* in the first of a historic series of leaders. 'Do they still maintain the unequal fight? . . . Unfortunately . . . the results agree too nearly with the fact of an invisible commander. Had the eye of a general fallen on the confusion in the harbour of Balaclava, or the impassable state of the road . . . we can hardly suppose that so able a man, as Lord Raglan undoubtedly is, would not have prevented such errors and neglects'.[14] With greater emphasis a more direct indictment was made a week later: 'It can no longer be doubted or even denied that the expedition to the Crimea is in a state of entire disorganization – affairs are going from bad to worse . . . Lord Raglan has scarcely been seen since the battle of Inkerman . . . It is a crime in a War Minister to permit an officer to remain for a single day in the nominal discharge of duties which has brought a great and victorious army to the verge of ruin'.[15]

Enhanced by the despatches of their correspondent Mr W. H. Russell who – in the braided uniform of the 'disembodied militia' – saw what was going on and wrote vividly and with passion about the sufferings of the British troops, these public denunciations hastened the downfall of the Government. They had their disadvantages, of course, also. With such publicity, free beer and all the artful devices of the recruiting sergeant failed to bring forward the young men that were needed by 'Queen and country'. Nor was it altogether wise to present the Russians with so much useful information. 'We have no need of any spies,' a Russian declared on one occasion, 'we have *The Times*.' Nevertheless the overall effect of the newspaper's leaders was beneficial, and there is little doubt that they helped to save the lives, relieve the suffering and restore the efficiency of the British troops in the Crimea. It was all very well for the Duke of Newcastle, Secretary of War, to rail at the 'ruffianly *Times*' and to appeal to the editors of newspapers for patriotic reticence; the irrepressible truth was emerging.

Up to this time Newcastle's relations with Raglan had been extremely cordial, but when he saw that a political storm was blowing up criticisms began to creep into his letters and despatches to the Crimea. On 6 January 1855 the Government's complaints were formally presented. Apart from an indirect indictment of Raglan himself it was suggested that his Adjutant-General (Estcourt) and Airey (the Quartermaster-General) might advantageously be relieved of their duties. Raglan replied to the effect that nothing short of actual recall would ever remove him from his command; he deplored the aspersions cast on his officers, and he not only defended Airey but spoke of him in terms of the highest possible commendation. However there can be no doubt that Raglan had been deeply hurt by the allegation that he saw nothing of his men, that he was entirely ignorant of their sufferings, and that he remained 'invisible' in his own comfortable quarters. Prodded by this reproach Raglan started to show himself more often about the camps. But his visits were never more than once a week and not so often if the weather was bad.

No one ever doubted that 'old Raggles' was a kind, warm-hearted individual with an unselfish devotion to duty. It is unlikely that the British army has ever had such a gentleman as its commander-in-chief. But Raglan was more than a gentleman. He was a patrician with roots in the eighteenth century. Proud, reserved, master of his emotions, remote from the rough and tumble of everyday life, Raglan was a complete aristocrat. His attitude towards the officer corps – British, French and Russian – reflect his class consciousness and his loathing of spies and deserters is equally characteristic. The tragedy was that such admirable qualities made Raglan unfitted to the command of an army shivering on the Heights above Sebastopol. The British army did not want a good-tempered old gentleman; what they needed was a younger man, a dynamic iron-fisted individual who was less of a gentleman and more of a cad – someone who was ruthless, energetic, imperious, who would feed and clothe his men, keep them warm and stand up for their rights even if it entailed dismissing his best friend. At sixty-seven Raglan was not, and never could be, that type of man. He was incapable of storming, threatening, abusing and shouting when told that something was not possible. Indeed the occasions when he is known to have shown his anger or even to have raised his voice are few and far between.

Unfortunately it was not only his character that made Raglan unsuited to the command. For nearly forty years he had served as a staff officer, a Whitehall warrior, and he had never commanded a company or a squadron let alone a battalion or regiment. In this time he had developed into a perfect civil servant – patient, urbane, tactful, conciliatory, loyal to his subordinates, averse to change, and – worst of all perhaps – he had acquired the civil servant's instinctive dislike of committing himself. Allied to a propensity for understatement this last quality often made him appear not merely vague but positively indifferent. Nor was he a good mixer; his conversations with the rank and file were always difficult and stilted and even to his staff he seemed distant – always courteous, but formal.

A poor commander-in-chief can have a good staff, it is said, but a good commander-in-chief cannot have a poor staff. Unfortunately the staff on which Raglan depended was largely composed of his own nominees (five members of it were related to him); men incapable or stupid, who successfully blended incompetence, indifference and ignorance. Few had had any training, of course – the Staff College at Camberley did not come into being until 1858 – but if they had had any inkling of the art of war Raglan's staff officers might have discounted some of his weaknesses.* As it was they did not know what was going on because they did not want to see what the ordinary soldier was suffering, or – if they did see – they seem to have considered that such suffering was unavoidable, irremediable and above all uncommunicable to Raglan. Confronted with one of Russell's accusatory articles one of them declared that the men were no worse off than they would have been at home, and with regard to food, rather better off. Such comments typified the attitude of Raglan's staff officers. Secure and comfortable in quarters in and around the neat little farmhouse where Raglan had his headquarters, his staff were immune to most of the problems that beset the rest of the army. And because they did so little in return for their security and amenities, they became objects of the army's loathing.

It is hard to believe that a man of Raglan's profound compassion really knew the full extent of the suffering experienced by his troops. It may be that this was a corollary of his not getting around sufficiently, his inability to mix well and his wish to keep out of the limelight. In extenuation, it has also been said that Raglan was compelled to spend long hours on paperwork – scribbling away laboriously with his left hand – because of the army's unprofessional organization and his lack of trust in, or the unreliability of, his staff.

A number of factors contributed to the marked difference in morale which existed between the British and French armies. To begin with the French had found Kamiesch to be far more suitable for the business of landing supplies than their ally found Balaclava. Here and at Kazatch extensive warehouses were built, together with hospitals and convalescent camps. Complete with a café-restaurant, supervised by a typical *Madame Henri* in black bombazine – 'La plus belle cantinière des Zouaves' – Kamiesch rapidly developed into a bustling shanty town. Because of its multitude of boutiques, run by

---

* A course at the Royal Military College, Camberley, catered for staff officers. Airey, and General Simpson who succeeded Raglan were two of the few who had taken it.

sharp-witted Levantines, and selling almost everything from wine to hair-oil, the French soldiers called it Friponville or Filonpis. The basic reason for French morale being higher than that of the British was largely due to the fact that they knew what war was like and how to look after their soldiers. Their tactics may not have compared with those of the British and some of their organization may be considered slipshod, but when British troops were overworked, hungry and in poor health, French soldiers were well fed, well clad, and relatively free from sickness. Because their ports were closer to their camps than Balaclava was to the British lines, their transport problem was, of course, easier. Moreover the shortage of transport and dreadful road between the British base and the Heights were crucial. Having said this however, there could be no doubt that the French organization was superior to that of the British.

The basic administrative problems – food supply and preparation, treatment of the sick and wounded – were all catered for at regimental level. Every regiment had a baker who distributed fresh bread daily, a surgeon who worked with the aid of an assistant, full medicine chests and an efficient mule ambulance service. In the French camp food was prepared collectively, whereas the British soldier was issued with individual rations which he had to prepare as well as he was able. This difference helps to explain how the French were able to keep up their health surprisingly well on one third as much meat as the British.* Only in mid-winter did the British adopt the technique of mass food production and as soon as they did so their circumstances began to improve. Even when the French food stocks were at their lowest, there was always enough meat for a full ration to be issued every other day. Dehydrated cakes of dried vegetables helped to reduce the transport demands. Nor did the French have to face a real breakdown in their transport arrangements for in addition to a properly organized wagon train they had built paved roads from Kamiesch and Kazatch to their siege lines on the plateau. Looking at these things the British marvelled. By comparison their own facilities were indeed entirely unfit for active service.[16]

With the arrival of 15,000 reinforcements in December the effective force of Canrobert's army was about three times the strength of that of the British, and in January Raglan estimated it to be four

---

* The British ration was 1½ lb. meat per day, that of the French ½ lb.

times as much. Cholera, scurvy, gangrene, fever, frost-bite and
dysentery had all exacted their toll of the men who had crossed the
Alma and survived the misty battle of Inkerman, and the drafts of
young recruits who started to arrive in November. Only the
Highland Brigade at Balaclava retained anything like its original
complement; those on the plateau front seemed to melt away. Duty
in the trenches was an ordeal comparable only in its miseries with the
trench warfare of the First World War. The horrors of modern
gunfire, of barrages and bombardments were unknown, but the men
of the Crimea in the winter of 1854–5 were sent to the trenches in a
state which no modern general would tolerate let alone the men
themselves. When they got there each soldier would sit in slush and
water with his back to the parapet; in the early part of the winter he
was there for two nights out of three. (And on one occasion the men
of the 46th Regiment spent six nights out of seven in the trenches.)
In twenty-four hours of such duty he was lucky to get three hours'
sleep.*

None but those of the hardiest constitution could stand it. In the
46th Regiment men were dying at the rate of three a day; out of the
708 men who had landed less than two months before, 108 were
dead by 10 December and 270 were sick. On the same day the 7th
paraded 354 officers and men out of 1,024 and early in January the
Grenadier Guards had only 128 men fit for duty. As the winter wore
on it became increasingly true that 'the finest army that had ever
left our shores' was nothing more than 'a contingent of the French'.
At the end of January it was only 11,000 strong, the sick and
wounded totalled 23,000, and a writer in *The Times* calculated that
by 15 March Raglan and his staff would be the sole survivors of the
British expedition.

In fairness to the French it must be said that they did a great deal
to help out their allies. Ambulances were lent, from Bruat's division
700 men were put to work on the road to Balaclava, and daily 800
other French soldiers carried up ammunition for the British.
Additionally the French took over the right of the British line,
enabling the British soldiers' spell in the trenches to be reduced

* The state of discipline may be judged by Colonel Egerton's Regimental Order issued on 21 November 1854. 'The utmost vigilance is
required on the part of the sentries in front of the Enemy, which cannot be
observed if they are suffered to muzzle themselves up like old Women, or
by tying Handkerchiefs on the Capes of their Coats round their heads
impairing the sight and hearing.'

from a twenty-four hourly stretch to twelve.[17] Raglan took all the help almost for granted. Reporting that 'the position of our troops is greatly improved by being relieved of part of the harassing duties they have had imposed on them,' Raglan continued '*but*, speaking confidentially, I am of the opinion, notwithstanding what General Canrobert says, that more might have been done.'[18] His idea of 'more' was for the French to take over the trenches every third night. For their part the French felt aggrieved at their allies' seeming lack of gratitude and even of interest. Those working alongside the French on the Balaclava road were not British, but Turks and Russian prisoners, and the French troops carrying ammunition up to the British guns on the plateau rarely saw any British troops employed on the same fatigue. Bosquet, seeing how his men were being used, reported to Canrobert 'the English seem not to take very much interest in these transport aids, for neither at Balaclava . . . nor at . . . Moulin . . . there were absolutely no English present.'[19]

At higher levels these suspicions were coupled with hints of bad faith. When the Duke of Newcastle asked his opposite number in Paris for a model of a certain type of cart which Canrobert's troops were using in the Crimea, Marshal Vaillant, the French Minister of War, said that he had no model but could provide drawings. But he advised against the use of such carts because the French had found them to be ill-adapted to the Crimean terrain and had perfected a better cart, numbers of which were now being built in Malta. When news leaked out that the French were providing themselves with a superior type of equipment and having it manufactured in British territory – at a time when the British authorities were only beginning to wake up to the idea of adopting an outmoded version of the same equipment – the British public was furious, and the subsequent outcry touched off fresh criticisms of Raglan. From the Crimea, Canrobert was penning glowing reports of his ally, and in Paris the Emperor told the British Ambassador, Cowley that he had the greatest admiration for Raglan. Privately, however, he commented that the British had 'an old woman' for a commander-in-chief.[20] Meantime while other British officers were wondering why he did not *order* the French to give more help, Raglan was hardly returning full measure for what he was getting. Writing to Lord Panmure – Newcastle's successor as War Minister – on 24 February 1855, he said 'I consider the presence of a Turkish force little short of 30,000 men at Eupatoria in the highest degree important, but General Canrobert is anxious to have a portion of it here. *I shall endeavour to prevent this,* and as Sir Edmund Lyons alone has the means of moving these Turkish troops and he agrees in my opinion, I hope we shall succeed in keeping Omar Pasha where he is . . .'[21]

While the sort of suspicion engendered by the attitudes described existed on the higher levels, the British and French troops themselves got on together remarkably well. Life in the French camp was difficult, but it was infinitely better than that in the British camps – a fact which was due primarily, as has been explained, to the supply lines running from the respective harbours. The British soldiers were astonished by the way their counterparts were able to live so well in such wretched surroundings, while to the French the British troops appeared woefully ignorant of how to look after themselves and afraid of work. Indeed the French soldiers' view would probably have been one of complete disgust, but they could not forget the British show of valour at the Alma, Balaclava and Inkerman. Naturally they resented having to help to build the Balaclava road and serve as porters for the British artillery. In time their grumbles were reflected in their attitude towards the British sick, and the wounded they carried down to Balaclava.

So far as military operations were concerned the siege could be considered to be at a standstill. Way back in November Raglan and Canrobert had decided that all they could do was to sit out the winter, and wait until better weather and reinforcements allowed a new attack to be mounted. During December (1854) and January (1855) it is doubtful whether their combined force could have repulsed a determined Russian attack in the Chersonese. Apart from occasional sorties across the lines on moonless nights, however, Menschikoff did not attempt any offensive action. Contrary to the belief that they were inured to cold the Russians in their trenches were just as distressed as the British and French in theirs and so had little inclination to fight. On occasions the cold even led to an unofficial truce when men from both sides would walk about in 'No Man's Land' without attempting to molest each other. The dreary bombardment continued spasmodically. But in Sebastopol military bands played in the boulevards and dandified officers strolled in the streets of the fashionable shopping area, while their elegant lady friends window-gazed at bonnets and mantles. Only the rumble of the guns and the occasional camel-wagon carrying dead to the cemeteries served to remind the inhabitants that the war was still going on. With good reason they felt safe. The garrison of the town was getting tired but under Todleben's direction the defences were growing stronger and there were rumours that the Emperor Nicholas himself was bringing an army corps of about 47,000 fresh troops to lift the siege.

The rumours were completely unfounded. Nicholas never had any intention of taking the field in person, and there was no army 47,000 strong preparing to march down to the Crimea. The war had revealed the cracks in the Tsar's glossy Empire, and Nicholas knew the system had failed. Although corruption and inefficiency existed on both sides, the Russian shortcomings were way ahead of those of the Allies. Despite the fact that Russian had 600 miles of railway, supplies took longer to reach the Crimea than by ship from England. Medical supplies were almost non-existent, there were weevils in the meat, mould in the biscuits, and the troops' boots were falling to pieces. Count Leo Tolstoy sent despatches back to St Petersburg praising the dogged courage of Menschikoff's men but Nicholas knew that his bureaucracy had been exposed as a fraud. In February 1855 he caught a cold on parade in St Petersburg; pneumonia developed and within a few days he was dead.

14

THE INFLUENCE OF
FLORENCE NIGHTINGALE*

'Much is she worth and even more is made of her.'
In Hospital, W. E. Henley

What Florence Nightingale accomplished during the war against Russia led to immense changes in the treatment of the British soldier. From her time onwards a milder era dawned in the life of Britain's army, and from the army, the development that she helped to bring about spread throughout the whole nation. And so, if only because this English nurse – 'rather nice looking, but not a bit pretty'[1] – was one of the best friends the British soldier has ever had, an account of the war would not be complete without some mention of her beneficent work.

Born in 1819, Florence Nightingale was thirty-five years old when she answered the call that was her destiny. At that time it seemed as if Providence had been preparing Miss Nightingale for the work she was to undertake – had indeed arranged all the circumstances of her life, including a long-standing friendship with Sidney Herbert, the then Secretary at War. A thoughtful but eminently practical woman, Florence Nightingale's main talent was her penetrating logic. Undeterred by hypocrisy and male bluster she could sweep away all the paltry subterfuges of officialdom to expose the real facts of the situation. During her training as a nurse in England and in Germany she had studied hospital organization, principles of sanitation, and the administration of schools and workhouses. And these subjects, somewhat outside the normal curriculum of a student nurse, were to prove of greater importance in her predestination than the conventional training in how to deal with the sick. In 1853 she was the

* For a recent popular study, see Mrs Cecil Woodham-Smith's *Florence Nightingale, 1820–1910*.

superintendent of an 'Establishment for Gentlewomen during Illness' in London's Harley Street, and was already showing the trait of impatience which made her so formidable and so invaluable. 'From committees, charity and schism – from the Church of England and all other deadly sins – from philanthropy and all the deceits of the Devil – Good Lord deliver us', she wrote.

During her time at the Gentlewomen's Establishment news of the inadequacy of the British army's medical system started to filter back to England. From private letters, articles appearing in the press, and the long nominal rolls of those who had died in hospital which were published by *The Times*, the British public was soon in no doubt as to the facts of the situation. Florence Nightingale and Sidney Herbert were both impressed by the need to make a personal contribution to relieve the suffering, and following suggestions put forward by correspondents to *The Times* Herbert offered Florence the job of forming a female nursing organization for service in Crimean hospitals. Thus it was that on 21 October 1854 she left London for Constantinople in charge of a party of thirty-eight nurses.

Recruiting nurses had not proved as easy as Herbert and Florence had expected. Time had been limited of course but Florence herself observed tartly that money was the only inducement. Yet the wages – ten to eighteen shillings a week according to experience – were not high, even if allowance was made for the fact that lodging and travelling expenses were provided free. And from the beginning it was made clear that discipline would be of a high order. Any nurse found guilty of 'neglect of duty, immoral conduct or intoxication' would forfeit her pay and allowances and the terms of her contract stipulated that she would devote her full time to her work.

Arriving in Constantinople on 4 November, Florence's nurses were just in time to receive the wounded from the battle of Balaclava. The British military hospital had been established at Scutari, a suburb of Constantinople on the Asiatic side of the Bosphorus. There, the long yellow building known as the Selimah Kishler housing Turkish artillery had appeared to be suitable accommodation and had been requisitioned. Known as 'The Barrack' this building, which was to acquire an ignominious reputation, could never have been suited to its purpose without considerable modifications which were not effected until news of the scandalous conditions and insufficient facilities available there had sparked off a scandal in Britain. About half a mile south of the Barrack a plot of land had been earmarked as a cemetery and this was well stocked by its unfortunate inmates and those of a smaller building – formerly the summer residence of a certain Haidar Pasha, from which it took its name. There, with the widow of an officer killed in the Crimea as matron, the sick and wounded officers were housed. Conditions here were never quite so bad as those in the Barrack because the patients' purses were longer and they were able to buy amenities not available to the troops. But they were bad enough. Early in 1855 the hulks of two old battleships were pressed into service to accommodate the overflow of casualties from the main hospitals, and later still another hospital was added to the complex when a building was taken over at Kulali, on the shores of the Bosphorus, four miles above Scutari.

At Scutari itself there were no proper landing places, only the rickety wooden piers, unrepaired and inadequate and of a type which may still be seen on some of the Greek islands. Transport of casualties from ship to shore and from the shore to the hospitals depended mainly on the assistance of whoever happened to be available: sailors, Turks, the few medical orderlies carried in the ships, and even on the efforts of the casualties themselves. In the enormous Barrack, the lines of beds extended for four miles and it was in this building that the most tragic scenes of the war were enacted. When Florence Nightingale arrived it was being used not only as a hospital but also as a transit camp, convalescent depot and home for the wretched wives separated from their regiments when Raglan sailed for the Crimea. Over and above the shortage of doctors and equipment this fact was an added administrative complication.

In the long, dark wards of the Barrack every form of misery and abomination was hideously multiplied. The mattresses on the beds, the tiles of the unglazed floor which was never washed, and even the plaster on the walls were soaked with liquid excrement. The building was standing in 'a sea of sewage'.[2] Lice, maggots, rats and countless other forms of vermin crawled or ran everywhere. Describing the conditions to Sidney Herbert Florence wrote graphically 'The vermin might, if they had but unity of purpose, carry off the four miles of beds on their backs and march them into the War Office'.[3] That staff was short, doctors especially, goes without saying. (In his evidence at a Court of Inquiry, Dr John Hall, the Inspector General of Hospitals and Raglan's Principal Medical Officer excused this fact by saying that 'the number of surgeons would be enough if we had no casualties'.) Shortage of the most elementary hospital equipment may be illustrated by the fact that twenty chamber pots were considered enough for the needs of 2,000 men. Lavatory accommodation was equally sparse and the drains of the privies which served as such were loaded with an immovable mass of excrement, from which 'the wind blew the sewer air up the pipes . . . into the corridors'. For a long time there was no operating theatre and surgeons amputated in the wards or corridors in the sight and hearing of all around. 'Some allowance must be made', said Dr Menzies – Hall's deputy as Inspector of Hospitals, 'for the confusion we were in.' Nor was it only equipment and supplies that were insufficient; method and decency were also lacking. The doctors worked unceasingly in the wards, protesting and exhausted. With insufficient equipment, short of drugs and without any hope of remedial activity on the part of their seniors, they had little hope of preventing the collapse of the system.

Many of the men who entered the hospitals were unable to speak, and had no identification marks, not even regimental insignia. They died anonymously or under names to which they had no right. Under a single name – that left by a careless orderly over the bed on which they died – it was possible for a dozen men to be shown dead, and the number recorded as such rarely tallied with the number who were actually buried.* More often than not death came as a merciful release for their sufferings were beyond imagination. After Inkerman the sick and wounded were lumped together in the same wards; and those who were only slightly wounded and who might have recovered caught the fevers from the others and were soon dead. Once a man entered the Scutari hospital 'all cheerfulness disappeared – he drew his blanket over his head and waited for the end.'

The dead were buried in the afternoon. About two o'clock, invalids capable of performing the duty would carry the corpses out of the wards to carts which waited to convey them to the cemetery. There 'a pit about ten feet deep and fourteen feet square [had been prepared to receive] . . . those who had died during the last twenty-four hours.' 'One row laid, the next covered, and the feet of those who deposited them necessarily trampled on the forms below'.[4]

* An average of 50 a day between September and November 1854.

Perhaps the nearest parallel would be the Great Plague. In February 1855 two out of every five men treated at Scutari died; at Kulali the death rate was one in two. In December 1854, at a time when Menzies was reporting to Dr Hall that '. . . our hospitals here are in first rate order as regards cleanliness and comfort and this opinion has been expressed in my hearing by various officers . . . I may also state that Lord William Paulet [the military commandant at Constantinople] on his first inspection . . . was also pleased to acknowledge that the establishment was in a most satisfactory order, and very different from what he had been led to expect . . .' over 2,000 men a month were dying. Menzies said nothing about this or even about the filth and squalor – although he did admit that some of the corridors in the Barracks were 'rather dirty'. (And adding in parenthesis that 'the other parts of the hospital, both passages and wards are in a perfect state of cleanliness . . .')[5]

To Florence Nightingale must go most of the credit for putting things right. At the same time, when assessing the value of her work it is important to remember that she took up her duties at a time when the conscience of Britain was demanding an immediate and effective reform of the British Army's medical services. If Florence Nightingale was providentially prepared for the occasion, so too was the occasion providentially prepared for her. Florence's magnificent intervention undoubtedly saved the lives of thousands of men but it would be wrong to suppose that she fought single-handed all the arrayed force of a cruel and obstinate reaction. Her principal enemies were the stupidity and incompetence of the senior medical officers who resented – understandably enough when one stops to consider the social background of the times – the criticism and interference of a woman. But she was invariably supported by the irresistible weight of public opinion, the patronage and approval of Queen Victoria – who spoke of her as 'that excellent and valuable person' – and the tremendous influence of *The Times* and the press generally.

Even the sentimentality of the Victorian era was an advantage. To the public the obdurate and essentially practical Miss Nightingale was depicted as the Lady with the Lamp, the shadow on the pillow, 'the soldiers' cheer, watched by angels with sweet approving smiles'. Her portrait appeared on paper bags and was reproduced in unrecognizable form on countless pieces of china. Babies, race-horses and streets were called Florence, and a best-selling biography – priced at one penny – was published which detailed 'her christian heroic deeds in the Land of Tumult and Death'. Florence herself, irritated and embarrassed by this effusive idolization, never seems to have appreciated that propaganda of this nature provided one of those peculiar advantages which made her absolutely invulnerable and almost invincible.

Her only public opposition was that of the prurient and theologically inclined, and they considered she was either brazen or unorthodox. 'Will it be believed, [queried a leader in *The Times*] that persons have been found of minds sufficiently impure and polluted to charge Miss Nightingale and her companions with want of delicacy and propriety? . . . She has aroused the *odium theologicum* in some, we hope not in many, parsonages in these realms. Poor lady! She is a Papist – she is an Anglican – she is a High Churchwoman – she is a Low Churchwoman – she is a Sublapsarian – she is a Supralapsarian . . . She is gone out not as a nurse, but as a Propagandist.'[6]

In fact the lady superintendent had started her work without any fluster whatsoever and with her customary inexorable efficiency. A less courageous woman might well have been daunted by what she found: dysentery cases dying at the rate of one in two; junior medical officers who were 'all cubs' and who resented being called away from their dinners on the arrival of wounded; a wash house 'admirably fitted by the Turkish authorities' which had been seized by the Commissariat and was being used as a store. But not Florence. Of the requisition system by which stores were issued it was said Treasury red tape would rather let twenty men die than permit a single infringement of rules. To get drugs, medicines and equipment for the wards the system demanded authorized signatures and counter-signatures. If these were not forthcoming, or not in order, whatever was being requisitioned was not let out of the store. When her nurses ran foul of this system soon after arrival Florence demonstrated that she was prepared to use violence if need be to get replacements for the rags of shirts which were the only clothing some of the patients possessed.

In late October 1854, an official Commission of Inquiry into the condition of the sick and wounded in Scutari had been appointed by the British Government, and its Commissioners arrived in Constantinople during the first week of November. Although Dr Hall tried to suppress information these men did a great deal of good work and their report – reticent and incomplete as it was – certainly had the effect of revealing a considerable amount of ugly truth and of speeding of departmental reforms. Reference to Miss Nightingale and her nurses was consciously discreet: 'We have reason to believe that the services of these hospital attendants have been extremely valuable'. The Commissioners were not prepared to commit themselves on the success or otherwise of a new-fangled corps of female nurses until it had proved itself. Their job, as they saw it, was to restrict their comments to more intelligible factors. And so: 'there was too much port wine in the hospitals, but the supply of doctors was inadequate'.

The Sanitary Commission followed the Hospital Commission and the members of the Sanitary Commission had exceptional powers. In consequence men were employed under their direction to clear the drains, tidy up the hospital area, and generally make the hospitals themselves decent and orderly. Without in any way detracting from the value of Florence Nightingale's work, it is fair to say that it was the Sanitary Commission which carried out the most urgent reforms and reduced the mortality rate. Yet without Miss Nightingale's representations to Sidney Herbert it is doubtful whether the Sanitary Commission would ever have been sent out from England, and it would appear that even if they were not actually dominated by her will its members were greatly influenced by her proposals.

As soon as Sidney Herbert realized that Florence Nightingale's nurses were a success he decided to reinforce them and in November another party was sent off to Constantinople. Having known Florence for over seven years it is somewhat surprising that he should have shown such poor judgement in doing so without consulting the woman whose influence in Scutari was now well established. In charge of the second party of forty-seven nurses was a Miss Mary Stanley, who till then had counted herself one of Florence's friends. Unfortunately she was on the way to becoming a convert to the Roman Catholic church and Florence had little patience with the teachings of Rome. The situation was further aggravated by the fact that Mary's party included a number of Roman Catholics and Mary herself had been appointed to a superintendency rank equivalent to her own.

When the contingent reached Scutari shortly before Christmas 1854 the situation was an uncomfortable one. From the very beginning the new nurses objected to Florence's domineering attitude; a few got drunk; and one – if her own story is to be believed – was grossly impertinent. As a temporary solution the new arrivals were diverted to the British naval hospital on the Bosphorus but this was a waste of talent and the situation was finally resolved by breaking up the contingent and distributing its members between the hospitals at Scutari and Balaclava. Fundamentally there was nothing except temperament involved; most of the new nurses worked well and some actually replaced incompetent or unruly members of Florence's original party. Florence herself was angry not so much with the nurses but with Herbert for sending them out without consulting her and with Mary Stanley for agreeing to accept an appointment equivalent to her own. Florence would not tolerate any rivals, and the wretched Mary Stanley ultimately had to return to England.

Among other volunteers to come to Scutari about this time was a certain Lady Alicia Blackwood and her husband the Reverend Dr Blackwood. Dr Blackwood took over as hospital chaplain while Lady Alicia – after she had shown that she was prepared to work under Florence's direction – was given charge of the soldiers' women in the hospital area. According to Lady Alicia there were about 260 or so of these women; all were in rags, covered with vermin and regarded by all and sundry as a 'great evil and difficulty'.[7] Most of them had come down from Varna and were the survivors of a very much larger party whose names and graves have never been recorded. When one of them died her grave was indicated merely by a crude cross on which was painted 'A Woman'. With no employment and no way of earning an honest living, nobody to look after them, or means of getting back to England – not even, it seems, with anyone concerned as to whether they were buried decently – their condition was deplorable. 'Their habits of intemperance had become such that almost anything they could get they would sell in order to purchase that dreadful poison Arak, which was sold in abundance by the Greeks who occupied every small available shed in the surroundings of the Barrack.'[8]

On the very first day of her mission Lady Alicia saw one of these women die 'on a heap of filthy black rags on a floor in a dark room containing about sixty women, from twenty-five to thirty men, and some infants'. No doctor had seen this woman and when she died her body was quickly rolled up, carried away in a piece of canvas and the vacant place taken by another.[9] Mercifully, the majority of children born in these crowded horrors were stillborn. As a result of Lady Alicia's exertions, however, a maternity ward was organized and most of the women were found jobs as hospital maids or in Florence's newly established laundry. (Up to then there had been no laundry and most of the hospital chores had had to be carried out by the patients themselves.)

Through the winter the hospital mortality rate rose ominously and if it had not been for Florence Nightingale it would have been worse. Gradually, however, kitchens, stores and wash-houses were organized; men were issued with soap and towels and fresh clothes were provided. Such accomplishments may seem very matter-of-fact. But none of them came easily and the story is told how Florence – unable to defeat regulations and confound imbecility – on one occasion engaged 200 workmen on her own responsibility to carry out repairs she considered were urgent. All this administrative work was undertaken in addition to her duties as a nurse, which sometimes kept her on her feet for twenty hours at a stretch.

> Miss Nightingale is in appearance, [wrote one who saw her in the wards of Scutari] just what you would expect in any other well-bred woman ... her manner and countenance are prepossessing, and this without the possession of actual beauty; it is a face not easily forgotten ... with an eye betokening great self possession, and giving when she wishes a quiet look of firm determination to every feature. Her general demeanour is quiet, rather reserved; still I am much mistaken if she is not gifted with a very lively sense of the ridiculous ... Her nerve is wonderful; I have been with her at very severe operations; she was more than equal to the trial. She has an utter disregard for contagion. I have known her spend hours over men dying of cholera or fever. The more awful to every sense any particular case, especially if it was that of a dying man, her slight form would be seen bending over him administering to his ease in every way in her power and seldom quitting his side until death released him.[10]

Much of the opposition to Florence's reforms stemmed from the army's senior medical officer, and a great and mutual hate developed between her and Dr Hall – whose award of a K.C.B. she declared could only mean that he had been appointed 'Knight of the Crimean Burial Grounds'. With her exacting critical faculty for analysing problems she wrote that the horrors of war were not wounds and blood and fever; they were 'intoxication, drunken brutality, demoralisation and disorder on the part of the inferior; jealousies, meanness, indifference, selfish brutality on the part of the superior'.[11]

Initially, in contrast with those of their ally, the French hospitals seem to have been well run. Sisters of Mercy 'with the freshest of complexions and the snowiest of caps' had been held as the example of how things should be run, and Florence Nightingale's nursing service had been formed to emulate their work. And up to the end of 1855 there is no doubt that the French sick and wounded were better off than those of the British. But while the latter were making a phenomenal recovery from a state of abject and inexcusable incompetence and misery, French development was in reverse. Having started the war with high standards of sanitation and medical treatment they failed to keep pace with the demands that were put upon them as the number of French troops in the theatre increased. In the winter of 1854–5 the health of the French troops was relatively good, while that of the British was in dire straits; by the following winter the position was reversed. For two reasons the plight of the French did not receive the publicity that had been accorded to the breakdown in the British medical services. First because a strict censorship was applied to the statistics released to the press; and, second, because public attention was diverted by the imminent fall of Sebastopol.

In the first three months of 1856 however fourteen French hospitals in the Constantinople region treated about 53,000 patients and of these 10,000 died – 80 per cent of them with typhus. In field hospitals in the Crimea deaths from disease in the same period ran to between 19,000 and 25,000. Typhus was the main scourge but cholera was also a problem; indeed the French army was never really free of the disease from the time that it had first ravaged the French ranks in Varna. The story of French suffering during those winter months of 1855–6 equalled the horrors of the British the winter before. But unlike the British the French misery did not prompt improvement. With only minor success, Canrobert tried to effect some administrative changes and Florence Nightingale and the British Medical Department offered aid. Except for port wine and beef extract the latter was refused and the situation was only corrected when Sebastopol fell and the French army was shipped home.

One piece of French organization which impressed the British was their method of clearing casualties from the battlefield and after Inkerman an attempt was made to copy it. But the organization known as the Ambulance Corps did not last long, and its history does not make good reading. Formed from old soldiers whose average age was forty-seven, ' . . . they were men . . . that fell into more habits of dissipation than the other soldiers'.[12] Whatever the age or habits of its members, the Corps was extinct by the beginning of 1855. According to Florence Nightingale they all 'died of delirium or cholera'.[13]

Finally, since this chapter is primarily concerned with Florence Nightingale, mention must be made of a shortcoming revealed in the Crimea with which she was indirectly associated and for which the British Army should continue to give praise. An army, Napoleon is supposed to have said, marches on its stomach, and reference to the way the British soldier was fed has already been made. Both the supply and preparation of his food were deplorable. Few British soldiers were, or are, culinary artists; indeed the French would say that this particular accomplishment has never been congenial to the British temperament. Even up to quite recently the British soldier has preferred to sit down to a badly cooked meal of half-burnt stringy beef than face a skilfully prepared dish of unfamiliar ingredients. But in the Crimea his food – especially that prepared in the hospitals – was often completely unpalatable, and the man primarily responsible for correcting this state of affairs was none other than a Frenchman.

This man, the chef of the Reform Club in London, joined Florence Nightingale in April 1855. Excitable and to the soldiers a somewhat absurd character, the good-natured but flamboyant Soyer had travelled to the Crimea at his own expense determined to show the army authorities how to make the most of their rations. He brought not only new ideas about cookery but a new stove to replace the mediaeval pattern camp kettles then in service. And this stove, which bears his name, has lasted to this day. (Soyer was dubbed a humbug by the die-hards of the old school: 'Soldiers,' said General Eyre, 'don't require such good messes as these while campaigning . . . you will improve the cook but spoil the soldier.'[14]*

---

* Of Soyer's work *Punch* said
    '. . . a cook can defy, you see,
    A commissariat's knavery.
    The soldier who saves a nation free
    Should have a ration savoury.'

To Florence Nightingale the British Army and British nursing service owes a great deal. Not only did she overthrow the antiquated and outmoded system of the Army Medical Department, she was also the founder of modern nursing. After the Crimean War soldiers' wives were never seen on active service again. Florence had made it clear that none of them who went to the Crimea were of sufficient use to serve the purpose which for so long had provided the pretext of their presence in the field – the care of the wounded. Reform came after the war and from Florence Nightingale's time onwards there dawned a milder era in the life of Britain's army, and from the army the influence of her work spread throughout the whole nation.*

* Tragically, Florence faded away after many years of growing weakness of the intellect, and when the Order of Merit – newly instituted in 1907 by King Edward vii – was brought to her in bed she scarcely recognized its import.

15

THE SIEGE:
THE FIRST PHASE

The bombardment of October 1854 and that which the battle of Inkerman prevented were both in the nature of artillery preparation for a somewhat belated assault on Sebastopol. And, as has been told, when the first failed to have the desired effect and the second to materialize, winter's wrath fell in full fury on the Allies and no assault was possible. As a result the operations before Sebastopol degenerated into a sort of siege – which is how they are usually described. Yet it must be made clear that by definition there was never a real siege as such. A siege proper postulates complete investment by a numerically superior force, with shortages of supplies and munitions for the garrison adding to its anxieties of bombardment and assault. Except for bombardment all of these conditions were wanting. With the northern and eastern approaches to the town wide open, Russian troops were able to march in and out at will, as Soimonoff's columns demonstrated; even the south side of the town was not completely covered. This situation continued until the Sebastopol defences were stormed and so far as the Allies were concerned the conditions analogous to a siege were confined to the build-up of their resources.

With operations at a standstill the royal personages in both allied armies appear to have decided that their wisdom and experience might be better utilized at home. In fact neither the Duke of Cambridge nor Prince Napoleon could have picked a less propitious time to leave the Crimea. With Britain's newspapers filled with grotesque details of the Crimean scandals, criticism of the Duke's action was inevitable.* Prince Napoleon's return was also

* The Duke's return was only part of Britain's attrition problem in her aged leadership corps. By mid-November few of the original commanders were still on active service. Generals Cathcart, Strangways, Goldie and Tylden were dead; Brown, Bentinck, Torrens and Adams had been wounded; others had returned home because of ill health and more were to follow. Even Sir John Burgoyne was recalled.

shrouded with suspicion. Despite Canrobert's testimony to the Prince's conduct, rumours and innuendoes suggesting cowardice had preceded his arrival in Paris.

Back in the Crimea, Raglan was still trying to persuade Canrobert to take over more ground from him. Meantime Burgoyne was pressing Raglan for a change in the whole system of operations. To him the Malakoff Bastion had always been the key of the Russian defences, but as long as the Inkerman plateau was in Russian hands he had recognized that any attack on it would be impracticable. After the battle of Inkerman, however, he had concluded that not only was an assault on the Malakoff feasible, but that by extending the siege works on the plateau it would be possible to seal the Tchernaya valley. Once this was done Russian reinforcements would have to cross Sebastopol harbour in order to get into the town. But French co-operation would be necessary and when it was suggested that they should take over some of the ground on the British left to leave Raglan's troops free to deal with the Malakoff, Canrobert refused to do so. What Canrobert had decided were the French objectives – the Central Bastion in the western sector of their front and the Flagstaff Bastion in the south-west corner – were relatively close to their base of Kamiesch and this suited them very well. If they were to take over the attacks of the Malakoff they would have to occupy the Inkerman plateau and the ridge next to it on the west of the Careening Ravine. As this would make for supply difficulties they did not relish the prospect. While agreeing that it would be advantageous to extend the proposed area of attack along a wider front, Canrobert rejected Burgoyne's proposal. On 26 January however, this decision was reversed when Marshal Vaillant, the French Minister of War, wrote to Canrobert ordering him to accept, and the French force was redeployed. By mid-February half of it had taken up position on the two ridges overlooking the Careening Ravine, while the other half remained on the ground originally taken up in October; and between these two halves the British held both sides of the Woronzoff Road. From the French point of view it was not an ideal situation, and with some justification Canrobert subsequently complained that it made for much of the French difficulties in the months that were to come.

February was the month in which the strength of the British army declined to its lowest, while that of the French rose to nearly 90,000 men. In March the British slowly began to recover. But until their allies were ready to move the French were not prepared to do anything on their own. Their interpretation of allied co-operation was joint action in all operations. Nevertheless there was a good deal of speculation as to what the next operation should be. At the beginning of the month Canrobert wrote to Vaillant to say that he thought the Malakoff could be captured without much difficulty. Meantime his chief engineer, General Bizot was telling Burgoyne that an attack on the Malakoff would be extremely hazardous until the hill in front of it (known as the Mamelon) was in allied hands. But if the Mamelon were captured the Malakoff would become an attainable objective, and the British would be able to attack the Redan. In fact the British engineers were all against any assault on the Redan. The nature of the soil precluded their trenches being pushed to within less than 400 yards of it, and it was reckoned that Russian fire – not only from the Redan itself but also from subsidiary strong points on either flank – would annihilate troops crossing this wide stretch of open ground. This was a detail whose importance was not evident until later. Meantime, with allied operations at a standstill the astute and energetic Todleben was moving heaven and earth to prepare for the assault he knew was bound to come. Intelligence information or clever deduction had led him to the conclusion that the Allies would change their plan and concentrate on the north-west corner of their front. And so, in the middle of February he started to bolster the defences in this sector. With a plentiful supply of labour, a sufficiency of tools and mechanized equipment, and a seemingly inexhaustible supply of guns, the work was effected at a speed at which the Allies could not compete.

A report that Tsar Nicholas had died reached the allied commanders on 6 March, and as it was thought that the news would have lowered the morale of the Sebastopol garrison the moment was considered propitious for an attack on the Mamelon. The British would press on with their preparations for an assault on the Redan, Bizot was told on 9 March by Sir Harry Jones, who had been given command of the siege operations after Burgoyne's departure. In the meantime the French should seize the Mamelon, and the following day was suggested as being a good time to attack. When the suggestion reached Canrobert, however, it was rejected; he was not prepared to mount an assault at such short notice. In the event this

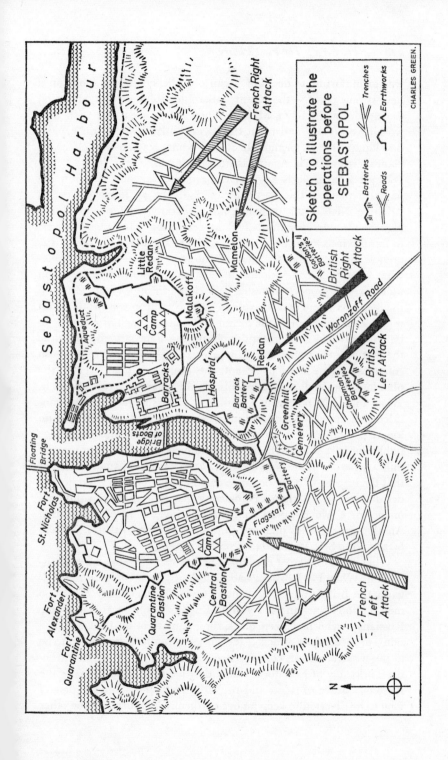

Sketch to illustrate the operations before SEBASTOPOL

Batteries — Trenches

Roads — Earthworks

CHARLES GREEN.

Sebastopol Harbour

French Right Attack

British Right Attack

British Left Attack

Rodgers's Batteries

Chapman's Batteries

Woronzoff Road

Little Redan

Mamelon

Malakoff

Camp

Redan

Aqueduct

Hospital

Barrack Battery

Greenhill Cemetery

Barracks

Bridge of Boats

Floating Bridge

St. Nicholas Fort

Flagstaff Battery

Camp

French Left Attack

Fort Alexander

Fort Quarantine

Quarantine Bastion

Central Bastion

N

was an unfortunate decision because Todleben started work on a
new strong point – the Kamtchatka Lunette – on the Mamelon
during the night of 11 March. When it was seen that with men
working on it day and night the Kamtchatka Lunette was rapidly
developing into a formidable strong point, Raglan himself urged
Canrobert to attack. Again Canrobert refused.

Never a particularly aggressive character, Canrobert was a much
harassed man at this particular period. On 27 January General
Adolphe Niel – an engineer, administrator and one of Louis
Napoleon's aides-de-camp – had arrived in the Crimea with powers
to inquire into, report on, and to a great extent take charge of, the
progress of operations. In Paris the Emperor had come to the somewhat unoriginal conclusion that Sebastopol would never be taken
unless it was properly invested and closed in on all sides. In itself
the idea was sound enough and as Louis Napoleon was firmly set on
it arrangements were made for an additional French army corps to
be concentrated at Constantinople during February. By the time
the first of these troops started to arrive Canrobert had either been
converted to, or come to accept, the Emperor's plan. In fact the
plan took a good deal of stomaching and Raglan never did accept it.
When Prince Napoleon had returned to Paris in January one consideration uppermost in the Emperor's mind was that there was no
longer a Bonaparte with the army. To maintain and encourage
public support of the dynasty – especially as one of its props was the
military nature of the Napoleonic Legend – it was virtually essential
that the imperial family be represented at the front. So what he had
decided was no less than a Napoleonic gesture – personal command
of the force which would complete the investment of Sebastopol.
Another aspect of his plan was for 20,000 of Omar Pasha's Turks to
be moved to Sebastopol to take part in the siege.

What use to make of the Turks had already created a lot of discussion. When the Russians had abandoned their campaign in Bulgaria the British navy had moved Omar Pasha's army of 55,000
men, 11,000 horses and 111 guns to Eupatoria. On 17 February, the
Russians – who had been blockading Eupatoria on the landward
side – unsuccessfully attacked the Turks with a force estimated to be
as large as 40,000. In consequence Raglan was in favour of letting
the Turks stay at Eupatoria where they were clearly disturbing the
Russians' peace of mind and probably causing a large number of
men to be diverted to keep an eye on them. Canrobert, on the other

hand, was all for moving the Turks into the allied sectors of the lines – garrisoning Eupatoria with some of the Sultan's troops from Egypt, if need be. Raglan was apprehensive. He thought that the Turks would probably promote sickness and disease; the Allies already had too many men too close together and the Turks who were to join them were 'not noted for their cleanliness in camp'. Raglan was also uncertain about the advisability of having Omar Pasha around. The situation was bad enough with just him and Canrobert trying to co-operate. To bring another independent commander whose troops were differently organized appeared to be compounding confusion and dissension. Moreover the fact that Omar Pasha, having been a marshal for over a year, regarded himself as senior to both Raglan and Canrobert, posed an additional problem. And as the French did not pay him the respect due to his appointment when he participated in allied conferences and councils, Raglan was hard put to keep everything on a cordial basis. However, as the strength of the French army was now three times that of the British and Omar Pasha himself favoured the idea of coming to Sebastopol, Raglan could hardly persist with his objections. And so at the beginning of April 20,000 Turks and thirty guns arrived.

On 6 April the British Secretary of State for War, now Lord Panmure, wrote to Raglan to say that the troops of another ally would be taking their place beside the British army in the near future. Count Cavour – already planning a united Italy – had persuaded King Victor Emmanuel of Sardinia to declare war against Russia so that he might be represented, on behalf of Italy, in the European Congress which would inevitably come at the close of the war. And so, early in May a 15,000 strong contingent of Sardinian troops, under General De La Marmora – who had been specifically ordered to place himself at Raglan's disposal – landed at Balaclava. Suspicion that the French wanted to take charge of the Sardinians had occasioned a great deal of correspondence and Panmure had gone out of his way to emphasize to Raglan that the Sardinians were 'sensitive lest they should be considered as mercenaries ... though they must act under your orders and be at your disposal. The Emperor has a design to lay his hands on them but this must never be allowed.'[1] With the arrival of the Sardinians, three regular regiments from the Mediterranean, which had been relieved by Militia volunteers, and some sizeable drafts of reinforcements the strength of the British army was now more on a par with that of the French.*

It was May before matters really started to improve for the British and until then Raglan was in a difficult position. Whenever the question of a full-scale assault came up in the councils of war, Raglan had to repeat that he was not ready. As a result the generals on both sides developed a hearty disrespect for each other, and all Raglan's tact and patience were needed to keep the peace between them. On occasions patience and civility broke down. When Canrobert opened one allied conference with the rhetorical under-statement of the campaign: 'Gentlemen, we are here for the capture of Sebastopol', Admiral Lyons was heard to say 'Oh! That's it, is it?' and his subordinate Admiral Stewart 'who was readily moved to unrestrained and boisterous laughter burst into an uncontrollable fit'.[2] In the British headquarters Canrobert was branded as a vacillating individual who 'never seems to know his own mind two days together'.[3] He had agreed on a major bombardment for 3 April but on 1 April asked to have it postponed until the 5th when he hoped Omar Pasha's troops would begin to arrive. There would then be less danger of an attack on the Allies near the Russian army of about 40,000 men on the Mackenzie Heights. Then, on 4 April, he asked for it to be put off until the 9th. Finally, when the bombardment did open on 9 April, all the allied batteries fired from a quarter past five in the morning until nearly noon – when Canrobert decided that not enough damage had been done to promise a

---

* At that time it was illegal to transfer men from one regiment to another. Furthermore only the first 25 infantry regiments of the British Line had two battalions. With the customary plea that the British economy would not stand the expense the British Government had disbanded much of the infantry and the law which had stood since the days of Cromwell had not been amended. 'Drafting' could take place between battalions of the *same* regiment but not between regiments, and so recruits could not be used as replacements for seasoned soldiers in regiments which were not on active service. In consequence a host of youngsters were sent to the Crimea, where they died for lack of training and experience.

Nor could the Militia, only re-raised by the Duke of Wellington a few years before be *sent* abroad, although militiamen might volunteer for service with the line and militia units might volunteer to serve abroad.

There was never any question of conscription. Britain was not prepared to go to that length, resorting instead to the time-honoured precedent of raising foreign mercenaries to make up the numbers. (Some 7,000 Swiss and German red-coated British infantry joined the army in the Crimea.)

successful assault.* Although Raglan favoured an immediate attack it was not feasible to launch one without Canrobert's agreement. When Raglan suggested that the assault should be made on the 14th Canrobert refused again.

Part of Canrobert's reticence stemmed from instructions he had received from Louis Napoleon. He was 'not to assault unless perfectly certain of the result being in our favour, but also not to attempt it if the sacrifice of life should be great'.[4] Apart from this Imperial restriction, however, the French generals were less inclined to irresponsible action than the British. On 18 April Raglan was again calling for an attack, but from his own ranks General Windham wrote 'This pleases many, but does not please me, nor did it the French. If we stormed we should be beaten'.[5] And a comment by the French Admiral Bruat illustrates how far apart the British and French staff were: 'The English have advanced their batteries to within 600 yards of the town and they and their General all want to go in! The French have got within 60 yards of the town and their General . . . won't go in!' On 24 April it was agreed that a combined attack would be launched on the 28th. Less than twenty-four hours later Canrobert again said 'Non' – this time because he reckoned that it would be prudent to await the arrival of the Imperial Guard and 20,000 other troops who were due shortly.[6] Writing home, a young subaltern named Gordon, who was to make his name in China and die in Khartoum, said that the French seemed to be afraid and were 'cramping the movements of the British'.[7] But if the British thought that the French were cramping their style, it was equally true to say that the French thought their allies – 'ces malheureux Anglais' – were nothing but a hindrance.

One of the factors responsible for the bitterness which had developed during the winter months was the relative proximity of the French trenches to those of the Russians. Since the end of 1854 the Russians had been making sorties against the Allies and a number of small but bloody engagements had been fought in which only the Zouaves had distinguished themselves. In addition to their sorties the Russians had also been pushing out their defences and building formidable batteries in the no man's land between the

---

* Canrobert's appreciation of the amount of damage done was correct. The French artillery had damaged the Mamelon and some of the outer defences but the British guns made little impression on the Redan. The Malakoff, protected by the Mamelon, was hardly damaged at all.

opposing lines. Nearly all the new works were in the French-held sectors of the front and because the French did not react quickly and aggressively towards their installations the British decided that the French were 'certainly . . . not the men we took them for'.[8]

Throughout March the Russians pushed their defences forward and as they reclaimed more and more land the British attitude towards their allies worsened. For the first time since the Alma, Raglan's men had found something about which they felt superior to the French. And in writing home nearly everybody dwelt on the 'disgrace' of the French and how they could no longer look up to them. Following the success of a Russian sortie on the night of 22 March, the French were not looking up to the British either. Because their allies had not guarded the Great Ravine on the French right flank the Russians had been able to attack the French flank. Guarding the ravine was a British responsibility and Canrobert and Bosquet had told the British brigade commander concerned that if it was not done properly the Russians could break through at this point – which was exactly what happened. Before this attack Raglan's appreciation of the situation in this sector implied that the French could not protect themselves, and that the British were needed to keep the French from being forced out of their trenches.

That the Russians were advancing their lines and building up their defences in front of the French rather than the British was largely fortuitous. On the French left they tried – successfully for a a time – to occupy and fortify a cemetery which lay outside the town's walls. If they had been able to do so permanently, their defence line would have been shortened. On the French right where most of their new defences were established, the Russian aim was to strengthen the Malakoff because – as Burgoyne, Niel and others had recognized – this really was the key to the defence line. Ironically the Malakoff was opposite the area originally assigned to the British but taken over later by the French.

The April bombardment, starting on Easter Monday, 9 April, lasted ten days. Easter had been celebrated in Sebastopol: 'In the afternoon joyous groups met on the bastions, making music, dancing and playing various games.'[9] And in the evening a military band gave a concert in the boulevard near the Khozarsky memorial. The French had also celebrated Easter; soldiers with bells announcing the hour of mass in the camps, flowers in the little wooden chapels where the altars rested on drums. 520 guns were employed on the allied side – of these only 123 were British; and they were answered by more than 900 guns from Sebastopol. About 2,000 tons of ammunition (165,000 rounds) were fired towards Sebastopol* and at the end of the ten days nobody could see any difference in the general aspect of Sebastopol. With the exception of the Flagstaff Bastion the bombardment had accomplished virtually nothing because Todleben had seen to it that any change inflicted during the day was repaired during the night. The total number of casualties were given as 6,131 Russians, 1,587 French and 263 British.[10] The large number of Russian casualties may be attributed to the fact that the Russian infantry was brought up to the front and kept under arms behind the batteries ready to repel the attack which never materialized, and to the fire of the allied mortars, which continued through the night when the guns fell silent, to deter the Russian working parties labouring to repair the day's damage. Among the French casualties was General Bizot, the French chief engineer, who was fatally wounded on 11 April.

Another long phase of uninspired routine followed this futile bombardment. Niel, in his role of special emissary, wrote to the Emperor to report that the bombardment had had little effect; that the capture of the Kamtchatka Redoubt on the Mamelon no longer had any value; that although the British had said that they were ready to storm the Redan across 700 yards of open ground, it was his opinion they would think better of it; and that finally a complete investment of Sebastopol was really the only solution. Although Niel's estimate of the damage done by the bombardment was very different from that of Todleben his opinion as to the futility of an assault until the British and French had sapped their way up to the Russian defences was sound. But the Flagstaff Bastion had been reduced to such a ruin that Todleben had given it up for lost on the 15th and on the 21st the French had dug their way forward to within 100 yards of it. But nothing came of this fact. (As has been related an assault was proposed for 28 April, postponed by Canrobert on the 25th and the next date fixed on the calendar for a general assault was 10 May. Canrobert, unable to resist the pressure applied by Niel on behalf of the Emperor was now regretting that he had been so eager to urge the British to open the bombardment so early.)

* The Russians fired about 90,000 rounds in return.

In Europe, April had been a busy month for the Emperor Louis Napoleon. On the 16th he and the Empress Eugenie had made a State visit to Britain where in a Council of War at Windsor Castle he put forward his proposals for bringing the war to a speedy and successful conclusion. The forces in the Crimea would be divided into four armies. One of these, comprising 30,000 Turks and Egyptians would occupy Eupatoria; a second – of 30,000 French and an equivalent number of Turks – would hold the existing lines in front of Sebastopol; and the other two would be the 'armies of operations'. Of these the first was to consist of 25,000 British, 5,000 French, the 15,000 Sardinians and, if possible, 10,000 Turks. With Raglan as its supreme commander this army would drive the Russians off the Mackenzie Heights and advance north towards Simpheropol. Meantime, the second – 70,000 men composed in part of French troops drawn from the army deployed in front of Sebastopol and in part from the reserve in Constantinople – was to go by sea to Aloushta on the eastern shore of the Crimean peninsula. From there it would advance on Simpheropol – across some very rugged and mountainous country, it might be added – to link up in some unexplained fashion with Raglan. Then, turning south the combined force would drive the Russians into the sea and capture Sebastopol.

The plan certainly showed some originality, and it was at least as good as any that the French generals had suggested. Having been mooted in March it had been bandied about between Paris, the Crimea and London. In Paris the French cabinet had been quick to point out that if the Emperor went to the Crimea in person he could not return without a victory; failure in the field – which was possible – would be far more disastrous if he were there in person. Moreover now that Nicholas was dead the chances of a negotiated peace settlement were better than they had been for over two years. Vaillant believed that it was politically desirable for the Emperor to stay at home but thought that if he did go to the Crimea – 'where they all dream of a Marshal's baton but do nothing'[11] – Canrobert and Raglan would be compelled to adopt a joint plan and act on it. The Empress, having been warned by a fortune-teller, was apprehensive and tried to talk Louis Napoleon out of going. In the Crimea, Canrobert, who had received the details of the plan with mixed feelings, had said that for Louis Napoleon to come to the front would be 'a very false move'. Raglan thought that the Emperor's proper place was at home and commented: 'He would be mistaken if he supposed that he could at once on arrival achieve a great success.'[12] In London, however, the British Government seemed willing to judge the plan on its merits, and the Prime Minister, Palmerston, said that Raglan should 'enter into cordial concert and dispassionate consultation with Canrobert on the subject of this plan ...'[13]

Thus, by the time Napoleon presented his grandiose plan to the assembled gathering at Windsor – which included Palmerston and Burgoyne as well as the Queen and Prince Albert – the plan had had a considerable airing. 'We discussed at great length the state of affairs in the Crimea and everybody seemed to arrive at one opinion as to the inexpediency of the Emperor's going there' Panmure said afterwards.[14] Louis Napoleon stressed the importance of achieving unity of action and the belief that his presence in the Crimea might be able to effect it, and then listened in silence to the Prince Consort. Prince Albert was relaying Raglan's advice to build up allied forces in Eupatoria – an idea which Napoleon regarded as strategically weak. He was prepared to give up the idea of going to the Crimea himself but not the rest of his plan. Only he, he felt, could make the generals show some initiative and on 28 April (1855) he ordered Canrobert to carry it out.* He still considered that the divided command of the allied armies was the fundamental cause of their failure, and never ceased to point out that if he were there he would be able to control the armies and ensure unity of action.

Where the Emperor was undoubtedly right was in his conclusion that some top-level co-ordination of the allied war effort was urgently needed. After a year of the alliance, disagreement, dissension, distrust and suspicion were at hand at every turn. Windham, serving with the British 4th Division wrote that while there was no real leader in either army, the French were worse off, having 'as much prejudice and more conceit'.[15] Panmure's view of his allies was clearly indicated in a letter to Raglan on 26 March: 'I have my suspicions of them and only hope you will not be induced to give way to them one inch more than you consider right. It is all very well to talk of the necessity of keeping a good understanding with the French but I have no notion of doing so to our own risk.'[16]

---

* It has been suggested that the Emperor never intended to go to the Crimea but used the threat of it to gain social acceptance for himself and Eugenie with the British royal family. (*Undercurrents of the Second Empire*, Vandam, pp. 129–33, 144–7.)

Meanwhile the British were beginning to emerge from the slothful mire of misery into which they had sunk. Health was improving, a railway from Balaclava to the base camps was almost complete, and an attempt to smarten up the troops had been made in April. Orders that men should pipeclay their belts and black their boots made the old soldiers grumble but this in itself was an indication of the partial return of health and cheerfulness.* The redcoats were not yet fully recovered but songs could again be heard in their camps: 'Cheer, boys, cheer!', 'Annie Laurie', and 'There's a good time coming!' The dark and airless huts that were now being provided were better than the tattered old tents, and the Sanitary Commissioners (whose ideas were culled from the French camps) were busily improving them. In December Queen Victoria had authorized the presentation of a silver medal and gratuity of £5 or £10 to men specially selected for distinguished service. (Known as the Distinguished Conduct Medal, this decoration was distinct from the one introduced ten years previously – which was intended primarily for good, faithful and efficient service in time of peace.) During the same month she also ordered one sergeant in every regiment to be promoted to the rank of ensign and another to be awarded a gratuity of £20 in recognition of the services of the non-commissioned officers in the campaign so far.† Minor things in themselves, they undoubtedly contributed to the improvement in morale that was now developing.

Early in the New Year Admiral Lyons had suggested that an expedition might be sent to seize the straits at Kertch, on the eastern end of the Crimean peninsula. Russian shipping bound for the Sea of Azov had to go through these straits and the admirals of both navies believed that if the straits were brought under allied control the flow of Russian supplies to Sebastopol would be seriously hampered. When the idea was first mooted Raglan had said that he thought such an expedition should come after the town had been

---

* A free issue of boots and clothing was made to the British troops in January. It was very welcome. In December as much as 30 shillings was being paid for a pair of socks.

† The Victoria Cross – a modest bronze symbol of the highest, most supreme courage and self-sacrifice – was not instituted until January 1856 although the first awards were back dated. Until the D.C.M. and V.C. were instituted the only way in which an N.C.O. or private soldier could be rewarded for highly meritorious conduct was by a monetary grant. For officers there was no decoration to commemorate a deed of remarkable courage at this time.

Roger Fenton's 'L'Entente Cordiale', showing British and French soldiers fraternising before Sebastopol during the winter of 1855.

The evacuation of wounded Turks, March 1855. The Turks had no stretchers or ambulances.

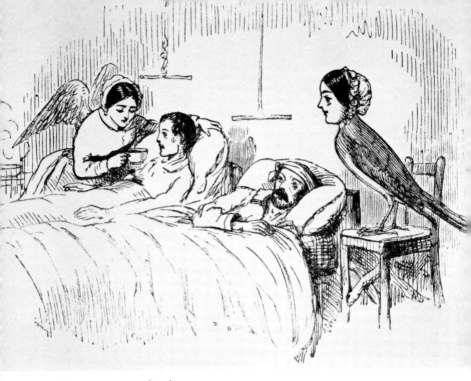

Two contemporary drawings:

Wounded soldiers and Nightingales.

'Tête d'Armée', or 'How the British Generals stormed the Great Redan'. Generals Simpson, the G.O.C., with a hood over his head; Jones, the engineer, wearing a nightcap; and Airey, the Quartermaster-General, with a handkerchief over his cap, watching the battle on 8 September, 1855.

assaulted. But, as the assault was put off time and time again, the British commander-in-chief gradually came to accept the idea and began to urge it on the French. Canrobert however was not interested in an allied blockade of the Sea of Azov. His main concern was for the siege and, he maintained, if he and Raglan had not the strength to take Sebastopol they could ill afford to dissipate their energies on Kertch. Nevertheless, after a good deal of hesitation, Canrobert yielded to Raglan's insistence and a joint expedition was planned for 3 May. Realizing that Anglo-French relations were strained Canrobert tried to ease them by agreeing to Sir George Brown commanding the expedition – although three-quarters of the troops would be French. In charge of the French contingent it was proposed to send General d'Autemarre who got along well with the British. Raglan was delighted, not only that the operation was going to take place but also that his old Peninsula War friend, Brown, was going to command it. Optimistically he wrote to London 'General Canrobert and myself are on the best of terms and he has today (1 May) yielded to my earnest recommendation that the Kertch enterprise should go forward'.[17] The French had agreed to provide 8,500 men and three batteries of artillery, but when the time came to embark on 3 May only 7,000 infantry and two batteries were ready to go. Carrying supplies for three weeks the expedition set out, sailing north past Sebastopol in the hope of deceiving the Russians and then doubling back towards Kertch.

Unfortunately, just one week before the expedition sailed, the Crimea was connected by telegraph with the outside world and this fact brought its miscarriage. Over the cable from Varna came a message to Canrobert from the Emperor ordering him to send Admiral Bruat and every available ship he could lay his hands on to Constantinople immediately; Louis Napoleon wanted the French reserves concentrated there to be moved to Sebastopol. Canrobert was also instructed to assume supreme command – which meant taking Raglan under his orders – and send a division to Aloushta as soon as the reserve arrived at Kamiesch; he was then to get ready for an offensive in the north of the Crimea. Above all Canrobert must not divert any troops from the main task in hand, the reduction of Sebastopol. As nobody in Paris had been told about the plans to attack Kertch, the Emperor could not have realized what his message implied. But to Canrobert it could only mean one thing.

9—TVW

Never really enthusiastic about the operation, he went to Raglan and told him that he was compelled to recall the men under d'Autemarre. In a three-hour discussion lasting till 1 a.m. on 4 May Raglan pointed out that the Emperor had sent the message without knowing the expedition had set out and that it would now be within sight of its destination. Better, he said, to let matters ride for a time; if anything went wrong Canrobert could always blame him. Mollified, Canrobert returned to his camp to find another telegram from the Emperor awaiting his attention; Canrobert was to concentrate all his forces and not to lose 'a single day'. To the French commander an order of this nature meant that he had no choice in the matter – the only thing he could do was recall Admiral Bruat with d'Autemarre's unit on board. And so, at 2.15 a.m. a French staff officer galloped up to the British headquarters to tell Raglan that he had sent a fast boat after the expedition with an order calling for the return of the French contingent.

Although the recall only applied to the French, obviously it was impossible for the British contingent to continue alone. Bruat himself believed that the venture would have been a success, and the British naval commanders tried to persuade him to emulate Nelson and turn a blind eye to Canrobert's order.[18] But Bruat was not prepared to disobey. The British officers were all furious, and in his anger the choleric Sir George Brown was barely restrained from knocking the innocent d'Autemarre down.[19] Admiral Lyons, a picture of frustrated rage, declared that Canrobert 'has spoiled one of the most promising coups that could have been', and to Raglan he wrote that he was 'grieved and disappointed beyond measure at having the cup dashed from my lips by General Canrobert'.[20] The troops, who were not told why the expedition was turning back felt thwarted, and Anglo-French relations – stressed enough already, especially after the recent futile bombardment – were brought almost to breaking point by the fiasco. According to Pélissier Raglan was 'hurt and irritated'; in England, the Minister of War, Lord Panmure, observed that Canrobert was 'utterly incapable of high command', and a statement from Buckingham Palace announced that Louis Napoleon's order to Canrobert had been issued 'without concert with us'.[21]

Few of those who blamed Canrobert appreciated his difficulties. Over the newly installed telegraph cable he was peppered with instructions from the Emperor at all hours of the day and night, and the strain wore him down. As commander-in-chief of the French army he was now as good as finished.

Bewildered and overwrought he re-presented Louis Napoleon's plan at an allied council of war. It was an unfortunate time but Niel was encouraging its adoption, and Canrobert himself felt that the plan had merit. It was clear that a unified command was more necessary than ever before and in his view the Emperor could secure this. If he was not to come to the Crimea an alternative *supremo* would have to be found. Turning to Raglan, Canrobert suggested that he would be best fitted for the appointment. After all Raglan was a field-marshal and nearly seventy years old, while he – Canrobert – was but a lieutenant-general and only forty-five. Surprised, Raglan tentatively accepted. After reflection, however, he said that he did not want the job since he did not fully subscribe to the Emperor's plan. Dejected and despondent, Canrobert cabled the Emperor to say that his cherished plan could not go ahead because Raglan would not co-operate.

By now Canrobert had had enough, and on 16 May he addressed a telegram to the Emperor: 'My health and spirit, tired by constant tension, no longer permit me to carry the burden of immense responsibility. My duty towards my Sovereign and my country forces me to ask you to give to General Pélissier, an able leader with great experience, the letter of command that I have for him. The army that I leave is intact, energetic and confident, and inured to war. I request that Your Majesty leave me a place of combat at the head of a simple division.'[22]

As it was unexpected, Canrobert's resignation and request for demotion caught the Emperor by surprise. His immediate reaction was to give the command to Niel but Marshal Vaillant persuaded him that Pélissier was the better man. And so Pélissier and Canrobert changed places – Canrobert taking over Pélissier's corps while Pélissier became the new commander-in-chief of the French army. From this moment the conduct of the campaign was to change in a way which Louis Napoleon could not foresee.

THE SIEGE:
THE SECOND PHASE

Pélissier was a man of a very different stamp from Canrobert. Sixty-one years old, stocky, rude and resolute, he was a fighter and no diplomat. The troops called him 'tin-head', and when he spoke to them it was in their own language, often addressing them as a 'lot of bastards' – terminology which seemed to have a special appeal for him since he was apt to refer to himself as 'that bastard Pélissier'. In spite of the primitive simplicity of his oral style however, he was by no means incapable of eloquence and when he wanted to impress he could pen well-phrased letter's and reports. Pélissier was a professional, and unlike his predecessor not the man to share his command and authority with anybody else – not even an emperor. Jealous of interference he would tolerate advice only when he had asked for it and he was not prepared to consider proposals from amateurs in Paris.

When Pélissier took over, the strength of the French army in Turkey and the Crimea amounted to about 120,000 men. (The total allied force amounted to about 224,000 men of which only 32,000 were British. The rest was made up with 17,000 Sardinians, 55,000 Turks under Omar Pasha's command and about 20,000 miscellaneous Turks including the garrisons of places like Kars). His first major action was to reorganize the French contingent, and General Reynault de Saint-Jean d'Angély – the commander of the Imperial Guard which had been shipped to Turkey, a brigade at a time – was named as the commander of the 22,000 French reserve corps in Constantinople. And Canrobert, who had swapped places with Pélissier and who had now decided that he did not want a corps command, was posted back to his old division – now the 1st Division of Bosquet's Second Corps. His second major action was an attempt to repair the damaged relations with the British. Despite the fact that Vaillant had written to tell him that the Kertch operation was finished and must not be reconsidered, Pélissier decided that it should go ahead. Canrobert, who treated orders from Paris like the Holy writ, would have accepted Vaillant's order without question. But Pélissier's reaction was to write back to Paris, saying 'Your orders, Marshal, are impossible to carry out . . . possession of Kertch . . . [is] necessary . . . and I have therefore ordered the expedition to proceed.'[1]

By now it was evident in Paris that a firmer hand was guiding the French army in the Crimea. And in London news that a second Kertch expedition was being organized caused Panmure to write to Raglan and say '. . . a new spirit has been infused into your French allies.'[2] Indeed there was little doubt that Pélissier had strong clear views of the strategic problems confronting the Allies and he began to put them into action as soon as he had taken the reins of command. 'We will give the Russians a sound thrashing', he said,[3] ordering Bosquet to get ready for a major assault. 'Such is my irrevocable will'.[4] He would begin, he declared, by capturing the Mamelon and Mount Sapoune (above the Careening Ravine). 'I do not conceal that this . . . will cost us definite sacrifices; but cost what they may I intend to take them' he wrote to Bosquet. 'It is not up to you my dear general, to decide the importance of such a result . . . All this is perhaps very difficult, but it is possible, and I have irrevocably decided to attempt it.'[5] This statement was intended to make it clear to Bosquet and to the other generals that Pélissier intended to run the campaign in his own way. Vaillant, comparing him with Canrobert, said that the difference between the two men was that Pélissier would be prepared to lose 14,000 men for a great result in one operation 'while Canrobert would lose the same number by driblets without obtaining any advantage'.[6]

On 22 May, to initiate his new aggressive policy, Pélissier ordered a night attack on a new line of Russian positions which had been established in some hitherto vacant ground between the Great Central Bastion and the head of Quarantine Bay. Six thousand men were flung into the assault which had to be repeated five times before the French finally gained their objective. As callous as he was even Pélissier described the bayonet fighting in this action as 'terrible'. And as an introduction to Pélissier's methods, it was a costly enterprise. The Russians were said to have lost over 3,000 men in fighting but although this could not be verified it was certain that the number of French soldiers killed, wounded or captured, was

2,303. When he heard about it in Paris, the Emperor said that in his opinion the engagement had not achieved anything sufficiently constructive to justify such losses. 'The loss was greater,' he told the British Ambassador in Paris, 'than that at Austerlitz. I would not have minded if it had been to produce a decisive result, but to see the bravest soldiers perish in such indecisive combat was terrible.'[7] And Pélissier, whose blunt audacity over the telegraph had already shaken the Emperor, was told that all future operations must conform to the overall royal plan. Pélissier's reply, apocryphal perhaps, was to cut the telegraph cable after sending a message to say that he could not do his job properly if he was tied to the end of an electric wire.

The second expedition to Kertch landed unopposed at Kamish Burun on 25 May. Omar Pasha had wanted to lead it and to have the force consist mostly of Turks. But this was unacceptable to both Raglan and Pélissier, who reckoned that Turkish troops would only be of any use if Kertch were to be occupied permanently. (In the event the expedition was sent out under the same officers as before – Brown, Lyons, d'Autemarre and Bruat – and was made up of 3,000 British, 7,000 French and 5,500 Turks.) After destroying the coast defence batteries, the Russian troops withdrew west along the main road to Russia and the admiral commanding the Russian flotilla in the Bay of Kertch – having burned ten of his fourteen ships – made a dash for the Sea of Azov. From Kamish Burun the Allies then moved on to Yeni Kale at the northern entrance to the straits, looting, burning and ravaging the countryside *en route*. (This disgraceful behaviour was aggravated by the fact that Sir George Brown either refused or was unable to keep his men in order.) With the troops firmly established at Yeni Kale the allied fleet sailed into the Sea of Azov to destroy – in this case quite legitimately – a large number of ships and an immense accumulation of stores. By mid-June the expedition could be considered to have been a complete success from the military point of view, and it is unfortunate that it was marred by the discreditable behaviour of the invaders. Leaving the Turkish contingent with 1,000 British and the same number of French to garrison Kertch the remainder of the expedition now returned to the Crimea.

Meantime, on the very same day the Kertch expedition had landed, troops under Brunet and Canrobert had attacked Russian outposts at Tchorgun on the northern side of the Tchernaya valley.

The attack was successful and when it was over a French division and 20 squadrons of cavalry moved up to the Fedukhine Heights; and, with the deployment of the Sardinians on the right of the French, the threat of interference to preparations for the grand assault on Sebastopol was greatly lessened.

As was to be expected Niel had been carefully watching the development of Pélissier's strategy and reporting back to the Emperor. Moreover, when he realized that what Pélissier was planning did not conform to the Emperor's overall strategy, he had said so to Pélissier on a number of occasions. Pélissier was prepared to accept only so much criticism, before administering a stinging rebuke. Turning on Niel at an allied conference Pélissier told him that he was not there to advise him but to obey orders. He was the commander-in-chief and Niel was a subordinate. If he continued to interfere, Pélissier assured him, he would have him sent home – forcibly if necessary. Furthermore, from that time on he was not to communicate with the Emperor without Pélissier's express permission. Having been put in his place in front of British generals, Niel was both humiliated and furious and the volume of his reports to Paris grew rather than decreased. Reporting his rebuke to the Emperor, he said that the latter's instructions were being flagrantly disregarded.

There was no doubt that Pélissier was ignoring instructions from Paris. From his viewpoint however, it was all very well for the Emperor to amuse himself making plans, but it was his job to run the army. In Paris, Louis Napoleon reacted predictably. Impatient and irritated with Pélissier as a result of Niel's reports he wired the French commander in the Crimea on 31 May. And the cable started off in the same vein as that which Pélissier had used to Niel: 'There is no question of a discussion between us, but of giving and receiving an order. I do not say to you "Carry out my plan"; I do say "Yours does not appear adequate to me". It is absolutely essential to invest the place without losing time. Tell me what means you are going to use to attain it.'

Pélissier replied immediately. He was only too willing to follow the Emperor's instructions, he said. But the terrain and uncertainty of British co-operation made a full-scale investment all along the line (such as the Emperor suggested) impossible. To attempt it would be to expose not only the Allies' military weakness to the Russians, but probably also the fact that they were at cross purposes. As he saw it each commander-in-chief had a different goal. The Turks had been ready for peace ever since the Russians had evacuated the Principalities; the British were concerned only with the maritime aspects of the war; the Sardinian contingent was too small to be of any real military worth, and apart from the fact that its presence was but a political move it depended almost entirely on the British. The basic problem was that France could not take Sebastopol on her own and had to have help from one of these allies; his plan depended on using the British troops already in the trenches.

Pélissier's reply was a penetrating, truthful but disconcerting appreciation of the problems confronting the Allies; it could also be considered an insubordinate riposte to the telegram of 31 May. But because it was the truth the Emperor had no ready answer.

Throughout this period Pélissier had not lost sight of his main objective and had been drawing up plans for an attack on the Mamelon on 7 June. It was to be primarily a French operation, but Raglan had promised complete co-operation. The British were to assist in the bombardment and to attack the Russian outpost known as the Quarries in advance of the Great Redan. Everything was nearly ready on 3 June when Pélissier received a cable from Louis Napoleon. In unmistakable language the Emperor stated his objections to the projected attack and went on

'For the welfare of France and for the glory of our arms you are at the head of the finest army which perhaps has ever existed. You are assured of an immortal reputation but it is necessary to do something great. The conduct of the siege comes closer to the qualifications of the general commanding the engineers [Niel] ... If you want to continue the siege without surrounding the place you will only succeed after fierce and bloody struggles which will cost you your best troops ... In accordance with the British Government which writes the same thing to Lord Raglan I order you positively not to persist at all with the siege without having completely invested the place. You are then to consult with Lord Raglan and Omar Pasha to ensure the most effective offensive, be it by the Tchernaya or against Simpheropol. In laying out the course to follow we leave both of you the widest latitude on the means that you employ.'[8]

Until 8 June, when the Mamelon had been successfully assaulted, Pélissier chose to ignore this message. Then, in reply he said that he had only just received the Emperor's order to change his plans because the message had been delayed.

On 6 June the allied artillery had pounded the Mamelon and the Quarries all day long, and next day Raglan rode up to Cathcart's Hill to watch the battle. Apart from his own party – which included Lady Paget among distinguished visitors who were living on the *Caradoc* in Balaclava harbour – Cathcart's Hill was crowded with other sightseers. Since the end of April the Crimean battlefields had become a regular tourist attraction. Apart from picnics and races near Balaclava, excursions to the Inkerman ridge were organized and just behind the front line elegant ladies on horseback and elderly gentlemen in check trousers and straw hats were not an uncommon sight.

On 7 June it would seem that the tourists got their money's worth. By five o'clock, the Kamtchatka Lunette on the Mamelon had been battered to ruins and the Quarries were in a similar position. The machinery of war was nowhere near so deadly and destructive as it is today, but it would be wrong to think of the guns that were used in the Crimea as toys. While the artillery of 1855 was not radically different from that used in the Peninsular War, within their own limits the guns were accurate and effective. Smooth-bored and muzzle loaded, they fired a variety of projectiles at medium or long ranges. The solid iron ball – the 'round shot' most frequently used—was a deadly and erratic missile which often changed its course when it struck an intervening object and ricocheted. (A ricochet was not always accidental, and it was possible for a skilful gunner to drive a ball almost horizontally round the angle of a fortification.) People with a quick eye were able to see a round shot flying towards them, or bowling and bounding over the ground. If they acted with sufficient alacrity it was possible to get out of its way. But if the shot did hit, its effect was terribly destructive; with a peculiarly distinctive thud bodies would be cut in two or heads and limbs knocked off. As there was nothing in those days comparable to the disruptive effect of modern high explosive the effect of a bombardment on earthworks or fortifications usually depended on concentration – the battering of the work by a large number of shot fired continuously and accurately.

To repel infantry or cavalry at close quarters guns were loaded with grape or canister – bunches of smaller balls, clamped with long screws between metal plates or loaded into a cylindrical case.

Shells were occasionally used instead of solid shot, but these were more properly the projectiles of howitzers or mortars. The gun was fired by means of a copper friction tube, detonation being effected by pulling a lanyard. After firing the gun would be run back, cooled off, sponged out and reloaded – a process which took up a good deal of time and it usually involved the resighting of the gun for every shot. Mortars and howitzers fired explosive shells – hollow spherical projectiles containing a bursting charge of black powder, and provided with a crude time fuse. This fuse usually consisted of a wooden plug with a powder channel down the middle. Drilled into the side of the plug was a series of holes which were filled with clay or putty. The composition of the fuse burnt at the rate of an inch every five seconds, and in order to time the explosion of the shell one of the stopped holes in the plug was bored out: so that the flame of the burning composition would be able to set off the bursting charge at the required time. (If the holes were left unpierced the fuse would burn down to the bottom of the plug, exploding the shell thirty seconds after firing.)

In many ways the shell was the most effective missile used in the war; deadly, demoralizing and immensely spectacular. A 'whistling dick' from a Russian battery could annihilate a couple of men without leaving any trace of them and a direct hit could split a cannon completely in two. Then there were novelties like the 'bouquet' which consisted of a number of small shells or grenades enclosed in a larger one. When the main container burst these would go on exploding on the ground or in the air at uncertain intervals. There was also a 'light ball' which was used to illuminate the battle zone at night, an incendiary 'carcass', and large rockets, fired out of tubes, which also carried grenades or solid balls. These were the guns and missiles used in the bombardment of Sebastopol and there was no gun or missile on the allied side to which the Russians did not have a counterpart; indeed the Minié rifle – the best weapon of the period and the only real novelty – was supplied with commercial impartiality to both.

Returning to the battle on 7 June. Soon after 6 p.m., the sightseers on Inkerman Ridge saw the rocket fired which was the signal for the assault to begin. Led as usual by the Zouaves, two French brigades raced across the open ground towards the Mamelon, while a third brigade on their left rushed the Kamtchatka Lunette. Pouring over the ramparts and parapets into the Russian fortifications the French troops carried their objective and, some of them driven on by their own crazy momentum, pressed on to the Malakoff itself. Here the attack was not only checked but swept back in disorder. Taking advantage of the situation the Russians now pressed forward and the French were even driven out of the Lunette. But Bosquet still had three brigades in reserve and after another brief bombardment a second attack was launched which re-captured the Mamelon and this time it was held. Meanwhile, two columns of British troops, 200 men of the 2nd and Light Divisions in each, had attacked the flanks of the Quarries, while two other columns similarly composed assaulted from the front. The Russians were swept out in the first rush, but when some of the British made the same mistake as the French and pursued them towards the Redan they too were ill placed to resist a counter-attack. Like the French the redcoats were forced back and there were some sticky moments. But the Quarries positions were held, and from them the British were now able to shoot directly into the embrasures of the Great Redan itself.

Throughout the night the British troops worked to link up the Quarries with their old trenches. Because there was so much rock near the surface progress was slow, and to build up the parapet of the new position the men had to use half-filled gabions, piles of stones and even the bodies of dead Russians. With their ranks thinned by the casualties of the battle, the men were tired and many who flopped down from sheer fatigue could not be woken up, when just before daylight the Russians launched another counter-attack. Noise rather than shooting drove it back. Colonel Campbell of the 90th Regiment kept his bugler blowing a succession of calls, while the officers shouted and emptied their revolvers into the advancing mass of Russians. Ten yards from the parapet the Russians wavered and halted. Their officers tried to drag them forward but they had started to trickle back, and by eight o'clock the British were still holding the Quarries. The first move towards the storming of Sebastopol had been carried out with complete success.

On 8 June the bombardment was resumed, and next day Raglan urged Pélissier to press on with his plans for an all-out attack on Sebastopol. Queen Victoria sent her congratulations to the French commander-in-chief, and Pélissier was pleased with this recognition of the French effort. But as his own Emperor had not so far expressed satisfaction he cabled Paris demanding to know whether Louis Napoleon was going to send 'félicitations' on the success of his soldiers or not. The Emperor replied on June 14 'I wished before sending congratulations on the brilliant success to learn how great the losses were. I am informed of the figure by Saint-Petersburg. I admire the courage of the troops but I would observe to you that a battle fought to decide the fate of the entire Crimea would not have cost you more. I persist then in the order which I had the Minister of War give you, to make all your efforts to enter resolutely into a field campaign.'[9]

This peevish telegram put Pélissier into a fit of unbridled rage. Throwing aside what slim vestige of tact and moderation he had exercised previously, he retaliated with a wire to the Emperor with a blunt expression of his feelings:

'Sire, in giving me the command ... Your Majesty told me ... to conform as much as possible to a former plan which the English had clearly modified in their attacks. Everything has been done in accord with them and we have gone hand in hand. Our plans have been made clear to you and have succeeded ... My conviction is that this is the only path to follow. In this situation, the radical execution of your orders ... is impossible ... Your Majesty must free me from the narrow limits to which he had assigned me or else allow me to resign a command impossible to exercise in co-operation with our loyal allies at the somewhat paralysing end of an electric wire ...'[10]

After sending this and a similar cable to Vaillant, Pélissier waited for a response which he expected would clear the air one way or another. On 17 June when none had been received, he wired again to Vaillant to say that he had waited patiently for a reply, and in the absence of one the final orders were being sent out for a major attack to take place the next day with the British against the Malakoff and the Great Redan. Pélissier and the Emperor had reached a crisis in their relations and before it was settled events were to complicate the issues further and heighten the Emperor's temper.

Pélissier's problems were not confined to his communications with Paris; he was also having trouble with his corps and divisional commanders. At a post-mortem on the Mamelon operation of 7 June, General Beuret, the commander of the 2nd Corps' artillery, proffered his resignation, after a dressing down, because Pélissier considered his guns had failed to give proper support. And General Mayran, an old and tried veteran of Algeria, went off with tears in his eyes and bitterness in his heart following a scathing censure of his conduct in the attack. Bosquet, who had imprudently retained a plan of the Malakoff found in the pocket of a dead Russian officer was also put in his place. Pélissier requested acidly, 'Be so good as to bring yourself down to the horizon of discipline, and remember that every captured plan is to be handed over to the commander-in-chief'. Bosquet was livid with rage. In fact there was more to the quarrel which ensued than the matter of the captured plan. Pélissier suspected that Bosquet was in league with Niel whom he knew had been writing to Paris in defiance of his orders. In the event the outcome was extremely serious. Bosquet was removed from the 2nd Corps, and given the relatively unimportant command of the Corps d'Observation operating near the Tchernaya valley – his place being taken by General Saint-Jean d'Angély, commander of the reserves. Because d'Angély was of the Imperial Guard Pélissier knew that the transfer would flatter the Emperor if the attack on the Malakoff was successful. This change, the result of mere spite, was probably the greatest single factor contributing to the failure of the offensive which was now being planned. To remove Bosquet at such a critical moment was undoubtedly a great mistake. Bosquet had studied the terrain and defences of the Malakoff for several months, and his preparations reflected the dangers which he foresaw; while the new commander had only thirty-six hours to acquaint himself with conditions, and a staff which resented the loss of Bosquet. Canrobert gave his opinion that Bosquet got the sack for consistent criticism of Pélissier's ideas; Bosquet himself reckoned that Pélissier deliberately removed him in order to get all the credit if the Malakoff assault were successful. He made no mention of the map incident but emphasized that his corps had the best troops and blamed his downfall on Pélissier's supreme egotism.[11]

By 15 June the allied troops knew that a big push was in the offing. Pélissier's plan, agreed with Raglan, was for an attack on the Malakoff by the French on 18 June followed by a British attack on the Great Redan. The operation was to begin with a bombardment on the 17th, and followed by an assault at six o'clock the following morning. In accordance with this arrangement the guns opened fire at daybreak on the 17th. By sunset when the Russian guns on the

Malakoff had been silenced, those on the Great Redan seemingly out of action, and heavy damage evident all along the line, it was assumed that the bombardment had been eminently satisfactory. Raglan was optimistic, Pélissier ebulliently confident. At eleven o'clock that night the French commander-in-chief cabled Vaillant: 'Tomorrow, the 18th, at break of day, in concert with the English, I assault the Great Redan, Malakoff and its dependent batteries.'[12] The battle would be fought on the fortieth anniversary of Waterloo, an occasion which both allied commanders separately saw as an auspicious occasion on which to commemorate the glory of the past.

For some unaccountable reason Pélissier decided to change the arrangements regarding the artillery fire and the hour of attack, only a few hours before the assault was due to be launched. Instead of attacking at dawn his troops would go in at 3 a.m. Not having been consulted or given any forewarning of the change, Raglan was justifiably annoyed. He 'feared' it was unwise, he said, and that it might bring about a state of confusion. He was right. Inevitably the change meant a speed-up in the preparations, and Raglan had very little time in which to draft a new set of orders and have them circulated. Thus Pélissier had compromised the situation by two extraordinary blunders: first the removal of Bosquet; and then a change of plan – which involved an assembly and an advance in pitch-black darkness, followed by an assault without any artillery support. Leaving aside the question of changing commanders at a critical time, it needs little military comprehension to appreciate that the altering of the hour of attack only a few hours before it was due to begin was a very serious blunder. And there was a third factor which also had a grave effect on the situation. At sunset on 17 June Raglan and Pélissier – together with their artillery and engineer advisers – had assessed the damage inflicted by the allied bombardment and concluded that the projected operation had every prospect of success. In fact they had over-estimated the effect of their guns and under-estimated Todleben's resources. During the night the Russians had not only repaired but actually improved the defences, and on the Malakoff guns had been mounted above its parapets in positions from which they could fire down on infantry advancing towards the bastion. For these reasons Pélissier's decision to let the French advance without any preliminary bombardment of the Malakoff turned out to be sheer folly.

The night of 17 June was calm, dark and extremely warm. In

Sebastopol it was quieter than it had been for some time and people said afterwards that they could hear the sea breaking along the rocks of the northern shore of the town. Until two o'clock in the morning when Russian buglers sounded the assembly in the Karabel barracks behind the Malakoff, only the tramp and shuffle of their troops moving up to the bastions and ramparts in preparation for the attack which the Russians knew was about to be launched, disturbed the peaceful quiet.

The French 2nd Corps was to deliver the attack; General Mayran on the right, General Brunet in the centre, General d'Autemarre on the left; a reserve of the Imperial Guard was located – events were to show unwisely – at a considerable distance in the rear. Things did not seem to go right from the very beginning. Brunet's division was held up while d'Autemarre's men were drinking their soup; and one of his brigades, losing its way in the darkness arrived late at the forming up place. Mayran, eager to begin the battle was nervously alert and showing signs of impetuosity.

With engineers assembling their assault equipment – ladders, woolpacks, gabions and irons – there had been great activity in the British lines since the afternoon. But by two o'clock in the morning nearly all the British troops were in position, ready for the attack. As yet there was no sound of any action – only the dull shuffling, the creak of leather and the occasional rattle of a scabbard or rifle butt which indicated the slow movement of the troops along the trenches. In the heavy darkness the men waited quietly in the appointed places talking in low voices or smoking their stubby grey pipes. These men were expecting an artillery prelude, a crashing bombardment which would kill or demoralize the Russians and smash a way for their advance. Soon they were to realize that someone had blundered again.

Raglan and his staff left the British army's headquarters a little after 2 a.m. With the customary indifference to danger Raglan had selected a position on the Woronzoff ridge near one of his mortar batteries. It proved to be a dangerous observation post but from it he was to have an excellent view of the battle. At the French headquarters horses were saddled by midnight. Pélissier usually walked his horse, but he was late in starting and had to trot in an effort to reach his own observation post – the Right Lancaster Battery on Victoria Ridge, now in the sector taken over by the French and about a mile south-east of the Mamelon – before the action started. He had to cover four miles, and although Pélissier went as fast as his horse would take him, it soon became evident that he could not arrive in time to give the signal for the attack. About 2.45 a.m., as he rode on in the darkness, there was a sharp rattle of musketry on the extreme right of the French line. The attack had started before he could send up the four star shells which were the signal for the co-ordinated assault to begin.

What had happened was that a light in the sky which appeared to come from the area of Pélissier's observation post had led to Mayran ordering the attack to go in. Why this light was mistaken for four star shells is not clear. According to some it was caused by the glowing fuse of a single ascending shell; according to others it came from a Congreve rocket. Whatever it was the fiery omen was fatal. Mayran was impatient and anxious not to incur Pélissier's wrath again and although his officers tried to restrain him he was convinced that the signal had been given, and ordered his men forward. On the face of it fifteen or twenty minutes might not seem to have been all that important especially as the assault was being made without artillery cover. The trouble stemmed from the fact that Brunet's units were not yet ready to move forward in the centre. The attack followed the general plan, troops entering the fray as soon as they were able. But it was not the co-ordinated assault it should have been. Details of what took place remain obscure; they were probably obscure to those who were involved. In the event, Pélissier, raging obscenely, was still trotting up towards the Lancaster Battery when Mayran's infantry started their fatal charge. (In fact it was not so much a charge as a stumbling, wild advance which ended in butchery.) As the Russian guns roared all along the Karabel front great slashes and ribbons of quivering light cut through the darkness, and Mayran's men were struck down in the open by blast after blast of grape and canister. Within five minutes of leaving the start line, Mayran himself had been mortally wounded and his division had fallen back and was trying to rally behind the position from which they had started the assault.

When Pélissier did reach the Lancaster Battery he ordered the rockets to be set off immediately. When they broke, in a spangle of green and white fire high above the battle zone, his staff waited anxiously for a corresponding movement of troops and the cheering sound of a general advance. When none came Pélissier must have realized that his change of orders was the basic cause of the confusion. Brunet was not ready, d'Autemarre was not ready; and when they were able to advance it was to destruction. By the time Brunet's battalions trudged forward, a grey uncertain light was illuminating the scene of action and this permitted the Russian gunners to see their targets. Within seconds the head of the French column was floundering in a storm of canister, grape and rifle fire; Brunet was fatally wounded, and his troops – like those of Mayran – were thrown back. On Brunet's left, d'Autemarre's men achieved an initial success. Reaching the Russian defences, west of the Malakoff, they broke through and for a time a regiment of Chasseurs was involved in some lively street fighting among the houses in the Karabel suburb. But the troops coming up behind, caught on the glacis of the Malakoff, suffered heavy casualties from the withering fire of the Russians and anti-personnel mines which were known as *fougasses*.

By daybreak it was clear that accident and incurable disorder were leading to catastrophe. The assault had collapsed. But Pélissier hesitated to give the order to retire.

It was now Raglan's turn to blunder. Seeing that the French were in difficulties he ordered the British attack to go in. Just why he did so seems almost as puzzling as why Pélissier decided to bring forward the hour of attack. Either he had second thoughts about the original arrangements, was misinformed, or made a faulty appreciation of the situation. Explaining his action later he wrote 'Of this I am quite certain, that if the troops had remained in our trenches, the French would have attributed their non-success to our refusal to participate in the operation.'[13] When the plans for the attack were finalized with Pélissier it had been decided that the British were not to advance until the Malakoff had been captured by the French. This would be announced by the flying of a tricolour from the Malakoff and it is said that a Russian flag was mistaken for the French colours. Whether this was so or not Raglan sent up the rocket which was his order for the British attack to begin. Like that of the French the assault started in a confusion from which it never recovered. Raglan's men were packed three deep in the trenches and they clambered over the parapet in a sprawling dislocated mass.* Many of them were mere boys with only a brief

---

* The confusion was increased by the pressure of large numbers of men who, though not on duty, had come into the trenches to see the others go off.

experience of discipline, and within a few minutes they were scattered and demoralized. At the foot of the hill was an abattis – a stockade of wood pointing outwards – and here the advance came to an abrupt halt. Nothing could induce the majority of the troops crawling in the tangle of the abattis to make an organized rush. Reinforcements were brought up, but when he saw the hopelessness of the situation Sir George Brown stopped them before they were pitched into the melee. Colonel Yea, the stalwart Fusilier who was now acting as a brigade commander was with them, and he was killed as he walked up to the Redan. It was all over when the men who had got to the abattis suddenly turned and raced back towards the trenches. There, screaming masses of wounded – for whom of course there was no adequate provision – were already crowding the trenches and many of these received additional injuries as this panic-stricken mob dashed back over them.

At about 8.30 a.m. Pélissier, having finally decided that he was unable to bring up his reserves quickly enough, ordered a general retirement. So far as the British were concerned no orders were needed, the retirement had already been effected. Raglan now rode across to the Lancaster battery to confer with Pélissier. The Frenchman was furious, blaming Mayran for attacking too soon and Brunet for not having been ready for the assault. Told that both of these had been killed he said that it was just as well because he would have had them both court martialled. Raglan, more in control of his feelings, attributed the failure to the allied under-estimation of Russian artillery strength. When a message from d'Autemarre arrived to say that the French losses had been too great – a remark which might apply perhaps to morale rather than the numbers of casualties – both commanders concluded it would be wise to abandon the attack and Pélissier issued his final orders to withdraw.

Allied losses in this grim fiasco had been heavy. 3,500 French and 1,500 British had been killed, wounded or taken prisoner. Moreover the position of both commanders-in-chief had become extremely precarious. Bosquet, still nursing resentment over his demotion promptly reported to the Emperor and said that in his view Pélissier's assaults were a waste of time and lives. As a result of this Napoleon wrote to Pélissier saying that his patience was exhausted, and that he would no longer allow his orders to be disobeyed and his soldiers' lives to be sacrificed. From that time on Pélissier would explain his plans in full, and do nothing of importance until he had first obtained telegraphic consent from Paris. Finally, if Pélissier was not prepared to do this he was to hand over the command to Niel immediately.

This letter, which would undoubtedly have brought Pélissier's dismissal was – fortunately for Pélissier – delayed by Vaillant, who was doing his best to temper matters between the Emperor and the French commander in the Crimea. And before it could be delivered the Emperor had received a placatory letter from Pélissier giving a politely worded explanation why the assaults had failed and a clear and concise appreciation of the existing situation. Mollified, Louis Napoleon cancelled his intention of relieving Pélissier and Vaillant was able to stop the Emperor's strongly worded admonishment. Meantime he had already written to Pélissier, explaining how insecure his position was and how close he was to being removed from his command. Pélissier was urged to send detailed reports to Paris, to try to co-operate with Niel, and – most important of all – to control his rebellious temper. Shaken by Vaillant's news Pélissier wrote back promising that all would go well in the future. He was a firm and loyal subject of the Emperor he declared, neither rebellious nor defiant.[14]

Raglan was also under a shadow. With a mood of dejection and humiliation prevailing in the British camps, the British commander-in-chief was a broken man in every sense of the word. Cholera and dysentery had again returned to the British army and in the week ending 23 June the local death rate had risen to 35 per cent of the entire force. On 20 June an officer of the Coldstream Guards visited Raglan at his headquarters. This officer knew Raglan well and was greatly shocked by his altered appearance. 'Do you not see the change in Lord Raglan?' he asked a group of staff officers as he left; 'Good God, he is a dying man!' Eight days later Raglan was dead. The cause of death was diagnosed as cholera and complications of acute diarrhoea, 'wear and tear and general debility'.[15] On 29 June Pélissier and Canrobert were among those who called at the British headquarters to pay their respects and according to witnesses, Pélissier stood by the bedside for nearly an hour 'crying like a child'. Combined with a touching general order to the French army announcing the death of Raglan this demonstration of grief helped to alleviate jealousies and bickering.[16] Later, Pélissier wrote in glowing terms of the departed Raglan, but it seems that he was not so carried away by emotion as to forget to report on the sanitation in the French army in the dispatch which announced Raglan's last rites.[17]

Most people recognized that the primary cause of Raglan's death was cholera but some of the British felt that his illness was caused by vexation and disappointment consequent on the failure of 18 June. And there is no doubt that Raglan felt himself compromised by it. He knew that he could not be regarded as a successful commander and he was conscious of acrimonious criticism in England. Replacement was a possibility he had to face. It seems unrealistic to attribute his death to concern over what had happened but there is little doubt that he had brooded over it.

In Paris the British Ambassador, Cowley, complained to the Emperor that if Pélissier had heeded Raglan's advice the attack on the 18th might well have succeeded. Louis Napoleon agreed with Cowley, and said in confidence that Niel and many other French officers had also agreed with Raglan's view. But the trouble was not so much that Raglan's sense of propriety prevented him from putting his ideas across to Pélissier, but that basically this disciple of Wellington was not really qualified to lead the British army. In a well-considered obituary his character was admirably summed up as that of a 'perfect gentleman, a brave soldier, a pure administrator, disinterestedly and nobly abandoning his ease and his habitual comforts at a time of life when they become to most men necessities. Lord Raglan has fallen a victim to his patriotism and his duty. That history will award him the title of a first rate general is perhaps improbable.'[18] This was probably as fair a judgement as could be passed on a man who others had said was distinguished for nothing but his amiable qualities.

THE FALL OF SEBASTOPOL

Raglan's successor was his chief of staff, General James Simpson. The peppery Sir Colin Campbell would have been a better choice and probably no one would have been more avidly acclaimed by the British army as commander-in-chief. But Campbell was no linguist and he was known to be cool towards the French. Unhappily also, he had never had a following either at the Horse Guards or at Raglan's headquarters where his contempt for the staff was notorious. Simpson was sixty-three, a colourless, reliably commonplace man. Like Raglan he was a Peninsular veteran; unlike him he had seen a little active service in India but years and experience had not done anything to improve his mediocre talents. He was frequently prostrated with gout, and no sooner had he assumed command than he was writing to Panmure to say that he regarded the appointment as temporary only, for he was sure that his health would 'give way'. In reply he was told neither to be 'oppressed by care, nor daunted by difficulty'.[1]

Difficulties there were in plenty. July 1855 was a month of despondency and moral deterioration in the Crimea. French troops were complaining of their leadership and saying that the British were not much use as allies. Cholera still prevailed in the camps (the French lost more than 1,600 men in July) and there was a lamentable decay in discipline, even among the officers. Between 13 and 21 July three British officers were court-martialled for being drunk on duty under arms and all were cashiered.*

People in Sebastopol were also feeling despondent. Although a Te Deum had been sung, and church bells rung to celebrate the repulse of the Allies on 18 June the initial mood of relief and cheerful confidence quickly gave way to one of gloomy resignation. And by the beginning of July despair was beginning to overshadow the mood of resignation. Talk of a floating bridge by which the town could be quickly evacuated and even a withdrawal to Perekop was now

---

* About this time sixpence a day extra pay was awarded to all British troops on active service.

current, and on 5 July Prince Gorschakoff ordered it to be built.*
By this time the numbers of sick and wounded in Sebastopol had
become a serious problem. There was a shortage of doctors, and as
the main hospital was overcrowded hundreds of wounded men had
had to be sent to hospitals in the interior where they had little
chance of recovery. A corps of nursing sisters was organized by
Grand Duchess Helen to help out, and an emergency hospital set up
in Fort Paul received most of the casualties from the Malakoff and
Redan. Officers' funerals were so frequent that all pomp and military music was forbidden. Admiral Nakhimoff died on 13 July from
wounds received three days before; Todleben was also wounded –
though not seriously – and he was recuperating in a villa near the
Belbec. Many buildings in the town had been destroyed by gun fire
but the cathedral was untouched and here officers and men of the
garrison could be seen kneeling reverently while coffins covered with
red velvet were placed in the aisles. Most of the elegant ladies had
gone, but it was not easy to get rid of the sailors' wives or families.
When they were sent away they returned, to establish themselves in
a shanty town of their own creation on the right bank of the
Tchernaya.

At the British headquarters Simpson had hardly settled into his
new appointment before he was confronted with an especially
tricky situation affecting allied co-operation. This time it was not the
French, but the Turks who were being difficult. On 11 July, Omar
Pasha had addressed a memorandum to the allied admirals and
generals saying that it was imperative for his army to move from the
Crimea to Asia Minor where the fortress of Kars, south-east of
Trebizond, urgently needed support.† In Silistria Omar Pasha had
been an independent commander with full authority, and he was
regretting ever having come to the Crimea; a campaign to relieve
Kars would give him an opportunity to regain his position. Moreover he did not like the French, and was unwilling to serve in a
subordinate role to a new and untried British commander-in-chief.
When his proposal to pull out of the Crimea was rejected at an
allied conference on 14 July, he was furious and he left next day for
Constantinople to take the matter up on a diplomatic level. And

---

* It consisted of eighty-six pontoons, each secured by a pair of anchors
and ran from Fort Nicholas on one side of the harbour to Fort Michael on
the other.
† See Chapter 18.

before leaving he ordered his troops to start concentrating on the coast. The idea of British, French and Turkish unity was becoming even more remote than it had ever been before.

What the British feared was that if Omar Pasha took his army off to Kars the allied position in the Crimea would be weakened, and so if he was to go some way would have to be found of replacing the men he would take with him. Only one solution seemed open: to transfer General Vivian's corps of auxiliary Turks to the Crimea – an arrangement which would have the advantage of reducing the number of commanders in the Crimea as Vivian could be 'ordered to do what Omar Pasha had to be begged to consider'.[2] Unfortunately the French were against it. St Arnaud's experiences with Turkish auxiliaries had not been especially successful, and in Paris it was rumoured that Vivian's Turks were an unruly lot and their officers were little better. Faced with this sort of situation Simpson was hopeless, and he was now saying that the plateau in front of Sebastopol would be indefensible in a second winter and that the Allies had better think about pulling back to better positions if the fortress held out much longer. Somehow or other he had gathered the impression that Pélissier shared his opinions, whereas the fact was that both Pélissier and the Emperor were, for once, in complete agreement about rejecting the ideas of both Omar Pasha and Simpson. As usual the Emperor wanted the best of two worlds. On 2 August 1855 he sent a memo to Vaillant, saying

'You must write to Pélissier: First, to consult always with General Simpson before undertaking anything; Second, to have better relations with Omar Pasha and try to use his troops; Third, to declare that the siege must be carried on; Fourth, to oppose any weakening of Ottoman forces in the Crimea. On this score, the English Government must perhaps hide the truth, but I know that in the French army it is said with a certain bitterness that the burden of the siege falls almost exclusively on us. We have 60,000 at the siege, the English have 12,000! The Turks for whom we are fighting are never in the trenches, no more than the Sardinians. They say that it was Lord Raglan who hindered Canrobert as [as well as] Pélissier from making a diversion which could have permitted investment of the fortress etc. etc. All this ought to be considered carefully. If now they still want to weaken the siege army by withdrawing Turkish troops they will create a justified alienation in the French army. Furthermore the great objective now is at Sebastopol and not at Kars'[3]

This statement put paid once and for all any speculation about raising the siege.

In August, while the question of Omar Pasha going to Kars remained unanswered, Queen Victoria paid a state visit to Paris. And, from the midst of feasts and balls, Vaillant sent a telegram to Pélissier telling him that the Emperor had informed him that 'both governments are agreed in not diminishing the Turkish forces before Sebastopol'.[4] Omar Pasha was not to get his army out of the Crimea until after the fall of Sebastopol.

On 4 July, Canrobert's 1st Division was ordered from the Tchernaya to replace the division that had been commanded by Mayran. Three days later Canrobert's men were in the trenches before the Malakoff and it was recognized that another attack was being formulated in which Canrobert's division would figure prominently. There was nothing wrong with Canrobert's troops, but Pélissier had now come to believe that the divisional commander himself was a problem. Until the latter part of his tour as commander-in-chief Canrobert had always been popular with the troops, and after demotion his old popularity – enhanced by his voluntary sacrifice for the benefit of France – returned. Every time he appeared at the front he was received enthusiastically, and the jealousy which this aroused among the officers who were now his superiors led to the decision to replace him. On 26 July 1855 Pélissier forwarded to Canrobert an extract of a message from Vaillant which said 'Tell General Canrobert that the Emperor invites him for reasons of health to return to France'. Canrobert was not prepared to go on such a flimsy pretext which bore a marked similarity to that which Prince Napoleon had used to leave the front.

'The condition of my health, [he wrote to Pélissier] though poorly, does not yet stop my activity in accepting a return to France. For this reason I would give our army a bad example, and I am offended, general, because of never having given any but good. If His Majesty, the Emperor, and you, general, think that the dignity of a higher command has suffered from the modest position now occupied by one who was for so long the commanding general of our grand army, and if you think that his presence in France would be more useful for the country and the Emperor, order it, and I will submit to your decision.'[5]

This letter was sent on to Paris with Pélissier's recommendation that Louis Napoleon could overcome Canrobert's scruples by ordering him to some position at Court, and on 28 July an order duly arrived recalling Canrobert to service in Paris. Canrobert accepted his lot and after a series of emotional farewells he left the Crimea on 4 August. His departure was a relief to Pélissier but there was a sincere regret among the lower echelons – despite the rumour that he was now leaving to take up an appointment as a Minister.

Canrobert's replacement was General MacMahon, who arrived in the Crimea on 18 August – having just missed an action which was in some ways one of the most important in the latter half of the campaign.* Because the British part in this battle of the Tchernaya was confined to an artillery diversion British histories concerned with the war against Russia pay scant attention to it. Partly because of the allied blockade in the Sea of Azov, and partly because a hard winter had limited the amount of grain and forage normally forthcoming from the steppe-lands, getting supplies to Sebastopol had become increasingly difficult for the Russians. Seen from St Petersburg this situation could improve only if allied pressure on Sebastopol was eased. In consequence, Prince Gorschakoff had been ordered to take the offensive. Gorschakoff himself was unenthusiastic about the idea of the attack; and Todleben, in his Belbec villa was very much against it. During the night of 15 August two divisions were concentrated on the Mackenzie Heights for an attack on Balaclava. Liprandi, the general who had commanded the Russian forces in the earlier action at Balaclava and who knew the ground extremely well, was given command of the main force, and it was decided that if he had any success the attack would be followed by a sortie from Sebastopol. Shortly before dawn on 16 August the rattle of musketry fire was heard on the hill near Tchorgun; in the chill, misty darkness Liprandi was already moving and driving back the Sardinian outposts. The French and Sardinians quickly formed up and when it was light they were ready to go into action. At first, the centre of the French line was pushed in at the Traktir

* For further details, see Appendix 7.

Bridge. The Russians crossed the river, not only by the bridge but by means of portable gangways placed across the stream at previously reconnoitred positions. Fighting up the slopes of the grassy Fedukhine Hills they tried to force their way up the road through the pass. But by six o'clock in the morning, Pélissier had decided that this was not a diversionary attack merely to draw troops away from Sebastopol and reinforcements were sent towards Traktir. An hour later these reinforcements had reached the Fedukhine Heights, and when the Russians made their final attack soon afterwards it was repulsed with heavy losses. As Gorschakoff had feared Russian casualties were over 6,000 men while French and Sardinian losses were only 1,451 and 250 respectively. More important to the Russians than the butcher's bill was the loss of morale and on 24 August Gorschakoff sent a despatch to the Minister of War in St Petersburg saying that it was folly to prolong the defence of Sebastopol. At that time he was again thinking of evacuation, although he was to change his mind a few days later.

In England there was a good deal of political uneasiness and popular discontent at this time. The Cabinet had just had the report of Colonel Tulloch and Sir John McNeill, who had been sent out to investigate conditions in the Crimea on behalf of the Government. The report suggested that many of the officers in the Crimean army, including some who had already gone – Cardigan, Lucan and Airey – were incompetent. Publication of the report was delayed until the following year, but its immediate effect was disturbing. Fortunately for the Government public attention was about to be diverted by the royal visit to Paris, where the Queen, the Prince Consort and their two eldest children were to be the guests of the Emperor. But the Government still had to face up to its problems and the Cabinet was wondering what to do about Simpson, whose letters made such pessimistic reading. Panmure, thoroughly fed up with Simpson's moans, wrote to him on 28 July 1855:

'Your letters have certainly been most disheartening, and have in my opinion done yourself a great injustice. It is impossible for a man feeling as you do to face the difficulties of any position or to cheer on others in the arduous task before them. If you are so weighed down by a sense of your own inability to bear the burden of command, you must write me so officially and request to be

relieved. It is neither fair to me, or yourself, to do otherwise ...
nothing on my part shall be left undone to make your position as
easy as I can ... But, my good friend, you must *lead*.'[6]

Who should succeed Simpson was now the question. One of the
potential candidates, the Duke of Cambridge, was rejected on the
grounds that 'he might fail in self control in situations where the
safety of the army might depend on coolness and self possession'.[7]
There was still Campbell, but he was again turned down. The choice
finally settled on General Codrington, and Simpson was instructed
to hand over to him if he felt that the command was becoming too
onerous. There the matter might have rested but for the fact that
Panmure's request for Simpson's opinion of Codrington as his
successor brought a reply on 14 August which was only partially
reassuring. 'He is, in my belief, the best general here; but I am in
full hopes not to be compelled by onus to act on your instructions at
the present time of very imminent chance of our being attacked;
for you must be aware of the very great disgust that will be occasioned to Bentinck, Campbell, Barnard and Rokeby, if Codrington is
called to the chief command. They will, of course, take the most
immediate measure to quit the army.'[8]

In France more assurances of allied goodwill and perseverance in
the war were in the making. Queen Victoria; the Prince Consort;
Bertie, the Prince of Wales; and Vicky, the Princess Royal, arrived
at Boulogne on 18 August in the royal yacht *Victoria and Albert*. It
was an extremely hot day, but Napoleon and all his royal carriages
were duly awaiting them and the royal party was given a tumultuous reception when the Emperor led the Queen ashore. It was two
days after the battle of the Tchernaya when the royal party reached
Paris; despatches had arrived and in the prevailing mood of exulta-
tion the people of the French capital received the British royal
family with unbounded enthusiasm. 'I felt quite bewildered but
enchanted', wrote the Queen afterwards. Just back from the seat of
war Canrobert who was said to be impressed by the Queen's
regality of manner made flattering remarks about the British;
'Victoria', he said in admiration, 'danced as well as her soldiers
fought.' 'Such an honest good man', the Queen wrote of him, 'so
sincere and friendly and so fond of the English, very enthusiastic,
talking with much gesticulation.'[9] Meantime, in the background of
balls and entertainment, the presence of the Prussian Minister at

Frankfurt, Bismarck, hinted of a future which Marshal de Castellane of the Emperor's staff mistakenly identified as a sympathy for Russia.

In the Crimea the Allies were completing their preparations for the final assault on Sebastopol. Gorschakoff's change of mind and decision to prolong the defence of the town may have been an honourable one, but even he must have realized that the town was doomed. He had been told that he could not expect reinforcements which could not reach him in time in any case, and the Allies were clearly in a position of local superiority. The French had already dug themselves into the slopes of the Malakoff, and whatever might happen on the British front opposite the Great Redan it was clear that the French should be able to storm the Malakoff. That an attack would not be long delayed was evident as the Allies had maintained a heavy bombardment of all the Russian positions ever since the battle of the Tchernaya.

On 3 September, Pélissier presided over an allied Council of War. The French trenches were now within twenty-five yards of the Malakoff, and batteries had been established on the town side of the Mamelon from which it was possible to fire at short range on the Malakoff. There was also a bullet-proof shelter for generals and a subterranean conference room.* All were agreed that the assault should take place as soon as practicable, and the date was set for 8 September. Bosquet would command the operation, and Mac-Mahon with the 1st Division was to lead the assault; the Imperial Guard would be posted in a reserve position from where it would be able to deliver a final and decisive blow. The allied fleets would also participate with a bombardment of Sebastopol's coastal defences. (In the event, this part of the operation was cancelled on the morning of the attack because of heavy seas.)

Simultaneously with the French assault on the Malakoff, the British were to attack the Great Redan and the arrangements that were made for this assault were much the same as those which had been made for 18 June. A force of 200 men would cover the advance of a ladder party of some 320 men. Once the ladders were in position against the walls of the strongpoint the main storming column

* On the night of 27 August there was a disastrous explosion in this chamber. 15,000 lb of gunpowder had been stored there for the forth-coming attack when a chance Russian shell exploded inside. Debris from the explosion landed in places as remotely removed as Sebastopol's Karabel suburb and the English camps in front of Balaclava.

(1,000 men) would follow; behind them would come a second storming party and behind them a consolidation group of 3,000 more men. Each group was made up in equal numbers of men of the 2nd and Light Divisions – both of which had been in front of the Redan for months, knew the ground well and were thought to have earned the honour of storming it. Regimental pride, the root of this decision, led to a blunder. Both divisions which had been in the thick of the fighting all through the campaign had suffered heavy casualties, and they had been filled up with young, raw recruits. Additionally, because the different assault groups were a mixture of units who had not rehearsed or trained together there was bound to be a lack of cohesion. The crowning mistake of all however stemmed from the fact that the British had not profited by their experience of 18 June, and widened their trenches in order to make a rapid advance possible.

On Bosquet's insistence the hour for the attack was set at noon. Noon seemed to be as good a time as any, because the chance of surprising the Russians was better than at the customary time of an attack – dawn, or just before dusk, when they were standing to arms. Moreover, it was reckoned that if the Russian field army decided to attack the Allies during the assault, in order to try to divert it, there would be insufficient time for them to reach the allied positions before nightfall. (Simpson, in particular, was worried about Intelligence reports that Gorschakoff's field army was planning another attack along the Tchernaya.)

At 11.30 a.m. on the morning of 8 September the daily bombardment was intensified, and after forty minutes of firing at a rate which was heavier than anything that had been experienced in the Crimea previously, it ceased. Bugles then sounded, drums rattled, and the attack against the Malakoff was launched – spearheaded by the Zouaves of the 1st Brigade of MacMahon's division. This time there was no repetition of 18 June. The Russians were completely surprised and by the time they had recovered enough to realize what was happening the leading Zouaves had crossed the twenty-five yards of open ground and were clambering over the ruins of the parapet into the bastion. Within ten minutes of leaving their trenches the Zouaves had planted a tricolour on the summit of the Malakoff, although the fighting still continued inside the bastion. As Pélissier had hoped, the assault had taken the Russians unawares. But they were fighting back and preparing a counter-attack.

Nevertheless the French were not going to give up this time and when a messenger was sent to MacMahon to ask if he felt he could hold the position, his reply became a modern classic in French military history: 'Tell your general,' he said, 'that I am here and that I am staying here.'[10]

On the right flank of the Malakoff the French were attacking two other points with little success. Two divisions advancing had stormed up to the Little Redan, but they were checked and eventually repelled. For six hours a bloody fight swayed and rolled along the shattered earthworks, and by the evening more than 1,000 French dead lay before the Little Redan. Bosquet sent up his reserves but they were caught in the open and cut down by canister fired from the guns of a mobile Russian battery or by the measured volleys of Russian riflemen in the trenches on either side of the bastion. Bosquet himself was wounded in the shoulder.

The hoisting of MacMahon's flag on the Malakoff had been the signal for the British to assault the Great Redan. The story of what happened was similar to that of 18 June – the only exception being that this time there were no last-minute changes and no mistakes about the signal for attack. The assault was also directed against four points instead of two, as it was expected that this would make it more difficult for the Russians to rush troops to the danger points as they had done previously. A contemporary account speaks of the men going forward 'with the greatest spirit'.[11] But an analysis of what actually took place seems to indicate that they went forward in a rabble and were driven back in a rout. Over and above the factors concerned with the organization of the attack which have already been mentioned, the British failure was due primarily to the fact that the troops had to cross over two hundred yards of open ground. Their trenches had not been pushed any closer than this because – it was alleged in excuse – of the obdurate and rocky earth. In all probability it was the British soldiers' incurable aversion to digging which contributed much to the failure.

After the repulse no further assault was possible, as the trenches were so crowded with wounded and disorganized stragglers that any movement was out of the question. An attack on the following day was contemplated but it never took place. Simpson reported the disaster as a 'most determined and bloody contest . . . maintained for nearly an hour and, although supported to the utmost, and the greatest bravery displayed, it was found impossible to maintain the position'. *The Times* blamed Simpson and said the 'unpardonable' failure was due to his not having pushed the trenches closer before the attack.[12] Whoever was to blame or why it was a tragedy, Clarendon, the Foreign Secretary, wrote

'Now I suppose the French will take it [the Great Redan] and will have a double crow over us, and we may expect heartburnings and recriminations. We have cut a poor figure lately and I expect we shall continue to do so as long as that worthy old gentlewoman, Simpson, is at the head of our affairs. I have a letter from Stratford [British Ambassador in Constantinople] today from headquarters saying that our army is living from hand to mouth and that we are even less prepared than last year for the winter while the French have vast stores of everything.'

On the Malakoff the Russians counter-attacked a number of times but they were not able to dislodge the French, and by two o'clock, when the last Russian attack had been repulsed, it was clear that MacMahon was immovable. Gorschakoff saw that he was defeated. Exhaustion was telling visibly on his men – as indeed it was on the allied troops. The guns and mortars were still firing, no longer in thundering salvoes but only with slow deliberate precision. Sebastopol had stood up to the Allies for nearly a year but the Russian commander did not consider that his men could hold out much longer, and orders for its evacuation were issued between five-thirty and six o'clock. Under the cover of darkness considerable quantities of stores were moved across the floating bridge which now spanned the harbour and the withdrawal was covered by a barrage of devastating fires and intimidating explosions. For two gripping hours the allied troops watched while Sebastopol burned and rocked with a series of convulsive explosions. By 8 p.m. it was clear that the Russians were pulling out, and an hour later Pélissier sent off a despatch telling of the victory of the Malakoff. When it arrived in Paris on the evening of 10 September the cannon in the Invalides were fired in celebration, a Te Deum was sung in Notre Dame, and Vaillant wrote to Pélissier to say that the Emperor had promoted him to Marshal of France. For Bosquet and MacMahon who had played dominant roles in the attack on the Malakoff and were largely responsible for the victory there was no mention of any reward. Admiral Bruat was promoted from Vice-Admiral to Admiral, and Simpson was awarded the Legion of Honour – a *quid pro quo* for the British Government giving the Order of the Bath to Pélissier and Bosquet.

In Britain news of the fall of Sebastopol reached London about the same time as it arrived in Paris and until the sad revelation of the British disaster came, there was a lot of heedless rejoicing. Guns were fired from the Tower and in St James's Park; at Balmoral, Prince Albert put a match to a ready-laid bonfire, and whisky flowed – producing in the words of the Queen 'great ecstacy'. When news of the repulse on the Great Redan was received however, public reaction was one of despondency and gloomy wrath. It mattered little that Sebastopol had fallen; the British campaign in the Crimea had ended ignominiously.

Major-General Lord George Paget (above)
A French vivandière (right)
The chaotic Balaclava-Sebastopol road during
the winter of 1854/55 (below).

Naval actions: Bomarsund (*above*); Kronstadt (*below*)

18

SECONDARY THEATRES

In March 1854 almost every ship of the French navy was in the Black Sea; so too was the greater part of the British Navy. And while the allied armies at Varna remained inactive it was left to the fleets to prosecute the war. But after bombarding Odessa in April there was very little activity until the time came to shepherd the armies across to the Crimea and stand guard outside Sebastopol.*

While the greater part of the Russian navy was deployed in the Black Sea, a powerful fleet estimated at about 'thirty sail of the line' lurked in the Baltic. To stop this fleet getting out into the North Sea and English Channel was the responsibility of a hurriedly assembled scratch fleet of sailing ships and steamers, and the 68-year-old Sir Charles Napier – 'Fighting Charlie' to some, 'Dirty Charlie' to others because of his disregard of dress and uniform – was appointed to command it. It was not exactly a prepossessing fleet. The best ships were in the Black Sea, as were the best of the Royal Navy's seamen, and when Napier accepted the command he made it clear that he did so only because he considered it his duty. To man the ships a vigorous recruiting drive had to be instituted and the men who were enlisted were for the most part half-starved specimens whom the army had rejected. It is to their credit and that of the Royal Navy that they were turned into seamen in so short a time.

On 10 March, eighteen days before war was declared on Russia, Napier sailed from Portsmouth. Before he left, Queen Victoria had reviewed this fleet of once-magnificent ships, inadequately manned and short of ammunition and Napier is reputed to have promised her that he would be in Kronstadt, the Russian naval base in the Gulf of Finland, within a fortnight – or he would be in heaven. In

---

* In June 1854 two British steam gunboats, H.M.S. *Firebrand* and H.M.S. *Fury*, raided Sulina a Bessarabian village at the mouth of the Danube and destroyed the Russian coast defence batteries there. Otherwise the Black Sea fleet's activities were restricted to routine patrolling and blockade duties.

the event he was in neither, and if he did make such a promise it is quite certain that he never had any intention of keeping it. Kronstadt was a popular objective among the armchair strategists not only because it was considered to be one eminently suited to a nation whose strength was founded on sea power, but also because its fall would see the eclipse of Russian power in the Baltic. This, it was believed, would induce the opportunist Sweden to throw in her lot with the allies. But Kronstadt was a powerful fortress whose granite casemates bristled with cannon. It was garrisoned by well-armed resolute troops, and Napier knew full well that it would be futile to attempt an operation against it.

In fact his orders said nothing about an attack on Kronstadt. He was to seal the Baltic, and – if possible – to destroy the Russian fleet that had wintered in the Gulf of Finland. By 20 March the fleet had reached Copenhagen where 'the Danes were excessively pleased with him [Napier] for taking off his hat on landing'.[1] Eight days later when war was declared it was off Kiel, ready to stop Russian ships going into the North Sea. From Kiel the fleet sailed up the Baltic and split up into three squadrons, one to blockade what is now the Gulf of Danzig, one in the Gulf of Riga and the third watching the mouth of the Gulf of Finland.

Several raids were staged. The dockyards at Uleaborg and Brahestad in the Gulf of Finland were destroyed, and by June when Admiral Perseval Deschenes brought a French fleet into the Baltic to join Napier, talk of an attack on Kronstadt was revived. But apart from a brief appearance off the base on 29 June 1854 the allied fleets gave Kronstadt a wide berth. Napier's over-confident raiders had suffered a sharp reverse at the tiny port of Gamla Karleby 100 miles south of Uleaborg. Because Gamla Karleby lay at the end of a narrow, shallow bay, Napier's warships had to lie five miles off the shore and so were unable to give the raiding force of sailors and marines the artillery support that was essential to their operation.

To Napier it was apparent that for future operations of this nature troops would be needed. No British troops were available but the French undertook to provide 11,000 if Britain would provide the ships to move them in. And so on 11 July a French division under General Baraguay D'Hilliers sailed from the French Channel ports to join Napier and Deschenes. The scene was now set for a more ambitious operation and on 21 June the ships of the combined fleets threaded their way through the narrow waters of the Aland (now Ahvenanmaa) islands to assault Bomarsund.

Most of the Aland islands, which lie at the mouth of the Gulf of Bothnia and which had been ceded to Russia in 1809, were uninhabited. But at Bomarsund there was a good harbour from which hostile ships could control the Swedish coastal trade. The port was dominated by a single fortress, flanked by massive towers whose red granite walls were nine feet thick. Each tower had twenty-four guns – eighteen, twenty-four and thirty-two pounders – and another ninety-two guns were emplaced in a battery above the harbour. Altogether it was a formidable objective. Nevertheless Napier and Deschenes decided that it was more suited to their resources than Kronstadt, or Helsinki or even the latter's outer defended port of Sweaborg. If something had to be attacked in order to pacify public opinion in London and Paris an operation against Bomarsund was much more likely to succeed.

On 21, 26 and 27 June the fleets bombarded the Russian defences and when they sailed away it was claimed that they had 'half-destroyed' the fortifications and killed a large number of the garrison. How this conclusion was arrived at remains a mystery because the Russians were returning the fire up to the moment the fleets sailed away. The final attack which was made in August took the form of a combined sea and land assault. A French force some 3,000 strong was landed at Tranvick Bay, four miles south of the harbour, while another combined Anglo-French force of about the same strength landed at a cove near Hulta, two miles to the north. Following a brief skirmish the French had got some sixteen-pounder guns into position by dawn on 13 August and were shelling the town. Meantime Deschenes' flagship, the *Inflexible*, and four British gunboats the *Edinburgh*, *Blenheim*, *Hogue* and *Ajax* were bombarding the outer defences. When the garrison commander of one of these, Fort Tsu, hoisted a white flag, there was a short truce but when the Russians learned that unconditional surrender were the only terms on which the allies were prepared to stop fighting the truce was concluded and the battle resumed.

After an all-night cannonade the land assault went in on the morning of 14 August. Fort Tsu soon fell, and was occupied by the French. (It had been booby-trapped and an exploding mine killed a large number of the French during the afternoon.) The main fortress and the rest of the town surrendered that night and with their wives and families the garrison, 2,245 strong* marched down to the harbour to be evacuated to Britain as prisoners of war.

Following this success the defences at Bomarsund were destroyed and for the rest of the summer operations were again confined to routine patrolling and minor raids. Then, with the approach of winter the fleets sailed for home. Having made no contest to engage the allied control of the Baltic during the summer it was too late to do so when ice locked their fleet in the Gulf of Finland.

In 1855 another and more effective fleet was sent out to prosecute a second blockade of the Baltic. Napier was no longer in command of the British element. He had been at loggerheads with the Admiralty from the moment he had been appointed and the modest results of his operations the previous summer had not impressed an ill-informed British public anxious for a quick and spectacular victory at sea. Dundas, who had been recalled from the Black Sea to become Second Sea Lord, was given the command of the new fleet and much was expected of him. Nor was it wrong to expect more than Napier had achieved, for the fleet which sailed for a rendezvous with the French in the Gulf of Finland was a very different fleet from Napier's scratch force. With the Russian Black Sea fleet confined behind its own barriers in Sebastopol, Dundas had been able to withdraw ships and crews from the main British fleet off the Crimean coast. As a result he had collected the best ships and best sailors of the whole Royal Navy. Yet Dundas, while paying lip service to the need for an attack on the Russian naval bases in the Gulf of Finland, was determined that he was not going to lose ships or men unnecessarily. He had seen the negligible effects of broadsides on the granite forts of Sebastopol and the damage occasioned to his own ships when attempts were made to reduce coast defences by battleships, and he was not going to pit his ships against the granite walls of any Russian naval base, not even to please *The Times*.

When the idea of a strike at the heart of the Russian Baltic Fleet, Kronstadt, was revived Dundas firmly turned it down. If he had had his way, he would also have rejected the pet project of the First Sea Lord, Sir James Graham, which was a plan for an attack on the subsidiary fortress of Sweaborg. Against his better judgement, however, he agreed to a bombardment and on 6 August, with Dundas

* The garrison was made up of native-born Finns from the Finland Regiment, the 10th Regiment of Imperial Line.

commanding the British ships and Admiral Penaud the French, the allied fleets dropped anchor off Sweaborg.

What constituted the fortified locality of Sweaborg covered six islands located about three miles south-east of Helsinki (then known as Helsingfors). The importance of the place stemmed from the fact that it dominated the channel to Helsinki, and because of this the islands had become nothing but a huge fortress. Cannon and ramparts bristled everywhere, but the nub of the fortifications was centrally located on the island of Vargon. Here, in a massive granite citadel which had been hacked out of the solid rock, 810 cannon and a garrison of 12,000 men waited for the Allies to make their move. When they arrived on 6 August, neither Dundas nor Penaud were especially anxious to make any move. At Penaud's suggestion the bombardment which had been proposed for the following day was postponed until a mortar battery could be set up on one of the islands in the Sweaborg group which had not been occupied by the Russians. When this was ready on the morning of the 9th a signal from Dundas's flagship gave the order to open fire and for three days and two nights British and French guns and mortars kept up an incessant cannonade. During that time 1,000 tons of iron balls, shells and rockets were hurled into an area of three square miles, and 100 tons of gunpowder were used to project them. And at the end of the action the Allies claimed that the Russians had suffered 2,000 casualties. (The Russians themselves said that only one man – a Cossack – was killed, but that about 1,000 men were injured, none seriously.) Casualties in the allied fleets were few, but when they sailed away nearly all the guns were worn out, and their mountings needed to be replaced.

Sweaborg could hardly be considered to be a successful operation. Dundas's excuse for not following up the bombardment with another on Helsingfors was that he was concerned about the 'innocent' civilian population and the town's beautiful cathedral.

That was virtually all there was to the war in the Baltic. The Russians showed little initiative and never dared to venture out while the Allies were anywhere near. Perhaps the most distinguishing feature of the whole business was the Russian use of mines – then called torpedoes – off Kronstadt and the earliest known 'minesweeping' operations.

Elsewhere naval operations were relatively minor. A British flotilla patrolled the White Sea and blockaded Archangel, and in the

Pacific there was an Anglo-French flotilla which saw some action. Commanded by Rear-Admiral David Price, the operations of this force were directed against the Russian Pacific Squadron, under Rear-Admiral Putiatin, based on Petropavlovsk in the Kamchatka region north-west of Japan. On 30 August 1854 an attack, launched on Petropavlovsk was broken off when Admiral Price committed suicide, and in May the following year a force of 700 sailors and marines which was landed on a beach outside the base, was forced to withdraw after suffering 200 casualties. From here, Price's successor sailed off to investigate a report that the Russians had established a base at Sitka in Alaska. And by the time the report was found to be untrue the war was over.

Undoubtedly the most important of the secondary operations against Russia took place in Asia Minor. From just outside Batumi on the Black Sea to Ararat on the Persian border there was 150 miles of Turkish frontier with Russia. The main town in the region of what was then Turkish Armenia was centred round the ancient fortress of Kars, eighty miles south-east of Batumi and roughly the same distance south-west of Tiflis. In the summer of 1854 a Russian army advanced into Turkish Armenia, and on 29 July it attacked a Turkish division deployed in front of Kars at a place called Byazid. Largely because of bad leadership the Turks were driven back, losing a considerable quantity of equipment in the process. But the Turkish commander at Kars, Zarif Mustapha Pasha, was determined to recoup his losses and in August he struck back at the Russians with an army of 22,000 Turkish infantry, 4,000 cavalry, 11,000 Bashi-Bazouks, 4,500 irregular cavalry and fifty-two guns. Against this force Prince Bebutoff, the Russian commander who had failed to exploit his success at Byazid, had an army of 20,000 infantry, 5,000 of the ubiquitous Cossacks, about 18,000 irregulars and sixty guns. Twenty miles east of Kars the two forces clashed. After a five hour battle the Turks again fell back on Kars, however, having suffered about 2,000 casualties and lost about another 2,000 men as prisoners to the Russians. The battle was lost not so much because of the superior tactics of Prince Bebutoff, it was said, but because Zarif was bewildered by the rival plans of his foreign advisers. Fortunately for him the Russians who had also suffered heavy losses again failed to follow up their success and the Turks were given another opportunity to rally. At this point the British decided to take a hand and a gunner, Colonel Fenwick Williams, was appointed as Raglan's liaison officer with Zarif. Williams had spent a number of years with the Turkish army and knew the Kars area well. With him went another gunner, Major Teasdale, as aide-de-camp and a Dr Sandwith who had been appointed Inspector-General of Hospitals in Asia Minor. At Constantinople, Williams was told by Raglan that his duties were to report back to him on the organization and condition of the Turkish army in Armenia, and to establish good relations with any French military mission which might turn up in the area.

Williams and his entourage arrived in Kars in September 1854 – just about the time of the battle of Alma – and was met by General Guyon, an Irishman serving in the Ottoman army. Guyon had gone to Kars to try to put some heart into Zarif's army and what he had to tell Williams was a story of disillusionment. Desertion was rife among the troops, who were in rags and whose pay was months in arrears. Hospitals were non-existent or useless; the whole garrison was in an incredible state of inefficiency. (The latter statement was quickly confirmed by Dr Sandwith. Oriental indifference combined with graft were the basic causes of the situation. Turkish officers rarely bothered about their hospitals. Fatalism also played its part. Many of the wretched patients died because they had decided that their hour had come, that death was their *khismet*.)

To a man like Williams only one course of action was open: to take over himself; and this is what he proceeded to do. A review of the resources available in Kars produced astonishing revelations. After inspecting the infantry whose combatant strength he had been told was 22,000, a head count showed that there were less than 15,000 on parade. Yet 33,000 rations were being charged for daily. Weapons were obsolete and in poor shape; the men were untrained as well as badly clothed and poorly fed; and their officers, prone to hit the bottle, were for the most part unfitted to lead. Williams' problem was to persuade the Turks themselves to put things on a better footing. Fortunately for him there were several European officers in the Turkish army besides General Guyon: so far none of them had been able to make much headway against Turkish incompetence and corruption but with the stimulus Williams now provided matters slowly began to change.

Much had also to be done to improve the defences of Kars. In 1828 when the Russians had captured the place its fortress had enjoyed an entirely unmerited reputation for strength. Since then little had been done. The old Turkish walls still stood and on the Karadagh mountain which loomed over the fort on one side and on the Tachmasb Heights on the other there had been some attempt to dig a few trenches. But these had been badly located and in any case were incomplete. With the winter approaching there was little that could be done at that moment. Nevertheless if Kars was to be held and a Russian invasion of Armenia halted the defences would have to be put in order. Teasdale was set to work on this until he was replaced in the following spring by Colonel Lake of the Madras Engineers who had been sent to Williams as his engineer adviser. Meantime Zarif had been replaced by a new commander-in-chief, Wassif Pasha, and two more British officers had joined Williams.

With the advent of spring and the melting of the snows Lake set about completing the work on the defences that Teasdale had begun and by the end of April it seemed as if the Russians had missed their opportunity. The defences of Kars were in order and the troops were in a better state than they had ever been. But in May the feast of Ramadan brought a set-back.* Digging and training eased up and the Turks were in no condition to fight.

At the beginning of June the Russians started to advance and by the 15th Williams estimated that an army of 30,000 was camped in the hills east of Kars. Shortly afterwards the Russians attacked and the Turkish outposts were driven in by Cossacks who only stopped when they came under the fire of the guns of the fortress. Losses on both sides were trivial and the morale of both sides had been boosted by this action – the Russians because of their success, and the Turks because it seemed that they were safe inside Kars.

Williams' anxiety now was whether Kars could withstand a siege. He had ordered all grain stocks in the surrounding districts to be requisitioned, but this had not been done; he had asked for supplies from the Turkish base at Erzurum, but these had not been forth-coming; he had called for a reserve of ammunition but this had not been provided. Now it was too late.

On 18 June, when great columns of Russians debouched from the hills and fanned out round the fortress it was obvious that the real

* This is the ninth month of the Mohammedan year and it is rigidly observed as thirty days' fast during the hours of daylight. This means neither food nor drink from sunrise to sunset and although the Koran permits its abrogation in travel and in war the pious Moslem will invariably observe the rules of fast.

attack was about to be launched. Williams was determined to hold out as long as he could, but he was not hopeful about the eventual outcome. (In Constantinople the authorities had already decided that resistance would collapse.) And General Mouravieff, who had replaced Prince Bebutoff was quietly confident. Having drawn a cordon round Kars he marched south, cut the road to Erzurum and began to collect the supplies which Turkish incompetence had left to them.* Inside the fortress Williams soon discovered that he was worse fitted for a leisurely investment than he had originally thought. Not only were the books recording false figures regarding supply stocks, hundreds of non-combatants – whose ejection to neighbouring villages he had ordered weeks before – were still with him.

Other than a few minor skirmishes nothing happened in July. The Russians sat patiently just outside the range of the Turks' weapons and Williams did not attempt a sortie against them. The Turks were not sufficiently well trained or equipped – mentally or physically – for aggressive action and it was better to let them stay secure within the walls. On 7 August the Russians attempted a probing attack but judging by the numbers involved it was intended more as a bait to lure the defenders out. When they refused to be drawn Mouravieff marched his army towards Erzurum, halting for some odd reason eighteen miles from it. Possibly the move was but a reconnaissance in force but it was enough to scare the foreign residents into packing up and leaving for Trebizond. Meanwhile Mouravieff, having collected all the local grain supplies and posted detachments in the main passes back to Kars, made a leisurely return to the scene of the siege. With twenty-eight battalions of infantry, 5,000 cavalry and forty-eight guns he knew that he could storm the fortress if need be. But he believed that the prize would fall into his lap without any fighting; sooner or later Williams' supplies would run out.

And so the siege continued. Desertion due to short rations was Williams's main enemy as the summer wore on, and when cholera appeared in the garrison he began to doubt whether the end was in sight. Well he might. By the end of August Mouravieff's main army had returned from the foray into Armenia and had pitched its camp round Kars. Rations in the fortress were cut back and to eke them out the 700 cavalry horses that Williams had retained were

* At Yeni-Keuy, fifty miles from Kars, the Russians found six weeks' supply of biscuit, wheat and barley for their army.

slaughtered. As August gave way to September and no reinforcements or relief appeared to be forthcoming from Turkey, Williams was still determined to hang on.

Williams had no way of knowing, but the allied generals had already decided the fate of the garrison. At a meeting on 14 July they had rejected a plan for 25,000 Turkish infantry and 3,000 cavalry to go to Kars, whose defence Omar Pasha had maintained was essential to the security of Constantinople. To the British and French – especially the French – the withdrawal of so many Turks would have weakened the allied position in the Tchernaya, leaving the Baidor valley and Balaclava exposed to a Russian attack. Kars was important but from the allied point of view not so important as the Crimea. As they were not strong enough to fight in both regions the Crimea must take priority. Sebastopol was the objective and until it was captured the Turk would not be permitted to get his army out of the Crimea.

Just before dawn on 29 September, nearly three weeks after the fall of Sebastopol General Kmetz, one of the Austrian officers in the Turkish army reported that he thought he could hear movement in the direction of the Tachmasb Heights. Mouravieff had grown tired of waiting and decided to attack.

If there was one thing that Williams had tried to instil in the garrison it was to act quickly in an emergency and the Turks were soon under arms. Both Lake and Teasdale who had been up most of the night had heard nothing until they were alerted by a Turkish gun firing on a mass of Russians advancing in the dim light towards the western defences of the fortress on Tachmasb. Realizing that they had been spotted the grey mass broke into a run. The Turks opened fire all along their trenches and the guns fired chain shot as the grey masses approached. Nevertheless one of the Turkish batteries was overrun and as soon as it ceased to fire the Russians swarmed against the parapet of the main redoubt nearby. The situation was only retrieved by a vigorous counter-attack led by Teasdale. On the right of this position the Russians had also broken through but again a vigorous attack, led this time by Kmetz, routed the assailants. When the action was over 850 corpses which included a high proportion of officers covered the acre of ground where most of the fighting had taken place.

Meantime the Russians had launched another attack on the south side of the fortress and while this was being fought off a third Russian force which had assembled behind the Tachmasb Heights advanced to attack the Turkish positions on the cliffs which looked down on Kars. This, the main attack, was directed against the most vulnerable side of the Kars position and it was repelled only with the greatest difficulty. A regiment of Russian dragoons was hurled against the Turks to try to break through but the garrison held out. By noon the battle was virtually over. Out of the 35,000 Russians who had attacked the 10,000-strong garrison more than 6,000 dead were buried by the Turks alone and the Turks themselves had suffered nearly 1,500 casualties.

After the battle the siege continued and despite the shattered condition of the Russians and the state of the now starving garrison no attempt was made to relieve Kars. And so on 25 November Williams was obliged to capitulate. Evacuation was out of the question as the Turks, reduced by now to a diet of two-fifths of the Turkish ration (barely sufficient to sustain life even when it was in full issue) and grass roots, were dying of starvation. On 27 November Williams and his officers dined amicably with Mouravieff and on the following day the Russians took possession of Kars.

Only one other major action outside the Crimean peninsula remains to be mentioned. After the fall of Sebastopol the Allies decided to attack the ports on the river Bug. The intention was to destroy Russian shipping and hamper Russian activities in much the same way as the operation in the Sea of Azov had hampered the flow of supplies to Sebastopol. At Kinburn, east of Odessa, three forts on a long narrow spur of the mainland defended the estuary at the mouth of the rivers Dnieper and Bug. And eighty miles up the Bug lay the town of Nicolaev where much of the Russian fleet was built and where many of its sailors were recruited. On 7 October an allied force of 10,000 troops sailed from Kamiesch Bay for Kinburn. In command of the force, which was predominantly French, was General Bazaine* and the British contingent comprised 17th, 20th, 21st, 57th and 63rd Regiments of the Line

---

* Achille Bazaine, forty-four years old, and destined to become a Marshal of France, is best remembered for his surrender of Metz to the Germans in 1870. An ex-sergeant of the Foreign Legion, veteran of Algeria and the Carlist war in Spain, Bazaine commanded the original Foreign Legion contingent of the French army in the Crimea. With him went his young beautiful Spanish wife, Soledad and her piano. Apart from the fact that the Emperor was keen on the expedition to Kinburn, it had the added advantage of freeing Soledad for Pélissier's pleasure.

and two battalions of Royal Marines. Arriving off Kinburn on 14 October the fleet of transports and warships dropped anchor about three miles west of the fort and that night an Anglo-French flotilla forced its way past the fort into Dnieper Bay. On the 16th the troops were landed above the forts to isolate them from reinforcements; the ships opened fire and on 17 October Kinburn and its forts surrendered. Eighty guns were captured and the fort of Oczakoff was blown up by its own garrison.

For some weeks after this the allied gunboats cruised ostentatiously off the Bug and Dnieper estuaries while the troops remained in possession of Kinburn. Louis Napoleon thought it would be a good idea to use Kinburn as a base for further operations. But the time for new bases was past; the war was entering its final phase.

19

FINALE

The allied campaign in the Crimea virtually ended with the occupation of Sebastopol. No battle followed; nor was there much heart left for fighting. After their evacuation of the main part of the town, the Russians dug themselves in on the heights north of the harbour and for the Allies the question was what to do next. Pélissier and Simpson both assured their respective governments that there was little that could be done immediately, and that any attack on the Russians in their present positions would be costly and uncertain to bring success. There was some discussion as to whether it would be possible to move them by threatening their communications with an advance from the allied right; or, alternatively, by sailing the allied armies round to Eupatoria and manoeuvring from there. But in either case it was not considered advisable to follow the Russians beyond the line drawn east and west from Eupatoria to Simpheropol. Burgoyne, still active in London, gave his opinion that it would be better to wait until the winter, when their own supply problems would compel the Russians to evacuate the Crimea.

From Paris, Pélissier was bombarded with telegrams from the Emperor suggesting a host of alternatives for further action and as a result of constant pressure General Bazaine was sent to occupy Kinburn. This pleased Louis Napoleon as he saw Kinburn not merely as a block to communications between Nicolaev, Kherson and Odessa, but also as a threat to the rear of the Russians still in the Crimea. Pélissier raised a whole cascade of objections to all his other suggestions and the Emperor found this irritating at first – although Pélissier's arguments eventually led him to change his opinion about allied objectives in the war. To the men in the field, Pélissier and Simpson, it now seemed safest to do nothing beyond occupying Sebastopol, and the town was parcelled out among the Allies.

On 22 September there was a brief action at Kertch in which a few French and British cavalry beat off some Cossacks, and occasionally

the Allies exchanged shots with the Russians across Sebastopol
harbour – with the object apparently of showing each other that
they were still at war. But all life had gone out of the campaign
and thoughts were turning homeward. Omar Pasha was finally
allowed to take his army to Asia Minor to save Kars – which he
failed to do. The British, having got their army back to health and
strength, declared that they were ready to get on with the war,
and the French said that they were just marking time. By November,
however, sentiment in France was against a continuation of the
fighting, and the Emperor had become aware of his nation's hope for
peace. In Paris he admitted privately to the British Ambassador that
France could not afford to continue much longer, and in London
the French Foreign Minister bluntly told Palmerston that France
was exhausted. As she had suffered more and contributed more than
Britain, the Emperor therefore really had no choice in the matter;
a peace settlement must be concluded. Feigning surprise, Palmerston replied that Britain did not keep large armies during peace
time and because of this had been slow to get started. But now, with
150,000 men under arms, she was ready to begin the war in real
earnest.[1] Popular feeling in Britain backed this view and the general
opinion was that the Russians should be given a sound beating in
the field before the armies came home. Louis Napoleon, however,
was now beginning to realize that he could justify France's continued sacrifice only if the war was to take on more Napoleonic
aims – or, at least, ones that could be more readily recognized as
French national objectives. Poland, Italy, or the left bank of the
Rhine, would be far more effective grounds for further sacrifice
than anything in the Black or Baltic seas. The French, unlike the
British, did not have interests in the Far East which were threatened
by Russia. The campaign in the Crimea had been undertaken by
Louis Napoleon mainly to establish his new dynasty on a foundation
of glory. That objective had been attained when the Malakoff was
captured and Sebastopol fell.

The imminent approach of winter sufficed as an excuse for
further inaction. Various plans were discussed for operations against
the Russians dug in on the Mackenzie Heights and in January 1856
the reconnaissance of the south-eastern shores of the Black Sea was
made to look for disembarkation points and at the roads in Asia
Minor. Meanwhile a Franco-Russian *entente* had been evolving to
the detriment of British interests and objectives. On 16 November,

Prince Napoleon made an address about French achievements in the Crimea which made no reference whatever to the British army being there. No real hatred existed between France and Russia and only duty kept them both at war. The diplomatists were busy; peace was in the air, and on 16 January 1856 Russia accepted the good offices of Austria as a step towards the negotiations of a peace treaty.

Meantime Codrington, who had taken over from Simpson, was ordered to continue preparations for further operations in the spring. The allied forces in the Crimea were to be divided into two independent armies: one commanded by Pélissier, composed primarily of French troops, but with the Sardinians and a token British force, would operate from Eupatoria; the other, under Codrington, and composed of British troops, the British mercenaries and some French, would operate from Sebastopol.

During the winter Louis Napoleon spent a great deal of time in consultation about the reorganization of the whole French army. His objective was to give the Imperial Guard more stature and responsibilities. (This reorganization was condemned later by historians who believed that the army was never really the same after 1855. The Imperial Guard had been a gesture and a reminder of the First Empire. To make it now a more basic element in the army was in fact trying to make the souvenir become the thing of which it was really only a symbol.[2] Forty years had passed and to try to maintain the methods and arms of the age which ended with Waterloo was to court disaster.) A more pressing problem was posed by Bosquet and Canrobert. Both had set their eyes on a marshal's baton and with some reluctance the Emperor finally decided to give it to them.

For the French army in the Crimea the winter of 1855–6 was a tragic one. The Russians had been defeated but sanitation had got out of hand and the epidemic which broke out as a result went unchecked. The situation was similar to that of the British in the preceding winter. The British army was now healthy and comfortable: 'well-fed, well-clothed and well-sheltered . . . the English soldiers were a great contrast to those of the previous winter; no one would have taken the smart clean troops on the plateau of Sebastopol in January 1856 to have been of the same race and nation as the care-worn, over-worked and sickly soldiers guarding the trenches in January 1855.'[3] By this time also a better class of recruit had come in and the ranks were filled not with boys but with men. Between January 1854 and March 1856 nearly 70,000 recruits – nearly half volunteers from the Militia – had been enlisted. But the numbers were short of the establishment voted by Parliament – 40,000 short in March 1855 – and for this reason the British Government had decided to raise a foreign legion of Swiss, Germans and Italians. Recruiting of Swiss and Germans began in 1855 and by 31 March, nearly 10,000 men had been engaged and 4,000 of these were actually sent to the Crimea.* Another recruiting centre was opened in Turin and by March 1856, 3,000 Italians had been recruited and sent to Malta. Yet another recruiting centre was opened at Niagara and a number of Americans were enlisted there. Finally, 20,000 Turks were enlisted into British officered units, so that in the spring of 1856 Codrington had about 90,000 men under his command and another 18,000 had been collected at Aldershot preparatory to joining them. The British infantry was also being issued with a new rifle, the Enfield, which was an improvement on the Minié.

On 28 February 1856 Austrian mediation brought an armistice which came into effect on 14 March, and on 30 March the Treaty of Peace itself was signed. Among other things this treaty called for the Allies to return to the Russians Sebastopol, Balaclava, Kamiesch Eupatoria, Kertch, Kinburn and other occupied areas, and for Kars to be given back to Turkey. The Black Sea was neutralized: 'Its waters and ports formally interdicted to the flag of war'; the maintenance of naval arsenals on its shores was forbidden, and ships of war were denied entrance into or passage through the Bosphorus or the Dardanelles. The Danube was to be an open waterway and there was to be a new adjustment of the Russian boundaries in Bessarabia. Finally, the signatory powers guaranteed the continuance of Ottoman suzerainty in the Principalities. By a separate agreement between Turkey and Russia, each of them was allowed to maintain in the Black Sea half a dozen light steamers of no more than 800 tons, and four steam or sailing vessels of not more than 200 tons. To complete the package, the Sultan issued a firman declaring that he was ready to improve the condition of all Christian peoples within his empire. But there was not a single reference in the treaty

---

* None of the mercenaries saw any action and this was the last occasion that the British army recruited men from a continental power. After the war many of the Germans settled in South Africa.

or in any of the subsidiary agreements to the question of the Holy Places – the ostensible cause of the war.

The allied evacuation of Sebastopol began almost before the ink on the treaty was dry. While it was in progress, reviews and races took the place of battle. Pélissier, Codrington and the Russian commander-in-chief, General Lüders, played host to each other; while the allied and Russian troops fraternized in the taverns. Finally, on 17 April, there was a grand military review at which Lüders took the salute.

As the allied troops departed, Russian units relieved them. The last of the British army left the Crimea on 12 July; the last of the French had departed on the 4th. So the troops went home. Officers who had taken part in the campaign were soon cheerfully planting Crimean crocuses or listening in their drawing rooms to renderings of Lindhals' 'Alma, a Battlepiece for the Pianoforte'. And in Jerusalem there were riots in the Church of the Holy Sepulchre; the people whose grievances had brought the war and who now found they were ignored had decided to settle their affairs in their own way.

EPILOGUE

Our God and soldiers we alike adore
Ever at the brink of danger;
Not before;
After deliverance, both alike requited
Our God's forgotten and our soldiers slighted.

Francis Quarles 1592-1655

For the rebuilding of Sebastopol the Russians engaged an American engineer, Colonel John C. Gowen, who had succeeded in refloating the American man-of-war *Missouri*, which had sunk at Gibraltar. The harbour had to be cleared and it seems that there was nobody in Russia capable of tackling the job. It took Gowen six years, but at the end of that time he had salvaged every vessel.

Politically the results of the war were almost as intangible and contradictory as the aims and causes which had precipitated it. Britain gained nothing and lost influence in Europe. Russia lost influence and prestige, and the saying that Russia was a colossus with feet of clay became a European commonplace. (This was a dangerous delusion which had fatal results for Germany in the Second World War.) Perhaps the most important outcome was the return of France, after forty years, to a position of diplomatic dominance in Europe. Symbolic of the change was that reference to 'the Emperor' now signified Napoleon III of France, whereas before the war it would have meant Nicholas I of Russia.

Much of the credit for this rise in France's reputation must go to her army and its leaders. Compared with that of Britain, the French army was better organized, its troops generally more experienced and adaptable, and its regimental officers technically more efficient. Of the French generals, St Arnaud – appointed to the command of the French Expeditionary Force because of past service to Louis Napoleon – lacked the qualities needed for a general on whose decisions depend the fate of 30,000 men. But for most of the time he was a mortally sick man. Canrobert, ambitious and confident when St Arnaud was in charge, proved weak and vacillating when he took over as commander-in-chief. Pélissier, a law unto himself, was the best leader and the most energetic. Of these three it was Pélissier who was the most deserving of a marshal's baton, and it is interesting to speculate on the course of the campaign in the Crimea if he had succeeded St Arnaud in October 1854.

The trouble with the British generals was that most of them lacked technical competence. Brought up in an atmosphere that was serenely remote from the fevered striving after mechanical progress that was going on around them, elderly and dignified, they had spent too many years signing documents and taking the salute at reviews to be expected to display the ill-bred pushfulness of mill-owners. Arrogant in manner and outlook, there was no doubting their personal disregard of danger and in a crisis most of them used their initiative boldly and aggressively. Compared with the French divisional commanders, the British generals were less professional but often more enterprising.

For real lack of enterprise, however, the Russian commanders far exceeded the allies. The Battle of the Alma was the decisive battle of the campaign and it was not lost by the British and French because the Russians allowed them to win. On two occasions during the battle the Russians had an opportunity to turn it in their favour – with a cavalry attack on the British left flank, or by Kiriakoff following up when Canrobert refused battle with his column. If both moves had been made when the opportunities presented themselves the result would have been devastating. Blame for this must be considered to lie primarily with the volatile Menschikoff, who was too nervous to attempt any daring move throughout the whole campaign. Gorschakoff was equally unenterprising and only Todleben really made a move for himself and he was worth a division of troops in Sebastopol.

Of the regimental officers the Russians were also the least prominent, mainly because they were submerged in the grey amalgam of the regimental columns. The Russian regimental officer was not much less of an automaton than the men under his command. Everything that was required of him – his behaviour, his method of command – was laid down by an authority that ultimately stemmed from the Tsar himself. Because of the accident of his birth, the Russian officer was classed in one of the higher of the fourteen social ranks to which every Russian was assigned, but he was given no rein to use his initiative or individuality. On the allied side the French regimental officers, accustomed to field conditions in Algeria, were able to look after themselves and their men better than their British counterparts, who tended to act as if they were still on the parade ground. Once disencumbered of social distractions there could be no doubt of their courage and purposefulness however. (But old habits die hard and it is perhaps in keeping with the British character to recall the subaltern's call for assistance at the height of the Battle of Inkerman: 'I say – we haven't been introduced but I think we met at Lady Palmerston's last year – we're in the devil of a mess . . .'[1])

It was the British private soldier who was the hero of the campaign. He did not have the colour and dash of the Zouave, the stolidity of the Russian 'Muffin Cap', or the fatalism of the Turk; but it is difficult to believe that any of these three would have endured what the British soldier had to endure in and out of battle. In battle the Russians – driven perhaps by the duress of their suppressive discipline – stood in their columns time and time again to receive devastating punishment before they yielded. The French troops with plenty of experience of the privations and dangers of active service, were more cautious; they were conscripts and in or out of the line they accepted only what hardships they had to accept. But the British soldier – illiterate, rigidly disciplined,* and a social outcast – was long-suffering as well as being stolid and shrewd. Possibly this stemmed from the fact that he was a volunteer, and the subconscious realization of the fact that he was where he was because he had elected to become a soldier more or less of his own free will led him to accept the conditions of the Crimea in a mood of resigned fortitude. The long-term soldiers who started the campaign were trained to a degree of perfection that reduced movements and bearing in battle to a drill. Yet they were not automatons like the Russians; beneath the surface there was something more than mere automation waiting to respond when the demand was made. Out of the line the British soldier behaved with the same long-suffering fortitude as he showed in battle. He was averse to digging – not to work in general as the French said – and he suffered a thirst which needed

* By modern standards discipline would be considered Draconic. Some regiments had given up flogging; nevertheless more than 3,000 floggings were inflicted during the campaign. In February 1856 a soldier guilty of murder was publicly hanged in Sebastopol – 150 men from every regiment being detailed to attend the execution.

much slaking. (It is said that empty beer bottles, relics of the siege, could be picked up round Balaclava many years afterwards. And there is a story of the Irishman, who sold his boots for drink and then blacked his bare feet before going on parade – in the hope that his crime would escape detection and that he would be able to pick up another pair from a casualty.)

It was the inarticulate manner in which her soldiers stood up to hardships that roused Britain's national conscience to make amends for the country's neglect of the army. For the first time ordinary citizens seemed to become aware of what manner of men soldiers really were. Tales of their struggles in the trenches and of their agony in the hospitals roused the British nation as never before. Yet, contrary to popular belief it was not the muddle and agony of the Crimea which brought reform to the British army. In 1856 some attempts were made to tidy up the military departments, but public demands for sweeping changes were disappointed and apathy would doubtless have descended if the British Government had not been shocked a second time by the Indian Mutiny. This established the inability of a regular army of about 150,000 men to police an Empire of 3 million square miles, even though the legendary supremacy of the British Navy still remained to shelter those who opposed any radical alterations in the army. Between 1859 and 1862, however, when France took the lead in the production and development of ironclad warships even this comforting illusion of naval invulnerability was suddenly shattered, and the Admiralty had to admit Britain's temporary inferiority. It was the combination of these three blows against national complacency – the war against Russia, the Indian Mutiny and the naval race with France – which caused mountainous controversy in Parliament and the Press. Even then it was not until 1868, when Edward Cardwell became Secretary of State for War in a new Gladstone administration that any effective reforms were undertaken. (A timid attempt to form a reserve of trained soldiers was made in 1859 and fear of a French invasion led to a revival of the old Volunteers, but these two measures appear like mice in comparison with the work of Cardwell.) After they had been put into effect it was said that never again would the anonymous Englishman in the ranks – or anywhere else – be quite so anonymous. Perhaps he was not *quite* so anonymous in 1900 as he was fifty years before but after every war there is always some return to anonymity.

Industrial development and mechanical progress got into their stride in Europe during the first half of the nineteenth century and by 1853 industry was being mechanized, steam was displacing sailpower and a network of railways already covered Britain. Other countries were making strenuous efforts to follow her lead and the spirit of mechanical invention was beginning to make itself felt in the arts of destruction. The natural aversion of the military leaders to innovation slowed the clock of progress. Fortunately for the British and French infantry they were not able to stop it altogether and the allied troops went into battle at the Alma equipped with the Minié rifle. This was a long-range weapon, whose rate of fire was slow compared with Peninsula War standards – and still slower compared with those set by Frederick-William 1 for his Prussian infantry.

Up to the time of the 1870s the application of science to warfare was mainly concerned with the range, precision, and rapidity of fire of the infantry and artillery weapons. Of course the soldiers could not help reaping the benefit of civilian progress. The railway had become a factor of ever increasing importance in the transport and supply of armies even before the war in the Crimea, and the telegraph which both Pélissier and Raglan loathed so much symbolized a revolution in military communications.* For the first time in the history of war the surgeon's knife lost half its terror when the anaesthetic chloroform came into common use and Florence Nightingale compelled the reluctant authorities to reform the murderous inefficiencies that made the hospital more deadly than the battlefield.

But these were gifts from civilian life – 'fall-out' from progress in the social and industrial spheres – which would have come to the soldiers in time without the war against Russia. What the war did was to stimulate the development of weapons, whose effect was to make firepower more than ever the master of the battle. In 1866 the Prussian needle-gun – a primitive breech-loader – brought the collapse of Austrian military power in the course of a few weeks. Four years later, in the Franco-German war, the French had got a greatly superior rifle in the *Chassepot* and a few machine guns. But

---

* The telegraph being a novelty was sometimes used in a novel way. Raglan was once awakened at midnight on receipt of a cable from the Secretary of State for War which read: 'Captain Jarvis has been bitten by a centipede. How is he now?'

they were hopelessly out-numbered and out-generalled, and the Germans had a compensating advantage in the possession of rifled breech-loading artillery, which invariably silenced the French guns.*

Despite the lessons of the Crimea and the fact that science was thrusting a phenomenal multiplication of firepower into the hands of their gunners and riflemen, the military leaders of all the great powers continued to cling to tactics that had been obsolete in Napoleon's time and were now merely suicidal. The American Civil War – conducted by improvised armies of civilians without military traditions – provided fertile soil for the growth of new ideas and demonstrated that to conduct an attack – even with greatly superior forces – against infantry properly dug in was to stage a massacre. (Considering the attraction that the war has had for modern strategists from Sir Basil Liddell Hart down, surprisingly few lessons were derived from this war by the military authorities in Britain. The probable explanation lies in the contempt felt in military circles for untrained, irregular soldiers, irrespective of their nationality. †) The idea of attacking a column and breaking through by sheer weight of numbers remained an obsession. In naval circles similar ideas prevailed, and it was a long time before the admirals could be persuaded that powerful guns and torpedoes made shock tactics – ship against ship – obsolete. (The arguments of those who clung to these ideas were strengthened in 1866 when an Austrian wooden ship rammed – or at any rate collided with – an Italian ironclad and sank her.) It was not until the *Dreadnought* type of ship came into being that the ram was discarded.

The ending of the Franco-Prussian war gave the military authorities of all countries an excuse for braking the application of science to war and there was a tendency to revert to the ideas that were in vogue before the war against Russia – particularly in regard to uniforms. That the lessons of the Alma, let alone 1870, had not been taken to heart was shown seven years later at Plevna when the

---

* Zola's *La Débâcle* gives a ghastly account of the annihilation of a French battery at Sedan by Prussian artillery beyond its range.

† Writing on the military influences of the American Civil War a modern historian concludes that 'It is unlikely that the Civil War, though widely studied in England (i.e. for the latest developments in artillery and fortifications) had any direct bearing upon official doctrine.' *The Military Legacy of the Civil War: the European Inheritance*, Jay Luvaas, Chicago University Press, 1959, p. 115.

Russian commanders drove up their men in mass formation to be mown down in the time-honoured style by the no means progressive Turks. Four years later (1871) Sir George Colley in South Africa gave an instructive demonstration of the fact that the British army had learnt hardly anything and forgotten a good deal since Sebastopol. By the turn of the century the manoeuvres of European armies would have reassured even Sir George Brown and Lord Cardigan.

APPENDIX 1

Provisions of the Straits Convention, closing the Dardanelles to Non-Turkish warships, signed by the Great Powers in 1841

1. That the straits of the Bosphorus and the Dardanelles, in conformity with the ancient usages of the Ottoman empire, shall remain permanently closed against all foreign vessels of war as long as the Ottoman Porte shall enjoy peace.

2. The Sultan declares, on his side, that he is firmly resolved to maintain immovably the ancient rule of the empire, in virtue of which it is forbidden to vessels of war of all nations to enter the Dardanelles or the Bosphorus, and in virtue of which these straits remain for ever closed, as long as the Ottoman Porte shall be at peace.

3. His Majesty the Emperor of Austria, and their Majesties the King of the French, the Queen of Great Britain, the King of Prussia, and the Emperor of Russia, on their part engage to respect that resolution of the Sultan, and to act in conformity with the principle there expressed.

4. The ancient rule of the Ottoman empire being thus established and recognized, the Sultan reserves to himself the right to grant firmans of passage to small vessels of war, which, in conformity with usage, are employed in the service of ambassadors of friendly Powers.

5. The Sultan reserves to himself the right to notify the terms of this treaty to all the Powers with which he is on terms of amity, and to invite their accession to it.

APPENDIX 2

Order of Battle at Alma, 20 September 1854

I. RUSSIAN ARMY

Commander-in-chief: General Prince Alexander Sergeievich Menschikoff

Commander of Eastern sector (Russian right): General Kvetzinski

Commander of Central sector: General Prince Mikhail Dmitrievich Gorschakoff

Commander of Western sector (Russian left): General Kiriakoff.

Eastern sector (Russian Right Flank)

4 battalions Kazan Regiment ⎫
4 battalions Vladimir Regiment ⎪
4 battalions Sousdal Regiment ⎬ 13,000 infantry
4 battalions Uglitz Regiment ⎪
2 battalions sailors ⎭

Brigade of Hussars ⎫ 3,400 cavalry
2 regiments Cossacks of the Don ⎭

5 batteries of field artillery (40 guns)

14 heavy guns

Central sector

4 battalions Volhynia Regiment ⎫
3 battalions Minsk Regiment ⎪
4 battalions Borodino Regiment ⎬ 10,000 infantry
1 battalion riflemen ⎪
4 batteries field artillery (32 guns) ⎭

Western sector (Russian Left Flank)

4 battalions Moscow Regiment ⎫
4 battalions Taroutine Regiment ⎬ 10,000 infantry
4 battalions reserves ⎭

3½ batteries field artillery (28 guns)
Detached at Ulukol Akles: 1 battalion Minsk Regiment
½ battery field guns (4 guns)

2. FRENCH ARMY

Commander-in-chief: Marshal Armand Jacques Leroy de St Arnaud
1st Division: General François Certain Canrobert
2nd Division: General Pierre François Joseph Bosquet
3rd Division: General Prince Jerome Charles Napoleon
4th Division: General Élie Frédéric Forey
8½ batteries field artillery (68 guns)
9,000 Turks

Each French division was normally composed of two brigades; each brigade of five battalions, of which one at least was a 'rifle' battalion; and two batteries of six guns. The establishment of a battalion was 952 men; that of the Chasseurs de Vincennes 1,250 (ten companies of 125); of the Zouaves (eight companies) 1,000 men. Consequently, at full strength a brigade was about 5,000 and a division 10,000.

3. BRITISH ARMY (Comprising one battalion of each regiment named)

Commander-in-chief: Field-Marshal Lord Raglan (the Hon. Fitzroy James Henry Somerset)

Front Line:
   2nd Division (Lieutenant-General Sir George De Lacy Evans)
      Right brigade:
      (Brigadier-General Adams)
         41st Regiment
         49th Regiment
         47th Regiment   } 5,000 infantry
      Left brigade:
      (Brigadier-General Pennefather)
         30th Regiment
         55th Regiment
         95th Regiment
      Light Division (Lieutenant-General Sir George Brown)

Right brigade:
(Brigadier-General Codrington)
   7th Regiment
  33rd Regiment
  23rd Regiment
Left brigade: } 5,000 infantry
(Brigadier-General Buller)
  19th Regiment
  88th Regiment
  77th Regiment

Second Line:
  1st Division (Lieutenant-General His Royal Highness the Duke of Cambridge)
    Right brigade:
    (Brigadier-General Bentinck)
      Grenadier Guards   } the Brigade
      Scots Fusiliers   of Guards
      Coldstream Guards
    Left brigade:
    (Brigadier-General Sir Colin Campbell)   } 5,000 infantry
      Royal Highland Regiment
      42nd (The Black Watch)   the
      93rd Argyll & Sutherland   High-
      Highlanders   land
      79th Queen's Own Cameron Brigade
      Highlanders

Reserve:
  3rd Division (Major-General Sir Richard England)
    Right brigade:
    (Brigadier-General Sir J. Campbell)
      1st, 4th, 28th, 38th Regiments
    Left brigade:
    (Brigadier Sir W. Eyre)
      44th, 50th, 60th, 68th Regiments
  4th Division (Major-General Sir George Cathcart)
    Right brigade:
      20th, 21st, 63rd Regiments

Left brigade:

46th, 56th Regiments, 1st Rifle Brigade

Cavalry: (Major-General Lord Lucan and Brigadier-General Lord Cardigan)

4th and 13th Light Dragoons

8th, 11th and 17th Hussars

Artillery:

8 batteries field artillery (64 guns)

1 troop horse artillery (4 guns)

APPENDIX 3

The bombardment of Sebastopol, 17 October 1854

The allied fleets took up positions near the harbour entrance and the British fleet came into action in the following order:

	Ship	*Guns*	*Commanded by*	*Towed by*
1.	*Albion*	90	Captain Stephen Lushington	*Firebrand*
2.	*Arethusa*	50	Captain Symonds	*Triton*
3.	*London*	90	Captain Charles Eden	*Niger*
4.	*Sanspareil*	70	Captain Dacres	
5.	*Agamemnon*		Admiral Lord Lyons Captain Mends	
6.	*Rodney*	90	Captain C. Graham	*Spiteful*
7.	*Bellerophon*	78	Captain Lord George Paulet	*Cyclops*
8.	*Queen*	116	Captain Mitchell	*Vesuvius*
9.	*Vengeance*	84	Captain Lord Edward Russell	*Highflyer*
10.	*Trafalgar*	120	Captain Greville	*Retribution*
11.	*Britannia*	120	Admiral Sir J. D. Dundas Captain Carleton	*Furious*

Each of the ships was towed into action by a steamer lashed along the port side.

The following are the names of the French line-of-battle ships which followed the British fleet into action. (The French moved in two columns; *Jupiter* leading the port column, *Napoleon* the starboard column.)

	Ship	*Guns*		*Ship*	*Guns*
1.	*Jupiter*	82	3.	*Suffren*	82
2.	*Bayard*	82	4.	*Ville de Marseilles*	70

	Ship	Guns		Ship	Guns
5.	Marengo	70	10.	Valmy	114
6.	Jean Bait	80	11.	Ville de Paris	114
7.	Algier	70	12.	Friedland	114
8.	Napoleon	90	13.	Morte Bello	114
9.	Henry IV	100	14.	Charlemagne	80

APPENDIX 4

Order of Battle and Dispositions at Balaclava, 25 October 1854

On the morning of 25 October, the 95th Highlanders were drawn up on the rising ground in front of the gorge leading to Balaclava. There they were joined by a detachment, about seventy strong, of invalids from the Guards Brigade. The Turks occupied the line of recently constructed redoubts on the ridge which ran east to west across the Balaclava plain. The Brigade of Heavy Cavalry – comprising the 4th and 5th Dragoon Guards, 1st and 2nd Dragoons and 6th Inniskilling Dragoons – under Brigadier-General Scarlett was camped half a mile west of the Highlanders, and the Light Cavalry – 4th Light Dragoons, 8th and 11th Hussars, 13th Light Dragoons and 17th Lancers – under Brigadier-General Lord Cardigan camped further west. The 1st, 2nd, 3rd, 4th and Light Divisions were all camped on the heights, and committed to the siege operations. (See Appendix 2 for the list of regiments.)

The Russian troops destined for the attack assembled in the Tchorgoun Valley on 23 October. They consisted of four regiments of the 12th Infantry Division, with cavalry and thirty-six guns. (The Odessa; the Ural; the Ukraine; and the Azoff Infantry Regiments; one battalion of the Dnieper Chasseurs; sixteen squadrons of Hussars; one regiment of Uhlans; ten sotnias of Cossacks of the Ural and Don; and thirty-six guns. Each regiment consisted of four battalions of 800 men each.)

This force was divided into two main columns for the attack. Column A, sub-divided into two small columns commanded respectively by General Scuderi (with the Odessa Regiment and six guns) and General Rykoff (with a brigade of cavalry, the Ural Regiment and two horse artillery batteries) advanced from the Traktir bridge. Column B, also sub-divided into two smaller columns under the respective commands of General Levontski (the Ukraine

Regiment, and ten guns) and General Semiakin (Azoff Regiment, the Dnieper Chasseurs and sixteen guns) advanced direct from Tchorgoun.

The right flank of Columns A and B was protected by a force under General Shabokritski. Under his command was the 1st Brigade of the 16th Infantry Division, comprising three battalions of the Vladimir Regiment, four battalions of the Sousdal Regiment with fourteen guns. Shabokritski deployed his troops on the southern slopes of the Fedukhine Hills.

The Russian left flank was protected by a force under Major-General Gribbe (three battalions of the Dnieper Regiment, the regiment of Uhlans, a sotnia of the Cossacks and ten guns). This force moved from Tchorgoun and occupied the village of Kamara.

When the Russian advance was reported Raglan ordered the British 1st and 4th Divisions to move down to the plain. The 4th Division took up a position near the Woronzoff road, while the 1st Division – descending the precipitous slopes of the plateau further south – moved across the plain in columns of companies, wheeled into line to form a line on the left of the 93rd Highlanders. Subsequently the 1st Division turned to face Canrobert's Hill ready to advance and retake the redoubts abandoned by the Turks. With the exception of the 42nd and 79th Highlanders, however, all the troops returned to their camps on the plateau.

APPENDIX 5

Order of Battle and Dispositions at the Battle of Inkerman, 5 November 1854

I. BRITISH

At the beginning of November the order of battle of the British army was as follows:

Cavalry (Earl of Lucan)

Heavy Brigade: (Scarlett)	4th and 5th Dragoon Guards, 1st and 2nd Dragoons, 6th Inniskilling Dragoons.
Light Brigade: (Cardigan)	4th Light Dragoons, 8th and 11th Hussars 13th Light Dragoons, 17th Lancers.

Infantry

1st Division: (H.R.H. the Duke of Cambridge)	Guards Brigade (Bentinck)	3rd Battalion Grenadier Guards 1st Battalion Coldstream Guards 1st Battalion Scots Fusilier Guards
	Highland Brigade (C. Campbell)	42nd, 79th, and 93rd
2nd Division: (Evans)	1st Brigade (Adams)	41st, 47th, and 49th
	2nd Brigade (Pennefather)	30th, 55th, and 95th
3rd Division: (England)	1st Brigade (Campbell)	1st Royals, 38th, and 50th
	2nd Brigade (Eyre)	4th, 28th and 44th
4th Division: (Cathcart)	1st Brigade (Goldie)	20th, 21st, 57th, and 68th
	2nd Brigade (Torrens)	63rd, 1st Battalion Rifle Brigade, 46th, 2 Companies

Light Division: (Brown)

- 1st Brigade (Codrington) — 7th, 23rd, and 33rd
- 2nd Brigade (Buller) — 19th, 77th, 88th, 2nd Battalion Rifle Brigade

Artillery

7 batteries,* and two 18-pounders, with the divisions on the plateau

2 troops (Captains Maude and Brandling) and 1 battery (Barker) at or near Balaclava.

Engineers

3rd, 4th, 8th, 10th and 11th Companies

Total strength in the five British infantry divisions about 22,000 men

The troops were disposed as follows:

(a) The *2nd Division*, on the right, camped with its right on the ridge overlooking the valley of Tchernaya.

(b) The *1st Division* was split up, with the Highland Brigade camped near Balaclava and the Guards Brigade further divided with Grenadiers and Scots Fusilier Guards on the left rear of the 2nd Division and the Coldstream on the Sapoune Heights overlooking the Fedukhine Hills (supporting French troops occupying a newly-constructed fort called Canrobert's Redoubt.)

(c) The *Light Division* was encamped on the left of the Guards Brigade, with its 1st Brigade, under Codrington, near the head of the Karabelnaya Ravine and Buller's 2nd Brigade between the ravine and the Woronzoff Road.

(d) The *Naval Brigade*, under Captain Stephen Lushington, was on the left of the Woronzoff Road.

(e) The *4th Division* was on the high ground between the Woronzoff Road and the small ravine which became known as 'The Valley of the Shadow of Death'. (This high ground was subsequently called Cathcart's Hill, in memory of the divisional commander who was buried there.)

* Captains Morris, Paynter, Wodehouse, Turner, Franklin, Swinton, and Townshend.

(*f*) The *3rd Division* was deployed on the left of the 4th Division as far as the precipitous cliffs of the Picket House Ravine.

(*g*) The *Light Brigade* was on the plateau near the Mill; the *Heavy Brigade* was near Kadikoi.

2. RUSSIAN

On 4 November the Russians had about 76,000 men deployed in and around Sebastopol. Menschikoff's plan was for 20,000 men under Prince Gorschakoff to demonstrate against Balaclava and stop the French (Bosquet's Corps d'Observation) sending any troops to help the British. At the same time General Timofief was to sally forth with part of the Sebastopol garrison of 20,000 and occupy the French who were engaged in the siege, and another 5,000 men were to hold the Mackenzie Heights.

The main force, of the remaining 31,000, was to attack the British, and for this two assault columns were formed:

Column A commanded by Lieutenant-General Soimonoff, had about 17,500 men of the Katherineburg, Tomsk and Koliwan Regiments under Major-General Wilboa; and the Vladimir, Sousdal, Uglitz and Butirsk Regiments under Major-General Shabokritski. (Each regiment had four battalions of about 800 men, and the column had twenty-two 12-pounder and sixteen 6-pounder guns.)

Column B under Lieutenant-General Pauloff, had a strength of 13,500 and consisted of the Borodino and Taroutine Regiments, with the Ochotzk, Yakutzk and Selensk Regiments under Major-General Ochterlony.

Actual Strengths were as follows:

Soimonoff's Column A: 28 battalions, 16,200 combatants
Pauloff's Column B: 20½ battalions, 13,500 combatants
Total Russian field force 48½ battalions or 29,700 men.

APPENDIX 6

Sebastopol, its environs and defences

Sebastopol harbour could accommodate the biggest ships of the Russian navy. From west to east it extended four miles inland; averaging three-quarters of a mile throughout its breadth; at its entrance – between Forts Constantine and Alexander – it was 1,000 yards wide.

On the north side of the town *Fort Alexander* stood at the southern entrance to the harbour, 500 yards east-north-east of Quarantine Fort. It mounted eighty-four large calibre guns. 500 yards further east stood *Artillery Fort* which – with the Alexander and Quarantine forts – formed the extreme right of the Russian defensive works round the town. The most powerful of the harbour defences however, was *Fort Nicholas*. Separated from the Artillery Fort by a small bay, it was a strong stone casemated strongpoint built in three tiers and capable of mounting 192 guns of large calibre. Standing on a promontory between the Great Harbour and Arsenal Creek it served as a defence to both. *Fort Paul* which stood on the opposite side of the harbour entrance to the Arsenal Creek, was also a stone casemated battery mounting eighty guns in three tiers.

Along the eastern edge of the docks in 'Dockyard Creek' was a block of three-storied buildings which had been built originally as stores and magazines. In the latter phases of the siege the Russians used these buildings as hospitals – because they were out of range of allied fire, and because it had become increasingly difficult to move the wounded to the north shore.

In addition to Forts Alexander, Artillery, Nicholas and Paul, the entrance to the Great Harbour was defended also by the *Wasp Fort* on the top of the cliffs north of Fort Constantine. It mounted only eight guns but they were of large calibre and proved a great source of annoyance to the allied fleets whenever their ships came within range of its guns. A battery, called *Telegraph Battery* – mounting seventeen guns at first but twenty-eight subsequently – was erected between Wasp Fort and Fort Constantine during the siege.

Fort Constantine at the northern entrance to the harbour was, like Fort Nicholas, a casemated strongpoint mounting 104 guns in three tiers. During the bombardment it suffered considerable damage but, owing to a shoal extending a considerable distance out to sea, no line-of-battle ships could get within 900 yards. (When the *Agamemnon* tried to do so she grounded on the edge of this shoal.) Further along the northern shore was a battery of twenty field guns, dug in and known as the *Earthern Battery*. Next to it, further east, was the stone fort called *St Michael's* with ninety-six guns. In the last three weeks of the siege, between this fort on the north and Fort Nicholas on the south side, the floating bridge was constructed that was to ensure the safe retreat of the garrison when the time came for them to abandon the town. *Fort St Catherine* mounting eighty-four guns, which stood 1,100 yards further east of St Michael's Fort was the last of the permanent defensive works on the north shore of the harbour.

After the Alma the Russians sank four of the oldest line-of-battle ships across the harbour mouth between Forts Constantine and Alexander. (When one of these vessels broke up, a fifth was sunk in its place.) Subsequently a floating boom of spars and masts, lashed together was placed a little higher up the harbour, and later still a second line of ships was sunk below the line where the long bridge was eventually constructed. As an additional protection against an attack by the allied fleet the remaining line-of-battle ships moved to berths above the site of the bridge and their guns trained on the entrance to the harbour. At the time of the capture of the town all these ships were either burned or sunk. During the siege steamers plied between the north and south sides taking reinforcements and provisions to the town and returning with the sick and wounded. When the town was abandoned these steamers were all sunk or run ashore.

Fort Severnaya, or the Great Northern Fort (known to the Allies as the *Star Fort*) stood on the high ground north of St Michael's and St Catherine forts. It mounted 120 guns, but – unlike the shore batteries and forts which stood out exposed with their stone walls and tiers of guns – this fort, from the allied positions on the south side, was almost concealed. A permanent strongpoint, with bastions and curtains and surrounded by a broad ditch, it afforded protection to the shore batteries below it, and formed the centre of a strong defensive position in case of an attack by land from the north. At the time of the Alma it stood as an isolated work but under Todleben's direction it was strengthened by a line of earthworks running west to the sea and eastwards across a ravine to a point about a mile east of Fort Catherine. These lines protected the points of communication with the town itself. Prince Menschikoff established his headquarters in them, near the harbour; and two houses south-west of Fort Severnaya, also near the harbour, were appropriated by the Grand Dukes at the time of the Battle of Inkerman.

On the high ground north of the harbour the Russians dug a large number of trenches. Those on the heights immediately overlooking the harbour not only protected the harbour but enabled the Russians to cover the French lines of approach to the Volhynian and Selensk Redoubts (commonly known as the White Works). Other trenches, further inland, provided an external defensive line towards the north, on the extreme left of which was a battery overlooking the sea and defending the mouth of the Belbec. During the early part of the siege many of Sebastopol's population moved to the north side where it was safer, and camped outside and east of Fort Severnaya. At a later period of the siege and after the fall of the town they moved still further to camps on the Mackenzie Heights.

On the southern side the extreme left flank of the main line of Russian defences was the Artillery Fort already described. About 1,000 yards south was the *Quarantine Bastion* (referred to by the Russians as No. 6). Standing about 190 feet above sea level this fort was connected with the Artillery Fort only by a crenellated wall (Cathcart's 'low park wall') but this was subsequently strengthened by a rampart in its rear. Several batteries (the Schemiakin batteries) were dug in on the ridge of ground running north-west in front of the Quarantine Bastion. Half-way between the Quarantine and Central Bastions was an advanced position – known as the 'Lunette Butakoff' – which flanked the long intervening curtain and behind it was a redoubt which was intended to serve as a second line of defence if the first were forced.

1,200 yards from the Quarantine Bastion stood the *Great Central Bastion* (No. 5) with its two flanking 'lunettes' – the Schwartz on the left flank and the Balkin on the right. In front and parallel to the two bastions a valley ran into the Quarantine Harbour. 1,000 yards

further on was the *Flagstaff Bastion* (No. 4). With its flanking position
this strongpoint covered 300 yards of ground; in front of it the
Russians laid an 8-foot belt of 2 inch thick planks studded with
6-inch nails with points upward. (This primitive obstacle seriously
impeded the French assault troops.) About 300 yards behind the
Flagstaff Bastion were the so-called Garden Batteries, and behind
them other batteries whose role was the support of the Flagstaff
Bastion. In the early part of the siege the French directed their main
attack against this strongpoint, the Central Bastion and the Schwartz
Lunette on its left flank, and against the Lunette Butakoff and left
face of the Quarantine Fort. In the attack against the two latter
objectives they encountered strenuous opposition, and it was this
that led them to direct their attention to the Malakoff and Little
Redan.

Separated from the French attack against the western parts of the
town by the deep Sarandanakin or Picket House Ravine, the British
attacks were directed against the south-eastern part of the Russian
defences – consisting of the Creek Battery, the Barrack Battery and
the Great Redan. The *Creek Battery* together with the batteries
erected in front of it on the precipitous sides of the adjoining hills,
defended the approaches down the Woronzoff Road and the Picket
House Ravine, and commanded all the level ground to its front. This
battery, being in the rear and partially concealed, was less exposed
to direct attack, and at the end of the siege was seen to have suffered
very much less than the adjoining Flagstaff and Redan Batteries.

At the eastern extremity of the Creek Battery the ground rose
abruptly to a height of about 200 feet, where the right of the *Barrack
Battery* was located; from there the ground covered with batteries
gradually rose in an easterly direction for a distance of about 850
yards in a direct line to the salient angle of the *Redan* (No. 3). Many
traverses and bunks had been constructed within the Redan and the
adjoining works, but the Redan itself was not enclosed in the rear.
In position in these works, at the time of the capture of the place,
there were more than 200 guns and mortars of different calibre.
From the left of the salient angle of the Redan the Russian works fell
back, and extended, in a northerly direction, nearly 800 yards,
falling towards the Karabelnaya Ravine.

The Karabelnaya Ravine separated the works of the Redan from
the *Malakoff* and *Gervais Battery*: the latter starting on the edge of the
right bank of the Middle Ravine; from where the ground gradually

rose to the commanding position occupied by the Malakoff (called by the Russians the Korniloff Bastion). The Malakoff occupied the summit of this position and extended in a north-north-westerly direction about 400 yards, with an average breadth of 150 yards – becoming narrower towards the rear. A deep ditch was sunk round the whole position, the parapets were strengthened by numerous traverses, and along the parapets other traverses – some of ten and twelve feet high – formed the roofs of bombproof galleries for the garrison to retire to during the heavy bombardments to which it was constantly subjected.

From the Malakoff a long curtain, nearly 700 yards in length, extended to the *Little Redan* (No. 2) and from this work the Russian lines ran north-east 650 yards to the *'Maison en Croix'* – a strongly fortified post 170 feet above the sea. From this point, the lines gradually fell to a bastion on the extreme left at the western entrance of Careening Creek, on the top of a cliff forty-five feet above sea level.

In front of the main line of works round the western part of the town the Russians had no strong advanced positions except at the cemetery; but in front of the three principal works of the eastern side they had, during the progress of the siege, established themselves in three strong positions considerably in advance of their main line, in the Quarries, 450 yards in front of the Redan; in the Mamelon, 650 yards in front of the Malakoff, and in the White Works (called the Selensk and Volhynian Redoubts) 900 and 1,300 yards respectively in front of the Little Redan. During the early spring of 1855, the French tried to take the White Works, but without success; and it was not until the successful attack of 7 June that the whole of these positions fell into the hands of the Allies. The Russians, on several occasions, attempted to retake them, but from that period they had to trust to their main line for defence, and consequently during the last three months of the siege the Russians were observed to be continually strengthening their internal defences.

APPENDIX 7

The Battle of the Tchernaya, 16 August 1855

Despite their success in repelling the allied assault on 18 June, many Russian officers in Sebastopol considered the town was untenable. A plan for the withdrawal of the garrison to the north side of the harbour and the Mackenzie Heights was submitted to the Tsar, but Alexander II refused to sanction it until one more attempt had been made to force the allied position. The Battle of the Tchernaya was the result.

As Prince Gorschakoff considered that the Inkerman Ridge was now too strongly held to offer much of a chance of success in that direction, he decided to try to oust the French from the Fedukhine Hills. These were occupied in depth – two divisions under Generals Vinois and Camon forward with three brigades under General de Chasseloup Laubat in reserve. The Sardinians were occupying Mount Hasfort with outposts on the hills west of Tchorgoun; the Turks had some observation posts over the Tchernaya at Alsu; some French cavalry under General d'Allonville was occupying the Baidar valley.

At dawn on 16 August the Russian army was seen advancing: General Read with the 3rd Corps d'Armee* against the French, and General Liprandi with the 6th Corps d'Armée† against the Sardinian position. The 2nd Division of the Reserve‡ was stationed on the Mackenzie Heights; the 4th Division was to support Liprandi's Corps; and the 5th Division support General Read.

* The 3rd Corps d'Armée was composed of the 7th Division under General Outschakoff, and of the 12th Division under General Martineau.

† The 6th Corps d'Armée was composed of the 6th Division under General Bellegarde, and of the 17th Division under General Vesselitsky.

‡ The Reserve consisted of the 4th Division under General Chipiloff, 5th Division under General Wrancken, and the 2nd Division of the Reserve under General Montressor.

On the left, Liprandi advanced with his 6th Division under General Bellegarde by the valley of the Schiuliu, and took up a position on the heights east of Tchorgoun; from here, with his artillery, he took the Sardinian outposts on the opposite hills, in reverse; while his 17th Division under Vesselitsky, coming over the hills, attacked them in front. The Sardinian outposts fell back but their batteries on Mount Hasfort checked any further advance of the Russians in that direction.

The morning was foggy when General Read advanced with the 7th and 12th Divisions, against the Fedukhine Heights. The 7th Division moved against the extreme left and left centre of the French, crossed the Tchernaya and the canal, and had started to climb the western part of the heights when they were met by two French brigades, under Generals Verge* and Wimpfen,† and were forced back in disorder over the Tchernaya. The 12th Division, in two columns, attacked the Traktir Bridge, forced its garrison to retire, crossed the river and the canal, and had already nearly gained the heights on both sides of the road. They were, however, met on the French left of the road by General Failly's brigade‡, and on the right by General Faucheur's brigade§, which formed the extreme right of the French position. After a fierce struggle these troops forced the Russian columns back again over the Tchernaya. The Sardinians had in the meantime advanced towards the right of the French, and taken up a position near the river, their artillery shooting up the Russians on the opposite side. The Turkish artillery from the heights above Alsu kept the Russians in check in that direction, and the English Cavalry under General Scarlett, with some heavy field guns, moved up from Kadikoi to join the French and Sardinian Cavalry.

The 12th Russian Division having been driven back once, was brought forward a second time – supported by the 5th Division – in order to try to force the French from their position near the Traktir bridge. At the same time the 17th Division belonging to Liprandi's corps, having driven in the Sardinian outposts, advanced down the

* The left Brigade, under General Verge, consisted of the Algérine Chasseurs, and of the 6th and 82nd Regiments of the Line.
† The right Brigade, under General Wimpffen, consisted of the 3rd Regiment of Zouaves, and of the 50th Regiment of the Line.
‡ General Failly's Brigade consisted of the 95th and 97th Regiments.
§ General Faucheur's Brigade consisted of the 19th Regiment of Chasseurs, and of the 2nd Regiment of Zouaves.

hill and attacked the extreme right of the French position and the left of the Sardinians, in order to force a passage across the river and secure the approach to the plain of Balaclava. General Cler at that time brought up his reserves on the right, and the French succeeded in driving the Russians opposed to them back again over the Tchernaya. This move was supported by two Sardinian battalions belonging to Trotti's division, who retook possession of the advanced posts which had been abandoned in the early part of the day.

APPENDIX 8

Prints and pictures of the Crimean war

So many pictures and prints illustrating the Crimean conflict have been produced that it is practically impossible to compile a complete list.

1. *Paintings and Sketches*

If only because it was the last important campaign in which British soldiers fought in full dress uniform the Crimea remained a popular subject with artists for many years. In consequence there is an abundance of military paintings and sketches of military life and military personalities associated with the war against Russia. In the London clubs with old-established military connections, art galleries in London, Paris and elsewhere – including, it is understood, the U.S.S.R. – in the Royal Collection, Buckingham Palace and Windsor, at the Staff College Camberley, at Chelsea Hospital and in private homes such paintings of varying quality are to be found.

In 1874, the *annus mirabilis* of her art life, Elizabeth, Lady Butler, was commissioned to paint *Calling the Roll after an Engagement in the Crimea* (subsequently renamed by the public as *The Roll Call*) – a picture for which Queen Victoria had a special affection. (For many years *The Roll Call* was kept at Osborne House, Isle of Wight and later at St James's Palace. It now hangs in the Officers' Mess of the Staff College at Camberley, but a copy of it – probably painted by H.R.H. Princess Louise *c*. 1897–8 – is in the National Army Museum Sandhurst.) Another of her pictures *Balaclava* hangs in the Queen's Park Gallery Manchester, and a third *The Return from Inkerman* (used on the jacket of this book) is in the possession of the Ferens Art Gallery in Hull. Lady Butler's attention to historical facts, and her accuracy in the details of uniforms, animal stances and battle backgrounds brought her international repute as a military painter.

Those wishing to try to capture something of the soldiers' background to the war in the Crimea would do well to look at her paintings.

Not unnaturally Florence Nightingale, the 'Lady with the Lamp' was a popular subject with painters, and there is an especially good painting *Queen Victoria Presenting the First Victoria Cross in Hyde Park 26 June 1857* in the Royal Collection.

2. *Plates and Prints*

There is a plethora of plates and prints and only the better known ones are referred to in the following catalogue.

1. *The Battle of the Alma about 3 o'clock p.m. on the 20th Septr 1854* . . . Lithograph, 17½ by 24¾, in colours. By Edmund Walker after Orlando Norie. Published in London 10th November 1854 by Rudolph Ackermann.

A fine large plate showing the Guards and Highlanders advancing and guns of the Royal Horse Artillery moving to a flank.

2. *The Grand Charge of the Guards on the Heights of the Alma, Septr. 20th, 1854.* Lithograph, 13 by 20, in colours. By and after L. Huard from a sketch taken on the spot by an English Officer. Published in London 1st November 1854 by E. Gambart & Co.

References in the title show the Duke of Cambridge and also Lord Raglan giving orders to Captain Maude, R.H.A., concerning his battery.

3. *An Episode at the Battle of the Alma 20th Septr., 1854.* Lithograph, 12¼ by 21¼, in colours. By A. Laby after A. F. de Prades. Published in London 23rd January 1855 by J. S. Welsh.

Represents officers of the Scots Fusilier Guards planting their colours on the Heights of the Alma.

4. *The Battle of The Alma.* Lithograph, 10½ by 17½, in colours, by Stannard & Dixon after Thomas Packer. Published in London 16th October 1854 by Stannard & Dixon.

5. *The Battle of Balaclava* . . . (25th October 1854). Lithograph, 17¼ by 26, in colours. By Edmund Walker after Orlando Norie. Published in London 1st January 1855 by Rudolph Ackermann. Shows the Scots Greys supported by the Enniskillings [sic] assisting the Light Cavalry charging dense masses of Russians.

6. *The Cavalry Charge at Balaclava, Octr., 25th 1854.* Lithograph, 13¼ by 19½, in colours. By and after Ed. Morin. Published in London, 28th November 1854 by Paul & Dominic Colnaghi & Co.

A vivid and artistic rendering of the Charge of the Light Brigade.

7. *Battle of Balaclava, Brilliant Charge of the Scots Greys, Octr., 25th, 1854.* Lithograph, 10½ by 15¼, in colours. By and after Augustus Butler. Published in London 6th January 1855 by Stannard & Dixon.

8. *The Battle of Inkerman* (5th November, 1854). Lithograph, 20 by 33¾, tinted. References in title margin. By E. Walker after Le Bihan.

A large plate of the whole battlefield showing the Guards in the foreground pressing back the Russians.

9. *The Soldiers Battle. Inkerman Novr., 5th, 1854.* Lithograph, 18 by 26½, in colours. Published in London 27th June 1855 by Paul & Dominic Colnaghi & Co.

A large plate showing the Allies advancing (the Guards in the foreground) on the Russians; the Reserves of the latter are shown in dense masses on the banks of the river Tchernaya.

10. *Battle of Inkerman . . .* Lithograph, 17½ by 26, in colours. By Edmund Walker after Orlando Norie. Published in London 22nd January 1855 by Rudolph Ackermann.

Shows the Coldstream Guards sustaining the Russian attack and General Bosquet's French Division in the distance coming to their relief.

11. *The Fall of Sebastopol.* Lithograph, 19¾ by 38, in colours. By Day & Son after William Simpson. Published in London 28th January 1857 by Paul & Dominic Colnaghi & Co.

A very fine plate showing the defences in flames with the Russians retreating in the distance.

12. *Burning of Sebastopol and Retreat of the Russians, 7th Septr., 1855.* Lithograph, 22½ by 38¾, in colours. By E. Walker after a sketch by Oswald W. Brierly at the time. Published in London 1st June 1857 by Paul & Dominic Colnaghi & Co.

Shows the Russian army evacuating the city which is in flames, over the bridge of boats.

13. *Sebastopol – The Storming of the Great Redan.* Lithograph, 11¾ by 31½, in colours. Published in London by Dickinson Bros. No particulars.

Shows the British entering the Russian fortifications.

14. A pair of lithographs, 17 by 26¾, tinted.

(a) (From the side of the Allies)

(b) (From the Russian side)

Both by and after Thos. Packer. Published in London 18th April 1855 by Stannard & Dixon.

An interesting pair of plates showing (a) the lines of the Allies from the redoubts over Balaclava harbour; and (b) Sebastopol and the allied fortifications from the north.

15. *The Siege of Sebastopol.* [sic] Lithograph, 12½ by 21½, in colours. By and after Vincent Brooks.

16. *Siege of Sebastopol [sic] from the new 32 pounder battery above the left attack Picquet House.* Lithograph, 13½ by 20, in colours. By E. Walker (Oct 22, 1854) after Capt. M. A. Biddulph, R.A. Published in London 17th November 1854 by Paul & Dominic Colnaghi & Co.

17. *Description of a view of the City of Sebastopol, the assaults on the Malakhoff and the Redan etc.* Woodcut, 11 by 18, panorama key and letterpress. By Henry C. Selous after Robert Burford from sketches by Capt. Verschoyle, Grenadier Guards. Published in London 1856 by W. J. Colbourn.

18. *The Officers' Portfolio of the Striking Reminiscences of the War. From drawings, photographs and notes taken on the spot.* 21 lithographs, average, 12 by 18, in colours. Published in London by Dickinson Bros.

(a) Balaclava. (Showing fleet and sentries in winter).

(b) Arrival of fresh troops at Balaclava.

(c) The Malakhoff.

(d) Close Quarters. (Bayonet attack by Guards on Russians.)

(e) Sebastopol from the rear of the Great Redan.

(f) The Storming of the Great Redan. 11¾ by 31½. (See No. 13).

(g) Rifle party skirmishing.

(h) Troops in review in rear of 21 Gun Battery.

(i) Repulse of the French from the Little Redan.

(j) Salient of the Redan, Midnight.

(k) Removing the wounded from the Great Redan.

(l) Traktir Bridge after the battle of the Tchernaya.

An artistic set, cut and mounted, with the titles written in by hand as was often the case with lithographs, enclosed in a portfolio decorated with a group of soldiers of the Allies amid ruins bearing the word 'Sebastopol' stamped on the cover. It is not known whether it was issued in book form but the publication is scarce. The plates not described are incidents and scenes connected with the operations.

19. *The Seat of the War in the East . . . First Series.* By William Simpson. With illustrated title page, 39 lithographs, average, 10 by 16, in colours with keys and descriptive letterpress. By various engravers after W. Simpson. Published in London 1855 by Paul & Dominic Colnaghi & Co.

(a) The Cavalry Affair of the Heights of Bulganak – The First Gun, 19th Sepr. 1854.

(b) Charge of the Heavy Cavalry Brigade, 25th Octr. 1854.

(c) Second Charge of the Guards when they retook the Two Gun Battery at the Battle of Inkerman.

(d) A Sentinel of the Zouaves, before Sebastopol. [sic]

(e) Charge of the Light Cavalry Brigade, 25th Oct. 1854.

(f) Sebastopol from the east or extreme right of English attack.

(g) A quiet night in the Batteries . . .

(h) The New Works at the Siege of Sebastopol on the right attack . . .

(i) A hot day in the Batteries.

(j) A hot night in the Batteries.

(k) Russian rifle pit.

20. *The Seat of the War in the East . . . Second Series.* By William Simpson. 41 lithographs, average, 11 by 18, in colours with keys and descriptive letterpress. By various engravers after W. Simpson. Published in London 1856 by Paul & Dominic Colnaghi & Co.

(a) Disembarkation of the Expedition to Kertch at Kamish Bournou and the blowing up of St. Paul's Battery.

(b) Battle of the Tchernaya, 16th August 1855.

(c) The attack on the Malakoff. (By the French).

(d) The Interior of the Redan . . .

(e) Interior of the Malakoff with the remains of the Round Tower.

(f) Redan and advanced trenches of British right attack.

(g) Bastion du Mat, from the Central Bastion.

Two fully illustrated volumes which give a complete record of the events with detailed key outlines of the important plates interleaved. Those not described represent scenes and incidents connected with the operations.

A reduction of this work in two volumes was also published at the time.

SOURCE NOTES

PROLOGUE
1 'Le fond de la grande question est toujours la Qui aura Constantinople?' *Lettres inedites de Napoleon Ier*, Leon Lecestre, Tome i, No. 286.
2 *Russian Wars with Turkey*, F. S. Russell, p. 5.
3 *Nicholas I et Napoléon III*, L. Thouvenel, p. 280.

CHAPTER 1   THE BELLIGERENTS
1 *Russian Wars with Turkey*, F. S. Russell.

CHAPTER 2   THE ARMIES TAKE THE FIELD
1 *Napoleon's Maxims of War*, General Burnod, p. 121.
2 *Crimea*, C. E. Vulliamy, p. 71.
3 *Select Committee*, p. 246.
4 *Select Committee*, p. 246.
5 *Ibid.*, p. 115.
6 *Lettres du Maréchal de St Arnaud*, II, p. 307.
7 *The Invasion of the Crimea*, A.W. Kinglake, II, p. 249.
8 St Arnaud, II, p. 310.

CHAPTER 3   OBJECTIVE SEBASTOPOL
1 *Memoirs of an Ex-Minister*, Earl of Malmesbury, I, p. 438.
2 *Life of Vice-Admiral Edmund, Lord Lyons*, S. Eardley-Wilmot, pp. 144–8.
3 St Arnaud, II, p. 451.
4 *Letters from Headquarters*, S. G. J. Calthorpe I, pp. 115–16, II, p. 43.
5 *Diary of the Crimean War*, F. Robinson, p. 53.
6 Vulliamy, p. 79.
7 Montaudon, p. 241.

8 St Arnaud II, p. 314.
9 Calthorpe I, p. 108.
10 *Turkey and the Crimean War*, Admiral Slade, p. 285.
11 *With the Green Howards in the Crimea*, by an Anonymous Soldier of the 19th Regiment.
12 Slade, p. 279.

CHAPTER 4   CALAMITA BAY
1 Robinson, p. 146.
2 *A Diary of the Crimea*, George Palmer Evelyn, pp. 79–80.
3 Ibid.
4 *The Past Campaign*, M. A. Woods, p. 92.
5 *The Eastern Question*, J. A. R. Marriott, p. 240.
6 St Arnaud II, p. 411.
7 *The History of the War Against Russia*, E. H. Nolan I, p. 94.
8 *The Reason Why*, C. Woodham-Smith, p. 178.
9 St Arnaud II, p. 489.
10 Evelyn, p. 82.

CHAPTER 5   THE MARCH TO THE ALMA
1 *Reminiscences of an Officer of Zouaves*, J. J. G. Cler, pp. 172–3.
2 *Crimean War Reader*, Chesney, p. 96.
3 *The Destruction of Lord Raglan*, C. Hibbert, p. 47.
4 Hibbert, p. 51.
5 *Records of the Royal Welsh Fusiliers*, pp. 72–3.
6 *A Voice from the Ranks*, T. Gowing, p. 16.
7 Hibbert, p. 57.
8 Kinglake II, p. 251, and Hibbert, p. 58.

CHAPTER 6   THE BATTLE OF THE ALMA: THE FIRST PHASE
1 *Battles of the Crimean War*, W. B. Pemberton, p. 40.
2 Letter written by Captain Alfred Tipping.
3 Narrative of Major G. R. Lidwill, The Green Howards (19th Regiment).
4 Gowing, p. 16.
5 *93rd Highlanders*, Cavendish, p. 94, and Hibbert, p. 83.
6 *Souvenirs de la Guerre de Crimée*, Ch. A. Fay, p. 64.
7 *The Battle of the Alma*, P. Gibbs, p. 89.

CHAPTER 7   THE BATTLE OF THE ALMA: THE SECOND PHASE

1 *The Crimean War from First to Last*, D. Lysons, p. 92.
2 *The King's Own: The Story of a Royal Regiment*, L. J. Cowper, p. 96.
3 *The Battle of the Alma: through an Officer's Eyes*, Lidwill, p. 8.
4 *The Royal Highlanders at Alma*, McSally.
5 *A Voice from within the Walls of Sebastopol*, R. A. Hodasevitch, p. 62.
6 Lidwill, p. 10.
7 Pemberton, p. 47.
8 *The War in the Crimea*, E. B. Hamley, p. 57.
9 Lidwill, pp. 11, 12.
10 According to Kinglake, who was there. (See MacMunn, p. 63.)

CHAPTER 8   THE BATTLE OF THE ALMA: THE THIRD PHASE

1 St Arnaud II, p. 494.
2 *The Origin and History of the First or Grenadier Guards*, General Sir F. W. Hamilton, p. 72.
3 McSally, p. 4.
4 *Gorschakoff* quoted by Kinglake II, p. 475, and Hibbert, p. 86.
5 St Arnaud II, p. 342.

CHAPTER 9   THE FLANK MARCH

1 Slade, p. 300.
2 *Extracts from the Letters and Journal of General Lord George Paget during the Crimean War*, p. 28.
3 Calthorpe I, p. 189.
4 *Hospital Report 1855*, p. 91.
5 Hibbert, p. 88.
6 Calthorpe I, p. 200.
7 *Crimean Diary*, C. A. Windham, p. 6.
8 *The Crimean Papers of Lord Raglan*, quoted in Hibbert, p. 92.
9 *Défense de Sebastopol*, E. I. Todleben I, pp. 230–9. Report of a conversation between H.M. Consul in Poland and Prince Gorschakoff.
10 St Arnaud II, p. 500.
11 Kinglake III, p. 14.
12 St Arnaud II, pp. 501–2.
13 Calthorpe I, p. 224.
14 Kinglake IV, p. 90.

15 *The Reason Why*, Woodham-Smith, p. 203.
16 *Hospital Report*, p. 160.
17 Vulliamy, p. 109.
18 St Arnaud II, p. 590.
19 *Le Maréchal de Saint Arnaud, 1798–1854 d'après sa Corréspondance et des Documents inédits*, M. Quatrelles l'Epine II, p. 437.
20 *Ibid.*, p. 444.
21 *Military Opinions of General Sir John Fox Burgoyne*, G. Wrottesley; R. E. Journal I, p. 17.

CHAPTER 10   SEBASTOPOL AND THE FIRST BOMBARDMENT
1 Pemberton, p. 71.
2 Hodasevitch, p. 99.
3 *The Crimean Papers of Lord Raglan*, quoted in Hibbert, p. 107.
4 *Materials for a History of the Defence of Sebastopol*, Zhandr, p. 227.
5 *The Russian Account of the Battle of Inkerman*, Anon, p. 3.
6 *Le Général Comte Todleben*, A. Brialmont, p. 2.
7 Todleben I, p. 267.
8 *Ibid.*, p. 272.
9 Slade, p. 317.
10 Zhandr, p. 243.
11 Windham, p. 36.
12 Fay, p. 89.
13 *Le Maréchal Canrobert: Souvenirs d'un Siècle*, C. G. Bapst II, p. 302.
14 *Royal Engineers Journal* I, p. 113, App. 16.
15 Calthorpe I, pp. 275–6.
16 Zhandr, p. 274.
17 Todleben I, p. 329.
18 *Ibid.*

CHAPTER 11   BALACLAVA: THE BATTLE OF THE SABRES
1 *Hansard*, pp. 3, 137, 744.
2 *Hansard*, pp. 3, 137, 745.
3 Kinglake IV, p. 248.
4 *Extracts from the Letters and Journals of . . . Lord George Paget*, p. 170.
5 Kinglake V, p. 233.
6 *The Charge of the Light Brigade*, Lord Tennyson.
7 *The Reason Why*, Woodham-Smith, p. 262.

CHAPTER 12   INKERMAN: THE 'SOLDIERS'' BATTLE

1 Calthorpe I, p. 334–5.
2 *Letters from the Black Sea during the Crimean War 1854–1855*, L. G. Heath, p. 103.
3 Calthorpe I, pp. 333–5, 339–43.
4 Pemberton, p. 145.
5 *Report of the Hospital Commissioners 1855*, p. 86.
6 *Ibid.*
7 *United Service Magazine III* (1854), p. 324.
8 Calthorpe I, pp. 392–6.
9 Calthorpe I, pp. 406–7.
10 Bapst II, p. 526.
11 *Despatches and Papers relative to the Crimean War*, F. Sayer, p. 49.
12 *Lettres du Maréchal Bosquet à sa Mère 1829–1858*, IV, pp. 204–5.

CHAPTER 13   WINTER 1854–55

1 Calthorpe I, p. 385.
2 *Report of the Sanitary Commissioners 1857*, II, p. 159.
3 *Ibid.*, III.
4 *Report of the Select Committee on the Army before Sebastopol 1855*, IV, p. 35.
5 *The War in the Crimea*, Hamley, pp. 166–7.
6 Bapst II, pp. 385–6.
7 *The Eastern Question*, K. Marx, p. 498.
8 *The Commissariat in the Crimea*, W. Filder, p. 169.
9 Calthorpe I, p. 439.
10 *A Visit to the Camp before Sebastopol*, R. C. McCormick, p. 54.
11 Vulliamy, p. 182.
12 Bapst II, p. 395.
13 *Letters from Camp*, C. F. Campbell
14 *The Times*, 23 December 1854, p. 9.
15 *The Times*, 20 December 1854, p. 6.
16 Campbell, p. 29 and *The Crimean in 1854 and 1894*, E. Wood, pp. 173–216.
17 Campbell, p. 34.
18 *The War in the Crimea*, Hamley, pp. 175–7.
19 Fay, p. 158.
20 *The Greville Memoirs, Part 3*, C. F. G. Greville, pp. 212–13.
21 *The Panmure Papers*, G. Douglas and G. D. Ramsay I, pp. 77–8.

CHAPTER 14   THE INFLUENCE OF FLORENCE NIGHTINGALE

1 *The Elton Papers:* vide Hibbert, p. 265.
2 *Report of the Select Committee on the Army before Sebastopol 1855*, II, p. 382.
3 *Florence Nightingale*, E. T. Cook I, p. 200.
4 *The War in the Crimea*, Hamley, p. 154.
5 *Sir John Hall*, S. M. Mitra, pp. 338–40.
6 *The Times*, 18 January 1855, p. 6.
7 *Report of the Select Committee on the Army before Sebastopol 1855*, II, p. 382.
8 *Narrative of Residence on the Bosphorus*, Blackwood, p. 56.
9 *Ibid.*, p. 51.
10 *Scutari and its Hospitals*, Osborne, pp. 25–6.
11 Cook, p. 276.
12 *Report of the Select Committee on the Army before Sebastopol 1855*, II, p. 93.
13 Cook, p. 226.
14 *The British Soldier*, H. de Watteville, p. 160.

CHAPTER 15   THE SIEGE: THE FIRST PHASE

1 *The Panmure Papers* I, pp. 134–45.
2 S. Eardley-Wilmot, p. 391.
3 Calthorpe II, p. 210.
4 Calthorpe II, pp. 187–9, 195–6.
5 Windham, p. 126.
6 Calthorpe II, p. 208.
7 *General Gordon's Letters from the Crimea*, D. C. Boulger, p. 33.
8 Lysons, p. 178.
9 Todleben II, p. 105.
10 Todleben II, p. 170.
11 *Mémoirs du Comte Horace de Viel Castel I*, p. 195.
12 *The Panmure Papers I*, pp. 112, 130, 141.
13 *Ibid.*, p. 174 and Hamley p. 219
14 *The Panmure Papers I*, p. 176.
15 Windham, p. 127.
16 *The Panmure Papers I*, pp. 110–11.
17 *The Panmure Papers I*, p. 179.
18 Calthorpe II, pp. 219–22.
19 *From the Fleet in the Fifties*, Mrs Tom Kelly, p. 312.
20 Heath, p. 199.

21 *Le Maréchal Pélissier*, Derrecagaix, pp. 346–7 and *The New Buonaparte Generals*, B. D. Gooch, p. 199.
22 Souvenirs du Général Comte Fleury I, p. 268.

CHAPTER 16   THE SIEGE: THE SECOND PHASE
1 Viel Castel I, p. 206.
2 *The Panmure Papers I*, p. 202.
3 *Souvenirs et Campagnes*, Motte Rouge II, p. 357.
4 Kinglake VI, p. 24.
5 *Histoire de la Guerre de Crimée II*, pp. 185–7.
6 *The War in the Crimea*, Hamley, p. 230.
7 *Napoleon III the Modern Emperor*, Sencourt, p. 159.
8 Derrecagaix, p. 396.
9 Derrecagaix, p. 431.
10 Derrecagaix, p. 432.
11 *Lettres à sa Mère*, Bosquet IV, p. 260.
12 *Histoire du Second Empire*, P. De La Gorce I, p. 405.
13 *The Panmure Papers I*, p. 245.
14 Derrecagaix, p. 462.
15 Heath, p. 209 and Boulger, p. 51.
16 Calthorpe II, p. 363.
17 *Le Moniteur*, 1 July 1855.
18 The Spectator, Vol 28, p. 705.

CHAPTER 17   THE FALL OF SEBASTOPOL
1 *The Panmure Papers I*, p. 316.
2 *The Panmure Papers I*, p. 328.
3 Rousset II, p. 327.
4 *Ibid.*, p. 333.
5 *L'Expédition de Crimée*, C. L. Bazancourt II, p. 374.
6 *The Panmure Papers I*, p. 316.
7 *The Panmure Papers I*, p. 282.
8 *Ibid.*, p. 348.
9 *Life of the Prince Consort*, Martin III, p. 324.
10 Derrecagaix, p. 505.
11 *The Times*, 23 October 1855.
12 *British Battles*, Anon III, p. 130.

CHAPTER 18   SECONDARY THEATRES
1 *British Battles*, Anon III, p. 92.

CHAPTER 19   FINALE
1 *St Petersburg and London 1852–64*, Eckstaedt I, p. 181.
2 Rousset I, p. ix.
3 Calthorpe II, p. 433.

EPILOGUE
1 *All Sir Garnet – A Life of Field Marshal Lord Wolseley*, Joseph H
Lehman, p. 62.

BIBLIOGRAPHY

So much has been written and published about the war against Russia that the historian's main difficulty is to decide which sources are the most accurate and revealing. What follows consists largely of published personal narratives, and many of the standard works have been omitted. Not included also are many of the reports which followed the numerous investigations into the plight of the British army during the winter of 1854–5, and a vast amount of periodical literature such as Hansard's *Parliamentary Debates* which was concerned primarily with diplomatic aspects of the war as well as contemporary newspaper and magazine reports. (Those of the latter which have been included are considered to be of special interest.)

Many of the books listed are not easy to procure and for the reader who wishes to pursue the subject of *The Vainglorious War* it is suggested that the best sources in the United Kingdom are the libraries of the British Museum, the Ministry of Defence and – for members – the Royal United Service Institution.

ADYE, Lieut.-Col. J., *A Review of the Crimean War*, Hurst & Blackett, London 1860.

AIRLIE, Mabell, Countess of, *With the Guards We Shall Go*, *A Guardsman's Letters in the Crimea*, Hodder & Stoughton, London 1933.

ALEXANDER III, Emperor of Russia, *Souvenirs de Sebastopol, recueillis et rédigés par S.M.I. Alexandre III, Empereur de Russie*, St Petersburg 1894.

ALISON, Sir A. *On Army Organization*, Wm Blackwood & Sons, Edinburgh 1869.

ANICHKOV, *Der Feldzug in der Krim*, E. S. Mittler & Sohn, Berlin 1857.

ANON, *The Russian Account of the Battle of Inkerman* (Translated from the German), John Murray, London 1856.

ARMAND, Dr A., *Histoire Médico-chirurgicale de la Guerre de Crimée*, Paris 1858.

AUBRY, Octave, *The Second Empire*, Longmans, Toronto 1940.

BAPST, Constant Germain, *Le Maréchal Canrobert: Souvenirs d'un Siècle*, Édition Plon, Paris 1898.

BARNES, Major R. Money, *A History of the Regiments and Uniforms of the British Army*, Seeley Service & Co., London 1950.

BARTHETY, Hilarion, *Le Maréchal Bosquet*, Paris 1894.

BAUDENS, M. L. *La Guerre de Crimée: les Campements, les Ambulances, les Hôpitaux*, Amyot, Paris 1858.

BAUDENS, M. L. *Souvenirs d'une Mission Médicale a l'Armée d'Orient*, Amyot, Paris 1857.

BAZANCOURT, Cesar Legat, Baron de, *Cinq Mois devant Sebastopol*, Ed. Amyot, Paris 1855.

BAZANCOURT, Cesar Legat, Baron de, *L'Expédition de Crimée jusqu'à la Prise de Sebastopol*, Ed. Amyot, Paris 1836.

BEDARRIDES, J. P., *Journal Humoristique du Siège de Sebastopol*, 2 vols., Librairie Centrale, Paris 1867.

BELL, Major-Gen. Sir G., *Rough Notes by an Old Soldier*, vol. 2, Day, London 1867.

BENSON, A. C. and ASHER, Viscount, eds., *The Letters of Queen Victoria (1837–1861)*, John Murray, London 1907.

BIDDULPH, H. ed., 'The Expedition to Kertch 1855', *J.S.A.H.R.* XXI (1942) pp. 128–35.*

BIDDULPH, H., 'The Fall of Sebastopol', *J.S.A.H.R.* XIX (1940) pp. 197–9.*

BIDDULPH, H., 'The Assault of the Redan', *J.S.A.H.R.* XXI (1942) pp. 52–4.*

BONNER-SMITH, D. and DEWAR A. C. eds., *Russian War 1854, Baltic and Black Sea – Official Correspondence*, London 1943.

BORMANN, Major-Gen. C., *The Shrapnel Shell in England and in Belgium with some reflexions on the use of this projectile in the late Crimean War*, Brussels 1859.

BOSQUET, Pierre F. J., *Lettres du Maréchal Bosquet 1830–1858*, Paris 1894.

BOSQUET, Pierre F. J. *Lettres du Maréchal Bosquet à sa Mère 1829–1858*, Pau 1877–9.

* *Journal of the Society for Army Historical Research.*

BOSQUET, Pierre F. J., *Lettres du Maréchal Bosquet à ses Amis 1837–1860*, Pau 1879.

BOTHMER, Gen-Leut. Graf von, *Der Russische Krieg*, Berlin 1877.

BOUCHER, Henri, *Souvenirs d'un Parisien*, Paris 1909.

BOULGER, D. C. ed., *General Gordon's Letters from the Crimea, Danube and Armenia*, D. C. Boulger, London 1884.

BOURNAND, François, *Le Maréchal Canrobert*, Paris 1895.

BRACKENBURY, G., *The Campaign in the Crimea*, P. & D. Colnaghi & Co, London 1855–6.

BRIALMONT, Gen. A., *Le Général Comte Todleben, sa Vie et ses Travaux*, Brussels 1884.

BRUNON, J., ' "Balaclava". La charge de la Brigade Legers', *Revue Historique de L'Armée* X (1954) pp. 217–40.

BRYCE, C., *England and France before Sebastopol, looked at from a medical point of view*, John Churchill, London 1857.

BUZZARD, T., *With the Turkish Army in the Crimea and Asia Minor*, J. Murray, London 1915.

CABROL, J. F., *Le Maréchal de Saint-Arnaud en Crimée*, Paris 1895.

CALLWELL, E. E., *The Effect of Maritime Command on Land Campaigns since Waterloo*, W. Blackwood & Sons, Edinburgh 1897.

CALTHORPE, S. G. J., *Letters from Headquarters; or the Realities of the War in the Crimea*, J. Murray, London 1856.

CAMPBELL, C. F., *Letters from Camp to his Relatives during the Siege of Sebastopol*, R. Bentley & Son, London 1894.

CARTER, Thomas, *Curiosities of War and Military Studies*, Groombridge & Sons, London 1860

CARTIER, V., *Un méconnu; le Général Trochu*, Paris 1914.

CARY, A. D. L. and STOUPPE MC CANCE, *Regimental Records of the Royal Welsh Fusiliers*, Published for the R.U.S.I. by Forster Groom & Co., London 1923.

CASE, Lynn, M. *French Opinion on War and Diplomacy during the Second Empire*, University of Pennsylvania Press, Philadelphia 1954.

CASSAGNAC, B. A. G. de, *Souvenirs du Second Empire*, Paris 1879–82.

CASTELLANE, Esprit V. E. B., Maréchal Comte de, *Campagnes de Crimée, d'Italie, d'Afrique, de Chine et de Syrie 1848–1862: Lettres addressées au Maréchal de Castellane par les Maréchaux Baraguay d'Hilliers, Niel, Bosquet, Pélissier, Canrobert, Vaillant et les Généraux Changarnier, Cler, Mellinet, Dousi, etc.*, Plon, Paris 1895–8.

CASTELLANE, Esprit V. E. B., *Journal du Mareschal de Castellane 1804-1862*, Plon, Paris 1897.

CLER, J. J. G., *Reminiscences of an Officer of Zouaves*, New York 1860.

CLIFFORD, Sir Henry Hugh, *Henry Clifford V.C., his letters and Sketches from the Crimea*, Michael Joseph, London 1956.

CLODE, Charles, *The Military Forces of the Crown*, John Murray, London 1869.

COLLINS, H. P., 'The Crimea: the fateful Weeks', *Army Quarterly* LXXI (Oct. 1955) pp. 86-96.

COLVILLE, R. F., 'The Baltic as a Theatre of War: the Campaign of 1854' *R.U.S.I.J.* LXXXVI (1941) pp. 72-80.*

COLVILLE, R. F., 'The Navy and the Crimean War', *R.U.S.I.J.* LXXXV (1940) pp. 73-8.*

Companion to the Almanac and Yearbook, London 1854-6

COOK, Sir Edward T., *The Life of Florence Nightingale*, Macmillan, London 1913.

COWPER, Colonel L. J. ed., *The King's Own*, vol. 2, Privately printed at the University Press Oxford, 1939.

DAHLGREEN, Lt. J. A., *Shells and Shellguns*, King & Baird, Philadelphia 1857.

DE GUICHEN, Vicomte, *La Guerre de Crimée – 1854-1856 et l'attitude des puissances Européennes*, Paris 1936.

DELAFIELD, Richard, *Report of Major Richard Delafield*, U.S. Senate Documents, 36th Congress, 1st Session A.S. 10/4, Washington 1860.

DE LEUSSE, Paul, *Souvenirs: Sebastopol – Reichshoffen*, Paris 1950.

DELUZY, Leon, *La Russie, son Peuple et son Armée*, Tanera, Paris 1860.

D'HAUTERIVE, Ernest, 'Corréspondance Inédite de Napoléon III et du Prince Napoleon' *Revue des Deux Mondes* XVIII pp. 763-96, XIX pp. 51-85, 519-45, Paris 1923-4.

DE NAVACELLE, H. Fabre, *Précis des Guerres du Second Empire*, Paris 1887.

DE NOE, Louis R. J., Vicomte, *Les Bachi-Bazouks et les Chasseurs d'Afrique*, Paris 1861.

DERRECAGAIX, Gen., *Le Maréchal Pélissier, Duc de Malakoff*, Chapelot, Paris 1911.

DEWAR, A. C. ed., *Russian War 1855 – Black Sea Official Correspondence*, D. Bonner-Smith, Navy Records Society, London 1943.

* *Journal of the Royal United Service Institution.*

DOUGLAS, G. and RAMSAY, G. D. eds., *The Panmure Papers. Begin a selection from the Correspondence of Fox Maule, 2nd Baron Panmure, afterwards 11th Earl of Dalhousie*, Hodder & Stoughton, London 1908.

DUBERLY, Frances Isabella, *Journal during the Russian War*, Longman, Brown, Green and Longmans, London 1855.

DU CASSE, Pierre E. A., Baron, *La Crimée et Sebastopol de 1853 à 1856: Documents Intimes et Inédits*, Ch. Lavauzelle, Paris 1892.

DU CASSE, Pierre E. A., Baron, *Précis Historiques des Opérations Militaires en Orient de mars 1854 à Septembre 1855*, Ch. Lavauzelle, Paris 1856.

EARDLEY-WILMOT, A. P., *What our Transports did in the Crimea*, Edward Stanford, London 1867.

EARDLEY-WILMOT, Sydney, *Life of Vice-Admiral Edmund Lord Lyons*, Samson Low & Co., London 1898.

EARP, G. Butler, *The History of the Baltic Campaign of 1854*, Ed. by G.B.E., London 1857.

EGGERTON, Hon. Algernon, *Notes from his Diary*, (Unpublished and held by the Ministry of Defence Library, London).

EWART, Lieut-Gen. J. A., *The Story of a Soldier's Life*, vol. I, Sampson Low, London 1881.

FALLS, Captain Cyril, ed., *A Diary of the Crimea: by George Palmer Evelyn*, Gerald Duckworth & Co, London 1954.

FAY, Ch. A., *Souvenirs de la Guerre de Crimée 1854–1856*, Berger-Levrault, Paris, 1869.

FENWICK, K. ed., *Voice from the Ranks: a Personal Narrative of the Crimean Campaign*, Folio Society, London 1954.

FERAY-BUGEAUD D'ISLEY ET TATTET, *Lettres inédites du Maréchal Bugeaud*, Paris 1923.

FILDER, William, *The Commissariat in the Crimea*, W. Clowes & Son, London 1856.

FLEURY, Émile Félix, Général Comte, *Souvenirs du Général Comte Fleury*, Paris 1897.

FORTESCUE, Hon. J. W., *A History of the British Army*, vol. XIII, Macmillan, London 1930.

FORTESCUE, Hon. J. W., *A History of the 17th Lancers*, Macmillan, London 1895.

GESSCKEN, Friedrich Heinrich, *Orientalischer Krieg 1855–1856*, Berlin 1887.

GIBBS, Peter, *The Battle of the Alma*, Weidenfeld & Nicolson, London 1963.

GOOCH, Brison D., 'A Century of Historiography on the Origins of the Crimean War', *American Historical Review* LXII (1965) pp. 33–58.

GOOCH, Brison D., 'The Crimean War in Selected Documents and Secondary Works since 1940', *Victorian Studies* I (1958) pp. 271–9.

GOOCH, Brison D., *The New Buonaparte Generals in the Crimean War*, Martinau Nijhoff, The Hague 1959.

GOWING, Timothy, *A Soldier's Experience*, Benham & Co., Colchester 1883.

GOWING, Timothy, *A Voice from the Ranks*, Heinemann, London 1954.

GRANDIN, Leonce, *Le dernier Maréchal de France*, Paris 1895.

GRANDIN, Leonce, *Les Gloires de la Patrie Française: Le Maréchal de MacMahon*, Paris 1894.

GRAVIÈRE, DE LA, *La Marine d'aujourd'hui*, Paris 1872.

GRAZEBROOK, R. M. ed., 'Letters from Sebastopol 1855', *J.S.A.H.R.*, XXXII (1954) pp. 30–33.*

GREVILLE, Charles F. G., *The Greville Memoirs*, Longmans & Co, London 1888.

GRETTON, G. le M., *The Campaigns and History of the Royal Irish Regiment from 1684–1902*, William Blackwood & Sons, London 1911.

GUEDALLA, Philip, *The Second Empire*, Constable & Co., London 1922.

GUEDALLA, Philip, *The Two Marshals*, Hodder & Stoughton, London 1943.

GUYHO, Corentis, *L'Empire Inédit –1855*, Paris 1892.

HACKETT, Captain J., *Journal, 18th September to 10th November 1854*, (unpublished journal held in the Ministry of Defence Library, London).

HAMLEY, General Sir Edward Bruce, *The War in the Crimea*, Seeley & Co, London 1891.

HAMLEY, General Sir Edward Bruce, *The Campaign of Sebastopol*, London 1855.

HANOTEAU, Jean and BONNOT, Emile, *Bibliographie des Historiques des Regiments Français*, Paris 1913.

HARDY DE PERENI, Marie J. F. E., *Afrique et Crimée 1850–1856*, Paris 1905.

* *Journal of the Society for Army Historical Research.*

HEATH, Leopold George K. C. B., *Letters from the Black Sea During the Crimean War, 1854–1855*, R. Bentley & Son, London 1897.

HENDERSON, Gavin B., *Crimean War Diplomacy and other Historical Essays*, Jackson, Son & Co, Glasgow 1947.

HIBBERT, C., *The Destruction of Lord Raglan*, Longmans, London 1961.

HITCHCOCK, F. O., 'The Light Brigade: was the Blunder Worth While?', *Army Quarterly*, LVIII (July 1949) pp. 194–204.

HODASEVITCH, R. A., *A Voice from within the Walls of Sebastopol*, John Murray, London 1856.

HORSETZAY, General A. von, *A Short History of the Chief Campaigns in Europe since 1792*, John Murray, London 1909.

HOWARD, Herbert E., 'Lord Cowley on Napoleon III in 1853', *English Historical Revue* XLIX pp. 502–5, London 1934

HUEBNER, Josef Alexander Graf von, *Neun Jahre der Erinnerungen eines oesterreichischen Botschafters in Paris unter dem Zweiten Kaiserreich 1851–1859*, Paris and Berlin 1904.

HUME, John R., *Reminiscences of the Crimean Campaign with the 55th Regiment*, (Privately printed for the Regiment), London 1894.

JAGOW, Kurt ed., *Letters of the Prince Consort 1831–1861*, New York 1938.

JERROLD, William Blanchard, *The Life of Napoleon III*, 4 vols, London 1874–82.

JOCELYN, Colonel J. R. J., *The History of the Royal Artillerie*, London 1911.

KELLER, Werner, *Are the Russians ten feet tall?*, Thames & Hudson, London 1961, (Droemersche Verlagsanstalt, Munich 1960).

KELLY, R. D. K., *An Officer's Letters to his Wife during the Crimean War*, Elliot Stock, London 1902.

KELLY, Mrs Tom, *From the Fleet in the Fifties*, Hurst & Blackett, London 1902.

KINGLAKE, Alexander William, *The Invasion of the Crimea. Its Origin and Account of its Progress down to the Death of Lord Raglan*, William Blackwood, Edinburgh 1863–80.

KOWALEWSKI, Egor Petrovitch, *Der Krieg Russlands mit der Turkei*, Leipzig 1869.

LADIMIR, Jules, *La Guerre en Orient et dans la Baltique*, Paris 1857.

LA GORCE, Pierre de, *Histoire du Second Empire*, Paris 1899.

LAKE, Sir Harry Atwell, *Kars and Our Captivity in Russia*, Richard Bentley, London 1856.

LAMARCHE, H., *L'Europe et la Russie*, Paris 1857.

LA MOTTE ROUGE, Joseph-Edouard de, *Souvenirs et Campagnes*, Paris 1895–8.

LAMY, Etienne, *Etudes sur le Second Empire*, Paris 1895.

LANCASTER, T. J., 'A Letter from the Crimea', *Fortnightly*, November 1854, pp. 336–7.

LANE-POOLE, Stanley, *Life of Stratford Canning: Viscount Stratford de Redcliffe*, Longmans, Green & Co., London 1888.

LAWS, M. E. S., 'Beatson's Bashi-Bazooks', *Army Quarterly* LXXI (1955) pp. 80–5.

LEBRUN, General, *Souvenirs des Guerres de Crimée et d'Italie*, Paris 1889.

LOIZILLON, Henri, *La Campagne de Crimée: Lettres Écrites de Crimée*, Paris 1895.

LYSONS, David, *The Crimean War from First to Last*, John Murray, London 1895.

MACMAHON, M. E. P. Maurice de, *Memoires du Maréchal MacMahon Duc de Magenta*, Paris 1932.

MACMUNN, George, *The Crimea in Perspective*, G. Bell & Sons, London 1935.

MAGEN, Hippolyte, *Histoire du Second Empire*, Paris 1878.

MARTIN, Louis, *Le Maréchal Canrobert*, Paris 1895.

MARX, Karl, *The Eastern Question*, Published in London in 1897 and reprinted by Franklin, New York 1968.

MASQUELEZ, M., *Journal d'un Officier de Zouaves*, Paris 1858.

MAXWELL, Peter Benson, *Whom Shall We Hang? The Sebastopol Inquiry*, James Ridgeway, London 1855.

McCORMICK, R. C., *A Visit to the Camp before Sebastopol*, New York 1855.

MERRILL, James M., 'British–French Amphibious Operations in the Sea of Azov, 1855', *Military Affairs*, XX (1956) pp. 16–27.

MICHOFF, Nicholas V., *Bibliographie des Articles de Périodiques Allemands, Anglais, Français et Italiens sur la Turquie et la Bulgarie*, Sofia 1938.

MITRA, S. M., *The Life and Letters of Sir John Hall*, Longman & Co, London 1961.

MOLENES, Paul de, *Les Commentaires d'un Soldat*, Paris 1860.

MONEY, Edward, *Twelve Months with the Bashi-Bazouks*, Newman and Co, London 1857.

NAPIER, Admiral Sir C., *The History of the Baltic Campaign of 1854*, Richard Bentley, London 1857.

NICKERSON, Hoffman, *The Armed Horde 1793–1939*, New York 1940.

NIEL, Adolphe, *Siège de Sebastopol: Journal des Opérations du Genie*, Paris 1858.

NIGHTINGALE, Florence, *Notes on matters affecting the Health, Efficiency and Hospital Administration of the British Army*, Harrison and Sons, London 1858.

NIGHTINGALE, Florence, *Subsidiary Notes as to the Introduction of Female Nursing into Military Hospitals in Peace and War*, Harrison and Sons, London 1858.

NOLAN, E. H., *The History of the War against Russia*, James Virtue, London 1857.

PACK, Colonel R., *Sebastopol: Trenches and five months in them*, Kirby and Endean, London 1878.

PAGET, George A. F., *Extracts from the Letters and Journal of General Lord George Paget during the Crimean War*, John Murray, London 1881.

PAGET, George, A. F., *The Light Cavalry Brigade in the Crimea*, John Murray, London 1881.

PARMENTIER, Capt. T., *Descriptions topographiques et stratégiques du Théatre de Guerre Turco-Russe*, Paris 1854.

PEMBERTON, W. Baring, *Battles of the Crimean War*, Batsford, London 1962.

PETROV, Gen.-Major A. N., *Der russische Donaufeldzug im Jahre 1853–1854*, St Petersburg 1891.

PORTER, Major-Gen. W., *Life in the Trenches before Sebastopol*, Longman, Brown, Green & Longmans, London 1856.

POWELL, Harry, *Recollections of a young soldier during the Crimean War*, Privately printed: A. R. Mowbray & Co., Oxford (date not given).

QUATRELLES L'EPINE, Maurice, *Le Maréchal de Saint-Arnaud, 1798–1854 d'après sa Correspondance et des Documents inédits*, Paris 1928–9.

RAMBAUD, A., *History of Russia*, 3 vols., Dana Estes & Co., Boston 1882.

RANKEN, Major G., *Six Months at Sebastopol*, Charles Westerton, London 1857.

REID, Douglas-Arthur, *Memoirs of the Crimean War*, St Catherine Press, London 1911.

REILLY, Major-Gen. W. E. M., *Siege of Sebastopol. An account of the Artillery Operations conducted by the Royal Artillery and Naval Brigade before Sebastopol in 1854–1855*, W. Clowes & Son, London 1859.

REVOL, Lieut-Col. F. J., 'Etudes sur le Haut-Commandement en Crimée', *Revue Militaire Française* VII pp. 73–109, 234–56, 289–313, VIII 51–82, Paris 1923.

ROBBINS, M., 'The Balaclava Railway', *Journal of Transport History*, pp. 28–43 and II pp. 51–2 London 1953 and 1955.

ROBINSON, Frederick, *Diary of the Crimean War*, Richard Bentley, London 1856.

ROSS-OF-BLADENSBURG, John Foster George, *The Coldstream Guards in the Crimea*, A. D. Innes & Co., London 1896.

ROUSSET, Camille, *Histoire de la Guerre de Crimée*, Paris 1897.

ROUX, François-Charles, 'La Russie et l'Alliance Anglo-Française après la Guerre de Crimée', *Revue Historique*, pp. 272–315, Paris 1909.

ROUX, François-Charles, 'La Russie, la France et la Question de Orient après la guerre de Crimée', *Revue Historique*, pp. 272–306, Paris 1912.

ROY, I. J. E., *Histoire du Siege et de la Prise de Sebastopol*, Tours 1875.

RUSSELL, Major Frank S., *Russian Wars with Turkey*, Henry S. King & Co., London 1877.

RUSSELL, William Howard, *The British Expedition to the Crimea*, George Routledge & Sons, London 1858.

RUSSELL, William Howard, *General Todleben's History of the Defence of Sebastopol 1854–1855*, George Routledge & Sons, London 1865.

SAINT ARNAUD, Leroy de, *Lettres du Maréchal de Saint Arnaud*, Paris 1858.

SANDWITH, Humphrey, *A Narrative of the Siege of Kars*, John Murray, London 1856.

SAYER, Frederic, ed., *Despatches and Papers relative to the Crimean War*, J. Harrison, London 1857.

SCHIMMELFENNIG, A., *The War between Turkey and Russia: A military Sketch*, John Murray, London 1854.

SHADWELL, Lawrence, *The Life of Colin Campbell, Lord Clyde*, John Murray, London 1881.

SHEPPARD, Edgar, *George, Duke of Cambridge*, John Murray, London 1906.

SHEPPARD, Eric William, *A Short History of the British Army*, Constable, London 1950.

SHRIMPTON, C. (Late Surgeon-Major French Army), *The British Army and Miss Nightingale* (English edition: A. W. Galignaci, Paris 1864.) Baillière Bros, New York 1864.

SKENE, J. H., *With Lord Stratford in the Crimean War*, Richard Bentley, London 1883.

SLADE, Adolphus, *Turkey and the Crimean War*, Smith Elder & Co., London 1867.

STEPHENSON, Sir F. C. A., *At Home and on the Battlefield: Letters from the Crimea, China and Egypt* (Collated and arranged by Mrs Frank Pownall), John Murray, London 1915.

STERLING, Lieut-Col. A., *The Story of the Highland Brigade in the Crimea*, John Murray, London 1895.

STEVENS, N., *The Crimean Campaign with the Connaught Rangers*, Griffiths and Forran, London 1878.

STEWART, P. F., *History of the 12th Royal Lancers, 1715–1945*, London 1950.

TANC, M. X., *Histoire Diplomatique de la Guerre d'Orient en 1854*, Paris 1864.

TARLE, E. V., *Saint Petersburg (Crimean War)*, Moscow, Leningrad 1950.

TAYLOR, A. H., 'Letters from the Crimea', *R.U.S.I.J.* (1957) pp. 79–85, 232–8, 399–405.*

TAYLOR, A. J. P., *The Struggle for Mastery in Europe, 1848–1918*, H. Hamilton, Oxford 1954.

TEMPERLEY, Harold, 'The Treaty of Paris of 1856 and its Execution', *Journal of Modern History* pp. 378–414, 523–43, London 1932.

THOUMAS, General Charles, *Les Transformations de l'Armée Française*, Paris 1887.

THOUVENEL, L., *Nicolas Ier et Napoléon III: les Préliminaires de la Guerre de Crimée, 1852–1854 d'après les Papiers inédites de M. Thouvenel*, Paris 1891.

THE TIMES (London) 1854–6, *The Letters of The TIMES Correspondent from the Seat of War in the East*, George Routledge, London 1855.

TODLEBEN, Graf Eduard Ivanovitch, *Défense de Sebastopol*, St Petersburg 1863–74.

TOOLEY, Sarah A., *The Life of Florence Nightingale*, New York 1905.

TULLOCH, A. M., *The Crimean Commission and the Chelsea Board*, Harrison, London 1857.

* *Journal of the Royal United Service Institution.*

TYLDEN, G., ' "Balaclava": "C" Battery, R.H.A. and the Light Brigade', *J.S.A.H.R.*, XXII (1944) pp. 260–1.*

TYLDEN, G., 'The Crimea in 1855 and 1856', *J.S.A.H.R.*, XXV (1947) pp. 23–6.*

TYLDEN, G., 'The Heavy Cavalry Charge at Balaclava' , *J.S.A.H.R.*, XIX (1940) pp. 98–103.*

VAILLANT, Jean B. P., *Rapport à l'Empereur par le Maréchal Ministre de la Guerre sur l'Ensemble des Dispositions Administratives Auxquelles a donné Lieu la Guerre d'Orient*, Paris 1856.

VETCH, Colonel R. H., *Life, Letters and Diaries of Lieut-General Sir Gerald Graham, V.C., G.C.B.*, William Blackwood, Edinburgh 1901.

VIEL CASTEL, Comte Horace de, *Mémoires du Comte Horace de Viel Castel sur le Règne de Napoléon III*, Paris 1883.

VIETH, F. H. D., *Recollections of the Crimean Campaign and the Expedition to Kinburn in 1855*, John Lovell, Montreal 1907.

VULLIAMY, C. E., *Crimea*, Jonathan Cape, London 1939.

WALDY, W. T. Jervis, *From Eight to Eighty: the Life of a Crimean Veteran*, John Murray, London 1914.

WATTEVILLE, Colonel H. de, *The British Soldier*, J. M. Dent & Sons, London 1954.

WHEATER, W., *Historical Record of the 7th, or Royal Regiment of Fusiliers* (Printed for private circulation), Leeds 1875.

WHITTON, Lieut-Col. F. C., 'Williams of Kars', *Blackwood's Magazine*, April 1936, London 1936.

WIGHTMAN, J. W., 'One of the Six Hundred on the Balaclava Charge, Printed in *The 19th Century*, Vol. X, p. 850.

WILLIAMS, Captain G. T., *Historical Records of the 11th Hussars (Prince Albert's Own)*, George Newnes, London 1908.

WILLIAMS, R. L., 'Louis Napoleon: a Tragedy of Good Intentions', *History Today*, pp. 219–26, London 1954.

WIMPFFEN, General de, *Crimée – Italie*, H. Galli, Paris 1892.

WINDHAM, Sir C. A., *The Crimean Diary and Letters of Lieut-Gen. Sir C. A. Windham KCB*, Keogan Paul, French, Trubner & Co., London 1897.

WOLSELEY, F. M. Viscount, *The Story of a Soldier's Life*, Constable & Co., London 1903.

WOOD, General Sir Evelyn, V.C., G.C.B., G.C.M.G., *The Crimea in 1854 and 1894*, Chapman and Hall, London 1896.

* *Journal of the Society for Army Historical Research.*

WOODHAM-SMITH, Cecil, *Florence Nightingale, 1820–1910*, Constable & Co., London 1950.

WOODHAM-SMITH, Cecil, *The Reason Why*, Constable & Co., London 1953; New York 1954.

WOODS, M. A., *The Past Campaign*, Longmans, Brown, Green & Longmans, London 1855.

WRIGHT, H. P., *Recollections of a Crimean Chaplain*, Wilkins Clowes & Co., London 1857.

WROTTESLEY, George, *Life and Letters of Sir John Burgoyne*, John Murray, London 1873.

WROTTESLEY, George *The Military Opinions of General Sir John Fox Burgoyne*, John Murray, London 1859.

ADDENDUM

AN AMATEUR, *A Trip to the Trenches in February and March 1855*, Saunders & Otley, 1855.

BRACKENBERG, George, *The Campaign in the Crimea*, Longman, Brown, Green, 1854.

CHESNEY, Kellog, *Crimean War Reader*, Frederick Muller, 1960.

GIBBS, Peter, *Crimean Blunder*, F. Muller, 1960.

ST AUBYN, Hon. Giles, *The Royal George 1819–1904*, Constable, London 1963.

INDEX